D1714758

Bioarchaeology of Spanish Florida

The Ripley P. Bullen Series
Florida Museum of Natural History

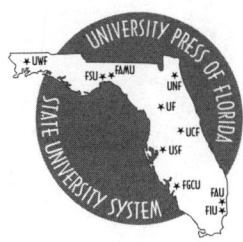

Florida A&M University, Tallahassee
Florida Atlantic University, Boca Raton
Florida Gulf Coast University, Ft. Myers
Florida International University, Miami
Florida State University, Tallahassee
University of Central Florida, Orlando
University of Florida, Gainesville
University of North Florida, Jacksonville
University of South Florida, Tampa
University of West Florida, Pensacola

Bioarchaeology of Spanish Florida

The Impact of Colonialism

edited by Clark Spencer Larsen

Foreword by Jerald T. Milanich, Series Editor

University Press of Florida

Gainesville · Tallahassee · Tampa · Boca Raton
Pensacola · Orlando · Miami · Jacksonville · Ft. Myers

Copyright 2001 by Clark Spencer Larsen
Printed in the United States of America on acid-free paper
All rights reserved

06   05   04   03   02   01   6   5   4   3   2   1

Library of Congress Cataloging-in-Publication Data
Bioarchaeology of Spanish Florida: The impact of colonialism /
edited by Clark Spencer Larsen; foreword by Jerald T. Milanich.
p. cm. — (Ripley P. Bullen series)
Includes bibliographical references and index.
ISBN 0-8130-2088-3 (alk. paper)
1. Indians of North America—Anthropometry—Florida.
2. Indians of North America—Missions—Florida. 3. Indians of
North America—Florida—Antiquities. 4. Human remains
(Archaeology)—Florida. 5. Ethnoarchaeology—Florida.
6. Florida—History—Spanish colony, 1565–1763. 7. Florida—
Antiquities. I. Larsen, Clark Spencer. II. Series.
E78.F6 B525 2001
975.9'01—dc21   00-048836

The University Press of Florida is the scholarly publishing agency
for the State University System of Florida, comprising Florida
A&M University, Florida Atlantic University, Florida Gulf Coast
University, Florida International University, Florida State Univer-
sity, University of Central Florida, University of Florida, Univer-
sity of North Florida, University of South Florida, and University
of West Florida.

University Press of Florida
15 Northwest 15th Street
Gainesville, FL 32611–2079
http://www.upf.com

Contents

Figures

Histology figures (color plates follow page 206)

Tables

Foreword

The European expansion into the Americas that began in the late fifteenth century had far-reaching consequences for the native societies of the Western Hemisphere. In the southeastern United States, the conquest began in earnest with the founding of Spain's La Florida colony.

Situated on the northern frontier of Spain's American empire, the relatively small Florida colony sought to secure its hold on the land and its people through a system of Catholic missions built among the Indians of the region and administered by Franciscan friars. Beginning in the late sixteenth century and continuing well into the 1700s, more than 150 mission churches served the Guale, Apalachee, and Timucua Indians across northern Florida and south-central and coastal Georgia. The missions were a major arena of Spanish-Indian interaction for nearly two centuries.

The story of those Spanish missions began to be revealed only in the 1930s when historians began to delve in the archival records of the colony. By the late 1940s, archaeologists had joined them and several missions were actually located and excavated. Since the 1970s, historians and archaeologists working in tandem have provided us with new perspectives on the missions and their impact on the native populations they served. The findings of these scholars have now appeared in more than a handful of volumes, many published by the University Press of Florida since the late 1980s. But there is still much to learn.

One source of new information regarding the colonization of the southeastern Indians comes from the people themselves. Using the latest scientific techniques, scientists have analyzed the mortal remains of a large sample of Indians who lived and died at the missions and who were interred in the floors of their mission churches. Led by Clark Spencer Larsen, bioarchaeologists working with mission populations have uncovered intriguing facts about the people's health and diet, the hardships imposed by Spanish labor drafts, and the demography, death, and population history, to name just a few topics. In this comprehensive volume, Larsen and other outstanding scholars present the results of their investigations, crafting the most comprehensive bioarchaeological study of colonialism ever undertaken in the Americas.

What makes this particular book so valuable is the comparison of the mission population with populations representing the pre-Columbian ancestors of the Guale, Apalachee, and Timucua Indians. Such a comparison provides a biological and cultural context for understanding the impact of colonialism on the mission-period Indians.

Larsen and his team of scientists have broken new ground in our understanding of the Columbian exchange. Their work has set a high standard, one that certainly will stimulate additional discussion and research.

Jerald T. Milanich
Series Editor

Preface

What happened to Native Americans when Europeans arrived, beginning in the late fifteenth century with Columbus and his crews? This question is one of the most frequently asked regarding the European settlement of the New World, especially in relation to the tremendous impact on health, lifestyle, and population on native peoples. In this book, we take a close look at the record of this impact provided by the study of skeletal remains of the native peoples living in the region called La Florida. This was one of the earliest regions to be contacted by Europeans following Columbus's landfall, and it offers some compelling insight into the impact of European contact on native New World peoples.

This book presents the results of a long-term collaborative bioarchaeological study, the La Florida Bioarchaeology Project, which I have directed since the early 1980s. Bioarchaeology, a branch of anthropology that combines both biological (physical) anthropology and archaeology, is used to investigate the details of Spanish colonialism and its implications for health and lifestyles of native peoples living on the Atlantic coast and in northern Florida. Specifically, we address long-standing issues relating to post-Columbian health and lifestyle changes for native populations. The chapters are not intended to represent an exhaustive study of remains of Indians living in the region. Rather, we focus on a defined research agenda that we believe represents a picture of population history, health, and lifestyle.

The project started out as an effort to understand the impact of European colonization and missionization of the Guale Indians living on St. Catherines Island off the coast of Georgia at Mission Santa Catalina de Guale. Eventually, it developed into a large-scale project to examine numerous mission populations and compare them with pre-contact inhabitants of La Florida. From the beginning, the project has been a team effort involving scientists from a number of institutions in the United States and elsewhere. We envisioned the project as an important step in gaining a more comprehensive understanding of the colonial period than is available from the documentary record alone.

The book is organized into five major segments. First, John Worth presents an ethnohistorical overview of La Florida, focusing on areas and issues of colonization and missionization that can be addressed by study of skeletal remains, such as health, lifestyle, and labor. Accompanying this is my overview of the pre-contact and mission era populations, the nature of lifeways before and after the arrival of Europeans, and the mortuary and human biological record in the region.

One of the fundamental components of health and well-being is diet. In the second segment, we provide details on dietary reconstruction based on analysis of carbon and nitrogen stable isotope ratios. These findings provide new perspective on dietary change and nutritional inference before and after contact.

The two chapters that follow explore the ramifications of dietary change. The manner in which the prehistoric and mission-era populations used their teeth to process food is indicated via microwear analysis by Teaford and coworkers. The manner in which food is acquired and workload in general leave an enormous impression on the skeleton. Ruff and Larsen assess the impact of changes in workload before and after contact via study of bone biomechanics.

In the three contributions making up the fourth segment, we examine the impact of lifeway on health and quality of life by looking at microscopic and macroscopic indicators of growth disruption in teeth (Simpson; Hutchinson and Larsen) and the impact of missionization on iron status and incidence of anemia (Schultz and coworkers).

Lastly, Griffin and coworkers examine evidence of biological associations between groups in the American Southeast to assess the relationships in the broader region, with a closer look at prehistoric and contact populations living on the Atlantic coast, especially in the region occupied by the Guale.

The book concludes with Phillip Walker's discussion of the general findings of the La Florida Bioarchaeology Project and its implications for understanding the northern frontier of New Spain extending from Florida to California, the region of the Americas called the Spanish Borderlands. He takes special note of the variability in the contact experience for native groups across this vast territory, emphasizing the point that bioarchaeology offers important and unique insight into major adaptive shifts and biological consequences of new events and new peoples thrust upon the landscapes and peoples of the New World. Key among the findings is the fact that the contact experience goes far beyond European-introduced contagion and population collapse. Indeed, the biological consequences of contact for native peoples are complex, they involve many factors, and they continue to be part of the social, cultural, and biological landscapes of the Americas today.

•   •   •

Preliminary versions of the chapters in this volume were presented as papers in a symposium I organized for the 1997 annual meeting of the American Association of Physical Anthropologists, held in St. Louis, Missouri.

Many people deserve special recognition for their help in contributing to the research presented. The work entailed a great deal of excavation done in collaboration with a number of ongoing archaeological projects. On St. Catherines Island, Georgia, I directed the excavation of the Santa Catalina mission cemetery as part of a collaborative project on the archaeology of the Spanish mission complex directed by David Hurst Thomas. On Amelia Island, Florida, I co-directed the excavations of two mission cemeteries— Santa Catalina de Amelia (and the associated ossuary) and Santa Maria de Yamasee—with Rebecca Saunders and Jerald Milanich in their study of the mission period. Excavation of the cemetery at San Luis de Apalachee in Tallahassee, Florida, I co-directed with Bonnie McEwan. All of these projects offered expansive insight into the mission period and represented the kind of collaboration that is required for meaningful bioarchaeological research. In the course of these excavations, I had the great pleasure of working with many capable individuals who served as assistant field directors. I especially thank Katherine Russell, Dale Hutchinson, Scott Simpson, Mark Griffin, and Hong Huynh.

Primary funding for fieldwork came from the Edward John Noble and St. Catherines Island Foundations (for St. Catherines Island), the University of Florida and Dr. and Mrs. George Dorion (for Amelia Island), and the Florida Department of State, Bureau of Archaeological Research, and the National Endowment for the Humanities (for San Luis de Apalachee). Mr. and Mrs. Frank Y. Larkin have taken special interest in my work on St. Catherines Island and elsewhere over the last 25 years. On St. Catherines Island, former superintendent John Tobey Woods Jr. and current superintendent Royce Hayes were especially helpful in the day-to-day activities and concerns of the fieldwork.

I thank the following curators and their institutions for their permission to study the collections under their care and to undertake the analyses described in this book: David Hurst Thomas, American Museum of Natural History; Jerald Milanich, Florida Museum of Natural History; Douglas Ubelaker and Donald Ortner, Smithsonian Institution; David Hally, University of Georgia; and Bonnie McEwan, David Dickel, and James Miller, Florida Bureau of Archaeological Research.

The laboratory research and analysis have been generously funded by the National Science Foundation over the last couple of decades (BNS-

8406773, BNS-8703849, BNS-8747309, SBR-9305391, SBR-9601766). I am especially grateful to John Yellen and Jonathan Friedlaender at the NSF for their advice and help on grant proposal preparation and administration. At various times, the American Museum of Natural History and my home institutions (in chronological order, University of Massachuetts–Dartmouth, Northern Illinois University, Purdue University, and University of North Carolina) stepped in with significant support for the research. I also thank Michael Gannon and the Institute of Early Contact Period Studies at the University of Florida for support of the isotope analysis from St. Simons Island sites. A grant from the University Research Council at the University of North Carolina funded the production of color plates in chapter 8.

I thank my collaborators, many of whom are authors in this book: Dale Hutchinson, Mark Griffin, Katherine Russell, Margaret Schoeninger, Mark Teaford, Christopher Ruff, Scott Simpson, Nikolaas van der Merwe, Joseph Ezzo, Michael Schultz, Julia Lee-Thorp, Inui Choi, Dawn Harn, Rebecca Shavit, Joanna Lambert, Katherine Moore, Leslie Sering, Matthew Williamson, Marianne Reeves, Dawn Harn, Susan Simmons, Elizabeth Monahan Driscoll, Tiffiny Tung, Patricia Lambert, and Elizabeth Moore. Dale Hutchinson and Susan Brannock-Gaul prepared the maps for chapters 1 and 2.

Production of such a book requires an accommodating and encouraging press. I especially thank Senior Editor Meredith Morris-Babb and the University Press of Florida for their help, patience, and wisdom. I thank Jerald Milanich for his interest in the project and his invitation to include the book in the Ripley P. Bullen Series, arguably the most important book series devoted to the study of native peoples in the American Southeast.

My wife, Christine Larsen, has been enormously supportive of my work in Spanish Florida over the years. I thank her for her participation in fieldwork, her help in the laboratory, and her critical reading of drafts of manuscripts.

The Ethnohistorical Context
of Bioarchaeology in Spanish Florida

John E. Worth

As a topic for directed research, the biological consequences of "first contact" between Native Americans and Europeans in the southeastern United States present a remarkable opportunity to explore the relationship between the documentary and archaeological records, between historical texts and "hard" biological data. Authors of the rest of this volume explore and interpret a wide range of archaeological and biological data, most of it completely new, regarding the biological impact of Spanish exploration, colonization, and missionization on Native Americans living in and around the colony of Florida. In this connection, my intent in this first chapter is to provide an overview of the broader ethnohistorical context regarding these same Native American populations.

Even though the Florida colony during its first incarnation (1565–1763) never effectively expanded far beyond its 16th-century roots in the port city of St. Augustine, the establishment of this isolated outpost of less than 3,000 Spaniards living on the northern fringes of the broader Spanish empire ultimately resulted in massive and dramatic transformations among indigenous populations living within and beyond the Spanish colonial frontier. Although long-range exploratory expeditions were undertaken in the decades before and after the establishment of St. Augustine in 1565, the most significant and the longest-lived mechanism for direct contact and interaction between Spaniards and Indians in the Southeast was undoubtedly the Franciscan mission system, which operated between roughly 1587 and 1706, before the final retreat of the missions and the virtual depopulation of interior Florida by English-backed slave raiders.

During these decades, Franciscan missions acted as the primary mechanism for societal assimilation in the colonial system of Spanish Florida. As is explored later, mission populations formed what was in effect the local economic base of the Florida colony during the 17th century. If not producing economic expansion, they at least permitted a degree of stability and continuity otherwise not always possible given the unreliability of external supply lines. For Native Americans affected directly or indirectly by this system, however, the biological consequences were increasingly severe, both for individuals and for groups.

I address the biological consequences of missionization in a four-part discussion that draws heavily on ethnohistorical data, much of which has been either discovered or reevaluated only very recently. I begin with a brief review of the sociopolitical and economic systems of late prehistoric populations within the study area of Spanish Florida, providing a benchmark against which transformations of the mission period may be compared. Second, I review the timing and nature of pre-mission era contacts between Europeans and Native Americans in the region that would become Florida. Next, I examine the primary mission era (1587–1706), when aboriginal chiefdoms were assimilated into the developing colonial system of Spanish Florida, focusing on the pivotal role that mission populations played in that system. Finally, setting the stage for the contributions that follow, I provide a specific overview of the anticipated biological consequences of assimilation and participation in the Florida colonial system.

Because much of this material is explored in greater depth in my recent two-volume *The Timucuan Chiefdoms of Spanish Florida* (Worth 1998a, 1998b)—including a wide range of supporting primary documentation as well as secondary literature—many of the citations in this chapter direct readers to specific sections of these volumes, where there are more extensive citations of supporting materials. Nevertheless, I also include citations to major published references where readers can also explore specific topics.

Chiefdoms of the Late Prehistoric Southeast

Although a detailed description of the many and diverse Native American societies of the late prehistoric Southeast is far beyond my scope, it is possible to summarize both commonalities and variations present within the broader area that became Spanish Florida (fig. 1.1). Most of the indigenous societies directly or indirectly affected by the Florida colony during the 16th, 17th, and 18th centuries may be described broadly as agricultural chiefdoms. Each comprised at least a handful of distinct communities under centralized, hereditary leadership, and that the economic infrastructure

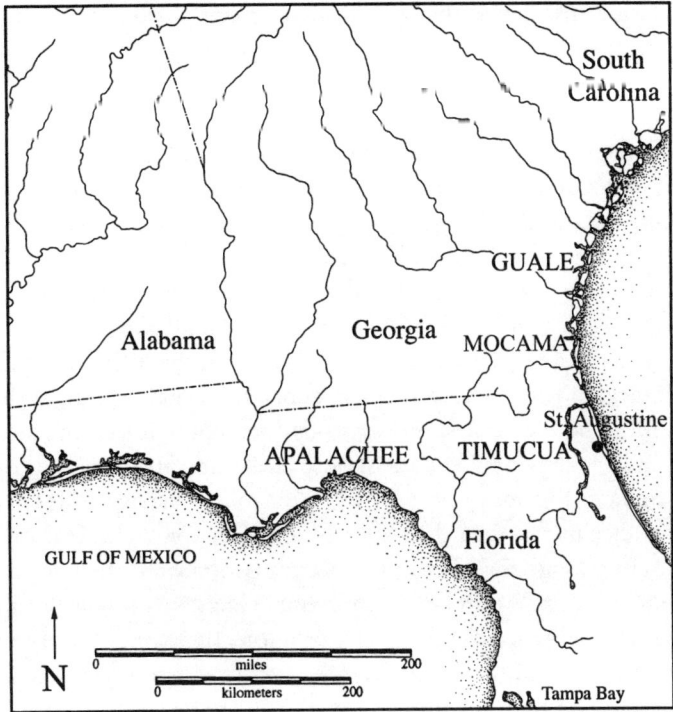

Fig. 1.1. Map of Spanish Florida.

of these societies was based in part on the appropriation of surplus labor
and agricultural products (especially maize) for the use of the chiefly matri-
lineage (Worth 1998a:1–18, 81–102, 162–68; and see Anderson 1994;
Widmer 1994).

While this is of course a gross oversimplification of an immensely complex and diverse range of socioeconomic systems, I would argue that the
term *agricultural chiefdom* is useful not only as a generalization but also in
calling attention to the fundamental characteristics of these societies that
made them more easily assimilated into the colonial system of Spanish
Florida. Specifically, most of the chiefdoms that were eventually assimilated as subordinate elements within a hierarchical system based on tribu-
tary labor and foodstuffs had been practicing some variation of this theme
for centuries prior to European contact. In effect, the agricultural chiefdoms of the late prehistoric Southeast were ideally suited to serve both as
breadbasket and as labor pool for the St. Augustine garrison, since each
political unit was already organized for the managed, hierarchical alloca-
tion of labor and foodstuffs. All that was required was the imposition of a

superordinate jurisdiction that would act to "skim" surplus labor and food for its own use.

This said, it must be noted that these agricultural chiefdoms varied considerably with regard to overall population size and settlement distribution, their degree of sociopolitical integration and centralized administration, and the relative contribution of agricultural products to the annual diet. There is considerable scholarly debate, for example, regarding the degree to which coastal chiefdoms such as the Guale and Mocama originally relied upon corn and other cultivated crops, as opposed to the rich abundance of estuarine and marine foodstuffs available in these productive environments (Larson 1980; Worth 1999; Larsen, this volume). Although documentary evidence clearly indicates substantial agricultural production in these areas by the earliest years of missionization during the late 16th century, there is only limited data to push these interpretations back to the very moment of European contact. Bioarchaeology may provide considerable assistance in this regard, especially regarding pre-contact differences and post-contact homogenization of Native American dietary regimes.

While a substantial number of aboriginal chiefdoms across the interior Southeast were exposed either directly or indirectly to brief European contact during one or more of several 16th-century exploratory expeditions, the geographic area encompassed by the long-lived mission system of Spanish Florida was somewhat more restricted. The mission system eventually included most of the present-day coast of Georgia and northern Florida, extending westward across the interior of southeastern Georgia and virtually the entire northern half of the state of Florida to its western extreme along the Apalachicola River basin. Major politico-linguistic groups eventually assimilated into the mission system included virtually all the Timucuan-speaking chiefdoms inhabiting the coastal, riverine, and lacustrine habitats of central, north-central, northern, and northeastern Florida as well as southeastern Georgia. The Muskogee-speaking chiefdoms of Guale and Orista-Escamaçu along the Georgia and South Carolina coast were impacted heavily by early coastal colonization around the city of Santa Elena (1566–87) as well as the later mission system. The populous Muskogee-speaking Apalachee chiefdom of northwest Florida was assimilated, as were elements of other chiefdoms to the west and north, including the Apalachicola chiefdom of southwest Georgia, which ultimately formed the core of the 18th-century Lower Creeks. Other groups along the southernmost frontier of Spanish Florida, including the Mayaca and Jororo of east-central Florida, were also impacted by the mission system (see Hann 1993).

Within this broad geographic area, Native American populations num-
bering in the many tens of thousands were directly assimilated or substantially affected by the mission system of colonial Spanish Florida. Here, the
primary mission era may be divided into roughly three broad periods: an
initial period of geographic expansion from 1587 until the 1630s; a period
of relative stasis (if not stability) from the 1640s through the 1650s; and a
period of contraction, aggregation, and retreat from the 1660s through
1706. These periods should not be considered mutually exclusive, however, especially since most of the overall elements of the mission system,
including the appropriation of surplus labor and food for Spanish use,
were in operation on a local and regional scale throughout most of the
mission era. Nevertheless, it must be emphasized that not all populations
were assimilated at once, and that not all served precisely the same function
in the overall colonial system. For this reason, the biological analysis of
archaeological human remains from any site or region must take into account the specific historical context and details of their involvement in the
mission system.

Finally, it should be noted that although missions were not established
beyond these geographic boundaries, significant numbers of refugees from
more distant regions ultimately settled within the mission system during
the final decades of the 17th century (Worth 1995, 1998b). Even though
some of these immigrants remained only a short time within Spanish Florida, their presence within and adjacent to established mission communities
undoubtedly resulted in at least some biological impact on local populations, particularly with regard to physical characteristics linked to ethnic
origin. In this regard, populations comprising the late 17th-century mission system of Spanish Florida originated from a geographic area much
larger than that which might be indicated by the distribution of mission
convents alone.

Exploration, Colonization, and Early Mission Efforts

The establishment of St. Augustine in 1565 represented the last and most
successful colonial effort undertaken by Europeans in the 16th century. It
followed more than half a century of initial exploration and failed attempts
at permanent colonization in this same region (see, e.g., Milanich 1995:
99–163, 1999:56–81; Hudson and Tesser 1994:36–122). All previous attempts involved some direct contact between indigenous Indians and immigrant Europeans, although the degree of biological impact resulting
from each is debatable. Nevertheless, since all these expeditions might be

argued to have posed at least some risk for localized epidemics, or even widespread pandemics, among Native American populations living in areas later missionized within the Florida colony, they must be mentioned here.

Following the 1513 discovery and naming of the Florida peninsula by Juan Ponce de León, there was a second failed attempt in 1521, resulting in his death from an arrow wound. That same year there was a Caribbean slaving expedition to the South Carolina and Georgia coast, followed by yet another failed colonial attempt there in 1526 under the direction of Lucas Vázquez de Ayllón, who also perished in the attempt. Pánfilo de Narváez also died in Florida during his failed expedition of 1528, as did Hernando de Soto, whose 1539–43 expedition succeeded primarily in establishing direct contact with a multiplicity of indigenous chiefdoms across the deep interior Southeast. Dominican friar Luís Cancer de Barbastro died on Florida's Gulf coast in a follow-up missionary expedition dating to 1549, and during the 1559–61 colonial attempt of Tristán de Luna, soldiers once again penetrated deep into the southeastern interior. The French garrison left in 1562 by Jean Ribaut along the South Carolina coast was also a complete failure, though the subsequent 1564 French colony at Fort Caroline near Jacksonville might well have survived had its Protestant inhabitants not been killed by Spaniard Pedro Menéndez de Avilés shortly after establishing St. Augustine just to the south. Before the French were extirpated, however, they did manage to send at least one small expedition to the deep interior Timucuan region of northern Florida.

This sort of limited contact continued even after 1565, including the two substantial expeditions of Juan Pardo launched from Santa Elena between 1566 and 1568, retracing much of de Soto's earlier route across the Appalachian summit. Later exploration into the interior was far more limited, but even these contacts between 1597 and 1628 might have had some biological consequences for Native Americans beyond the mission system.

While none of these early expeditions and colonial attempts resulted in the kind of long-term and in-depth contact and interaction that were ultimately established through the mission system, together they represent a prolonged period of episodic and repetitive, if limited, face-to-face contact between Europeans and Native Americans in the broader region that fell within or not far beyond the eventual colonial jurisdiction of Spanish Florida. In this sense, they form a sort of baseline for "first contact" that prefaced the era of missionization under primary consideration in this volume. Researchers are blessed with a relative wealth of documentation regarding the Native American groups encountered during many of these expeditions, but it is difficult to judge their subsequent biological impact, even as a sum total of all these contacts combined. Given that such contacts were normally brief and only rarely violent, and were followed by years or decades without further contact, the most likely source of biological impact is of course European pathogens, unwittingly introduced by passing explorers or colonists. Attempts to examine this question from an archaeological standpoint have generally relied upon indirect evidence for substantial regional population decline—(i.e., the cessation of public architecture after the 16th century, simultaneous reduction in site numbers and size, and abandonment of entire chiefdoms)—in the absence of clear and convincing direct skeletal evidence for European pathogens (Smith 1987). Nevertheless, there seems to be sufficient evidence to conclude that the sum total effect of early European exploration in many areas was regional population loss, in some cases severe. While there is only limited evidence to this effect for areas later directly assimilated into the mission system, the possibility nonetheless exists that missionized populations had already been exposed to earlier population loss due to the biological impact of 16th-century exploration. For my purposes here, however, I focus on biological changes that occurred in surviving populations during the primary colonial era of Spanish Florida (1565–1763) and more precisely during the primary Franciscan mission period (1587–1706).

It must be remembered that there was an intermediate period of Spanish colonial and missionary activity along the Atlantic coast between 1565 and 1587 and that the increased level of interaction during this period between Spaniards and Native Americans undoubtedly had biological consequences for the indigenous coastal populations. Points of direct contact were in operation at St. Augustine after 1565; at Fort San Mateo at the mouth of the St. Johns River between 1565 and 1568; at Santa Elena on Parris Island, South Carolina, between 1566 and 1587; and at Fort San Pedro on Cumberland Island between 1569 and the early 1570s. In addition, a handful of Jesuit missionaries were dispatched to work in coastal Orista and Guale between 1568 and 1570, followed by Franciscans in 1574–75. Although Franciscans remained as chaplains in both Santa Elena and St. Augustine through the 1580s, it was not until 1587 that formal mission convents were established directly within aboriginal villages (Lyon 1976, 1992; Hann 1996:50–72; Milanich 1999:82–103).

Interaction between Native Americans and Spaniards during this early colonial phase varied in its character and extent and, in any case, was markedly different from that which was established after 1587 with the onset of the primary mission era, especially with regard to labor, food production, settlement aggregation, and ethnic mixing. While relations between Spanish colonists and neighboring chiefdoms were often friendly or at least neutral, this early period was frequently characterized by hostility and outright warfare between Spaniards and Indians or between Indian allies of rival Spanish and French interests. To the south, in the district just west and north of St. Augustine, coastal Timucuans later known as the Mocama remained fierce allies of the French even through the 1570s, while St. Johns River Timucuans under chief Outina allied themselves with the Spanish, simultaneously making the Spanish enemies of the deep interior Potano, who were assaulted by Spanish forces in 1567 and 1585, supplementing earlier raids supported by the French in 1564 and 1565. Many of these antagonistic relationships manifested themselves in open warfare, undoubtedly resulting in numerous casualties and, in many cases, in the wholesale abandonment of villages and traditional territories.

To the north, in the vicinity of Santa Elena, the Orista-Escamaçu and Guale chiefdoms maintained amicable relations with Spanish colonists through this same period, ending abruptly in 1576 with a widespread revolt that resulted in the temporary abandonment of Santa Elena and its destruction by fire at the hands of Indian attackers. In the winter of 1579–80—following fierce reprisals by Spanish authorities, including the destruction of all major coastal villages—the rebels once again rendered obedience to the Spanish crown, paving the way for renewed interaction until Santa Elena was dismantled and abandoned in 1587.

Apart from the wounds and deaths resulting from conflicts during this period, the biological consequences of warfare might be anticipated to have been far more wide-reaching. Specifically, Spanish reprisals commonly resulted in the repeated burning of major Indian villages and the intentional destruction of their agricultural crops and stores of food. Thus there is good reason to suspect that both settlement and dietary patterns may have been significantly altered among Native American groups opposed to the Spanish during this period. This would certainly be the case for the Orista-Escamaçu and the Guale between 1576 and 1579 and probably for many of the coastal and interior Timucuans between 1565 and 1580.

In the absence of warfare, amicable relations between Spaniards and Native Americans during this period undoubtedly included reciprocal visits between chiefs or their representatives and Spanish officials, presumably including the exchange of gifts and food. Account records from the 1580s make it clear that Indians around Santa Elena, including parties from Orista-Escamaçu and Guale, did provide manual labor to the Spanish garrison in exchange for rations of wheat flour and occasional gifts of iron tools. Nevertheless, it seems clear that such tasks were normally limited to episodic construction projects associated with the fort and did not include the kind of farming activities that would characterize the later mission period. Spaniards did barter or appropriate Indian food on occasion but relied principally on their own external supply lines during this early period, in contrast to later decades when mission-based production flourished.

Missionary efforts during this early period were generally so short-lived and limited as to be virtually incomparable to the permanent convents established by Franciscans during the primary mission era. On account of hostilities, no early missionaries were sent among the Timucua, but the brief presence among the Guale and Orista-Escamaçu of a handful of Jesuits for less than two years and a few Franciscans for less than a year can hardly be given undue weight in comparison to the far lengthier interaction between the Santa Elena garrison and its Indian neighbors. Apart from the possible introduction of more epidemic diseases, the biological impact of these early missionary efforts must have been only minimal.

Missions and the Assimilation of Chiefdoms

The arrival of nine new Franciscan friars in 1587, resulting in the establishment of the first permanent Timucuan missions north of St. Augustine that same year, launched a missionary effort that would alter the destiny of the Florida colony. Missionization ultimately came to be the primary mechanism for the integration and assimilation of aboriginal societies on Florida's colonial frontier (Worth 1998a:35–76; Milanich 1999:104–29). The key to understanding the process by which Florida's Native American chiefdoms were assimilated, as well as the ultimate impact on the societies involved, lies in the structure and function of the broader colonial system of Spanish Florida. Viewed within the context of the vast colonial empire ruled by Spain during the 16th–18th centuries, Spanish Florida was a strategic military outpost on the northern periphery of a complex web of productive colonies centered on the Caribbean basin and mainland Central and South America. Lacking the economic productivity demonstrated by densely populated New World provinces bearing gold, silver, and other valuable commodities, Florida's primary function for the Spanish crown was strategic, guarding the shipping routes of the Bahama Channel, through which all the riches from the Americas traveled on their way to Spain. As a consequence, direct royal support for the Florida garrison town of St. Augustine was normally only barely sufficient for most of the garrison, and was occasionally lacking altogether, for which reason St. Augustine ultimately developed a reputation as a wretched frontier town to which few soldiers and colonists would relocate willingly. During the 17th century, external support became less and less reliable due to delays in the shipment of wheat, corn, and other products from New Spain and Havana and in the delivery of cash from the *situado*—the royal dole of silver coins from the coffers of Mexico. The inhabitants of St. Augustine were eventually left in the precarious position of having too many poor military families and not enough colonial farmers.

The ultimate survival of this garrison town was, therefore, based on an extensive support system, including not only periodic infusions of cash, armaments, provisions, and other supplies from other Spanish colonies external to Florida but also a vast pool of human and natural resources comprising greater Spanish Florida (see Worth 1998a:126–34, 210–14; Bushnell 1994). Without readily available internal sources of real wealth with which to supplement purchasing power based on cash derived from royal support, St. Augustine's Spanish population was in many ways almost wholly dependent upon Indian labor, both directly and indirectly, to make up for substantial shortfalls in vital foodstuffs (principally maize) and other supplies. As a consequence, the colonial system of 17th-century Spanish Florida was fundamentally based on the structural assimilation of largely self-sufficient centers of Native American population distributed across an unevenly productive landscape. In this sense, Florida's mission provinces served a pivotal function for the residents of St. Augustine: the maintenance of a vast Indian labor pool comprising an interconnected web of population centers subordinated beneath the Spanish crown and church. In effect, then, Florida eventually became not so much an independent Spanish outpost interacting with neighboring and autonomous Indian societies (as was the trend during the colony's first two decades) but was instead a broader community of interdependent Spanish and Indian populations woven into a functioning colonial system with its hub at the Atlantic port of St. Augustine.

At its core, the internal economic structure of the colonial system in 17th-century Florida revolved around the production and distribution of staple food crops, particularly maize. While this is of course a simplification of a much more complex economic system, local maize production does seem to have played a determining role in the overall structure of Florida's economic system, especially in the role of the mission provinces in that system. It was the production and distribution of Florida's yearly maize crop that constituted the primary economic relationship between St. Augustine and its mission provinces. Together, the mission provinces provided both surplus maize and surplus labor for producing more maize, all of which was subsidized at least in part using funds derived from Florida's yearly royal subsidy, the situado. While local officials often skimmed personal profits from all such transactions, the end result of this colonial system was the yearly production of substantial supplementary food reserves for the city of St. Augustine. Given existing limitations both in available Spanish agricultural labor in St. Augustine (including not only soldiers and their families but also royal slaves and prisoners) and in subsidy funds that could have been used to purchase staple foods from other Spanish colonies, Spanish officials ultimately came to rely on the food and labor provided by the mission provinces as a relatively inexpensive local solution to food supply problems in St. Augustine. In times of crisis, St. Augustine's maize reserves were the primary buffer against privation for the Florida colony.

One perpetual dilemma in the overall colonial food production system that developed in Florida was the fact that St. Augustine was situated in a comparatively unproductive region of Florida and had few resident Indians remaining by the first decades of the 17th century—presumably a consequence of demographic collapse due to early and prolonged exposure to European pathogens introduced at the port. The most productive areas in colonial Spanish Florida (in terms of both soil fertility and human population, since neither was useful alone) were located far to the west and north of St. Augustine, in the mission provinces of Apalachee and Guale. While surplus maize and other foodstuffs were regularly bartered with trade goods and transported by ship from coastal ports in these provinces, the initiation of the Spanish *repartimiento* draft labor system in Florida provided hundreds of Indian laborers who traveled to St. Augustine on foot across the less productive Timucuan mission provinces of Timucua and Mocama. A yearly draft of some 300 unmarried males from the mission provinces spent between four and seven months in the environs of St. Augustine to provide the labor force needed to produce the city's yearly maize crop. This important crop amounted to perhaps a million pounds of maize each year during the mid-17th century, providing something on the order of eight times the amount of surplus corn available annually from Apalachee and Guale (Worth 1998a:126–34, 176–97).

Neither local agricultural productivity nor the available labor pool was distributed evenly across all the mission provinces during the mission period. While Apalachee provided abundant maize and numerous laborers, Guale and Mocama seem to have provided comparatively fewer laborers, focusing instead on local maize production for barter by ship. The interior Timucuan missions, on the other hand, generally produced few laborers and little surplus maize, serving instead as a transportation corridor across the peninsula. These missions, for example, particularly those along the trans-peninsular road known as the Camino Real, nevertheless played a crucial role in the maintenance of the travel, transport, and communication network that effectively linked the population centers of Apalachee and St. Augustine into a functioning economic unit. As way stations along the primary east-west land transportation corridor in Spanish Florida, the Timucuan missions were links in the western mission chain, without which the colonial system would have been unable to function efficiently. Just as Apalachee was a major agricultural production center in the Florida colony, Timucua served as a major transportation corridor. Larger surpluses in Apalachee were purchased for the royal warehouses, whereas minimal surpluses in Timucua presumably served to ration travelers of all sorts, including Spanish soldiers and officers, Franciscan friars, repartimiento laborers, burden bearers, and couriers. Each province thus had a unique role in Florida's colonial system, making both Apalachee and Timucua interdependent parts of a broader society. A similar relationship existed between Guale and Mocama along the northern mission chain.

The driving force behind the entire economic system was aboriginal labor. Without resident aboriginal labor, the fertile soils of Apalachee and Guale could yield neither the agricultural surpluses regularly purchased by Spanish agents nor the subsistence base of resident Indian and Spanish populations, including friars and garrisoned soldiers. Without aboriginal labor, the missions of Timucua and Mocama could not produce the staple foods that supported resident and transient populations along the Camino Real, nor could they provide ferry services across the rivers and estuaries of northern Florida and coastal Georgia. Furthermore, without aboriginal labor from all these regions (particularly Apalachee), the yearly maize crop in St. Augustine would effectively vanish, leaving the Spanish residents of St. Augustine without any important local source of staple foods as a backup in case of the failure of external supply lines. Finally, without aboriginal labor on a local level, the Florida mission chiefs would have little real basis to their hereditary positions of leadership, undermining not only traditional aboriginal sociopolitical systems but also the overlying Spanish administrative structure on which the entire colonial system was based. In these fundamental ways, aboriginal labor was perhaps the most important commodity in 17th-century Spanish Florida. This interpretation, of course, has considerable bearing on the overall biological impact of the mission system.

Ironically, it was precisely this commodity that entered a free-fall decline during the 17th-century mission era. The fatal flaw in the colonial system of Spanish Florida was its substantial dependence upon stable aboriginal population reserves as a source of labor. Even as Native American chiefdoms were incorporated into the expanding colonial system through the process of missionization, they were simultaneously exposed to a variety of European plague diseases to which they possessed little resistance. As we shall see, epidemic population decline was soon supplemented by other forces leading to increased mortality, decreased fertility, and simple flight from the mission provinces. The 17th-century colonial system of Spanish Florida was thus characterized by an almost continual process of adaptation and change, driven by rampant demographic collapse in the mission provinces. This tragic phenomenon ultimately transformed the colonial system, setting up internal stresses that, at least in the case of the interior Timucuan missions, led to open rebellion and the subsequent wholesale transformation of the interior missions under Spanish guidance (Worth 1998b:38–116).

Internal change and adaptation served only as a preface to external forces that would eventually result in the rapid destruction of the mission system and its contraction to the area around St. Augustine by 1706. Beginning in 1659, immigrant northern Indians variously known as Chichimecos, Rickahockans, or Westos arrived along the frontiers of broader Spanish Florida, wielding English-supplied firearms in a campaign of terror that would ultimately transform the entire social geography of the Southeast (Milanich 1999:168–88; Worth 1995, 1997, 1998b:140–46). In 1661, they assaulted and destroyed Guale mission Santo Domingo de Talaje on the Georgia mainland, and subsequent raids forced the retreat and relocation of all mainland Guale missions to the barrier islands by the 1670s, including the aggregation and fusion of villages from a variety of locations. Simultaneously, a new confederacy of refugees from the deep interior called the Yamasees relocated first to the old Escamaçu province on the mission frontier, and by the late 1660s into the mission system itself, forming new island towns in Guale and Mocama and later in Apalachee and on the upper St. Johns River in central Florida. While the coastal Yamasees contributed substantially to the repartimiento labor draft, their involvement in the Franciscan conversion effort was minimal during their brief tenure among the mission Indians. Pirate assaults against these relocated coastal missions in 1683 and 1684 finally forced the retreat of all Guale and Mocama missions to Amelia Island and southward, while the Yamasees fled west and north, ultimately relocating back to Escamaçu as new slave raiders for the Scottish and English traders in Carolina.

With the destruction of the Westo after 1680 by Carolina settlers, the creation of a new alliance with the mission Yamasees in late 1684, and the establishment of trade relations among the nascent Lower Creek and the Cherokee between 1685 and 1690, the missions were subjected to yet another wave of slave raids in the western interior after 1685, beginning with Timucuan mission of Santa Catalina de Afuyca that year. The annihilation of all remaining Guale missions in 1702 and the rout of Apalachee in 1704 prefaced final raids in Timucua that forced the abandonment of all remaining missions by 1706. The mission era was effectively over, as the few hundred survivors huddled together as refugees in a handful of newly established mission towns within sight of St. Augustine (Hann 1996:296–325; Worth 1998b:147–58; Milanich 1999:188–95).

Anticipated Biological Consequences

Within the 119 years that constituted the primary mission period between 1587 and 1706, the mission system of Spanish Florida resulted in significant and widespread transformations among assimilated chiefdoms, many of which would be anticipated to result in biological consequences for Native American populations living in and around these mission communities. A considerable amount of scholarly research has already been directed at this question (Larsen et al. 1990, 1996; Larsen 1990, 1993; Hoshower and Milanich 1993), and this volume represents the most current data and thinking in this regard. Based at least in part on the results of previous bioarchaeological research, in combination with the comparative wealth of ethnohistorical data already discussed, the following discussion addresses the anticipated biological consequences of missionization, some of which can be and have already been examined and some of which remain to be explored or demonstrated. I intend this discussion more as an overall framework for understanding the broader scope of biological change among mission populations than as a precise list of predictions or hypotheses for scientific testing.

What precisely were the broader sociopolitical and economic consequences of missionization for aboriginal populations, and how might these changes have been reflected in the biological realm? Given the overall ethnohistorical context discussed, changes in the following areas might be expected to be evidenced within skeletal samples taken from mission-era populations. On an individual level, these morphological and compositional changes would be related principally to alterations in activity, diet, and biological stress (related to nutrition or disease); on a group or community level, changes might occur in demography (i.e., increased mortality and decreased birthrate), overall community health, and ethnic composition. Ultimately, the sum total of such biological changes would be expected to be reflected to greater or lesser degrees in mission-era skeletal samples from the various provinces or regions within the Florida mission system, particularly when compared with pre-mission-era samples from the late prehistoric or contact periods in these same areas.

Documentary evidence makes it abundantly clear that the most significant biological consequence of missionization in Spanish Florida was rapid and traumatic depopulation of all areas directly affected by the mission system, eventually resulting quite literally in extinction for all missionized populations. Although the causes, timing, and rate of depopulation undoubtedly varied from province to province, and even from village to village, global census data from Spanish Florida confirm unambiguously that indigenous population levels within the geographic area eventually encompassed by the mission system dropped effectively 100 percent between the early 16th and late 18th centuries. Using a rough estimate of perhaps 200,000 prehistoric Native Americans living in what would later become the Florida mission system, subsequent data suggest that these same populations eventually plummeted to less than 5 percent of their original level by the end of the primary mission period in the early 18th century. They declined to less than 0.1 percent by the time of their removal from Florida in the 1760s, when only 89 mission Indians (including many immigrant refugees from beyond the original mission system) boarded ships bound for Cuba with the Spaniards, not counting some 40 families of remnant Apalachee, Yamasee, and Creek Indians living around Pensacola who were shipped to Veracruz, Mexico, that same year. Later records demonstrate that the total surviving number of Florida Indians in Cuba and Mexico was just over 100, of whom many certainly died within a few years of their immigration (Worth 1998b:156–57; Hann 1988:314–16).

Despite this ultimate result, the extinction of the mission Indians was actually a comparatively gradual process, lasting many generations, during which surviving populations were subjected to a variety of biological transformations. In this sense, the detailed examination of skeletal populations from Florida missions represents a remarkable opportunity to explore the precise nature and timing of specific changes resulting from many different aspects of daily life in the assimilated mission chiefdoms.

The reasons for radical depopulation in the Florida mission provinces were undoubtedly numerous, and elsewhere I have outlined five principal categories that contributed to the observed demographic collapse among missionized Native Americans (Worth 1998b:8–26). These included death and declining health resulting from or influenced by (1) epidemic diseases, (2) exhaustion and exposure, in the context of the colonial labor system, (3) declining nutrition, and (4) frontier raiding, all of which resulted in an increased rate of mortality among mission populations. These factors were presumably supplemented by (5) reduced population growth influenced by an overall decrease in community health as well as by demographic transformations and also (6) intentional out-migration, in which individuals and families simply left the mission system to live beyond the reach of Spanish authorities.

For our purposes here, however, the simple death or absence of individuals or families from mission communities represents only one of many biological consequences evidenced for the mission period. In some ways, the overall depopulation of the missions represents the least intriguing of all biological transformations experienced, since it was actually the living, surviving populations that were forced to adapt and change during the courses of their lives, providing a far greater possibility that such life changes would be reflected in skeletal populations.

Such changes would be expected in several areas within the primary mission period, including transformations in diet and nutrition, activity and workload, community health, and (later) in the ethnic composition of local populations. Easily the most important dimension of the mission system in this regard was the colonial economy of broader Spanish Florida, already addressed. Two principal factors—the intensification of agricultural production in mission communities and the colonial wage-labor system—would be expected to have resulted in significant biological transformations among mission Indians. Given that the staple crop of Spanish Florida was maize, and that the local production and barter of mission maize eventually became one of the primary functions of the mission economy, it would seem likely that mission diets across Spanish Florida became far more uniform in their reliance upon agricultural products such as maize. In this sense, missionization probably served to minimize or even erase previous disparities in the relative contribution of maize and other agricultural crops to Native American diets in the various regions assimilated into the mission system. Inasmuch as maize served as the primary currency of the mission frontier, at least with regard to the garrison of St. Augustine, missionized chiefdoms and villages undoubtedly increased their maize crops substantially during the 17th century, in many cases probably growing far more than could ever be eaten by local residents. This agricultural intensification was enhanced by the introduction of iron tools such as axes for felling trees and hoes for cultivating fields, but it was the increased demand for maize in St. Augustine that prompted their widespread use toward this end. In the absence of the colonial barter economy, such iron tools held principally social value as visible symbols of chiefly alliances, but during the mission period their value was far higher in the realm of economic productivity (see Worth 1998a:38).

In the biological realm, the agricultural intensification spurred by the colonial economy served not only to render mission diets more homogeneous across Spanish Florida but presumably also to alter the nutritional composition of mission diets, resulting in specific changes generally associated with an increased reliance on starchy carbohydrates. In addition, dental health would obviously have declined, particularly given the sugars present in maize. All of these transformations would be expected to be reflected in skeletal populations and might be especially pronounced among Native American groups that had had little previous experience with a substantially agricultural diet.

Agricultural intensification in the missions also resulted in transformations in local aboriginal work patterns, which were of course supplemented by the simultaneous increase in wage labor associated with the annual repartimiento labor drafts. Not only were resident mission populations expected to provide the additional labor associated with increased local maize production, but they also served as the labor pool for the colonial labor system, which generally enlisted young, unmarried males for seasonal labor in the privately owned fields and ranches around St. Augustine and San Luis, for courier and burden-bearing services, and for canoe and ferry transportation in specific locations. In overall perspective, the colonial labor system would be expected to have resulted in substantial transformations in Native American labor patterns, reflected in the biological realm by alterations in the intensity, type, and frequency of activities associated with various tasks associated with manual labor. In this regard, several subpopulations can be identified within mission communities, distinguished in part by gender, age, and marital status. Specific tasks were generally associated with specific groups; young adult males would be expected to bear the imprint of increased upper-body activity associated with lengthy periods of digging and hoeing in agricultural fields and also increased lower-body activity associated with episodic long-distance travel on foot. Other groups not directly affected by the annual repartimiento draft—women, children, and older, married males—presumably took up the slack in the missions, providing manual labor in mission fields to make up for other laborers absent in St. Augustine during the growing season. All these transformations in labor patterns, while complex, should be reflected in the bioarchaeological record.

The colonial labor system had additional effects in the biological realm, particularly the seasonal and annual demographic profile of specific mission communities. Mission chiefs occasionally complained that most of the young males eligible for marriage lived or spent long periods of time in St. Augustine as wage laborers, leaving mission villages with a surfeit of unmarried young women (Worth 1998b:21–22). This, in turn, resulted in a decreased overall birthrate, leaving the mission Indians literally without any means to combat epidemic depopulation with a normal or increased birthrate.

Global depopulation in the Florida missions also produced secondary consequences that provided further fuel for biological change in surviving mission populations. Even as mission populations declined rapidly, Indian and Spanish authorities endeavored to counter this trend with a variety of strategies designed to maintain mission villages with sufficient population levels to survive as viable communities (Worth 1998b:27–37). One of these strategies was *congregación,* or the intentional contraction and aggregation of outlying satellite communities into central villages and administrative centers. Apart from resulting in the outright abandonment of many smaller subordinate villages and hamlets, this strategy, employed most commonly during the early and mid-17th century, ultimately resulted in the fusion of originally dispersed population centers into larger communities, all on a localized scale. In some cases, entire villages were voluntarily or forcibly relocated tremendous distances in order to repopulate strategic nodes in the travel and transport network of Spanish Florida. In the end, congregación and directed resettlement resulted in a significant transformation from a relatively dispersed settlement pattern to a far more centralized one, reducing the overall number of communities within the mission system from hundreds to only a few dozen, all within the space of just a few decades. This phenomenon, combined with the effects of agricultural intensification and the colonial labor system described, undoubtedly resulted in a degree of crowding and sedentism that may not have been present prior to the mission period, potentially compromising elements of overall community health.

Finally, beginning in the 1660s and continuing through the end of the primary mission period in 1706, Florida's mission communities were transformed by the advancing juggernaut of English-sponsored aggression and the technological advantages afforded these slave raiders by their flintlock muskets. Land-based aggression had several effects, including the further contraction of all remaining satellite communities and farmsteads into more compact and defensible mission villages and the further relocation and aggregation of exposed communities. In the Guale province, for example, no fewer than four formerly distinct mission villages lived together on the northern end of Sapelo Island between 1680 and 1684, including mainland Tupiqui and Satuache and the island towns of Guale and Sapala, originally located many miles apart from one another in the old Guale chiefdom (Worth 1995:34, 101).

Even more important, English-sponsored slave raiding also resulted in the immigration of significant numbers of Native Americans from more distant regions as refugees from the raiding. Without question the largest group of such refugees was the Yamasee confederacy, which coalesced along the northern mission frontier in the 1660s and which relocated en masse into the mission system by the 1670s (Worth 1995:18–30). Their brief tenure on the Georgia coast, and an even more ephemeral stay along the upper St. Johns River in central Florida, nonetheless resulted in the physical proximity of Native American populations from widely disparate geographic, ethnic, and even linguistic origins during the 1660s, 1670s, and early 1680s. Many of the converted Christian Yamasee even remained in the Tama mission in the Apalachee province, and while most of the Atlantic coast Yamasee evidently remained unconverted and unattached to their Guale and Mocama neighbors, demographic data from 1675 and 1681 population reports suggest that at least some intermarriage did occur, presumably introducing an element of biological diversity to local mission populations during this period (Worth 1995:34).

In conclusion, while the details of the initial biological consequences of missionization remain a fruitful subject for scientific research, as demonstrated in this volume, it must be remembered that the ultimate biological impact of the missions was extinction. All major regional provinces or districts assimilated into the mission system, including principally the Guale, Mocama, Timucua, Yustaga, Apalachee, and various "Freshwater" Timucuan chiefdoms of the upper St. Johns River drainage had been severely depopulated by the last decades of the 17th century; the few survivors who remained after the retreat of the missions in the face of English slave raiding by 1706 were gradually reduced to near total extinction by the 1760s, when the removal of only a handful of surviving mission Indians to Cuba and Mexico effectively marked the biological end of these populations in the southeastern United States. Nevertheless, the story of biological adaptation and change experienced by surviving generations of mission Indians during the 17th and early 18th century is one that is well worth studying, even if the end result was ultimately a tragic one.

References Cited

Anderson, D. G. 1994. *The Savannah River Chiefdoms: Political Change in the Late Prehistoric Southeast.* Tuscaloosa: University of Alabama Press.

Bushnell, A. T. 1994. *Situado and Sabana: Spain's Support System for the Presidio and Mission Provinces of Florida.* Anthropological Papers of the American Museum of Natural History 74.

Hann, J. H. 1988. *Apalachee: The Land Between the Rivers.* Gainesville: University Press of Florida.

———. 1993. The Mayaca and Jororo and Missions to Them. In *The Spanish Missions of La Florida,* ed. B. G. McEwan, 111–40. Gainesville: University Press of Florida.

———. 1996. *A History of the Timucua Indians and Missions.* Gainesville: University Press of Florida.

Hoshower, L. M., and J. T. Milanich. 1993. Excavations in the Fig Springs Mission Burial Area. In *The Spanish Missions of La Florida,* ed. B. G. McEwan, 217–43. Gainesville: University Press of Florida.

Hudson, C., and C. C. Tesser. 1994. *The Forgotten Centuries: Indians and Europeans in the American South, 1521–1704.* Athens: University of Georgia Press.

Larsen, C. S. 1993. On the Frontier of Contact: Mission Bioarchaeology in *La Florida.* In *The Spanish Missions of La Florida,* ed. B. G. McEwan, 322–56. Gainesville: University Press of Florida.

——— (ed.). 1990. *The Archaeology of Mission Santa Catalina de Guale*: 2. *Biocultural Interpretations of a Population in Transition.* Anthropological Papers of the American Museum of Natural History 68.

Larsen, C. S., C. B. Ruff, and M. C. Griffin. 1996. Implications of Changing Biomechanical and Nutritional Environments for Activity and Lifeway in the Eastern Spanish Borderlands. In *Bioarchaeology of Native American Adaptation in the Spanish Borderlands,* ed. B. J. Baker and L. Kealhofer, 95–125. Gainesville: University Press of Florida.

Larsen, C. S., M. J. Schoeninger, D. L. Hutchinson, K. F. Russell, and C. B. Ruff. 1990. Beyond Demographic Collapse: Biological Adaptation and Change in

Native Populations of La Florida. In *Columbian Consequences*: 2. *Archaeological and Historical Perspectives on the Spanish Borderlands East,* ed. D. H. Thomas, 409–28. Washington; Smithsonian Institution Press.

Larson, L. H., Jr. 1980. *Aboriginal Subsistence Technology on the Southeastern Coastal Plain during the Historic Period.* Gainesville: University Press of Florida.

Lyon, E. 1976. *The Enterprise of Florida: Pedro Menéndez de Avilés and the Spanish Conquest of 1565–1568.* Gainesville: University of Florida Press.

———. 1992. The Failure of the Guale and Orista Mission: 1572–1575. In *Columbus and the Land of Ayllón: The Exploration and Settlement of the Southeast,* ed. J. Cook, 89–104. Darien, Ga.: Darien News.

Milanich, J. T. 1995. *Florida Indians and the Invasion from Europe.* Gainesville: University Press of Florida.

———. 1999. *Laboring in the Fields of the Lord: Spanish Missions and Southeastern Indians.* Washington: Smithsonian Institution Press.

Smith, M. T. 1987. *Archaeology of Aboriginal Culture Change in the Interior Southeast: Depopulation during the Early Historic Period.* Gainesville: University Presses of Florida.

Widmer, R. J. 1994. The Structure of Southeastern Chiefdoms. In *The Forgotten Centuries: Indians and Europeans in the American South, 1521–1704,* ed. C. Hudson and C. C. Tesser, 125–55. Athens: University of Georgia Press.

Worth, J. E. 1994. Late Spanish Military Expeditions in the Interior Southeast, 1597–1628. In *The Forgotten Centuries: Indians and Europeans in the American South, 1521–1704,* ed. C. Hudson and C. C. Tesser, 104–22. Athens: University of Georgia Press.

———. 1995. *The Struggle for the Georgia Coast: An Eighteenth-Century Spanish Retrospective on Guale and Mocama.* Anthropological Papers of the American Museum of Natural History 75.

———. 1997. Integrating Ethnohistory and Archaeology among the Timucua: An Overview of Southeast Georgia and Northeast Florida. Paper presented at the 54th annual meeting, Southeastern Archaeological Conference, Baton Rouge, Louisiana.

———. 1998a. *The Timucuan Chiefdoms of Spanish Florida*: 1. *Assimilation.* Gainesville: University Press of Florida.

———. 1998b. *The Timucuan Chiefdoms of Spanish Florida*: 2. *Resistance and Destruction.* Gainesville: University Press of Florida.

———. 1999. Coastal Chiefdoms and the Question of Agriculture: An Ethnohistorical Overview. Paper presented at the 56th annual meeting, Southeastern Archaeological Conference, Pensacola, Florida.

2

Bioarchaeology of Spanish Florida

Clark Spencer Larsen

Christopher Columbus's landfall in the Bahamas in 1492 set in motion an extraordinary change in the lives and lifeways of native populations throughout the Americas. Many scholars assume that pre-Columbian peoples lived in a kind of paradise before the invasion of Europeans, suffering no disease, no malnutrition, and no demanding labor. Dobyns (1983:34) remarked, for example, that "before the invasion of peoples of the New World by pathogens that evolved among inhabitants of the Old World, Native Americans lived in a relatively disease-free environment. . . . Before Europeans initiated the Columbian exchange of germs and viruses, the peoples of the Americas suffered no smallpox, no measles, no chickenpox, no influenza, no typhus, no typhoid or parathyroid fever, no diphtheria, no cholera, no bubonic plague, no scarlet fever, no whooping cough, and no malaria."

To be sure, none of the horrific diseases Dobyns mentions was present in the New World before Europeans crossed the Atlantic for the first time. And, for most regions, the introduction of novel Old World pathogens led to shortened life spans and caused widespread suffering and death (Crosby 1972, 1986; Reff 1991; Cook 1998; and see Larsen 1994). Contrary to assertions of scholars relying on historical records, however, there is abundant evidence from paleopathological studies of skeletons from across the Americas that native populations were not novices to infectious diseases and poor health (see Verano and Ubelaker 1992; Larsen 1994). For example, human remains show pathological and molecular evidence of tuberculosis—lesions typical of the disease have been identified in North and South America in skeletons and mummies, and fragments of DNA from tubercular lesions on lung tissue from a pre-Columbian mummy match with modern *Mycobacterium tuberculosis,* the microbe that causes the disease (Salo et al. 1994). Importantly, studies of historic-era skeletons from throughout the Western Hemisphere reveal evidence for increased morbidity, especially in later prehistory with the introduction and adoption of agriculture (Larsen 1994).

Nor was it the case that pre-contact native diets were always adequate or workloads easy (Larsen 1994; various authors in Verano and Ubelaker 1992, Larsen and Milner 1994, and Baker and Kealhofer 1996). Abundant evidence from stable isotope analysis reveals a shift to plant carbohydrates and decreasing diversity of diet in many regions of the Americas, and osteoarthritis is severe in a number of regions.

The misperceptions about health and well-being of the pre-Columbian world are problematic because they establish an incorrect context for characterizing and interpreting the impact of European colonization on native populations: life for Native Americans went from good to bad. Moreover, the narrow focus on disease, dying, and death in historical scholarship has overshadowed other key areas of the contact experience and human biology, including the impact of population relocation and aggregation, changing activity and labor exploitation, dietary shifts and nutritional decline, and other factors. In this book, we offer that bioarchaeology—the study of human remains from archaeological contexts—presenting an important approach for constructing a more informed understanding of the biology of contact. Just as this record has shown that pre-contact Native Americans did not live in a disease-free setting, it has the potential to reveal important characteristics that collectively comprise the various life experiences that influence biology.

The Bioarchaeological Record of Contact

The human skeleton is a highly sensitive indicator of past life experiences, both within the individual and from the population in which that individual lived. Throughout the years of growth and development and adulthood, diet and nutrition, disease, lifestyle, and activity leave a record on the bones and teeth from which it is possible to reconstruct life history in highly informative ways (Larsen 1997).

Unlike written sources, which begin at the time of European contact, the biological record represented by skeletons is a continuous one, beginning from well before European contact and continuing through the contact period (e.g., various studies in Larsen and Milner 1994; Baker and Kealhofer 1996). This continuity allows us to compare and contrast pre-contact and post-contact conditions in ways that are not possible with written sources. This is not to say that the historical record is not an important source of information. Indeed, historical sources provide enormous insight into the lives and lifestyles of native peoples (and see Worth, this volume). When these sources are combined with the bioarchaeological record, we are in a position to gain a more comprehensive understanding of biological change and population decline in the post-Columbian world.

It has only been in recent years that human remains have been brought into the discussions about post-contact human biology. It is not surprising that human remains have not been part of the discussion about health and quality of life during the contact period in the Americas. For one thing, until the last couple of decades, physical anthropologists who study ancient skeletons have not been much interested in issues relating to lifestyle. Moreover, few large samples of well-documented contact-era skeletons had not been professionally excavated. Even if samples of skeletons had been recovered and studied by a physical anthropologist, the results of study were likely relegated to an appendix of an obscure (often unpublished) archaeological report. Finally, many of the methods used by bioarchaeologists as a matter of routine investigation today were not developed until the last decade or so (e.g., application of scanning electron microscopy to tooth wear). Indeed, in the present book, most of the research would not have been possible 20 years ago (and see Larsen and Milner 1994).

Realizing the potential of the study of human remains from mission sites for gaining a more comprehensive understanding of the biology of the contact period, I began the La Florida Bioarchaeology Project, starting with the excavation and study of a large series of skeletons from the 17th-century Santa Catalina de Guale mission, located on St. Catherines Island, Georgia (Larsen 1990; and see later discussion). The Santa Catalina skeletons represent the remains of persons from the Guale, the primary tribe living on the Georgia coast. Having spent much of the previous decade studying the skeletons of prehistoric Indians who were the ancestors of the Guale, I recognized that what we had learned about the pre-contact biological record (summarized in Larsen 1982, 1984) would provide an important backdrop for evaluating the biological consequences of the arrival of Europeans and establishment of mission centers for native populations. Previous to our work on the contact-era Guale, other mission cemeteries had been excavated in La Florida (see Larsen 1993), but the research on the Santa Catalina skeletal remains was the first to address issues that considered the larger scope of biocultural adaptation during the post-contact period.

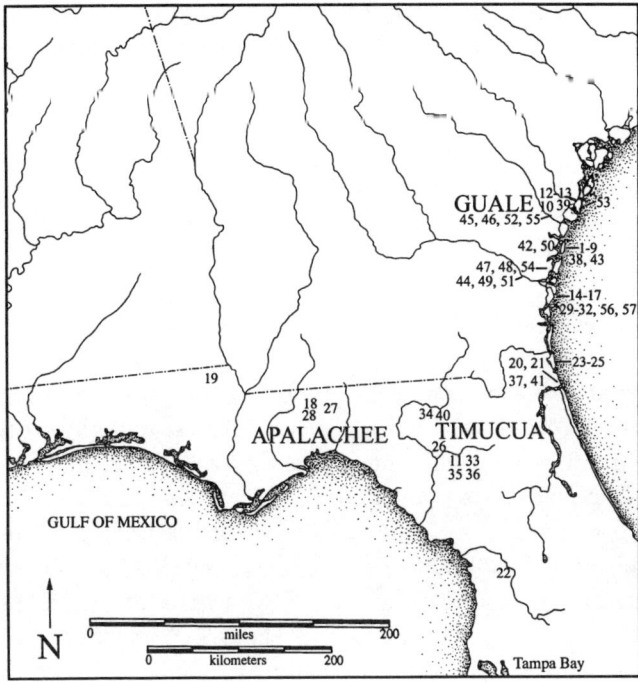

Fig. 2.1. Map showing locations of pre-contact and contact-era mortuary sites, La Florida Bioarchaeology Project. Names of the numbered sites are given in table 2.1.

Comparison of numerous pre-contact skeletons with those recovered from the St. Catherines Island mission, and follow-up research on the descendant Guale population from Santa Catalina de Guale de Santa Maria (herein called Santa Catalina de Amelia) on Amelia Island, Florida, indicated some fundamental changes in lifeway for native populations: (1) study of bone chemistry involving analysis of stable isotopes of carbon and nitrogen revealed a simultaneous increase in maize and decrease in seafood in the diet (Schoeninger et al. 1990; Larsen et al. 1992); (2) analysis of enamel defects caused by growth disruption revealed an increase in physiological stress (Hutchinson and Larsen 1988, 1990); and (3) analysis of structure of limb bones indicated an increase in workload, probably related to labor exploitation by Spaniards (Ruff and Larsen 1990; Larsen and Ruff 1994).

The historical record clearly indicated population decline over the period, both in size and in quality of life, in large part due to the impact of

European-introduced infectious diseases. Our study of skeletons indicated that the consequences of contact were complex and multifactoral. On the one hand, some of the changes we observed were clearly negative. On the other hand, we came to the realization that a new approach that considered how native populations adapted to new and changing circumstances could provide a more informed understanding of changes in native populations. For example, our analysis of bone structure showed that post-contact Guale made biological adjustments to the increased demands relating to food production and workload.

As our research unfolded, we recognized that post-contact human adaptation in Guale was only a small part of a larger picture of biocultural change that occurred across the complex cultural and biological landscapes of La Florida. We needed to look at the skeletons representing the other major tribal groups that came under the umbrella of missionization if we were to come to a broader understanding of a region sharing common life experiences and a common history of contact with a major European power.

A decade after the initial work began on the study of the remains from Santa Catalina on St. Catherines Island, we expanded the research program to include several other major tribal groups, especially the Timucua, who lived in northern Atlantic coastal Florida inland to north-central Florida, and the Apalachee, who occupied a large portion of the panhandle of Florida (fig. 2.1). Like the Guale, both these tribal groups have been extensively studied by historians, ethnohistorians, and archaeologists (see McEwan 1993; Bushnell 1994; Milanich 1995, 1996, 1999; Worth 1998, this volume; Hann 1988, 1996; Hann and McEwan 1998). The wealth of knowledge about the history and archaeology of these groups provides essential context for understanding human biological change based on the study of skeletal and dental remains from contact-era sites (and see Worth, this volume). The record is further strengthened by a collaboration among historians, archaeologists, and physical anthropologists toward a common goal of developing a greater understanding of the past in pre-contact and contact Spanish Florida (Gannon 1992).

The Biocultural and Archaeological Setting

As is pointed out by Worth in the preceding chapter, native peoples in Spanish Florida were among the first to be contacted by Europeans in the New World. The consequences for native populations of the earliest encounters are little known, owing to the brevity of these encounters between Europeans and Indians and to the lack of documentation. Almost certainly, these early contacts led to loss of life from epidemics and violence. Regarding the former, there is little direct knowledge from study of skeletons dating to the period. However, the evidence for violence is clearly displayed in skeletons with cutmarks probably made by Spaniards wielding metal-edged weapons (Tatham Mound, Florida; Hutchinson and Norr 1994).

Once Spain's long-term successes in the region began in 1565 with the founding of the first permanent European colony and capital of La Florida by Pedro Menéndez at St. Augustine, interactions between Indians and Europeans were more sustained. It was during the mission period, from 1587 to 1706, that the broader implications for post-contact native populations began to take shape.

The Mission Era

The provinces occupied by Guale, Timucua, and Apalachee contained most of the missions, but other tribes were involved, such as the Yamasee, a group representing an aggregation of various tribal entities who moved from Georgia and coastal South Carolina to Atlantic coastal Florida in the later 17th century (see Hann 1990; Worth 1995, this volume). The Guale occupied the Georgia coast and adjacent mainland from the mouth of the Savannah River southward to St. Simons Island (Jones 1978). Timucua province included the southern Georgia coast and the northern Florida Atlantic coast and extended westward to the Aucilla River (Hann 1990, 1996; Milanich 1996; Worth 1998). Apalachee province included the Florida panhandle west of the Aucilla River to the Ochlockonee River (Hann 1988, 1990). For much of this period, the principal mission centers were placed in strategic locations. On the Atlantic coast, Santa Catalina de Guale located on St. Catherines Island represented the principal northern outpost on the Atlantic seaboard until its abandonment in 1680. On the western end, missions extended beyond Apalachee province, but the primary center was in the heart of Apalachee at San Luis de Apalachee.

Santa Catalina de Guale was one of the longest-lasting missions, having been established in the period of Spanish geographic expansion in the late 16th century and continuing until 1680, when a large force of Yamasee Indians led by Colonel James Moore and British troops from Carolina attacked the mission and forced its abandonment. The survivors of the attack, Indians and Spaniards, ended up on Amelia Island, where Santa Catalina de Amelia was established by the summer of 1684 (Worth 1995). This followed more than 20 years of conflict with other native groups, slave raids, and other factors that characterize the third and final period of the mission era noted by Worth (this volume). The newly constructed mission on Amelia Island lasted only until 1702, when Colonel Moore and his associates repeated their attacks on Guale. Once again, the priests, garrison, and Indians retreated southward, this time to St. Augustine. This final retreat ended Guale as a province controlled by Spain. Guale represents a microcosm of the social, political, and biological changes characterizing the mission era as a whole.

Missionization of coastal Timucua was also early, but as Worth notes (this volume), Timucua was never an important region with regard to food or other types of production. Rather, the region and the native people occupying it served as an important link between the more productive Apalachee province to the west and St. Augustine on the Atlantic coast (see Worth, this volume).

Throughout the 17th century, a great deal of population movement of these and other tribes occurred. From Georgia, the Yamasee settled on Amelia Island in a village previously occupied by Timucua (known as Mocama) at the settlement of Santa Maria (Worth 1995). The locality and its mission is known as Santa Maria de Yamasee (Hann 1990; and see Worth 1995).

The Apalachee were first contacted by Narváez in 1528, followed by de Soto in 1539 (Hann 1988; Hann and McEwan 1998). Formal missionization did not begin in Apalachee province until the early 1630s, the second broad period of the mission effort (see Worth, this volume). Over the next several decades, key missions were established in the province, including the principal mission and western capital of Spanish Florida at San Luis de Apalachee (also called San Luis de Talimali) in 1656 (Hann 1988; Hann and McEwan 1998); some missions were moved from previous locations. At its peak in the mid-1670s, San Luis had a resident population of some 1,500 Apalachee and Spaniards (Hann and McEwan 1998). Although there were several missions west of San Luis in the Apalachicola River basin, this mission served as the main western anchor of Spanish colonization in the American Southeast.

Unlike most of the other missions in La Florida, where the population was mostly native and included a resident priest and perhaps a small garrison, San Luis had a sizable garrison of Spanish troops and various nonmilitary Spaniards and their families. San Luis and the other Apalachee missions were abandoned in 1704 during conflicts with British military and their Indian allies.

Archaeological Context for Interpreting Human Biology in Spanish Florida

In virtually no other region in the New World is the archaeology of contact between Europeans and native populations as well documented as it is in Spanish Florida. Especially during the last decade or so, the efflorescence of research activities focusing on archaeological and ethnohistorical documentation of mission sites and their key components (e.g., churches and cemeteries) has resulted in an unusually comprehensive picture of native lifeways (Thomas 1987, 1990; Jones et al. 1991; Larsen 1990; Weisman 1992; various authors in McEwan 1993; Hann and McEwan 1998).

Key to understanding human adaptation is the ability to characterize diet accurately. From numerous archaeological excavations, native foodways have been reconstructed based on the study of plant and animal remains recovered from pre-contact and contact-era sites in each of the three primary provinces of La Florida (Reitz and Scarry 1985; Reitz 1988, 1993; Scarry and Reitz 1990; Ruhl 1990; Scarry 1993). Prior to contact by Europeans and the mission period, archaeological evidence indicates a diversity of foods collected or produced for consumption across the region.

On the Georgia coast, the role of cultivars—and maize especially—has been interpreted in two different ways. Based on his reading of written documents dating to the 16th century, Lewis Larson (1980) regards maize as having been present in late prehistoric diets but suggests that it was never very important. Alternatively, in his reinterpretation of these and other sources, Grant Jones (1978) contends that maize was an important focus of diet, providing enough surplus food for storage and distribution in the Guale chiefdom.

The archaeobotanical record is only sparse for this region, making it impossible to determine the importance of maize in native diets. Stable isotope evidence from analysis of human bone samples from late prehistoric contexts, however, is unequivocal: maize was an important part of late prehistoric Guale diets, having been adopted after about A.D. 1000 or so (see Schoeninger et al. 1990; Larsen et al. 1992, this volume; Hutchinson et al. 1998). Moreover, microwear evidence from pre-contact and contact-era teeth indicates diet and tooth use consistent with a maize diet (Teaford 1991; Teaford et al., this volume).

Abundant archaeological evidence indicates that marine foods figured prominently in the diets of prehistoric and contact native populations in Guale, including a range of fish and shellfish (Reitz 1988). The importance of seafood in these Georgia coastal societies reflects the tremendous productivity of the estuarine and marine waters of the Georgia Bight (see Reitz

1988). Various terrestrial foods were also eaten prehistorically and historically, and deer especially provided an important source of protein (Reitz
1988). Archaeological excavations at Santa Catalina de Guale and other
contact era sites on St. Catherines Island have produced the remains of a
variety of Old World cultivars, including wheat, watermelon, peas, canta-
loupe, and grapes, along with New World cultivars, such as maize, beans,
squash, and gourd (Ruhl 1990, 1993). Additionally, various wild plants
are represented by acorns, persimmon, plum/cherry, amaranths, and che-
nopodium (Ruhl 1990).

Native groups living to the south of Guale occupied a diversity of landscapes, and the dietary variability reflected in archaeological plant and
animal remains shows this diversity. The coastal Timucua and Apalachee
ate various fish and shellfish. For other aspects of diet, the Timucua differed from the Apalachee and Guale in some key ways. Many of the
Timucua groups in the contact period either conducted no agriculture or
cultivation was a minor part of subsistence technology (Hann 1996; Worth,
this volume). In the archaeobotanical record, Newsom (1991) has found
for the area south of St. Augustine that domesticated plants (maize and
squash) are present only in post-contact contexts, indicating the possibility
that maize was eaten only during the mission period.

In contrast to Timucua, de Soto chroniclers and various later mission
accounts describe the rich agricultural soils and the overall productivity of
agricultural pursuits in Apalachee province (Bourne 1922; and see Hann
1988; Scarry 1993; Hann and McEwan 1998). For the prehistoric period
immediately preceding the mission period, charred corncobs and maize
kernels found at the Mississippian period Lake Jackson site suggest the
probable importance of agriculture several centuries before Europeans arrived (Ruhl 1990; Scarry 1993).

During the mission period, the apparent productivity of Apalachee
fields was a primary consideration for establishing missions in the region
(Hann 1988). When it became clear that the infertile soils of the region
surrounding St. Augustine were not going to produce enough food for the
growing town, Apalachee and its productive fields provided an obvious
solution, and Apalachee (and to a lesser extent Guale) became a source of
maize for the town (see Hann 1988; Scarry 1993; Hann and McEwan
1998; Worth, this volume).

Under the mission system, the Indians began producing food not only
for themselves but also for export and for support of priests, military, and
other Spaniards living at the missions and elsewhere. This increase in food
production may well have led to increase in agricultural food consumption

in the native population, a point we investigate in this volume via stable isotope analysis and other lines of evidence (see Larsen et al., this volume; Teaford et al., this volume).

Margaret Scarry's (1993) assessment of pre-contact and mission archaeological plant assemblages indicates specific patterns of diet and dietary change. She suggests that indigenous crops—especially maize—provided the staples for everyone's diet, a finding that is consistent with the documentary record. Her analysis of plant remains from the village area at San Luis de Apalachee, for example, indicates the presence of a relatively wide range of Old World cultivars (e.g., wheat, garbanzo, peach, fig, hazelnut). From the floor of the council house at San Luis, she found a diversity of plants, including maize, beans, sunflower, wheat, peach, hickory, acorn, and various wild fruits.

Analysis of animal food remains by Reitz (1990, 1993, n.d.) points to a diversity of animals being hunted and collected prehistorically and historically throughout the provinces of Spanish Florida. In the coastal setting, fish and shellfish provided an essential part of the diet. Inland, not surprisingly, these foods were far less important, but freshwater aquatic sources provided key foods for at least some regions (e.g., north-central Florida). In the missions, although there are some commonly used animals (e.g., deer), there are some distinctive differences between the three provinces. Written records indicate that horses, cattle, pigs, and chickens were raised by Indians living at the missions. However, the zooarchaeological remains indicate that these animals were likely a minor part of their diet, as distinct from what Europeans may have been eating.

No horse remains have been identified in mission contexts. Pig remains have been identified but infrequently (e.g., San Luis de Apalachee, Santa Catalina de Guale). Both pigs and cattle have been identified as abundant fauna at San Luis only; indeed, most of the biomass was derived from domestic mammals (Reitz 1990, 1993). This unusual composition of mammalian fauna likely reflects the diets of Spaniards and high status Indians living in or near the mission complex. Reitz's analysis reveals that most mission Indians ate a range of animals similar to what their prehistoric predecessors ate.

Native Lifeways in La Florida: A Case for Temporal and Geographic Variation

The analysis of food remains from pre-contact and mission archaeological sites indicates that a strong case can be made for shifts in diet and variation from one region to another. Primary changes from the pre-mission to the mission period include continued (intensified) use of maize in Guale and Apalachee provinces and the adoption of maize in Timucua province. These changes have important implications for health status and well-being of native populations both before and after contact.

Importantly, increased consumption of maize was likely related to increased production of this cultivar and other food crops. Increased production would necessarily have meant increased workload for Indians, a conclusion that is consistent with historical records indicating the practice here and elsewhere in New Spain of the highly exploitative draft labor system, repartimiento (see Weber 1992; Worth, this volume). The priests and Spanish crown quickly perceived the native populations of Apalachee, Guale, and Timucua as an important labor source. Adult men and women provided the essential labor for production of food crops and for its transport to St. Augustine and elsewhere in the provinces.

Another important aspect of the labor system introduced to La Florida by the Spanish was stresses relating to travel and carrying of heavy burdens. A network of roads and trails crisscrossed Spanish Florida, providing the routes for transport of goods around the provinces, linking communities in Timucua and Apalachee, and linking these communities with St. Augustine (Hann 1988; Worth 1998, this volume). Pack animals were not available until late in the mission period, and all burdens were carried on the backs of Indians. Indians carrying these burdens over long distances were exposed to some extremely physically demanding work. Moreover, food shortages for repartimiento laborers were a chronic problem. Royal treasurer Don Joseph de Prado summarized the problem for the native population and land transport:

> For lack of pack animals, the said Indians bring on their back and transport the fruits and goods of the land which are bartered and traded, a hard thing, which they refuse and resent so much, since it is commonly said that for this cause some absent themselves from among the Christians, and many others leave it off and refuse to be [Christians] in order not to experience similar labor, from which it has resulted in some dying on the roads in times of cold [weather], and there was a Christian Indian woman who, having had a male child, killed him without baptism in order not to see him made a slave. (Quoted in Worth 1998:14–15)

Native labor was an essential part of crop production and formed an essential part of the economic structure of La Florida. Governor Canzo reported to the crown in 1602–3: "But with all this and the grain from the maize, the labor that they endure in the many cultivations that are given is great, and, if it were not for the help of the Indians that I make them give, and they come from the province of Guale, Antonico, and from other cauiquwe, it would not be possible to be able to sow any grain" (unpublished transla tion provided by John H. Hann).

Fray Alonso Moral noted in his report in the 1670s about the conditions of life for natives carrying heavy burdens in Apalachee:

All the natives of those provinces suffer great servitude, injuries, and vexations from the fact that the governor, lieutenants, and soldiers oblige them to carry loads on their shoulders to the Province of Apalachee and to other areas and also to bring loads from those regions to the fort of St. Augustine. . . . Each year from Apalachee alone more than three hundred are brought to the fort at the time of the planting of the corn, carrying their food and the merchandise of the soldiers on their shoulders for more than eighty leagues. . . . This is the reason according to the commonly held opinion that they are being annihilated at such a rate. (Quoted in Hann 1988:140–41)

During periods of epidemics, supplying the native labor on which the Spanish were so dependent must have been a particular burden on the provinces, themselves already facing a reduction in the labor supply. One Spaniard noted in 1655 that the smallpox epidemic had diminished the repairs on the fort at St. Augustine:

The necessary wood must be cut and brought from the forests by Indians. This necessitates too much work for them as the distance which it must be carried on their shoulders is long. I now consider this manner of bringing it impossible because of the high mortality rate which has been the result of a series of plagues of smallpox which have afflicted the country for the last ten months. Many died as a result of this and of the trials and hunger which these unfortunate people suffered, and the province is quite destitute. (Quoted in Hann 1988:177)

We address the issue of labor exploitation by examination of biomechanical properties of long bones (Ruff and Larsen, this volume).

This shift to a diet involving a heavier reliance on maize also has important implications for nutritional quality and health for mission Indians. Maize, a carbohydrate, has a high sugar component, which is an important contributing factor to dental caries or tooth decay (Larsen et al. 1991; and see Larsen et al., this volume). Moreover, maize contains phytate, a substance that binds iron into a complex formation and prevents the absorption of this essential element (Lynch 1997). A dependence on maize can lead to insufficient iron bioavailability and reduced iron stores. If iron status is low, iron deficiency anemia can result. As a response to deficient iron stores, the body increases its red blood cell production, creating a bone pathology called porotic hyperostosis when it affects the outer layers of the cranial vault and cribra orbitalia when it affects the orbital roofs (Larsen 1997). These pathological conditions can also be caused by other agents, such as deficiencies of vitamins C and D (Schultz et al., this volume), but iron deficiency is a leading cause (Stuart-Macadam 1989).

Elsewhere, we have documented marked increases in porotic hyperostosis and cribra orbitalia in some of the mission populations, especially Santa Catalina de Guale, Santa Maria de Yamasee, and Santa Catalina de Amelia, suggesting that the dietary shifts played an important role in contributing to increased iron deficiency anemia (Larsen and Sering 2000; and see Schultz et al., this volume).

The ethnohistoric record and the overall evidence provided from archaeological excavations at mission sites and the interpretation of settlement changes indicate the presence of other stressful conditions that contributed to the decline of quality of life for mission Indians. A common theme throughout the record is the increased concentration of native population in and around mission centers. For some areas, this concentration—called congregación—was brought about by external forces, such as the relocation of Indians from one region to another. As already noted, Yamasee Indians from Georgia relocated to Amelia Island, in part due to pressures placed upon them from other groups in their home region. The reasons for this relocation are diverse. Some groups may have viewed the missions as a safe haven from rival tribes. Some may have viewed the availability of resources—perceived or real—in the missions as an attractive feature, enough to warrant moving to mission centers. Regardless of the cause of population relocation, the record suggests a long-term process of population resettlement and aggregation at mission centers. This process was at various times and various places an intentional practice of the Spanish authorities, serving to promote religious conversion and to facilitate population control (see Hann 1988; Worth 1998).

A well-known outcome of population concentration is the creation of poor living conditions that are conducive to the maintenance and spread of infectious pathogens. One has only to travel to a third world country and observe the deleterious effects of living in close, crowded conditions with no sanitation, poor hygiene, and poor diet. In these situations, disease is readily spread, infections are commonplace, and health overall is poor. In the missions of La Florida, a case can be made for poorer living circumstances than in prehistoric settings where population was likely more dispersed. At Santa Catalina de Guale on St. Catherines Island, for example, archaeological evidence indicates that the mission Indians living on the island were mostly concentrated in and around the vicinity of the mission (Thomas n.d.). This kind of settlement would have provided an ideal reservoir for the infectious organisms that contributed at various times to epidemics, increased mortality, decreased fertility, and population decline.

Infectious disease is problematic to study in archaeological remains, especially because acute infectious diseases kill the host long before skeletal changes appear in the affected individual. However, chronic infectious disease, both before and after European contact, has been well documented at the Irene Mound site on the north Georgia coast and elsewhere in the American Southeast (see Larsen 1994). The potential for tuberculosis to cause high morbidity and mortality in poorly nourished, highly stressed populations is well documented. Populations previously unexposed to tuberculosis are at risk, because particularly vulnerable genotypes have not been "winnowed out" by selective pressure. On the other hand, individual members of a population who have been previously exposed (even if no primary disease resulted) are at risk of contact with active infectious cases reactivating latest pathogens causing the disease. Venereal treponemal disease—syphilis—can cause a high rate of miscarriages, stillbirths, and neonatal and infant mortality. The endemic (nonvenereal) form of treponemal disease documented in the American Southeast (see Larsen 1994) would not have produced this effect, but the venereal form introduced from Europe and Africa to Native American populations who lacked protective immunities derived from previous exposure would have reduced efforts to replace lost population (see Walker, this volume). Infectious diseases of various sorts were clearly a leading cause of morbidity and mortality in this setting (and see Schultz et al., this volume).

Population relocation and aggregation, combined with poor sanitation, increased workload, reduced nutrition, and iron deficiency are a suite of factors that contributed to increased physiological stress during the mission period. Moreover, various accounts of other stressors occurring during the 16th century indicate an increasing stress burden during this time, including harassment by the Spanish military, piracy, and slave raiding. Organized raiding on mission Indians by unconverted Indians was a common problem throughout the mission period. Assaults in the first half of the 17th century in Timucua, for example, led to injury and death for many. Beginning in the 1660s, these raids were part of an organized campaign by English settlers to the north, which may have been linked to the market in Virginia and Carolina for slaves (Worth 1995, 1998, this volume).

These various negative factors likely contributed to increased stress loads in the native population. Physiological stress resulting from these factors has a negative impact on growth and development of the body tissues, including bones and teeth. The teeth provide a memory of growth stress during the years of growth and development, especially from about the time of birth, when the enamel of the permanent (adult) teeth begins to form, until about age 12, when the crowns of the teeth are fully formed (Smith 1991). The ameloblasts, the cells that produce the tooth enamel, are readily disrupted if the maturing person experiences either poor nutrition or disease or some combination of the two. As a result of the physiological stress, the ameloblasts either die and produce no enamel or they produce enamel at a much slower rate (Larsen 1997). We explore some of these issues in looking at the macroscopic and microscopic dimensions of dental growth disruption (Hutchinson and Larsen, this volume; Simpson, this volume).

Mortuary Archaeology and the Skeletal Samples

Within a period of well under a century following the establishment of the first missions among coastal Atlantic populations, Guale and Timucua, and later among inland Timucua and Apalachee, alterations in native belief systems were well in place. The rather dramatic shift in ideology from native to Christian is clearly played out in how the remains of deceased persons were treated. The archaeological record of mortuary behavior demonstrates the high degree of success of replacing native belief systems with Christianity, especially with respect to the remarkable uniformity of interment pattern observed in the mission cemeteries. Typically, once an individual died, an oval burial pit was excavated in the floor of the church (some mission cemeteries are located outside the church), and the remains of the deceased were placed in the pit, on the back, feet toward the altar and hands folded on the chests or abdomen (Larsen 1990, 1993). The burials are generally oriented parallel to the long axis of the church.

The oval pits containing remains are discrete units, usually prepared for the burial of one person. Over time, however, especially in missions with a long history of occupation, all available space for interment was used. At Santa Catalina de Guale, 52.4 percent of 226 graves were undisturbed by later burial intrusions (Larsen 1990). Disturbances to burials were due to placement of later burials. At mission cemeteries with relatively short historiou, the degree of disturbance was relatively low. At the descendent Santa Catalina missions on Amelia Island, most (92.5%) of the 121 interments were in undisturbed context (Larsen 1993). The other mission skeletal series lie somewhere between these two extremes. Disturbance of burials occurs throughout the mission cemeteries. However, relatively less disturbance is present in those burials located closest to the altar. For example, at San Luis de Apalachee, the very high status burials are largely undisturbed by later intrusions (and see Hann and McEwan 1998).

Variation in the Mortuary Record

There is some important variation in mortuary practices associated with mission-era sites. With the exception of two mission cemeteries, individual interments contain few grave goods. This pattern is consistent with church doctrine prohibiting burial of objects with deceased persons. Contrary to church practice, at Santa Catalina de Guale and San Luis de Apalachee, however, a number of burials contained grave offerings, some of which are highly elaborate. At Santa Catalina, these grave goods included thousands of beads, many of which were in formations representing rosaries, medallions depicting religious scenes, crucifixes, and finger rings. In addition, several burials contained elaborate domestic items, such as majolica vessels and plates, cloth, and mirrors (Larsen 1990; Thomas 1987, 1990, 1993).

Similarly, at San Luis, crucifixes, beads, a hand-carved crystal cross, and the remains of a metal knife were found with individual interments. At both Santa Catalina and San Luis, this elaborate material culture is associated primarily with high status individuals who had been buried in the altar area. A number of these high status individuals were also buried in wooden coffins specially prepared for individual deceased, including at least one person at Santa Catalina and no fewer than six persons at San Luis (Larsen 1990; Hann and McEwan 1998). At San Luis, two persons in coffins and a third person—probably a shroud interment—were buried with their heads oriented to the west, opposite all other individuals. Our estimates of number of individuals are 432 at Santa Catalina (Larsen 1993; the entire cemetery was excavated) and 210 at San Luis (Larsen and Tung, 1999; about 25% of the cemetery was excavated, including most of the altar end of the church). In all likelihood, these individuals either had high status within the native community or served some important religious function.

Exceptions to the practice of Christian-style burial during the historic period are represented at two sites. At the Pine Harbor site, located slightly inland from the mainland coast that faces St. Catherines Island, a large protohistoric burial mound was tested, revealing a series of burials placed in bundles and multiple-individual concentrations. These interments re flect pre-Christian, non-mission burial practices. Similarly, adjacent to and overlapping the Santa Catalina de Amelia cemetery on Amelia Island, Florida, a large pit containing the mostly disarticulated remains of nearly 60 individuals were recovered. At the bottom of the ossuary, two adult males, fully articulated, were found in the remains of a large wooden box held together by iron spikes. These remains are clearly from the contact period and likely predate the Guale and Apalachee missions. The pre-contact remains from the study region are drawn from a range of burial contexts, but mostly they are from burial mounds (see Larsen 1982).

Knowledge of the pre-contact mortuary record in the study area began in the middle and later 19th century (Jones 1859; Moore 1897; Larsen and Thomas 1978). An understanding of the mortuary record for the mission period began in the 1930s with excavations at the Nombre de Dios mission site in St. Augustine, Florida (Seaberg 1991). Over the remainder of 20th century—especially in the 1970s, 1980s, and 1990s—hundreds of skeletal individuals from the major provinces have been excavated from mission contexts (see review in Larsen 1993). These remains, along with an extensive pre-contact mortuary record, provide an important basis for characterizing, evaluating, and interpreting biocultural changes in La Florida.

For purposes of comparison, and in order to characterize temporal and geographic variation, we have first divided the pre-contact and contact-era skeletal samples into two broad groups corresponding to the boundary between the modern states of Georgia and Florida. This was done in large part because the Georgia populations are largely coastal (and from nearby mainland areas), whereas the Florida populations include both coastal and predominantly terrestrial adaptations. For the region as a whole, two key adaptive shifts took place over the time period for which human remains are present. They include the shift from a lifeway based exclusively on foraging—hunting, gathering, and fishing (for coastal settings)—to a lifeway based to varying degrees on farming. As noted, there appears to have been a high degree of variation in farming practices in the study area, ranging from little or no farming south of St. Augustine to full-scale farming in Apalachee. Agriculture develops across much of the landscape and should be regarded as an important adaptive change.

The next adaptive shift involved that which took place following the arrival of Europeans and especially during the period of missionization. The historical records and archaeological evidence clearly point to dietary shifts (related to more intensive farming) and other alterations in lifeway. Moreover, changes during the mission period were likely present (increased physiological stress, increased labor, and declining quality of life).

Reflecting the temporal and geographic variation in native foodways, for purposes of analysis we have divided the populations temporally and spatially into the following seven groups: (1) Georgia Early Prehistoric (400 B.C.–A.D. 1000); (2) Georgia Late Prehistoric (A.D. 1000–1550); (3) Florida Early Prehistoric (A.D. 0–1000); (4) Florida Late Prehistoric/ Protohistoric (A.D. 1000–1600); (5) Georgia Early Mission (A.D. 1600–1680); (6) Florida Early Mission (A.D. 1600–1680); and (7) Florida Late Mission (A.D. 1680–1700). These periods and the list of sites within each are summarized in table 2.1.

The Agenda

The skeletal samples from pre-contact and contact-era Spanish Florida form the comparative base for addressing the key issues discussed by the authors in the present volume. These issues can best be presented in a series of general questions relating to the two primary adaptive changes in the region—first the shift from foraging to farming and then the arrival of Europeans and establishment of missions. Four general questions frame the research presented in the following chapters: (1) When and how did diet change, and what are the implications for health and resource acquisition both before and after contact? (2) How did physical activity, workload, and behavioral strategy in general change, and what are the implications for health? (3) How did physiological stress change over the time frame, and how do these changes relate to shifts in lifeway? (4) What were the biological relationships of native populations in this setting? We address these questions via the examination of specific data sets, including stable isotope analysis for dietary reconstruction (question 1), biomechanical and dental microwear analysis (question 2), macroscopic and microscopic enamel and cranial pathology (question 3), and population history and biological distance analysis (question 4).

Although the research presented in this volume has a unified theme, it is important to point out that the research relating to each of the four questions has had a somewhat different history in the La Florida Bioarchaeology Project. The areas of dietary change, physical activity, and physiological stress (macrodefects) have been investigated since the beginning of the project nearly two decades ago. Thus, reflecting the time depth involved in the research program, we have relatively more data to draw

Table 2.1. Skeletal samples from Spanish Florida

Site	Location	Association	References	No.ᵃ
Georgia early prehistoric (400 B.C.–A.D. 1000)				
Deptford site	inland Georgia	Guale	Larsen 1982; DePratter 1991	10
Cedar Grove Mound B	inland Georgia	Guale	Larsen 1982; DePratter 1991	45
Cedar Grove Mound C	inland Georgia	Guale	Larsen 1982; DePratter 1991	46
McLeod Mound	coastal Georgia	Guale	Thomas and Larsen 1979; Larsen 1982	1
Seaside Mound I	coastal Georgia	Guale	Thomas and Larsen 1979; Larsen 1982	2
Seaside Mound II	coastal Georgia	Guale	Thomas and Larsen 1979; Larsen 1982	3
Cunningham Mound C	coastal Georgia	Guale	Thomas and Larsen 1979; Larsen 1982	4
Cunningham Mound D	coastal Georgia	Guale	Thomas and Larsen 1979; Larsen 1982	5
Cunningham Mound E	coastal Georgia	Guale	Thomas and Larsen 1979; Larsen 1982	43
Evelyn Plantation	inland Georgia	Guale	Larsen 1982	44
Sea Island Mound	coastal Georgia	Guale/Mocama	Larsen 1982	29
Airport site	coastal Georgia	Guale/Mocama	Larsen 1982	30
Cannons Point	coastal Georgia	Guale/Mocama	Martinez 1975; Zahler 1976	31
Charlie King Mound	coastal Georgia	Guale/Mocama	Larsen 1982	32
Florida early prehistoric (A.D. 0–1000)				
Melton Mounds	inland Florida	Timucua	Sears 1956; Smith 1971; Milanich 1994	33
McKeithen Mounds	inland Florida	Timucua	Milanich et al. 1984	34
Cross Creek Mound	inland Florida	Timucua	Smith 1971; Milanich 1994	35
Wacahoota Mound	inland Florida	Timucua	Milanich 1978	36
Henderson Mound	inland Florida	Timucua	Loucks 1976	11
Mayport Mound	coastal Florida	Timucua	Wilson 1965	37
Georgia late prehistoric/protohistoric (A.D. 1000–1550)				
Irene Burial Mound	inland Georgia	Guale	Caldwell and McCann 1941; Larsen 1982	12

Site	Location	Group	Reference	
Irene Large Mound	inland Georgia	Guale	Caldwell and McCann 1941; Larsen 1982	13
Irene Mortuary	inland Georgia	Guale	Caldwell and McCann 1941; Larsen 1982	13
Deptford Mound	inland Georgia	Guale	Caldwell and McCann 1941; DePratter 1991	39
Groves Creek	coastal Georgia	Guale	Larsen unpublished	53
Johns Mound	coastal Georgia	Guale	Larsen and Thomas 1982; Larsen 1982	6
Marys Mound	coastal Georgia	Guale	Larsen and Thomas 1982; Larsen 1982	7
Southend Mound I	coastal Georgia	Guale	Larsen and Thomas 1986	8
Southend Mound II	coastal Georgia	Guale	Larsen and Thomas 1986	38
North End Mound	inland Georgia	Guale	Moore 1897; Larsen 1982	47
Low Mound, Shell Bluff	inland Georgia	Guale	Moore 1897; Larsen 1982	48
Townsend Mound	inland Georgia	Guale	Moore 1897; Larsen 1982	49
Norman Mound	inland Georgia	Guale	Larson 1957; Larsen 1982	50
Lewis Creek	inland Georgia	Guale	Larsen 1982	51
Seven Mile Bend	inland Georgia	Guale	Larsen 1982; unpublished	52
Little Pine Island	inland Georgia	Guale	Larsen unpublished	54
Red Bird Creek	inland Georgia	Guale	Pearson 1984; unpublished	55
Oatland Mound	coastal Georgia	Guale/Mocama	Larsen 1982	56
Kent Mound	coastal Georgia	Guale/Mocama	Larsen 1982	57
Martinez Test B	coastal Georgia	Guale/Mocama	Martinez 1975	54
Indian Field	coastal Georgia	Guale/Mocama	Wallace 1975; Zahler 1976	15
Taylor Mound	coastal Georgia	Guale/Mocama	Wallace 1975; Zahler 1976	16
Couper Field	coastal Georgia	Guale/Mocama	Wallace 1975; Zahler 1976	17

Florida late prehistoric/protohistoric (A.D. 1000–1600)

Site	Location	Group	Reference	
Lake Jackson	inland Florida	Apalachee	Jones 1982	18
Waddells Pond	inland Florida	Apalachee	Gardner 1966	19
Leslie Mound	inland Florida	Timucua	Milanich et al. 1984	40
Tatham Mound	inland Florida	Tocobaga	Hutchinson 1991; Hutchinson and Norr 1994; Mitchem 1989	21

(continued)

Table 2.1—*Continued*

Site	Location	Association	References	No.[a]
Goodman Mound	coastal Florida	Timucua	Bullen 1963; Jordan 1963; Recourt 1975	4
Browne Mound	coastal Florida	Timucua	Sears 1959	20
Holy Spirit Church	coastal Florida	Timucua	Johnson n.d.	21
Georgia early mission (A.D. 1600–1680)				
Pine Harbor	inland Georgia	Guale	Larsen 1990	22
Santa Catalina de Guale	coastal Georgia	Guale	Thomas 1987; Larsen 1990	9
Florida early mission (A.D. 1600–1680)				
Ossuary at Santa Catalina	coastal Florida	Timucua	Larsen 1993	24
Santa María de Yamasee	coastal Florida	Yamasee	Larsen 1993; Saunders 1988	23
San Martín de Timucua	inland Florida	Timucua	Hoshower 1992; Weisman 1992	26
San Pedro de Patale	inland Florida	Apalachee	Jones et al. 1991	27
Florida late mission (A.D. 1680–1700)				
San Luis de Apalachee	inland Florida	Apalachee	Shapiro and Vernon 1992; McEwan 1993	28
Santa Catalina de Amelia	coastal Florida	Guale	Larsen 1993; Saunders 1988	25

a. The number refers to the site location shown in figure 2.1.

upon for these areas of inquiry. In contrast, it has only been within the last stage of the La Florida Bioarchaeological Project—the component of the project involving the study of all three tribal provinces (Guale, Apalachee, and Timucua)—that we have begun to investigate microscopic indications of physiological stress (enamel defects and cranial lesions) and tooth use. Therefore, the data sets for these areas are more restricted in scope. Biological distance analysis has been undertaken with Guale first in order to identify the potential for research on biological relationships across La Florida. Therefore, we present our findings on biological distance with regard to how Guale fits into the greater American Southeast. Our next stage of analysis will be expanded to include Timucua and Apalachee provinces. In a real sense, as with the scientific enterprise generally, the research presented is a work in progress, with some stages farther along than others.

Finally, the research questions are largely guided by which component of the skeleton is preserved and available for study. This point is especially underscored in our biomechanical analysis of long bones from La Florida (Ruff and Larsen, this volume). In this regard, in order for the long bone to be analyzed, it has to be nearly complete and the outer bone cortex has to be intact. The kind of bone preservation needed for this type of analysis is present almost exclusively for Atlantic coastal Georgia and Florida samples, mostly Guale (and Timucua, to a lesser extent). For the entire Apalachee sample, no long bones were preserved well enough for biomechanical study. On the other hand, the scope of research for dental wear and microdefects is greatly increased owing to the relatively better preservation of teeth. Similarly, stable isotope analysis requires only a small sample of bone for collagen extraction and isotope ratio determination. Therefore, where collagen is preserved, for most of the settings across Spanish Florida, we are able to identify biological signatures of diet.

This study is not intended to present all of what bioarchaeology can potentially contribute to our understanding of biocultural change. For example, we have presented studies of dental caries, infection, and demographic change elsewhere (Russell et al. 1990; Larsen et al. 1991; Larsen et al. 1992; Larsen and Harn 1994). We draw readers' attention to these studies in developing a broader consideration of adaptation and change.

Owing to the variable nature of the data sets—which is largely driven by the availability of human remains and specific parts of skeletons, preservation differences across the region, and the stage of research, preliminary or mature—we present in each chapter a listing of the sites used for analysis and how they relate to specific issues addressed within that chapter. A

44 | Clark Spencer Larsen

complete list of all sites involved in the book is presented in table 2.1 and
their locations in the study area are shown in figure 2.1.

The research results presented in the following chapters represent one of
the most comprehensive analyses of biocultural adaptation and change
relating to the consequences of European contact anywhere in the New
World. This body of data contributes to a growing bioarchaeological
record providing important details on the impact of major dietary shifts
and the arrival of Europeans in the New World (see various authors in
Verano and Ubelaker 1992, Larsen and Milner 1994, and Baker and Kealhofer 1996; Miller et al. 1999; review in Larsen 1994). Although the written sources provide insight into this important period of human history,
arguably it is the people themselves—represented by their mortal remains—who tell a key part of the story.

References Cited

Baker, B. J., and L. Kealhofer (eds.). 1996. *Bioarchaeology of Native American
    Adaptation in the Spanish Borderlands.* Gainesville: University Press of Flor-
    ida.
Bourne, E. G. (ed.). 1922. *Narratives in the Career of Hernando de Soto.* New
    York: Allerton.
Bullen, A. K. 1963. Physical Anthropology of the Goodman Mound. In *Papers on
    the Jungerman and Goodman Sites, Florida,* ed. D. F. Jordan, E. S. Wing, and
    A. K. Bullen, 61–71. Contributions of the Florida State Museum, Social Sci-
    ences, 10.
Bushnell, A. T. 1994. *Situado and Sabana: Spain's Support System for the Presidio
    and Mission Provinces of Florida.* Anthropological Papers of the American
    Museum of Natural History 74.
Butzer, K. W. 1993. No Eden in the New World. *Nature* 362:15–17.
Caldwell, J., and C. McCann. 1941 *Irene Mound Site, Chatham County, Georgia.*
    Athens: University of Georgia Press.
Cook, N. D. 1998. *Born to Die: Disease and New World Conquest, 1492–1650.*
    Cambridge: Cambridge University Press.
Crosby, A. W., Jr. 1972. *The Columbian Exchange: Biological and Cultural Con-
    sequences of 1492.* Westport, Conn.: Greenwood Press.
———. 1986. *Ecological Imperialism: The Biological Expansion of Europe, 900–
    1900.* Cambridge: Cambridge University Press.
Denevan, W. M. 1992. The Pristine Myth: The Landscape of the Americas in 1492.
    In *The Americas Before and After 1492: Current Geographical Research,* ed.
    K. W. Butzer, 369–85. Annals of the Association of American Geographers 82.
DePratter, C. B. 1991. *W.P.A. Archaeological Excavations in Chatham County,*

Georgia, 1937–1942. University of Georgia, Laboratory of Archaeology Series, Report 29.

Dobyns, H. F. 1983. *Their Number Become Thinned: Native American Population Dynamics in Eastern North America.* Knoxville, University of Tennessee Press.

Gannon, M. 1992. The New Alliance of History and Archaeology in the Eastern Spanish Borderlands. *William and Mary Quarterly* 49:323–34.

Gardner, W. M. 1966. The Waddells Mill Pond Site. *Florida Anthropologist* 19:43–64.

Hann, J. H. 1988. *Apalachee: The Land Between the Rivers.* Gainesville: University Presses of Florida.

———. 1990. Summary Guide to Spanish Florida Missions and *Visitas,* with Churches in the Sixteenth and Seventeenth Centuries. *Americas* 56:417–513.

———. 1996. *A History of the Timucua Indians and Missions.* Gainesville: University Press of Florida.

Hann, J. H., and B. G. McEwan. 1998. *The Apalachee Indians and Mission San Luis.* Gainesville: University Press of Florida.

Hoshower, L. 1992 Bioanthropological Analysis of a Seventeenth-Century Native American Spanish Mission Population: Biocultural Impacts on the Northern Utina. Ph.D. diss., University of Florida, Gainesville.

Hutchinson, D. L. 1991. Postcontact Native American Health and Adaptation: Assessing the Impact of Introduced Diseases in Sixteenth-Century Gulf Coast Florida. Ph.D. diss., University of Illinois, Urbana-Champaign.

Hutchinson, D. L., and C. S. Larsen. 1988. Determination of Stress Episode Duration from Linear Enamel Hypoplasias: A Case Study from St. Catherines Island, Georgia. *Human Biology* 60:93–110.

———. 1990. Stress and Lifeway Change: The Evidence from Enamel Hypoplasias. In *The Archaeology of Mission Santa Catalina de Guale: 2. Biocultural Interpretations of a Population in Transition,* ed. C. S. Larsen, 50–65. Anthropological Papers of the American Museum of Natural History 68.

Hutchinson, D. L., and L. Norr. 1994. Late Prehistoric and Early Historic Diet in Gulf Coast Florida. In *In the Wake of Contact: Biological Responses to Conquest,* ed. C. S. Larsen and G. R. Milner, 9–20. New York: Wiley-Liss.

Hutchinson, D. L., C. S. Larsen, M. J. Schoeninger, and L. Norr. 1998. Regional Variation in the Pattern of Maize Adoption and Use in Florida and Georgia. *American Antiquity* 63:397–416.

Johnson, R. E. N.d. Holy Spirit Church Site. Fieldnotes on file, Department of Anthropology, University of North Carolina, Chapel Hill.

Jones, B. C. 1982. Southern Cult Manifestations at the Lake Jackson Site, Leon County, Florida: Salvage Excavation of Mound 3. *Midcontinental Journal of Archaeology* 7:3–44.

Jones, B. C., J. H. Hann, and J. F. Scarry. 1991. *San Pedro y San Pablo de Patale:*

A Seventeenth-Century Spanish Mission in Leon County, Florida. Florida Archaeology 5.

Jones, C. C., Jr. 1859. *Indian Remains in Southern Georgia.* Savannah, Ga.: J. M. Cooper Company.

Jones, G. D. 1978. The Ethnohistory of the Guale Coast through 1684. In *The Anthropology of St. Catherines Island*: 1. *Natural and Cultural History*, by D. H. Thomas, G. D. Jones, R. S. Durham, and C. S. Larsen, 178–210. Anthropological Papers of the American Museum of Natural History 55.

Jordan, D. F. 1963. The Goodman Mound. In *Papers on the Jungerman and Goodman Sites, Florida,* ed. D. F. Jordan, E. S. Wing, and A. Bullen, 24–49. Contributions of the Florida State Museum, Social Sciences 10.

Larsen, C. S. 1982. *The Anthropology of St. Catherines Island*: 3. *Prehistoric Human Biological Adaptation.* Anthropological Papers of the American Museum of Natural History 57, pt. 3.

———. 1984. Health and Disease in Prehistoric Georgia: The Transition to Agriculture. In *Paleopathology at the Origins of Agriculture,* ed. M. N. Cohen and G. J. Armelagos, 367–92. Orlando: Academic Press.

———. 1993. On the Frontier of Contact: Mission Bioarchaeology in *La Florida.* In *The Spanish Missions of La Florida,* ed. B. G. McEwan, 322–56. Gainesville: University Press of Florida.

———. 1994. In the Wake of Columbus: Native Population Biology in the Postcontact Americas. *Yearbook of Physical Anthropology* 37:109–54.

———. 1997. *Bioarchaeology: Interpreting Behavior from the Human Skeleton.* Cambridge: Cambridge University Press.

——— (ed.). 1990. *The Archaeology of Mission Santa Catalina de Guale*: 2. *Biocultural Interpretations of a Population in Transition.* Anthropological Papers of the American Museum of Natural History 68.

Larsen, C. S., and D. E. Harn. 1994. Health in Transition: Disease and Nutrition in the Georgia Bight. In *Paleonutrition: The Diet and Health of Prehistoric Americans,* ed. K. D. Sobolik, 222–34. Southern Illinois University at Carbondale, Center for Archaeological Investigations, Occasional Paper 22.

Larsen, C. S., and G. R. Milner (eds.). 1994. *In the Wake of Contact: Biological Responses to Conquest.* New York: Wiley-Liss.

Larsen, C. S., and C. B. Ruff. 1994. The Stresses of Conquest in Spanish Florida: Structural Adaptation and Change before and after Contact. In *In the Wake of Contact: Biological Responses to Conquest,* ed. C. S. Larsen and G. R. Milner, 21–34. New York: Wiley-Liss.

Larsen, C. S., and L. E. Sering. 2000. Inferring Iron Deficiency Anemia from Human Skeletal Remains: The Case of the Georgia Bight. In *Bioarchaeological Studies in Life in the Age of Agriculture,* ed. P. M. Lambert, 116–33. Tuscaloosa: University of Alabama Press.

Larsen, C. S., and D. H. Thomas. 1978. The Prehistory of St. Catherines Island. In *The Anthropology of St. Catherines Island*: 1. *Natural and Cultural History,* ed. D. H. Thomas, G. D. Jones, R. S. Durham, and C. S. Larsen, 172–78. Anthropological Papers of the American Museum of Natural History 55, pt. 2.

———. 1982. *The Anthropology of St. Catherines Island*: 4. *The St. Catherines Period Mortuary Complex*. Anthropological Papers of the American Museum of Natural History 57, pt. 4.

———. 1986. *The Anthropology of St. Catherines Island*: 5. *The South End Mound Complex*. Anthropological Papers of the American Museum of Natural History 63, pt. 1.

Larsen, C. S., and T. A. Tung. 1999. Mission San Luis de Apalachee: The Human Remains. Report to the Florida Bureau of Archaeological Research, Tallahassee.

Larsen, C. S., R. Shavit, and M. C. Griffin. 1991. Dental Caries Evidence for Dietary Change: An Archaeological Context. In *Advances in Dental Anthropology*, ed. M. A. Kelley and C. S. Larsen, 179–202. New York: Wiley-Liss.

Larsen, C. S., C. B. Ruff, M. J. Schoeninger, and D. L. Hutchinson. 1992. Population Decline and Extinction in La Florida. In *Disease and Demography in the Americas*, ed. J. W. Verano and D. H. Ubelaker, 25–39. Washington: Smithsonian Institution Press.

Larsen, C. S., M. J. Schoeninger, R. Shavit, and K. F. Russell. 1990. Dietary and Demographic Transitions on the Southeastern U.S. Atlantic Coast. *International Journal of Anthropology* 5:333–46.

Larsen, C. S., M. J. Schoeninger, N. J. van der Merwe, J. M. Moore, and J. A. Lee-Thorp. 1992. Carbon and Nitrogen Stable Isotopic Signatures of Human Dietary Change in the Georgia Bight. *American Journal of Physical Anthropology* 89:197–214.

Larson, L. H. 1957. The Norman Mound, McIntosh County, Georgia. *Florida Anthropologist* 10:37–52.

———. 1980. *Aboriginal Subsistence Technology on the Southeastern Coastal Plain during the Late Prehistoric Period*. Gainesville: University Presses of Florida.

Loucks, J. J. 1976. Early Alachua Tradition Burial Ceremonialism: The Henderson Mound, Alachua County, Florida. M.A. thesis, University of Florida, Gainesville.

Lynch, S. R. 1997. Interaction of Iron with Other Nutrients. *Nutrition Reviews* 55:102–10.

Martinez, C. A. 1975. Culture Sequence on the Central Georgia Coast, 1000 B.C.–1650 A.D. M.A. thesis, University of Florida, Gainesville.

McEwan, B.G. 1991. San Luis de Talimali: The Archaeology of Spanish-Indian Relations at a Florida Mission. *Historical Archaeology* 25:33–41.

——— (ed.). 1993. *The Spanish Missions of La Florida*. Gainesville: University Press of Florida.

Milanich, J. T. 1978. Two Cades Pond Sites in North-Central Florida: The Occupational Nexus as a Mode of Settlement. *Florida Anthropologist* 31:151–75.

———. 1994. *Archaeology of Precolumbian Florida*. Gainesville: University Press of Florida.

———. 1995. *Florida Indians and the Invasion from Europe*. Gainesville: University Press of Florida.

———. 1996. *The Timucua*. Oxford: Blackwell Publishers.

———. 1999. *Laboring in the Fields of the Lord: Spanish Missions and Southeastern Indians*. Washington: Smithsonian Institution Press.

Milanich, J. T., A. Cordell, V. Knight, and B. Sigler-Lavelle. 1984. *McKeithen Weeden Island: The Culture of Northern Florida, A.D. 200–900*. Orlando: Academic Press.

Miller, E., C. M. Gagnon, and B. J. Baker. 1999. Contact Dynamics in the Mid-Atlantic and Northeast: A Bioarchaeological Perspective. Symposium, annual meeting of the American Association of Physical Anthropologists, Columbus, Ohio.

Mitchem, J. M. 1989. Redefining Safety Harbor: Late Prehistoric/Protohistoric Archaeology in West Peninsular Florida. Ph.D. diss., University of Florida, Gainesville.

Moore, C. B. 1897. *Certain Aboriginal Mounds of the Georgia Coast*. Journal of the Academy of Natural Sciences of Philadelphia 11.

Newsom, L. A. 1991. Archaeobotanical Analysis of Four Features from the 1990 South End Project at Fig Springs (8CO1), Columbia County, Florida. Report on file, Florida Museum of Natural History, Gainesville.

Pearson, C. E. 1984. Red Bird Creek: Late Prehistoric Material Culture and Subsistence in Coastal Georgia. *Early Georgia* 12:1–39.

Recourt, P. 1975. Final Notes on the Goodman Mound. *Florida Anthropologist* 28:85–95.

Reff, D. T. 1991. *Disease, Depopulation, and Culture Change in Northwestern New Spain, 1520–1764*. Salt Lake City: University of Utah Press.

Reitz, E. J. 1988. Evidence for Coastal Adaptations in Georgia and South Carolina. *Archaeology of Eastern North America* 16:137–58.

———. 1990. Zooarchaeological Evidence for Subsistence at La Florida Missions. In *Columbian Consequences: 2. Archaeological and Historical Perspectives on the Spanish Borderlands East*, ed. D. H. Thomas, 543–54. Washington: Smithsonian Institution Press.

———. 1993. Evidence for Animal Use at the Missions of Spanish Florida. In *The Spanish Missions of La Florida*, ed. B. G. McEwan, 376–98. Gainesville: University Press of Florida.

———. N.d. Vertebrate Faunal Remains from the St. Catherines Island Transect Survey. Unpublished report on file, Department of Anthropology, University of Georgia, Athens.

Reitz, E. J., and C. M. Scarry. 1985. *Reconstructing Historic Subsistence with an Example from Sixteenth-Century Spanish Florida*. Society for Historical Archaeology, Special Publication 1.

Ruff, C. B., and C. S. Larsen. 1990. Postcranial Biomechanical Adaptations to Subsistence Strategy Changes on the Georgia Coast. In *The Archaeology of Mission Santa Catalina de Guale*: 2. *Biocultural Interpretations of a Population in Transition*, ed. C. S. Larsen, 94–120. Anthropological Papers of the American Museum of Natural History 68.

Ruhl, D. L. 1990. Spanish Mission Paleoethnobotany and Culture Change: A Survey of the Archaeobotanical Data and Some Speculations on Aboriginal and Spanish Agrarian Interactions in La Florida. In *Columbian Consequences*: 2. *Archaeological and Historical Perspectives on the Spanish Borderlands East*, ed. D. H. Thomas, 555–80. Washington: Smithsonian Institution Press.

———. 1993. Old Customs and Traditions in New Terrain: Sixteenth- and Seventeenth-Century Archaeobotanical Data from La Florida. In *Foraging and Farming in the Eastern Woodlands*, ed. C. M. Scarry, 255–83. Gainesville: University Press of Florida.

Russell, K. F., I. Choi, and C. S. Larsen. 1990. Paleodemography at Santa Catalina de Guale. In *The Archaeology of Mission Santa Catalina de Guale*: 2. *Biocultural Interpretations of a Population in Transition*, ed. C. L. Larsen, 36–49. Anthropological Papers of the American Museum of Natural History 68.

Salo, W. L., A. C. Aufderheide, J. Buikstra, and T. A. Holcomb. 1994. Identification of *Mycobacterium tuberculosis* DNA in a Pre-Columbian Mummy. *Proceedings of the National Academy of Sciences* 91:2091–94.

Saunders, R. 1988. *Excavations at 8NA41: Two Mission Period Sites on Amelia Island, Florida*. Miscellaneous Project Report Series, 35. Florida Museum of Natural History, Department of Anthropology, Gainesville.

Scarry, C. M. 1993. Plant Production and Procurement in Apalachee Province. In *The Spanish Missions of La Florida*, ed. B. G. McEwan, 357–75. Gainesville: University Press of Florida.

Scarry, C. M., and E. J. Reitz. 1990. Herbs, Fish, Scum, and Vermin: Subsistence Strategies in Sixteenth-Century Spanish Florida. In *Columbian Consequences*: 2. *Archaeological and Historical Perspectives on the Spanish Borderlands East*, ed. D. H. Thomas, 343–54. Washington: Smithsonian Institution Press.

Schoeninger, M. J., N. J. van der Merwe, K. Moore, J. Lee-Thorp, and C. S. Larsen. 1990. Decrease in Diet Quality between the Prehistoric and Contact Periods. In *The Archaeology of Mission Santa Catalina de Guale*: 2. *Biocultural Interpretations of a Population in Transition*, ed. C. S. Larsen, 78–93. Anthropological Papers of the American Museum of Natural History 68.

Seaberg, L. M. 1991. Report on the Indian Site at the "Fountain of Youth," in St. Augustine. In *America's Ancient City, Spanish St. Augustine, 1565–1763*, ed. K. A. Deagan, 209–74. New York: Garland.

Sears, W. H. 1956. Melton Mound Number 3. *Florida Anthropologist* 9:87–100.

———. 1959. *Two Weeden Island Period Burial Mounds, Florida: The W. H. Browne Mound, Duval County; the MacKenzie Mound, Marion County*. Contributions of the Florida State Museum, Social Sciences, 5.

Shapiro, G., and R. Vernon. 1992. *Archaeology at San Luis*: pt. 2. *The Church Complex*. Florida Archaeology 6.

Smith, B. H. 1991. Standards of Human Tooth Formation and Dental Age Assessment. In *Advances in Dental Anthropology*, ed. M. A. Kelley and C. S. Larsen, 143–68. New York: Wiley-Liss.

Smith, S. D. 1971. A Reinterpretation of the Cades Pond Archaeological Period. M.A. thesis, University of Florida, Gainesville.

Stuart-Macadam, P. L. 1989. Nutritional Deficiency Diseases: A Survey of Scurvy, Rickets, and Iron-Deficiency Anemia. In *Reconstruction of Life from the Skeleton,* ed. M. Y. Iscan and K.A.R. Kennedy, 201–22. New York: Alan R. Liss.

Teaford, M. F. 1991. Dental Microwear: What Can It Tell Us about Diet and Dental Function? In *Advances in Dental Anthropology*, ed. M. A. Kelley and C. S. Larsen, 342–56. New York: Wiley-Liss.

Thomas, D. H. 1987. *The Archaeology of Mission Santa Catalina de Guale*: 1. *Search and Discovery*. Anthropological Papers of the American Museum of Natural History 63, pt. 2.

———. 1990. The Spanish Missions of La Florida: An Overview. In *Columbian Consequences*: 2. *Archaeological and Historical Perspectives on the Spanish Borderlands East,* ed. D. H. Thomas, 357–97. Washington: Smithsonian Institution Press.

———. 1993. The Archaeology of Mission Santa Catalina de Guale: Our First 15 Years. In *The Spanish Missions of La Florida,* ed. B. G. McEwan, 1–34. Gainesville: University Press of Florida.

———. N.d. Archaeological Survey of St. Catherines Island, Georgia. On file, Department of Anthropology, American Museum of Natural History, New York.

Thomas, D. H., and C. S. Larsen. 1979. *The Anthropology of St. Catherines Island*: 2. *The Refuge-Deptford Mortuary Complex*. Anthropological Papers of the American Museum of Natural History 56, pt. 1.

Thornton, R. 1987. *American Indian Holocaust and Survival: A Population History since 1492*. Norman: University of Oklahoma Press.

Ubelaker, D. H. 1992. North American Indian Population Size: Changing Perspectives. In *Disease and Demography in the Americas,* ed. J. W. Verano and D. H. Ubelaker, 169–76. Washington: Smithsonian Institution Press.

Verano, J. W., and D. H. Ubelaker (eds.). 1992. *Disease and Demography in the Americas*. Washington: Smithsonian Institution Press.

Wallace, R. L. 1975. An Archaeological, Ethnohistoric, and Biochemical Investigation of the Guale Aborigines of the Georgia Coastal Strand. Ph.D. diss., University of Florida, Gainesville.

Weber, D. J. 1992. *The Spanish Frontier in North America*. New Haven, Conn.: Yale University Press.

Weisman, B. R. 1992. *Excavations on the Franciscan Frontier: Archaeology of the Fig Springs Mission*. Gainesville: University Press of Florida.

Wilson, R. L. 1965. *Excavations at the Mayport Mound, Florida.* Contributions of the Florida State Museum, Social Sciences, 13.

Worth, J. E. 1995. *The Struggle for the Georgia Coast: An Eighteenth-Century Spanish Retrospective on Guale and Mocama.* Anthropological Papers of the American Museum of Natural History 75.

———. 1998. *The Timucuan Chiefdoms of Spanish Florida.* 2 vols. Gainesville: University Press of Florida.

Zahler, J. W., Jr. 1976. A Morphological Analysis of a Protohistoric-Historic Skeletal Population from St. Simons Island, Georgia. M.A. thesis, University of Florida, Gainesville.

3

Food and Stable Isotopes in La Florida

Diet and Nutrition Before and After Contact

Clark Spencer Larsen, Dale L. Hutchinson,
Margaret J. Schoeninger, and Lynette Norr

Over the last 20 years, the analysis of stable isotopes of carbon and nitrogen extracted from archaeological human bone has revolutionized our understanding of past diet and foodways (see Ambrose and Norr 1993; Schoeninger 1995; Larsen 1997). The present availability of a huge and growing data set based on the investigation of thousands of humans from a range of time periods around the world has resulted in a far more informed understanding of the history of diet.

The purpose of this chapter is threefold: (1) to present a regional reconstruction of diet from La Florida based on our analysis of stable isotopes; (2) to draw inferences about quality of nutrition and health in native societies in this setting; and (3) to indicate aspects of behavioral strategy and resource acquisition from about 400 B.C. through the early 18th century A.D. This study builds on earlier work based on an investigation of prehistoric and contact-era Guale from the Georgia coast (Schoeninger et al. 1990; Larsen et al. 1992b; Hutchinson et al. 1998). In particular, we address regional variation relating to two major developments: the shift from foraging to farming in later prehistory and the establishment of Roman Catholic missions among native populations beginning in the 16th century.

The Setting

La Florida—the Georgia coast and much of northern Florida—is today characterized by a high degree of ecological diversity, especially with regard to plants and animals and their habitats. These habitats range from the estuarine and marine settings of the coastlines of Georgia and Florida to the inland terrestrial settings of northern Florida. The Atlantic coastal region is dominated by a series of barrier and marsh islands with a wide range of subtropical plants and animals. Archaeological evidence indicates that throughout prehistory and into the contact period, marine foods, especially various fish and shellfish, provided a large part of people's diet. The sheer abundance of oyster and clam shells in archaeological settings in the region makes clear the importance of these resources to native populations. Other animal remains have been extensively documented from the coastal zone (Reitz 1988), indicating that a primary source of animal protein was white-tailed deer.

Owing to factors relating to preservation in subtropical climates, plant remains are not well preserved. With regard to maize, the record is virtually missing (Larsen 1982; Larsen et al. 1992b). This has led some to believe that agriculture was a minor part of subsistence economy among late prehistoric societies living on the Georgia coast (see Jones 1978). However, Jones's (1978) reinterpretation of key historical sources documenting lifeways at the time of initial contact in the 16th century indicates the contrary. That major changes in diet and lifeway in general took place prior to European contact is strongly suggested by changes in settlement and social organization, including increase in population size, population aggregation, and increasing social complexity after about A.D. 1000. It is during this time, for example, that we see the appearance and growth of a complex chiefdom at the Irene Mound site, a large Mississippian culture ceremonial and population center (Caldwell and McCann 1941).

The inland (terrestrial) zone of northern Florida is dominated by pine forests and hardwood hammocks with various rivers, lakes, and swamps (Myers and Ewel 1990). These settings provided a range of foods, including fish and shellfish and various terrestrial flora and fauna. In the northwestern and north-central region of Florida, well-drained loamy soils provided potentially productive agricultural lands for prehistoric populations, as for mission-period Indians living in the region and as is the case today (Brown et al. 1990). Various animal and plant remains have been found in archaeological sites from throughout the region (see Milanich 1994), but our understanding of maize is known mostly from corncob impressions on ceramic vessels. As on the Georgia coast, the paucity of plant remains in archaeological sites in Florida provides an inadequate picture of dietary change.

The archaeological evidence for population size and settlement patterns is different in some key ways in Florida than to the north in Georgia. This difference reflects regional variation in habitats and native cultures, suggesting that the trajectory of food use may also have been different. There are, however, some similarities between pre-contact Florida and pre-contact Georgia. For example, in later prehistory, a large Mississippian mound, ceremonial, and habitation complex flourished at the Lake Jackson site near present-day Tallahassee. The native population living at the Lake Jackson site was probably ancestral to the historically known Apalachee Indians living in the region at initial contact and during the mission period. Historical records suggest that mission Apalachee were prodigious agriculturalists, raising a variety of crops, including maize. We believe that the late prehistoric Lake Jackson site had its economic "roots" in agricultural production. But, again, actual evidence for diet and food use is largely unknown from the archaeobotanical record except that maize was present.

After the establishment of Spanish missions among native peoples in La Florida—especially among the Guale on the Georgia coast, Yamasee on the northern Florida Atlantic coast, Timucua in Atlantic coastal and interior Florida, and Apalachee in the Florida panhandle—historical documentation clearly indicates the importance of cultigens for native populations, for support of Spaniards at mission centers and elsewhere, and for export (see Hann 1988). Cultigens have been recovered from mission sites, confirming the presence but not the importance of maize and other crops (Scarry 1993).

The picture that emerges from our review of archaeological and historical sources is that, first, maize agriculture was adopted at some point in later prehistory but when and to what degree is unknown; and second, maize and agriculture in general likely took on an increased role in native foodways during the mission period (1587–1706). The purpose of this chapter is to provide a substantive basis for reconstructing and interpreting prehistoric and contact-era diets in order to address several fundamental questions about native lifeways: (1) When and how did diet for native populations change prior to European contact? (2) How did diet change with the arrival of Spaniards and the establishment of missions? (3) How did these changes vary across the cultural and environmental landscapes both before and after contact? Before addressing these questions, we review the substance of stable isotope analysis and the skeletal samples used.

Stable Isotope Analysis

Isotopes are chemical elements that differ in the number of neutrons in their atoms. Unstable isotopes of an element transmute over time (e.g.,

radioactive carbon, ^{14}C); stable isotopes of the same element do not transmute (^{13}C, ^{12}C). Most elements have two or more isotopes, but only about
10 elements have stable isotopes with biological significance. Of these elements, stable isotopes of carbon (^{13}C and ^{12}C) and nitrogen (^{15}N and ^{14}N)
have received the most attention with regard to biological meaning and
dietary reconstruction in archaeological studies.

Field and laboratory studies of animal species show that the ratios of the
stable isotopes of carbon and nitrogen found in their tissues reflect the
ratios in the foods they eat (see Schoeninger 1995; Norr 1995). This means
that humans should also retain these differences in their tissues, including
bone. Because stable isotope ratios vary only slightly between different
foods, the ratios are expressed in parts per thousand (or "per mil," $^{o}/_{oo}$) as
delta (δ) values in relation to an international standard (Pee Dee Belemnite,
or PDB, for carbon, and atmospheric nitrogen, or AIR, for nitrogen). ^{12}C/
^{13}C ratios (δ^{13}C values) vary depending on the photosynthetic pathway of
the plants consumed. In this region of the world, the economically important plants eaten by humans mostly have one of two types of pathways, C_3
or C_4, depending upon how efficiently carbon is extracted from atmospheric carbon dioxide (CO_2) and utilized by the plant during photosynthe-
sis. As a rule, C_4 plants discriminate less against the isotopically heavier
^{13}C from the atmosphere. This means that C_4 plants have less negative
isotope ratios than C_3 plants. In Georgia and Florida, most plants eaten by
people are of the C_3 variety. The major economically significant C_4 plant
for the prehistoric and contact periods is maize. During the contact period,
sugarcane—another C_4 plant—was eaten by some humans in the circum-
Caribbean region. However, to our knowledge, native populations living
in the missions of La Florida had minimal access to it, if any.

Nitrogen isotopic variation, measured as ratios of ^{15}N/^{14}N (δ^{15}N values),
distinguishes terrestrial and marine foods and their consumers, owing
mostly to the fact that nitrogen enters the ecological domain of these settings in different ways. Because of the differences in how nitrogen is acquired by terrestrial and marine organisms, there is a tendency for marine
organisms to have more positive δ^{15}N values than terrestrial organisms,
and these differences are ultimately reflected in the human consumers and
their bone tissue.

For coastal settings, carbon isotope ratios for maize and for marine
organisms overlap to a large extent, precluding clear dietary reconstruction
of the use of maize and marine foods. In the coastal zone of Georgia and
Florida, where native populations in later prehistory and at missions likely
ate both marine foods and maize, we cannot rely on stable isotope ratios of

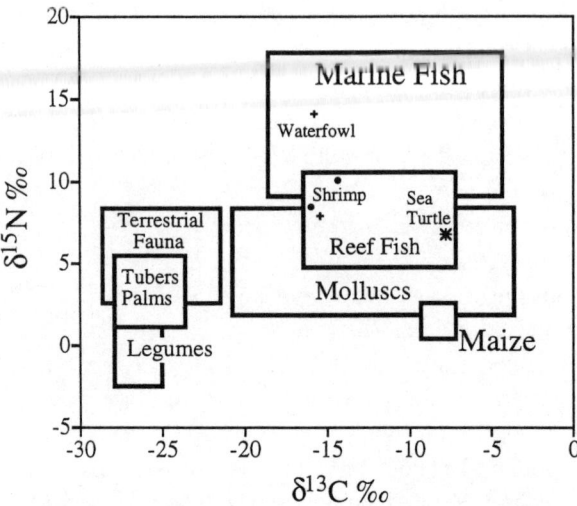

Fig. 3.1. Bivariate plot of carbon and nitrogen stable isotope ratios ($\delta^{13}C$ $\%_{00PDB}$, $\delta^{15}N\%_{00AIR}$) of major foods eaten by humans in the circum-Caribbean region. Following Tieszen 1991 and Wahlen 1994, 1.5 percent was added to the $\delta^{13}C$ value of the modern foods in order to compensate for ^{12}C enrichment of the atmosphere from burning of fossil fuels. Figure is adapted from Hutchinson et al. 1998;based on data from Keegan and DeNiro 1988; Norr 1990; Schoeninger and DeNiro 1984; Schoeninger et al. 1990; Hutchinson and Norr n.d.; Norr and Cooke 1998).

carbon alone. However, use of bivariate plots of stable isotope ratios of carbon and nitrogen circumvents this problem (Schoeninger et al. 1990). Therefore, for this study we have determined stable isotope ratios for both carbon and nitrogen in order to track the use of maize and seafood in native populations. A bivariate plot for stable carbon and nitrogen isotope ratios for some of the major foods eaten by humans from the circum-Caribbean region are shown in figure 3.1.

Our determination of carbon and nitrogen stable isotope ratios from human bone followed procedures developed earlier and published elsewhere (Schoeninger et al. 1990; Hutchinson and Norr 1994). Briefly, bone samples (mostly from long bones and ribs) were cleaned in the laboratory and the organic component (collagen) was extracted and analyzed via mass spectrometry. The quality of samples and appropriateness for this study were assessed by examining the collagen weight yield and the carbon to nitrogen ratios (Schoeninger et al. 1990; Ambrose and Norr 1992), which determine if the results are true biogenic signals of diet or artifactual due to postdepositional factors. Ratios were determined following standard equations:

$$\delta^{13}C = \left[\frac{(^{13}C/^{12}C)_{sample} - (^{13}C/^{12}C)_{PDB}}{(^{13}C/^{12}C)_{PDB}} \right] \times 1000^0/_{00}$$

$$\delta^{15}N = \left[\frac{(^{15}N/^{14}N)_{sample} - (^{15}N/^{14}N)_{AIR}}{(^{15}N/^{14}N)_{AIR}} \right] \times 1000^0/_{00}$$

The Skeletal Samples and the Populations They Represent

In order to identify temporal shifts and geographic/cultural variation, we divide the region temporally and geographically. Samples were acquired from 184 individuals from 28 archaeological sites from the following seven periods and locations: Georgia Early Prehistoric (400 B.C.–A.D. 1000), Florida Early Prehistoric (A.D. 0–1000), Georgia Late Prehistoric (A.D. 1000–1550), Florida Late Prehistoric/Protohistoric (A.D. 1000–1600), Georgia Early Mission (A.D. 1600–1680), Florida Early Mission (A.D. 1600–1680), and Florida Late Mission (A.D. 1680–1700). The isotope samples are summarized by location and period in table 3.1, and the individual stable isotope data are presented in table 3.2. The Georgia early prehistoric sample comes from five coastal (marine) sites from St. Catherines Island—McLeod Mound, Seaside Mound I, Seaside Mound II, Cunningham Field Mound C, and Cunningham Field Mound D—and one inland (terrestrial) population is represented by the Deptford site, located upriver from the mouth of the Savannah River. The Florida early prehistoric period is represented by the Henderson Mound, an Alachua-tradition site and also an inland site.

The Georgia late prehistoric period is represented by eight sites from St. Catherines Island (Johns Mound, Marys Mound, South End Mound I), St. Simons Island (Martinez Test B, Indian Field, Taylor Mound, Couper Field), and upriver on the Savannah River immediately north of the city of Savannah (Irene Mound site). These sites date from the locally known St. Catherines (A.D. 1000–1150), Savannah (A.D. 1150–1300), and Irene (A.D. 1300–1550) periods (see DePratter 1979). The Irene Mound samples are derived from two successive periods: from the earlier Savannah period (Burial Mound) and from the later Irene period (Large Mound and Mortuary).

Table 3.1. Samples used for stable isotope analysis (N = 184)

Site	Location	N
Georgia early prehistoric		
McLeod Mound	coastal Georgia	4
Seaside Mound I	coastal Georgia	1
Seaside Mound II	coastal Georgia	3
Cunningham Mound C	coastal Georgia	2
Cunningham Mound D	coastal Georgia	1
Deptford site	inland Georgia	11
Florida early prehistoric		
Henderson Mound	inland Florida	4
Georgia late prehistoric/protohistoric		
Johns Mound	coastal Georgia	10
Marys Mound	coastal Georgia	2
Southend Mound I	coastal Georgia	5
Irene Burial Mound	inland Georgia	10
Irene Large Mound	inland Georgia	1
Irene Mortuary	inland Georgia	10
Martinez Test B	coastal Georgia	2
Indian Field	coastal Georgia	2
Taylor Mound	coastal Georgia	9
Couper Field	coastal Georgia	7
Florida late prehistoric/protohistoric		
Lake Jackson	inland Florida	4
Waddells Pond	inland Florida	1
Browne Mound	coastal Florida	5
Holy Spirit	coastal Florida	4
Tatham Mound	inland Florida	20
Georgia early mission		
Santa Catalina de Guale	coastal Georgia	22
Florida early mission		
Santa Maria de Yamasee	coastal Florida	7
Ossuary at Santa Catalina	coastal Florida	8
San Martín de Timucua	inland Florida	2
San Pedro de Patale	inland Florida	5
Florida late mission		
San Luis de Apalachee	inland Florida	1
Santa Catalina de Amelia	coastal Florida	21

Table 3.2. Stable isotope ratios by individual

Lab no.	Site	Burial	Sex[a]	$\delta^{13}C^{0}/_{00}$	$\delta^{15}N^{0}/_{00}$
UCT389	McLeod Mound	13	F	-17.1	13.1
UCT391	McLeod Mound	15	F	-18.6	12.9
UCT392	McLeod Mound	16	F	-13.8	12.6
UCT393	McLeod Mound	17	F	-13.6	12.4
UCT385	Seaside Mound I	14	M	-15.0	—
UCT386	Seaside Mound II	11	M	-13.8	10.6
UCT387	Seaside Mound II	13	F	-15.7	—
UCT388	Seaside Mound II	14	F	-13.4	13.2
UCT394	Cunningham Mound C	1	F	-16.0	14.4
UCT395	Cunningham Mound C	3	F	-14.8	—
UCT396	Cunningham Mound D	2	M	-13.9	12.9
UCT334	Deptford site	4A	F	-13.4	11.3
UCT335	Deptford site	4B	F	-14.5	11.3
UCT382	Deptford site	8A	F	-18.6	10.7
UCT337	Deptford site	13	F	-17.5	9.6
UCT338	Deptford site	16	F	-17.7	—
UCT339	Deptford site	17	F	-16.7	11.6
UCT340	Deptford site	18A	M	-15.6	12.9
UCT341	Deptford site	22	F	-16.0	11.8
UCT342	Deptford site	28	M	-16.8	12.0
UCT343	Deptford site	29A	M	-17.1	9.6
UCT344	Deptford site	40	M	-12.6	10.4
UCT372	Johns Mound	1	M	-14.2	11.6
UCT379	Johns Mound	14	M	-13.4	13.1
UCT377	Johns Mound	16	F	-14.6	13.3
UCT376	Johns Mound	18	F	-13.9	13.6
UCT374	Johns Mound	26	I	-13.7	12.3
UCT370	Johns Mound	36	I	-14.1	13.0
UCT375	Johns Mound	37	F	-14.4	12.7
UCT378	Johns Mound	47	M	-14.3	13.5
UCT373	Johns Mound	B	M	-14.2	12.9
UCT371	Johns Mound	11A	M	-14.2	13.3
UCT380	Marys Mound	1	F	-14.3	11.8
UCT381	Marys Mound	5	F	-14.7	12.9
UCT349	Irene Burial Mound	2A	F	-14.0	9.6
UCT350	Irene Burial Mound	3	M	-13.3	10.4
UCT351	Irene Burial Mound	4B	M	-10.0	10.6
UCT353	Irene Burial Mound	5	M	-12.4	10.5
UCT352	Irene Burial Mound	7	F	-10.8	9.5
UCT354	Irene Burial Mound	9	F	-16.4	—
UCT355	Irene Burial Mound	12	F	-16.4	10.1
UCT356	Irene Burial Mound	14	F	-13.9	11.2
UCT357	Irene Burial Mound	16	M	-14.4	10.8
UCT358	Irene Burial Mound	72	F	-11.5	13.3
UCT359	Large Mound	8A	M	-17.4	10.7
UCT360	Irene Mortuary	64	M	-16.8	9.2

(continued)

Table 3.2—*Continued*

Lab no.	Site	Burial	Sex[a]	$\delta^{13}C^0/_{00}$	$\delta^{15}N^0/_{00}$
UCT361	Irene Mortuary	69D	M	-17.9	8.7
UCT362	Irene Mortuary	70	M	-17.0	10.4
UCT363	Irene Mortuary	74	F	-14.5	9.7
UCT364	Irene Mortuary	75	M	-13.7	10.2
UCT365	Irene Mortuary	107	M	-17.7	9.9
UCT366	Irene Mortuary	108	F	-17.0	9.6
UCT367	Irene Mortuary	109	M	-17.9	10.2
UCT368	Irene Mortuary	110	F	-15.6	10.0
UCT369	Irene Mortuary	111	F	-17.2	9.6
MS4843	Southend Mound I	5	M	-13.3	13.1
MS4844	Southend Mound I	6	F	—	12.5
MS4847	Southend Mound I	16	F	—	10.4
MS4850	Southend Mound I	24	F	-13.2	12.8
MS4851	Southend Mound I	27	F	-12.4	11.7
M386	Couper Field	2	F	-13.8	12.8
M382	Couper Field	5	M	-14.0	12.8
M387	Couper Field	7	F	-14.2	12.1
M383	Couper Field	8	M	-12.4	11.8
M384	Couper Field	11	M	-13.9	11.4
M388	Couper Field	13	F	-14.5	11.7
M385	Couper Field	15	M	-13.6	13.5
M371	Indian Field	4	M	-14.8	14.8
M372	Indian Field	5	F	-14.8	13.2
M369	Martinez Test B	2	M	-13.4	14.1
M370	Martinez Test B	3	M	-12.7	13.6
M376	Taylor Mound	2	F	-13.0	12.7
M373	Taylor Mound	3	M	-12.5	13.6
M377	Taylor Mound	4	F	-13.7	12.1
M378	Taylor Mound	5	F	-13.9	12.7
M374	Taylor Mound	6	M	-9.9	12.2
M375	Taylor Mound	8	M	-10.2	12.8
M379	Taylor Mound	9	F	-13.3	11.5
M380	Taylor Mound	11	F	-11.1	11.0
M381	Taylor Mound	379	F	-11.1	12.5
MS4610	Browne Mound	7	F	-12.4	14.0
MS4604	Browne Mound	11	F	-17.1	13.2
MS4608	Browne Mound	18	M	-12.3	14.2
MS4603	Browne Mound	19	M	-17.4	9.2
MS4607	Browne Mound	46	M	-13.4	13.2
MS4617	Holy Spirit	7	F	-17.3	12.2
MS4619	Holy Spirit	8	M	-18.1	—
MS4620	Holy Spirit	9	M	-19.4	12.8
MS4622	Holy Spirit	11	F	-17.1	11.8
MS4615	Henderson Mound	14	I	-17.9	9.0
MS4613	Henderson Mound	27	I	-16.1	11.2
MS4612	Henderson Mound	32	I	-13.2	9.1
MS4614	Henderson Mound	34	I	-16.3	11.9

Lab no.	Site	Burial	Sex[a]	$\delta^{13}C^o/_{oo}$	$\delta^{15}N^o/_{oo}$
DH39	Waddells Mill Pond	65	I	-12.8	10.4
MS4599	Lake Jackson	6	M	14,6	9.1
MS4600	Lake Jackson	7	F	-13.7	13.0
MS4601	Lake Jackson	10	F	-14.0	8.8
MS4602	Lake Jackson	16	F	-13.6	9.3
DH10	Tatham Mound	113	F	-17.5	10.9
DH7	Tatham Mound	127	M	-20.3	11.9
DH23	Tatham Mound	1	F	-18.8	11.8
DH48	Tatham Mound	2	F	-13.8	10.1
DH24	Tatham Mound	9	M	-18.7	12.0
DH8	Tatham Mound	14	F	-15.6	10.9
DH4	Tatham Mound	16	M	-13.9	11.4
DH11	Tatham Mound	17	M	-15.8	11.5
DH13	Tatham Mound	24	I	-18.4	12.0
DH9	Tatham Mound	30	M	-17.7	11.7
DH16	Tatham Mound	33	I	-16.9	10.8
DH1	Tatham Mound	42	I	-18.1	12.0
DH17	Tatham Mound	48	I	-18.6	12.0
DH14	Tatham Mound	51	M	-18.5	12.6
DH15	Tatham Mound	55	I	-19.1	11.9
DH6	Tatham Mound	56	I	-19.7	11.7
DH30	Tatham Mound	66	F	-17.8	10.3
DH42	Tatham Mound	77	F	-15.0	10.4
DH29	Tatham Mound	86	F	-17.3	11.7
DH12	Tatham Mound	120	I	-18.6	11.6
MS2835	Santa Catalina de Guale	9	F	-9.6	7.4
MS2836	Santa Catalina de Guale	18	M	-11.7	9.6
MS2838	Santa Catalina de Guale	22	F	-12.4	9.6
MS2839	Santa Catalina de Guale	39	M	-11.6	10.4
MS2840	Santa Catalina de Guale	41	M	-11.0	9.8
MS2841	Santa Catalina de Guale	46	M	-10.4	8.5
MS2844	Santa Catalina de Guale	58	F	-12.0	9.5
MS2832	Santa Catalina de Guale	60	F	-14.3	9.5
MS2848	Santa Catalina de Guale	64	F	-11.8	9.9
MS2849	Santa Catalina de Guale	74	M	-9.7	7.5
MS2850	Santa Catalina de Guale	88	F	-11.0	9.7
MS2851	Santa Catalina de Guale	98	F	-11.2	8.9
MS2857	Santa Catalina de Guale	99	F	-12.1	9.0
MS2861	Santa Catalina de Guale	107	M	-10.8	10.8
MS2865	Santa Catalina de Guale	123	F	-11.2	10.2
MS2862	Santa Catalina de Guale	160	I	-12.9	9.9
MS2869	Santa Catalina de Guale	169	M	-11.6	9.3
MS2871	Santa Catalina de Guale	219	I	-11.0	8.9
MS2876	Santa Catalina de Guale	235	I	-10.6	10.0
MS2879	Santa Catalina de Guale	276	F	-11.3	9.4
MS2877	Santa Catalina de Guale	294	M	-11.4	9.8
MS2859	Santa Catalina de Guale	111	I	-12.6	9.6
MS3280	Ossuary at Amelia Island	1	M	-12.1	9.8

(continued)

Table 3.2—*Continued*

Lab no.	Site	Burial	Sex[a]	$\delta^{13}C^0/_{00}$	$\delta^{15}N^0/_{00}$
MS3201	Ossuary at Amelia Island	2	M	-12.1	10.6
MS3282	Ossuary at Amelia Island	3	M	-11.5	10.0
MS3283	Ossuary at Amelia Island	4	M	-13.4	10.1
MS3284	Ossuary at Amelia Island	5	F	-12.8	10.2
MS3285	Ossuary at Amelia Island	6	F	-11.3	10.8
MS3286	Ossuary at Amelia Island	7	F	-12.4	9.4
MS3287	Ossuary at Amelia Island	8	F	-12.0	10.8
MS4575	Santa Maria de Yamasee	15	M	-12.0	14.5
MS4585	Santa Maria de Yamasee	16	F	-12.0	12.2
MS4586	Santa Maria de Yamasee	42	F	-11.6	11.9
MS4587	Santa Maria de Yamasee	51	M	-12.8	11.2
MS4588	Santa Maria de Yamasee	67	F	-12.0	9.5
MS4589	Santa Maria de Yamasee	74	M	-13.6	7.3
MS4590	Santa Maria de Yamasee	83	F	-12.5	9.5
MS4591	San Martin de Timucua	91	M	-12.7	7.9
MS4595	San Martin de Timucua	92	M	-12.1	9.4
MS4581	San Pedro y San Pablo de Patale	14	M	-12.2	9.0
MS4582	San Pedro y San Pablo de Patale	34	F	-14.2	5.8
MS4578	San Pedro y San Pablo de Patale	41	F	-10.2	8.7
MS4577	San Pedro y San Pablo de Patale	46	M	-10.0	9.6
MS4584	San Pedro y San Pablo de Patale	61	F	-11.0	6.4
MS4611	San Luis de Apalachee	3	M	-16.5	12.3
MS3248	Santa Catalina de Amelia	1	F	-11.1	10.9
MS3249	Santa Catalina de Amelia	6C	M	-10.2	11.0
MS3250	Santa Catalina de Amelia	7	F	-11.3	10.1
MS2832	Santa Catalina de Amelia	11	M	-12.4	9.8
MS3251	Santa Catalina de Amelia	15	M	-11.3	10.1
MS2834	Santa Catalina de Amelia	19	F	-12.1	8.8
MS3252	Santa Catalina de Amelia	20	F	-11.8	10.5
MS3254	Santa Catalina de Amelia	30	F	-11.1	9.6
MS3255	Santa Catalina de Amelia	34A	M	-10.9	9.8
MS3256	Santa Catalina de Amelia	36B	F	-11.3	9.4
MS3257	Santa Catalina de Amelia	45	M	-10.0	8.6
MS3258	Santa Catalina de Amelia	50A	F	-12.2	10.3
MS3271	Santa Catalina de Amelia	59B	M	-11.4	10.3
MS3272	Santa Catalina de Amelia	60	F	-12.2	9.6
MS3273	Santa Catalina de Amelia	65	M	-10.4	10.2
MS3274	Santa Catalina de Amelia	66	F	-12.5	8.3
MS3275	Santa Catalina de Amelia	73	M	-10.5	8.8
MS3276	Santa Catalina de Amelia	78	M	-12.5	11.6
MS3277	Santa Catalina de Amelia	88	F	-12.6	10.1
MS3278	Santa Catalina de Amelia	91	F	-12.1	9.7
MS3279	Santa Catalina de Amelia	95B	M	-12.5	10.9

a. F = female; M = male; I = indeterminate.

The Florida late prehistoric samples are from two interior sites, the Lake Jackson and Waddells Pond sites. The populations living there are the likely ancestors of the Apalachee Indians (Scarry 1990). The two sites are local variants of the Mississippian culture known as Fort Walton. Lake Jackson was a multi-mound, ceremonial, and village complex. The overall connection with the larger Mississippian sphere characteristic of the Eastern Woodlands in general is indicated by the type of mound construction, plaza, and ceremonial copper breastplates and other objects found at the site (Jones 1982). Two coastal Florida sites date to the same time period: the Holy Spirit Church site (also known as the McCormick site) and the Browne Mound in the region of the mouth of the St. Johns River on the Atlantic coast. Another key inland site—located in west-central Florida— is the Tatham Mound site, which contains a late prehistoric component (A.D. 1200–1450) and a later protohistoric (A.D. 1525–1550) component (Hutchinson 1991; Hutchinson and Norr 1994).

The contact period is represented by a series of skeletal remains from seven mission sites in Georgia and Florida. The earliest sample is from the Georgia early mission period, from Santa Catalina de Guale on St. Catherines Island. This is one of the largest and most extensively documented mission period skeletal samples in La Florida (see Larsen 1990). Two sites represent the Florida early mission period: Santa Maria de Yamasee on Amelia Island on the Atlantic coast and a protohistoric (mid-16th-century) ossuary of disarticulated remains adjacent to a Guale mission cemetery (Santa Catalina de Santa Maria), also on Amelia Island. Interior Florida of this period is represented by the San Martín de Timucua (also called Fig Springs) and San Pedro y San Pablo de Patale (also called Patale) mission sites. The Florida late mission period is represented by the Santa Catalina de Santa Maria (or de Amelia) site on Amelia Island and the interior site of San Luis de Apalachee (or San Luis de Talimali) in Tallahassee.

It is likely that the late prehistoric sites in coastal Georgia are ancestral populations of the mission period Guale. Likewise the late prehistoric Florida populations are ancestral to the Timucua to the east and the Apalachee to the west. The Santa Catalina population from St. Catherines Island (A.D. 1607–1680) are the ancestors of the later Santa Catalina population from Amelia Island (A.D. 1684–1702) (see Larsen et al. 1992a).

Temporal Comparisons of Diet

Temporal Comparison 1: Georgia Early Prehistoric to Late Prehistoric

Comparison of late and early prehistoric isotope values in inland and coastal Georgia reveals a simultaneous shift from more negative to less negative stable carbon isotope ratios and more positive to less positive stable nitrogen isotope ratios (tables 3.3 and 3.4, fig. 3.2). For the inland setting, $\delta^{13}C$ values increase on average from –16.0 to –15.1‰ and $\delta^{15}N$ values decline from 11.1 to 10.2‰. Similarly, for the coastal populations, the stable isotope ratios shift from more negative to less negative for carbon (from –15.1 to –13.4‰), but there is no appreciable change in $\delta^{15}N$ values (from 12.8 to 12.6‰). These findings indicate that the inland and coastal populations increased their C_4 (maize) consumption. For the coastal region, the slight change in nitrogen values indicates that there may have been a slight reduction in eating of marine foods, but it did not represent a major shift in diet; use of marine resources remained virtually unchanged over time.

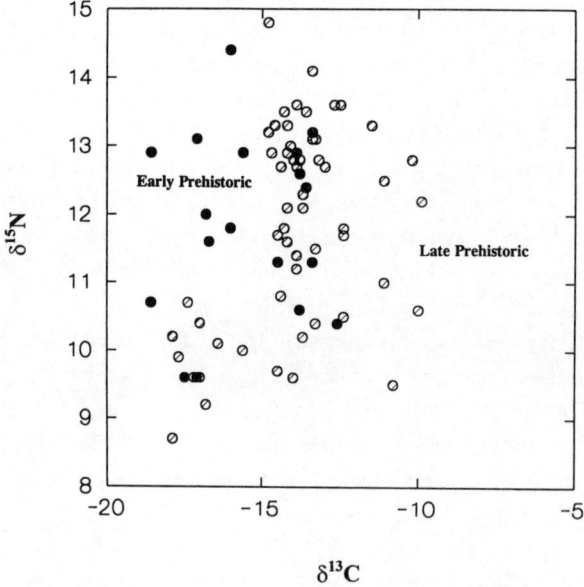

Fig. 3.2. Bivariate plot of carbon and nitrogen stable isotope ratios of Georgia early prehistoric (*filled circles*) and Georgia late prehistoric (*hatched circles*) individuals.

Table 3.3. Summary statistics of stable isotope ratios for Georgia early prehistoric

Region	N	$\delta^{13}C^0/oo$	S.D.	$\delta^{15}N^0/oo$	S.D.
Coastal Georgia					
Females	8	-15.4	1.8	13.1	0.7
Males	3	-14.2	0.7	11.8	1.6
Total	11	-15.1	1.7	12.8	1.6
Inland Georgia					
Females	7	-16.3	1.9	11.1	0.8
Males	4	-15.5	2.1	11.2	1.5
Total	11	-16.0	1.9	11.1	1.1

The differences between the coastal and inland settings are especially pronounced in the nitrogen values. The more positive values in the inland setting indicate lesser amounts of seafood in the diet than on the coast. These differences between coastal and inland settings indicate that diets were highly localized, with foods being extracted from ecological settings close to home.

Comparisons of isotope ratios of males and females reveals a clear difference between late prehistoric coastal males and females in $\delta^{15}N$ values (t-test, $p \leq 0.05$; males = 13.0%oo, females = 12.3%oo). This difference in nitrogen stable isotope values indicates differences in diet between late prehistoric men and women living on the coast.

Table 3.4. Summary statistics of stable isotope ratios for Georgia late prehistoric

Region	N	$\delta^{13}C^0/oo$	S.D.	$\delta^{15}N^0/oo$	S.D.
Coastal Georgia					
Females	19	-13.6	1.1	12.3[a]	0.8
Males	16	-13.2	1.4	13.0[a]	0.9
Total	37[b]	-13.4	1.2	12.6	0.9
Inland Georgia					
Females	10	-14.7	2.2	10.3	1.2
Males	12	-15.5	2.6	10.2	0.6
Total	22	-15.1	2.4	10.2	0.9

a. Statistically significant differences (t-test; $p \leq 0.05$).
b. Sex determination not possible for all individuals.

Temporal Comparison 2: Florida Early Prehistoric
to Late Prehistoric/Protohistoric

Some of the late prehistoric Florida populations show a clear shift in $\delta^{13}C$ values from the early prehistoric period, going from an average of –15.9 for the inland Henderson Mound to an average of –13.7 for the northern inland Waddells Pond and Lake Jackson sites (table 3.5). The $\delta^{15}N$ values remain essentially unchanged over time (10.4 to 10.1) for these inland groups. In contrast to these samples and those for the late prehistoric Georgia series, the $\delta^{13}C$ values determined for the late prehistoric Florida coastal samples are quite negative (–16.1), indicating little use of C_4 foods (maize) in diet or, more likely, none (table 3.5). Similarly, the late prehistoric/protohistoric Tatham Mound population, who lived in the central inland region (Florida Gulf), express very negative $\delta^{13}C$ values on average (–17.5), indicating no use of maize in their diets. There are significant sex differences in comparison of nitrogen stable isotope ratios for the inland samples from Florida (males = 11.9; females = 10.9), indicating differences in freshwater aquatic food consumption, with males eating more fish or shellfish than females. The source of these foods in this setting was probably interior lakes and streams (see Hutchinson and Norr 1994).

Table 3.5. Summary statistics of stable isotope ratios for Florida early and late prehistoric

Region	N	$\delta^{13}C$‰	S.D.	$\delta^{15}N$‰	S.D.
Inland Florida early prehistoric					
Total[a]	4	-15.9	2.0	10.3	1.5
Northern coastal Florida late prehistoric					
Females	4	-16.0	2.4	12.8	1.0
Males	5	-16.1	3.1	12.4	2.2
Total	9	-16.1	2.6	12.6	1.6
Northern inland Florida late prehistoric					
Females	3	-13.8	0.2	10.4	2.3
Males	1	-14.6	—	9.1	—
Total	5[a]	-13.7	0.7	10.1	1.7
Central inland Florida late prehistoric					
Females	7	-16.5	1.8	10.9[b]	0.7
Males	6	-17.5	2.3	11.9[b]	0.4
Total	20[a]	-17.5	1.8	11.5	0.7

a. Sex determination not possible for all individuals.
b. Statistically significant difference (t-test; $p \le 0.01$).

These findings from the Florida setting reveal some similarities, but mostly differences, in comparison with the Georgia settings. That is, in both settings, there is a temporal shift from a lifeway that had no use of maize prior to about A.D. 1000 to a lifeway in which maize figured prominently in diet during the final centuries prior to European contact. However, the change in diet in Florida appears to have been primarily restricted to pre-contact Apalachee, the large Mississippian center at Lake Jackson in particular. The late prehistoric Waddells Pond site also expresses clear evidence of maize consumption, but the site is represented by one individual only (see table 3.2). All other late prehistoric samples in Florida, however, show no appreciable change in diet in later prehistory, in marked contrast to the Georgia setting. This finding indicates that beyond the immediate influence of Mississippianization in Florida, no change in diet occurred, at least as can be determined from stable isotope analysis.

Temporal Comparion 3: Georgia and Florida Late Prehistoric to Mission

Comparisons of isotope values from the various mission populations with the late prehistoric Georgia and Florida populations shows dramatic changes, regardless of ecological setting. In this regard, all mission settings have less negative $\delta^{13}C$ stable isotope values and less positive $\delta^{15}N$ stable isotope values both as a group and in comparison with prehistoric populations from the same region (tables 3.4, 3.5, and 3.6; fig. 3.3). Moreover,

Table 3.6. Summary statistics of stable isotope ratios for Georgia and Florida missions

Region	N	$\delta^{13}C^0/oo$	S.D.	$\delta^{15}N^0/oo$	S.D.
Coastal Florida					
Females	19	-11.9	0.5	10.1	1.0
Males	17	-11.7	1.1	10.3	1.5
Total	36	-11.8	0.8	10.2	1.2
Coastal Georgia					
Females	10	-11.7	1.2	9.3	0.8
Males	8	-11.0	0.7	9.5	1.1
Total	22[a]	-11.5	1.0	9.4	0.8
Inland Florida					
Females	3	-11.8	2.1	7.0	1.5
Males	5	-12.7	2.4	9.6	1.6
Total	8	-12.4	2.2	8.6	2.0

a. Sex determination not possible for all individuals.

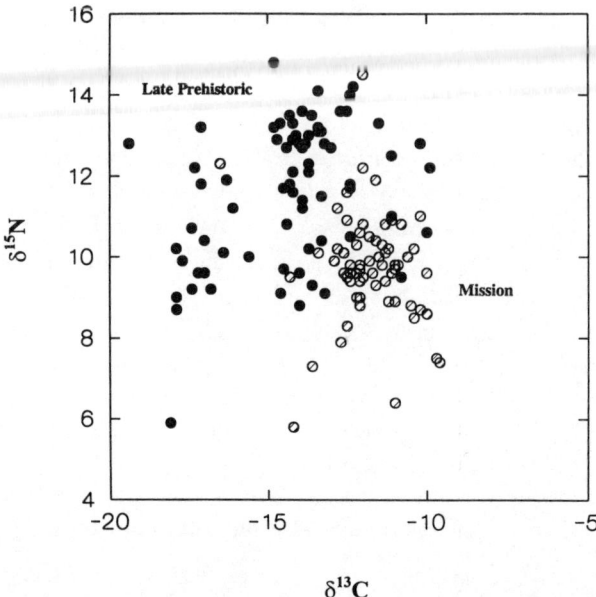

Fig. 3.3. Bivariate plot of carbon and nitrogen stable isotope ratios of Florida and Georgia late prehistoric (*filled circles*) and mission period (*hatched circles*) individuals.

regardless of the mission or its location in La Florida, the stable isotope values for carbon especially are statistically indistinguishable when comparing the missions: coastal Georgia (Santa Catalina de Guale, $\delta^{13}C$ = −11.5), coastal Florida (Santa Maria de Yamasee, Santa Catalina de Santa Maria Ossuary, Santa Catalina de Amelia, $\delta^{13}C$ = −11.8), and inland Florida (San Martín de Timucua, San Pedro y San Pablo de Patale, San Luis de Apalachee, $\delta^{13}C$ = −12.4) (t-test, $p \leq 0.05$). The only difference to emerge from these comparisons is a somewhat lower $\delta^{15}N$ value for the inland Florida missions (8.6) than in the coastal Florida and Georgia missions (10.2 and 9.4, respectively). This variation likely reflects the greater access to marine foods in the coastal setting than in the inland setting.

The less negative $\delta^{13}C$ values for all mission tribal groups across the region indicate a general pattern either of intensification of maize agriculture (e.g., Guale) or of shifting from predominantly C_3 foods to maize agriculture (e.g., Timucua). The generally less positive stable nitrogen isotope ratios reflect an overall reduction in marine food consumption. Thus, the dietary picture is one involving more carbohydrates from maize and less protein from seafood.

No clear sex differences in isotopic values emerge from these comparisons, suggesting that diets of males and females were broadly similar during the mission period. Moreover, comparison of early and late mission
samples shows little change over time (e.g., comparison of Santa Catalina
on St. Catherines Island with Santa Catalina on Amelia Island), suggesting
a similar level of use of maize and marine foods during the contact period.

Regional Variation in Diet

Regional Variation 1: Georgia Late Prehistoric

Although the change in isotope ratios of the late prehistoric period of Georgia can be characterized as one indicating a general increase in maize consumption, for both coastal and inland settings, one important exception to
this pattern was identified in our analysis. Predictably, the carbon stable
isotope ratios in the Savannah period (A.D. 1150–1300) component of the
Irene Mound site are less negative ($\delta^{13}C = -13.3$) than for the inland Georgia early prehistoric ($\delta^{13}C = -16.0$), indicating a marked shift in diet. This
pattern of change has been documented across the Eastern Woodlands of
North America and documents the spread and adoption of maize agriculture to this area of the Atlantic coast (and see Ambrose 1987; Smith 1989).
However, in the following Irene period (A.D. 1300–1450) there is a clear
and statistically significant reversal of this trend. The stable carbon isotope
ratios for the Irene period component are clearly more negative ($\delta^{13}C =
-16.6$), which almost certainly reflects a diet that contained far less maize
than during the Savannah period occupation of the site. This trend is not
seen in any other region of the overall study area of La Florida.

The change in diet within the Irene Mound community may be related
to circumstances specific to the Savannah River valley during this period.
Anderson (1994) has examined the late prehistoric (Mississippian) sociopolitical systems in the Savannah River valley, demonstrating a cyclical
pattern of appearance, expansion, and collapse of polities. The Irene
Mound site first made its appearance in the early twelfth century A.D.,
expanded over the next couple of centuries, and finally collapsed during
the first half of the 15th century, a full century before the arrival of Europeans in the region. Anderson argues that the last several decades or so of
the occupation of the Irene site represent a period of social and political
disarray and decline, which he relates to both internal and external circumstances. Internally, these Mississippian chiefdoms typically follow cyclical
episodes of power shifts and control of economic resources. In regard to

external circumstances, Anderson notes that this period was punctuated by environmental disruption caused by severe drought. He asserts that if rain full shortages were dramatic enough, crop failures would have resulted, forcing populations to use other (nondomestic) food resources. As with many other regions of the American Southeast, there was a general increase in population in this area during this time (see Larsen 1982), which would have resulted in additional pressures on food, population collapse, and the demise of the system. Thus, the abrupt shift in stable isotopic signatures in the Irene period may well reflect internal shifts in political organization and dietary change relating to climatic variation as seen elsewhere in the Southeast around this time (Schoeninger and Schurr 1998).

Regional Variation 2: Florida Late Mission

As already noted, the missions of La Florida show a generally uniform pattern of increasing (less negative) $\delta^{13}C$ values. These changes in stable isotope ratios reflect increasing maize consumption. One interesting possible exception to this pattern has been identified at the San Luis de Apalachee mission. We analyzed 10 bone samples from San Luis, but unfortunately with the exception of one individual, there was not enough collagen to produce meaningful results. The single exception was individual 3, a high status adult male, who had been interred near the altar on the western end of the church (Larsen et al. 1996). This person was one of six (from a total population of 210) who had been interred in a wooden coffin. All others were buried without coffins, probably in cloth shrouds. Moreover, this person was one of three who had been buried with their heads oriented to the west; all others were oriented with their heads to the east. Isotopic analysis of his collagen revealed a carbon stable isotope ratio of –16.5, indicating little maize in his diet. Abundant historical documentation indicates that the Apalachee Indians were eating maize (and other plant domesticates) in their diets (Hann 1988). Analysis of plant remains from various contexts at San Luis reveals the role of cultivars in native diets (Scarry 1993). For example, plant remains from the council house and other contexts at San Luis reveal a diverse (but not abundant) group of cultivars, including maize, bean, sunflower, wheat, peach, and a number of wild plants. Our analysis of this high status person indicates that he may have consumed these foods, but maize was not eaten on a regular basis.

We have also analyzed evidence of dental caries in the San Luis population. Generally speaking, populations eating large amounts of carbohydrates, such as maize, tend to have high frequencies of carious lesions (Larsen 1997). In the San Luis series, the total caries prevalence is relatively low, only about 4.5 percent (Larsen and Tung 1999), which is much lower than in other mission samples we have studied (see Larsen et al. 1991). For this setting, historical documentation may have exaggerated the importance of maize in native diets. The comprehensive analysis of plant remains from San Luis indicates the presence of maize, which may have been eaten in large quantities by some people. Individual 3 was apparently not among them.

Regional Variation 3: St. Catherines Island, Georgia

St. Catherines Island has been the focus of intensive archaeological, bioarchaeological, and ethnohistorical investigation, especially since the late 1970s. Owing to the longer history of bioarchaeological study there, especially regarding stable isotope analysis (see Schoeninger et al. 1990), the data base for analysis is more complete than for other sections of the study area discussed in this chapter. As such, the shifts in stable isotope ratios of carbon and nitrogen for St. Catherines Island provide one of the most detailed pictures of dietary change for this region of the study area and for North America in general. For the Early Prehistoric (400 B.C.–A.D. 1000:

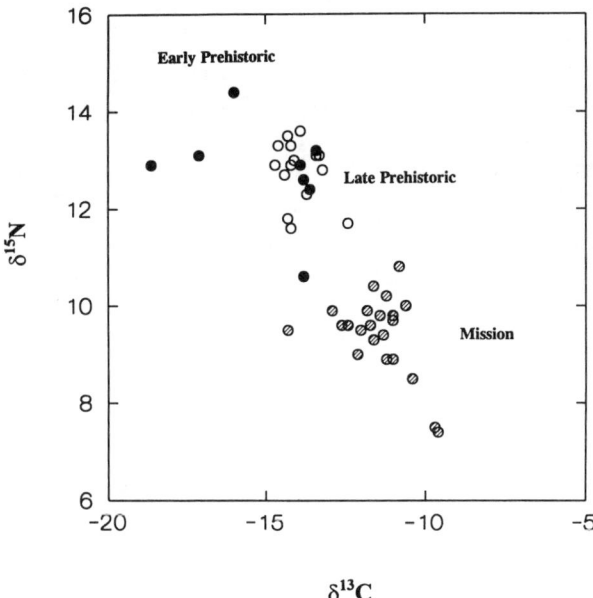

Fig. 3.4. Bivariate plot of carbon and nitrogen stable isotope ratios from St. Catherines Island, including early prehistoric (*filled circles*), late prehistoric (*open circles*), and mission (*hatched circles*).

McLeod Mound, Seaside Mounds I and II, Cunningham Field Mounds C and D) to Early Late Prehistoric (A.D. 1000–1150: Johns Mound, Marys Mound) to Late Late Prehistoric (A.D. 1300–1550: Southend Mound I) to Early Mission (A.D. 1600–1680: Santa Catalina de Guale), the δ^{13}C values rise steadily from –15.1 to –14.2 to –12.9 to –11.5, respectively, reflecting a gradual shift in diet from no maize to maize inclusion to intensive use of maize.

Bivariate plots of δ^{13}C and δ^{15}N values clearly show the highlights of change in diet over time for St. Catherines Island (fig. 3.4). Additionally, these comparisons highlight the contrast in later prehistory with developments taking place farther north and inland at the Irene Mound site, where there is a reduction in maize consumption, and to the south in Florida, where maize is not generally adopted until the mission period.

Dietary Change in La Florida

The use of stable isotope analysis as a tool for reconstructing diet in La Florida provides a compelling picture of dietary change and regional variation. Three principal findings emerge from this study. First, local factors are a huge influence in determining the kinds of foods eaten by native societies. This is especially clear in comparing coastal with noncoastal populations: coastal people ate more marine foods than noncoastal populations, even when the noncoastal population was located within a few kilometers of a coast (e.g., Irene Mound).

Second, there is an increase in use of C_4 resources—maize—in later prehistory, especially after about A.D. 1000. This finding is consistent with dietary changes documented via stable isotope analysis for much of eastern North America (Ambrose 1987). The change identified in the present study appears to be relatively uniform in the Georgia coastal region and adjacent mainland, and in the area of western (panhandle) Florida, but not elsewhere in northern and central Florida or in the final prehistoric period at the Irene Mound site. The finding that the late prehistoric/protohistoric Tatham Mound population from Gulf coast Florida ate predominantly C_3 foods corresponds with the accounts of early explorers in the region, who reported limited or no access to maize. One member of the de Soto expedition, Ranjel, remarked on their travels north from central Florida in the late 1530s that "they came to the plain of Cuaçoco, and the soldiers went into the corn fields and gathered the green corn with which they cheered themselves a little, for it was the first they had seen in that country" (Bourne 1922:64, cited in Hutchinson et al. 1998:409). This account clearly underscores the point that native populations living south of the present Florida-Georgia border—with the Apalachee being the primary exception—ate little maize prior to contact. Indeed, archaeobotanical remains recovered from various sites in northern Florida contain no evidence of maize prior to the contact era (see Ruhl 1990).

Third, and perhaps most striking, is the overall conflation of diet in the mission period, especially with respect to maize consumption. Put another way, the dietary change involved a shift from a heterogeneous food base in prehistory to a homogeneous food base in the mission period, involving more maize and less seafood. This pattern of dietary change that we have reconstructed from isotopic evidence is consistent with all ethnohistoric, biological, and archaeological evidence (see, for example, Hann 1988, 1996; Larsen 1990, 1993; Ruhl 1990; Scarry and Reitz 1990; Larsen et al. 1992b; Newsom and Quitmyer 1992; Bushnell 1994; Hudson 1997; and others). This is not to say that seafood and plants other than maize suddenly dropped out of diet in the mission period. Abundant archaeobotanical and zooarchaeological data indicate the contrary (Reitz 1993; Scarry 1993). Shellfish, fish remains, and many different kinds of plants found in mission site refuse attest to the fact that many different kinds of foods were consumed by native populations during the mission period. Nor do we intend to imply that diet was uniform across La Florida. Reitz (1990) argues, for example, that the diets at St. Augustine (Nombre de Dios) and St. Catherines Island (Santa Catalina de Guale) were substantially different, especially in the kinds of animals eaten.

That said, our findings based on assessment of stable isotope ratios of carbon and nitrogen indicate that maize played an increasingly important role in native foodways, and marine foods became less important for coastal populations, after contact and establishment of missions in Guale, Timucua, and Apalachee provinces of La Florida. The commonality of maize suggests a widespread pattern of shifting dietary interests.

Why, then, did maize become so much more important in the mission settings than before? We argue that this dietary change was largely brought about by cultural and social forces occasioned by the arrival of Spaniards in the region. That is, Spaniards came from a part of the world where agriculture was the primary means of acquiring food. European-introduced domestic animals were certainly part of the new landscape that emerged in La Florida, especially in the later 17th century. For example, cattle were introduced and beef was apparently available for consumption not only by Spaniards living in some areas of La Florida but also by the native population (Hann 1988). Thus, the protein derived from domesticated animals may have been important in some settings and may explain in part the relatively low prevalence of dental caries discussed for San Luis (protein is a known caries inhibitor). However, in many areas of La Florida, domesticated animals were rarely used, and they were not available to the native populations (e.g., Guale). The production of domesticated plants was a far more important enterprise, and the isotopic analysis reveals that the importance was widespread among native peoples.

We suggest that the change in diet was one aspect of a suite of behaviors encouraged or introduced to native populations as part of their conversion to Christianity. Spanish friars likely viewed agriculture as a component what it meant to be Christian, "civilized," and more like Europeans. These friars reoriented the economic system to one that involved more intensive agriculture. Moreover, the Spanish government and clergy viewed La Florida as a source of food for feeding the native populations inhabiting the missions but also for the support of the mission priests, the military garrison, and other non-natives. On occasion, crops were also required as tribute to the Spanish crown (Bushnell 1994). Historical sources indicate that crops grown in agricultural fields on St. Catherines Island were exported to St. Augustine, the capital of La Florida (see Jones 1978). We believe that these various circumstances involving increased maize production would have occasioned increased maize consumption.

Implications of Dietary Change for Biocultural Adaptation and Stress

The increased dependence on maize has profound implications for health, quality of life, and behavior both before and after contact. Maize is deficient in the essential amino acids lysine, isoleucine, and tryptophan (Whitney and Rolfes 1993). With these deficiencies, the consumer eats incomplete protein, which contributes to poor growth during the juvenile years. In addition, maize has phytate, which results in reduced availability of iron to the body tissues; iron absorption in maize-based diets is generally low (Ashworth et al. 1973). This reduced bioavailability can lead to iron deficiency anemia. Maize is also a carbohydrate, which is a predisposing factor to dental caries and poor oral health in general (Larsen et al. 1991). Thus, the clear understanding of diet in this setting provides an important context for understanding some of the health changes documented in this volume, such as porotic hyperostosis and cribra orbitalia (Schultz et al., this volume) and growth arrest (Hutchinson and Larsen, this volume; Simpson, this volume). Moreover, poor diets—and the associated poor nutrition— an exacerbate the effects of infection. Poor nutrition and infection have a synergistic relationship (Scrimshaw et al. 1968): malnourished people are more susceptible to infection, and people with an infection have a worsened nutritional status. Thus, the increase in infection seen in some of the mission populations (see Larsen and Harn 1994) may well have been influenced by the deteriorating quality of diet in this setting.

The decline in nutritional quality that we are inferring began before European contact, especially for Georgia. In the historical literature on decline in health and the population collapse in La Florida and elsewhere in the New World, historians have largely focused on the role of European-introduced infectious disease as the cause of decline in native population size (Cook 1998). However, we regard diet as being an essential factor for interpreting health changes and population dynamics in this critical period of human biological history.

Finally, the increased production of maize has clear implications for behavior, especially physical activity and workload. Spain viewed the native population living in La Florida as a labor source for a wide variety of activities, including agricultural production, building projects, and transport of materials and goods over long distances (see Hann 1988; Larsen 1990). After the arrival of Europeans, women played a more important role in agricultural production, including involvement in the fields. Our impressions from reading the historical literature on native labor in this setting suggest that workload for many—including both men and women—would have been demanding. Indeed, the repartimiento draft labor practice required able-bodied males to contribute labor with very little compensation. Thus, the shift in diet documented in this chapter provides important context for understanding skeletal changes relating to activity (Larsen and Ruff 1994; Ruff and Larsen, this volume).

Conclusions

This analysis of stable isotope ratios of carbon and nitrogen reveals fundamental changes in diet in the pre-contact and contact-era populations living in La Florida. Overall, these changes included a general increase in maize and decrease in marine food consumption. The pattern of change that we document via stable isotope analysis is one of a shift from regional diversity to uniformity and convergence of diet across the landscape. Precise knowledge of this dietary shift and its regional variations is central to understanding variation in health and activity in this diverse and complex setting.

Acknowledgments

Thanks go to David Hurst Thomas (American Museum of Natural History), Douglas Ubelaker (Smithsonian Institution), Jerald Milanich (Florida Museum of Natural History), and James Miller and Bonnie McEwan (Florida Bureau of Archaeological Research) for permission to study the skeletons housed under their care and to perform the analysis described in this chapter. Many of the samples were acquired in collaborative archaeological research programs with David Hurst Thomas (St. Catherines Island, Georgia), Kenneth Hardin, Jerald Milanich, and Rebecca Saunders (Amelia Island, Florida), Jerald Milanich and Jeffrey Mitchem (Tatham Mound, Florida), and Gary Shapiro and Bonnie McEwan (San Luis de Apalachee). Funding for fieldwork was provided by the St. Catherines Island Foundation, George and Dottie Dorion, Piers Anthony, and the Florida Department of State. Funding for laboratory analysis came from the University of Illinois, University of Wisconsin, Institute for Contact Period Studies (University of Florida), East Carolina University, and grants from the Florida Department of State, the National Endowment for the Humanities, the National Science Foundation, and the Margaret Cullinan Wray Research Fund.

References Cited

Ambrose, S. H. 1987. Chemical and Isotopic Techniques of Diet Reconstruction in Eastern North America. In *Emergent Horticultural Economies of the Eastern Woodlands*, ed. W. F. Keegan, 87–106. Southern Illinois University, Center for Archaeological Investigations, Occasional Paper 7.

Ambrose, S. H., and L. Norr. 1992. On Stable Isotopic Data and Prehistoric Subsistence in the Soconusco Region. *American Antiquity* 33:401–4.

———. 1993. Isotopic Composition of Dietary Protein and Energy versus Bone Collagen and Apatite: Purified Diet Growth Experiments. In *Prehistoric Human Bone: Archaeology at the Molecular Level*, ed. J. B. Lambert and G. Grupe, 1–37. Berlin: Springer-Verlag.

Anderson, D. G. 1994. *The Savannah River Chiefdoms: Political Change in the Late Prehistoric Southeast*. Tuscaloosa: University of Alabama Press.

Ashworth, A., P. F. Milner, J. C. Waterlow, and R. B. Walker. 1973. Absorption of Iron from Maize (*Zea maize* L.) and soya beans (*Glycine hispida* Max.) in Jamaican infants. *British Journal of Nutrition* 29:269–78.

Bourne, E. G. (ed.). 1922. *Narratives in the Career of Hernando de Soto*. New York: Allerton.

Brown, R. B., E. L. Stone, and V. W. Carlisle. 1990. Soils. In *Ecosystems of Florida*, ed. R. L. Myers and J. J. Ewel, 35–69. Orlando: University of Central Florida Press.

Bushnell, A. T. 1994. *Situado and Sabana: Spain's Support System for the Presidio and Mission Provinces of Florida.* Anthropological Papers of the American Museum of Natural History 74.

Caldwell, J., and C. McCann. 1941. *Irene Mound Site, Chatham County, Georgia.* Athens: University of Georgia Press.

Cook, N. D. 1998. *Born to Die: Disease and New World Conquest, 1492–1650.* Cambridge: Cambridge University Press.

DePratter, C. B. 1979. Ceramics. In *The Anthropology of St. Catherines Island: 2. The Refuge-Deptford Mortuary Complex*, by D. H. Thomas and C. S. Larsen, 109–32. Anthropological Papers of the American Museum of Natural History 56.

Gardner, W. M. 1966. The Waddells Mill Pond Site. *Florida Anthropologist* 19:43–64.

Hann, J. H. 1988. *Apalachee: The Land Between the Rivers.* Gainesville: University Presses of Florida.

———. 1996. *A History of the Timucua Indians and Missions.* Gainesville: University Press of Florida.

Hoshower, L. 1991. Bioanthropological Analysis of a Seventeenth-Century Native American Spanish Mission Population: Biocultural Impacts on the Northern Utina. Ph.D. diss., University of Florida, Gainesville.

Hudson, C. 1997. *Knights of Spain, Warriors of the Sun: Hernando De Soto and the South's Ancient Chiefdoms.* Athens: University of Georgia Press.

Hutchinson, D. L. 1991. Postcontact Native American Health and Adaptation: Assessing the Impact of Introduced Diseases in Sixteenth-Century Gulf Coast Florida. Ph.D. diss., University of Illinois, Champaign-Urbana.

Hutchinson, D. L., and L. Norr. 1994. Late Prehistoric and Early Historic Diet in Gulf Coast Florida. In *In the Wake of Contact: Biological Responses to Conquest*, ed. C. S. Larsen and G. R. Milner, 9–20. New York: Wiley-Liss.

———. N.d. Unpublished data on file, Department of Anthropology, University of Florida, Gainesville.

Hutchinson, D. L., C. S. Larsen, M. J. Schoeninger, and L. Norr. 1998. Regional Variation in the Pattern of Maize Adoption and Use in Florida and Georgia. *American Antiquity* 63:397–416.

Jones, B. C. 1982. Southern Cult Manifestations at the Lake Jackson Site, Leon County, Florida: Salvage Excavation of Mound 3. *Midcontinental Journal of Archaeology* 7:3–44.

Jones, B. C., J. H. Hann, and J. F. Scarry. 1991. *San Pedro y San Pablo de Patale: A Seventeenth-Century Spanish Mission in Leon County, Florida.* Florida Archaeology 5.

Jones, G. D. 1978. The Ethnohistory of the Guale Coast through 1684. In *The Anthropology of St. Catherines Island: 1. Natural and Cultural History*, by D.

H. Thomas, G. D. Jones, R. S. Durham, and C. S. Larsen, 178–210. Anthropological Papers of the American Museum of Natural History 55.

Keogan, W. F., and M. J. DeNiro. 1988. Stable Carbon- and Nitrogen-Isotope Ratios of Bone Collagen Used to Study Coral-Reef and Terrestrial Components of Prehistoric Bahamian Diet. *American Antiquity* 53:320–36.

Larsen, C. S. 1982. The Anthropology of St. Catherines Island: 3. Prehistoric Human Biological Adaptation. Anthropological Papers of the American Museum of Natural History 57, pt. 3.

———. 1993. On the Frontier of Contact: Mission Bioarchaeology in La Florida. In *The Spanish Missions of La Florida*, ed. B. G. McEwan, 322–56. Gainesville: University Press of Florida.

———. 1996. Unpublished data on file, Research Laboratories of Archaeology, University of North Carolina, Chapel Hill.

———. 1997. *Bioarchaeology: Interpreting Behavior from the Human Skeleton.* Cambridge: Cambridge University Press.

Larsen, C. S. (ed.). 1990. *The Archaeology of Mission Santa Catalina de Guale: 2. Biocultural Interpretations of a Population in Transition.* Anthropological Papers of the American Museum of Natural History 68.

Larsen, C. S., and D. E. Harn. 1994. Health in Transition: Disease and Nutrition in the Georgia Bight. In *Paleonutrition: The Diet and Health of Prehistoric Americans,* ed. K. D. Sobolik, 222–34. Southern Illinois University, Center for Archaeological Investigations, Occasional Paper 22.

Larsen, C. S., and C. B. Ruff. 1994. The Stresses of Conquest in Spanish Florida: Structural Adaptation and Change before and after Contact. In *In the Wake of Contact: Biological Responses to Conquest,* ed. C. S. Larsen and G. R. Milner, 21–34. New York: Wiley-Liss.

Larsen, C. S., and D. H. Thomas. 1982. *The Anthropology of St. Catherines Island: 4. The St. Catherines Period Mortuary Complex.* Anthropological Papers of the American Museum of Natural History 57, pt. 4.

Larsen, C. S., and T. A. Tung. 1999. *Mission San Luis de Apalachee: The Human Remains.* Report to the Florida Bureau of Archaeological Research, Tallahassee.

Larsen, C. S., H. P. Huynh, and B. G. McEwan. 1996. Death by Gunshot: Biocultural Implications of Trauma at Mission San Luis. *International Journal of Osteoarchaeology* 6:42–50.

Larsen, C. S., R. Shavit, and M. C. Griffin. 1991. Dental Caries Evidence for Dietary Change: An Archaeological Context. In *Advances in Dental Anthropology,* ed. M. A. Kelley and C. S. Larsen, 179–202. New York: Wiley-Liss.

Larsen, C. S., C. B. Ruff, M. J. Schoeninger, and D. L. Hutchinson. 1992a. Population Decline and Extinction in La Florida. In *Disease and Demography in the Americas: Changing Patterns Before and After 1492,* ed. J. W. Verano and D. H. Ubelaker, 81–95. Washington: Smithsonian Institution Press.

Larsen, C. S., M. J. Schoeninger, N. J. van der Merwe, K. M. Moore, and J. A. Lee-Thorp. 1992b. Carbon and Nitrogen Stable Isotopic Signatures of Human Dietary Change in the Georgia Bight. *American Journal of Physical Anthropology* 89:197–214.

Loucks, J. J. 1976a. Early Alachua Tradition Burial Ceremonialism: the Henderson Mound, Alachua County, Florida. M.A. thesis, University of Florida, Gainesville.

Martinez, C. A. 1975. Culture Sequence on the Central Georgia Coast, 1000 B.C.–1650 A.D. M.A. thesis, University of Florida, Gainesville.

McEwan, B. G. (ed.). 1993. *The Spanish Missions of La Florida*. Gainesville: University Press of Florida.

Milanich, J. T. 1993. *The Spanish Missions*. Gainesville: Florida Museum of Natural History.

———. 1994. *Archaeology of Precolumbian Florida*. Gainesville: University Press of Florida.

Myers, Ronald L., and John J. Ewel (eds.). 1990. *Ecosystems of Florida*. Gainesville: University Presses of Florida.

Newsom, L. A., and I. R. Quitmyer. 1992. Archaeobotanical and Faunal Remains. In *Excavations on the Franciscan Frontier: Archaeology at the Fig Springs Mission*, ed. B. R. Weisman, 206–33. Gainesville: University Press of Florida.

Norr, L. 1990. Nutritional Consequences of Prehistoric Subsistence Strategies in Lower Central America. Ph.D. diss., University of Illinois, Champaign-Urbana.

———. 1995. Interpreting Dietary Maize from Bone Stable Isotopes in the New World Tropics: The State of the Art. In *Archaeology in the American Tropics: Current Analytical Methods and Applications*, ed. P. W. Stahl, 198–223. Cambridge: Cambridge University Press.

Norr, L., and R. G. Cooke. 1998. Unpublished data on file, Department of Anthropology, University of Florida, Gainesville.

Reitz, E. J. 1988. Evidence for Coastal Adaptation in Georgia and South Carolina. *Archaeology of Eastern North America* 16:137–158.

———. 1990. Zooarchaeological Evidence for Subsistence at La Florida Missions. In *Columbian Consequences*: 2. *Archaeological and Historical Perspectives on the Spanish Borderlands East*, ed. D. H. Thomas, 543–54. Washington: Smithsonian Institution Press.

———. 1993. Evidence for Animal Use at the Missions of Spanish Florida. In *The Spanish Missions of La Florida*, ed. B. G. McEwan, 376–98. Gainesville: University Press of Florida.

Ruhl, D. L. 1990. Spanish Mission Paleoethnobotany and Culture Change: A Survey of the Archaeobotanical Data and Some Speculations on Aboriginal and Spanish Agrarian Interactions in La Florida. In *Columbian Consequences*: 2. *Archaeological and Historical Perspectives on the Spanish Borderlands East*, ed. D. H. Thomas, 555–80. Washington: Smithsonian Institution Press.

Saunders, R. 1988. *Excavations at 8NA41: Two Mission Period Sites on Amelia Island, Florida.* Miscellaneous Project Report Series 35, Florida Museum of Natural History, Department of Anthropology, Gainesville.

Scarry, C. M. 1993. Plant Production and Procurement in Apalachee Province. In *The Spanish Missions of La Florida,* ed. B. G. McEwan, 357–75, Gainesville: University Press of Florida.

Scarry, C. M., and E. J. Reitz. 1990. Herbs, Fish, Scum, and Vermin: Subsistence Strategies in Sixteenth-Century Spanish Florida. In *Columbian Consequences: 2. Archaeological and Historical Perspectives on the Spanish Borderlands East,* ed. D. H. Thomas, 343–54. Washington: Smithsonian Institution Press.

Scarry, J. F. 1990. The Rise, Transformation and Fall of Apalachee. In *Lamar Archaeology,* ed. M. Williams and G. Shapiro, 175–86. Tuscaloosa: University of Alabama Press.

Schoeninger, M. J. 1995. Stable Isotope Studies in Human Evolution. *Evolutionary Anthropology* 4:83–98.

Schoeninger, M. J., and M. J. DeNiro. 1984. Nitrogen and Carbon Isotopic Composition of Bone Collagen from Marine and Terrestrial Animals. *Geochimica et Cosmochimica Acta* 48:625–639.

Schoeninger, M. J., and M. R. Schurr. 1998. Human Subsistence at Moundville: The Stable Isotope Data. In *Studies in Moundville Archaeology,* ed. V. J. Knight, Jr., and V. P. Steponaitis, 120–32. Washington: Smithsonian Institution Press.

Schoeninger, M. J., N. J. van der Merwe, K. Moore, J. Lee-Thorp, and C. S. Larsen. 1990. Decrease in Diet Quality betweeen the Prehistoric and Contact Periods. In *The Archaeology of Mission Santa Catalina de Guale: 2. Biocultural Interpretations of a Population in Transition,* ed. C. S. Larsen, 78–93. Anthropological Papers of the American Museum of Natural History 68.

Scrimshaw, N. S., C. E. Taylor, and J. E. Gordon. 1968. *Interaction of Nutrition and Infection.* World Health Organization Monograph 57.

Sears, W. H. 1959. *Two Weeden Island Period Burial Mounds, Florida: The W. H. Browne Mound, Duval County; the MacKenzie Mound, Marion County.* Contributions of the Florida State Museum Social Sciences 5.

Shapiro, G., and B. G. McEwan. 1992. *Archaeology at San Luis:* pt. 1. *The Apalachee Council House, Florida.* Florida Archaeology 6.

Smith, B. D. 1989. Origins of Agriculture in Eastern North America. *Science* 246:1566–71.

Thomas, D. H. 1987. *The Archaeology of Mission Santa Catalina de Guale: 1. Search and Discovery.* Anthropological Papers of the American Museum of Natural History 63, pt. 2.

Thomas, D. H., and C. S. Larsen. 1979. *The Anthropology of St. Catherines Island: 2. The Refuge-Deptford Mortuary Complex.* Anthropological Papers of the American Museum of Natural History 56, pt. 1.

Tieszen, L. L. 1991. Natural Variations in the Carbon Isotope Values of Plants: Implications for Archaeology, Ecology, and Paleoecology. *Journal of Archaeological Science* 18:227–48.

Wahlen, M. 1994. Carbon Dioxide, Carbon Monoxide and Methane in the Atmosphere: Abundance and Isotopic Composition. In *Stable Isotopes in Ecology and Environmental Science*, ed. K. Lajtha and R. H. Mitchener, 93–113. Oxford: Blackwell Scientific Publications.

Wallace, R. L. 1975. An Archeological, Ethnohistoric, and Biochemical Investigation of the Guale Aborigines of the Georgia Coastal Strand. Ph.D. diss., University of Florida, Gainesville.

Weisman, B. R. 1992. *Excavations on the Franciscan Frontier: Archaeology of the Fig Springs Mission.* Gainesville: University Press of Florida.

Whitney, E. N., and S. R. Rolfes. 1993. *Understanding Nutrition.* 6th ed. Minneapolis–St. Paul: West Publishing Company.

Zahler, J. W., Jr. 1976. A Morphological Analysis of a Protohistoric-Historic Skeletal Population from St. Simons Island, Georgia. M.A. thesis, University of Florida, Gainesville.

4

Pits and Scratches

Microscopic Evidence of Tooth Use
and Masticatory Behavior in La Florida

Mark F. Teaford, Clark Spencer Larsen,
Robert F. Pastor, and Vivian E. Noble

Over the past 15 years, dental microwear analysis has grown to become a valuable part of the paleobiological and bioarchaeological "arsenal," yielding important inferences about diet and tooth use in a variety of animals (see, e.g., Puech 1984; Teaford and Walker 1984; Grine 1986; Solounias et al. 1988; Pastor and Johnston 1992; Lalueza et al. 1996; Teaford et al. 1996; Ungar 1996; King et al. 1999; Pérez-Pérez et al. 1999). Microwear analysis is based on the study of scratches and pits laid down on tooth surfaces during life. Thus, it does not require evolutionary assumptions about the "selective advantages" of morphological changes such as in cusp anatomy, size, and shape (Teaford 1994). That is, it provides evidence of diet and tooth use directly from tooth surfaces, even when there are no obvious differences in morphology in the samples being analyzed.

If a dentition has lain in the ground for hundreds or thousands of years, a potential problem lies in the distinction between postmortem wear and antemortem wear. Fortunately, previous studies have shown that postmortem and antemortem wear on teeth are distinguishable (Grine 1986; Teaford 1988b; Pastor 1993; King et al. 1999). Postmortem wear affects every surface exposed to taphonomic processes, whereas antemortem wear affects only certain surfaces of the tooth in a limited number of ways. For instance, the occlusal surface of a molar, and sometimes its buccal or lingual sides, are subjected to antemortem wear, depending on the food that is being processed (Grine 1986; Pérez-Pérez et al. 1994). By contrast, the inter-proximal facets should show a very different pattern of wear (von Radlanski 1988). If a tooth shows unusual microscopic patterns indicative of postmortem wear, it is excluded from analysis. As might be expected, the incidence of postmortem wear can vary dramatically from archaeological site to archaeological site (Lukacs and Pastor 1900, Pastor 1992, 1993, Pastor and Johnston 1992; Teaford and Leakey 1992), depending on various factors, such as depositional environment, excavation techniques, and tooth preparation.

The purpose of the present study is to use dental microwear analysis to document and interpret differences in diet and tooth use in a select sample of pre- and post-contact populations from Spanish Florida. As shown in other papers in this volume, populations from this region underwent dramatic changes in diet and resource use (see Larsen, this volume). Especially pertinent to the present investigation were the shift from foraging to farming prior to the arrival of Europeans and during the period of early contact and the intensification of maize agriculture in the mission period. How might these major adaptive shifts be reflected in tooth use as it is displayed in dental microwear? Previous work has shown that the answer to this question is not a simple one, largely because the process of dental microwear formation is complex. Changes in dental microwear can be caused by changes in diet, food preparation technique, ingestive behavior, or the abrasives in or on food (Puech et al. 1986; Pastor 1992; Ungar 1992; Lucas and Teaford 1995; Ungar et al. 1995; Teaford and Lytle 1996; Danielson and Reinhard 1998).

Experimental laboratory and field research on animals has shown that certain diets can yield characteristic microwear patterns. For example, animals that feed on hard objects tend to have more and larger pits on their molars (Teaford and Walker 1984; Teaford 1988a; Teaford and Runestad 1992); animals with fine abrasives in their diets (e.g., phytoliths) tend to have scratches on their molars (Walker et al. 1978); and animals with fibrous diets tend to show polished enamel surfaces with accentuated enamel prism relief (Walker 1981). However, the microwear of humans, with their variable diets and food preparation techniques, has proven to be difficult to characterize. Microwear for some human populations is similar to that in some nonhuman primates, such that those eating hard objects tend to have large pits on their molars and those eating fibrous diets tend to exhibit enamel polishing on their molars (Harmon and Rose 1988). Major dietary transitions have often been accompanied by major differences in food preparation techniques, such as the onset of cooking (Molleson et al. 1993), and this, in conjunction with individual variations in diet (Pérez-Pérez et al. 1994, 1999) and disproportionate abrasive effects of different food items (Molleson et al. 1993), has made interpretations difficult. Thus, in modern populations, agriculturalists might exhibit rough molar enamel surfaces with broad scratches and pits (Gordon 1986; Teaford and Lytle 1996) or fine microwear features (Molleson et al. 1993; Ungar and Spencer 1999), depending on methods of food preparation for specific foods. More recent populations with a high consumption of meat (e.g., Eskimos) might exhibit fine molar microwear features (Gordon 1986), large incisor microwear features (Ungar and Spencer 1999), or few microwear features (Lalueza Fox 1992), depending on which teeth and which surfaces are examined—molars or incisors and occlusal or non-occlusal surfaces.

For the purposes of this study, the most relevant previous work has involved analyses of archaeological samples bracketing certain dietary transitions. From the Old World, two main studies have looked at the transition from hunting-gathering to agriculture. Pastor (1993) found that hunting-gathering populations in South Asia exhibited relatively rougher molar enamel surfaces than did agricultural populations. Molleson and co-workers (Molleson and Jones 1991; Molleson et al. 1993) found that agricultural populations that depended on large-grained cereals showed larger pits on their molar enamel than did their hunting-gathering predecessors. The agricultural populations also exhibited more variable microwear patterns, perhaps indicative of more variable diets. In the New World, and more relevant to this particular study, Bullington (1991) looked at deciduous molar microwear in the transition to maize agriculture in the Lower Illinois River Valley. Comparisons of samples from Middle Woodland and Mississippian sites—representing hunter-gatherers and agriculturalists, respectively—suggested a more abrasive diet in the earlier Middle Woodland populations. Finally, in a pilot study for the present work, Teaford (1991) looked at a small sample of molars from archaeological sites along the Georgia-Florida coast. Those from the period before European contact showed more pits and larger scratches as compared with those from the later agricultural periods, suggesting a change in diet and tooth use. In the present investigation we seek to explore this issue in greater detail with a larger, broader data set.

Materials and Methods

As in many previous microwear analyses (Strait 1993; Teaford et al. 1996; Ungar 1996), the present work is based on scanning electron microscope (SEM) examinations of high resolution casts of teeth. The scanning electron microscope is used, rather than traditional light microscopy, because of its superior depth of focus (or depth of field) and therefore clearer representation of microwear. The casts are used because they allow the teeth to be examined at higher accelerating voltages (in traditional, high vacuum, non-environmental SEMs), which yield better images. The casts are extremely stable and yield excellent resolution of detail, below 0.1 microns (Teaford and Oyen 1989). Casts are also useful because it is often impossible to use rare museum teeth in analyses requiring gold-coating of the tooth or analyses in high vacuums.

The study began with one maxillary central incisor (I1) and one maxillary first molar (M1) from as many teeth as possible (second molars [M2] may occasionally have been used, as the distinction between M1 and M2 was sometimes difficult with isolated teeth). Only teeth showing average amounts of wear were used in the analyses. Slightly worn teeth and those showing dentin exposures over more than one-third of the occlusal surface were not used (see later discussion of postmortem wear and for the actual sample sizes used in the statistical analyses of microwear measurements). Dental impressions were taken with Coltene-Whaledent's President Jet Regular polysiloxane, and positive casts were made using Ciba-Geigy's Araldite cold-cure epoxy. All casts were then sputter-coated with 200 angstroms of gold and examined in an Amray 1810 scanning electron microscope in secondary emissions mode at an accelerating voltage of 20kV.

Tooth-Cleaning and Sample Sizes

The first thing that became apparent was that preservatives had been applied to many of the teeth, in amounts that varied between archaeological sites. Initially, the consolidant applied during and immediately following excavation—for the most part, polyvinyl acetate (PVA)—was detectable either with the naked eye or under a standard dissecting light microscope. Because acetone, or sometimes alcohol, is traditionally used to thin or remove PVA, cleaning of teeth to be used in the microwear analysis commenced with a gentle swabbing of the teeth with these solvents. For some of the sites, such as San Martín de Timucua (Fig Springs), this procedure worked relatively easily; most teeth were usable after one or two cleanings. For most of the other sites, PVA removal was more difficult. Initial cleanings removed most of the preservatives, but the remaining preservative proved extremely hard to remove—at least to the level necessary for dental microwear analyses.

Once these cleaning difficulties became apparent, teeth from a number of sites were cleaned quickly to determine which sites might yield teeth that could be cleaned easily. Only the Florida late prehistoric Lake Jackson site

Table 4.1. Samples used in dental microwear analysis

Site	Location	Molar (N)	Incisor (N)
Florida early prehistoric			
Mayport Mound	coastal Florida	9	0
Georgia late prehistoric			
Johns Mound	coastal Georgia	4	0
Indian Field	coastal Georgia	1	0
Irene Mound	inland Georgia	10	6
Irene Mortuary	inland Georgia	2	0
Irene site (no association)	inland Georgia	2	0
Florida late prehistoric			
Lake Jackson	inland Florida	6	4
Georgia early mission			
Santa Catalina de Guale	coastal Georgia	8	0
Florida early mission			
Santa Maria de Yamasee	coastal Florida	9	1
Ossuary at Santa Catalina	coastal Florida	12	7
San Martín de Timucua	inland Florida	20	11
Florida late mission			
Santa Catalina de Amelia	coastal Florida	9	0
Total		92	29

and Florida early Mission San Martín de Timucua fell into that category. Of the rest of the sites, we chose to focus on the larger collections that would facilitate statistical analysis. No samples are available for the Georgia early prehistoric period, but all other periods are represented by at least one site. Specifically, the samples used in this study for microwear analysis are from the following periods: Florida Early Prehistoric (A.D. 0–1000), Georgia Late Prehistoric (A.D. 1000–1550), Florida Late Prehistoric (A.D. 1000–1600), Georgia Early Mission (A.D. 1600–1680), Florida Early Mission (A.D. 1600–1680), and Florida Late Mission (A.D. 1680–1700) (see table 4.1).

Dental microwear analyses require exceptionally clean tooth surfaces so that the measured microwear is on the tooth surface, not in the preservative on the tooth surface. As a result, more information about the cleaning of these teeth will prove useful for future investigators. Gross levels of preservative were generally easy to recognize (see fig. 4.1). However, as cleaning progressed, the effects of the preservatives became far more insidious (see fig. 4.2). Coated teeth that were in good physical condition were wrapped

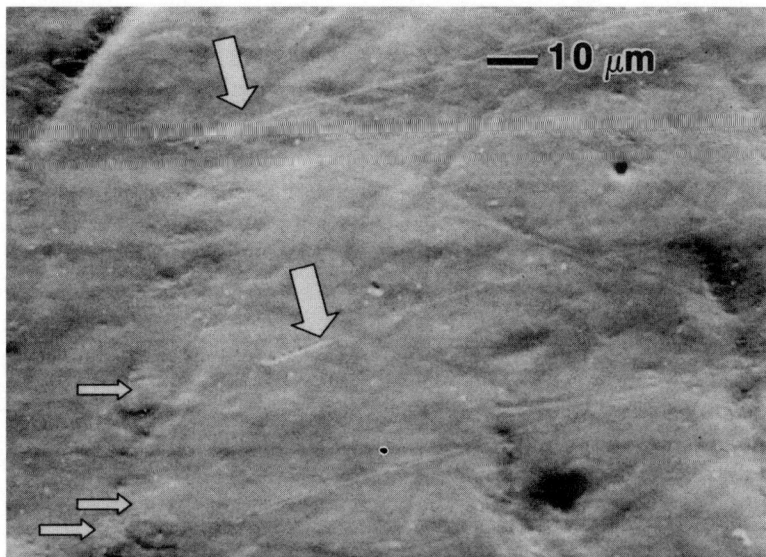

Fig. 4.1. Scanning electron micrograph of molar with obvious preservative coating (from inland late prehistoric site in Georgia; Irene Mound 79). Note general lack of fine detail, plus brush strokes (indicated by large arrows), and globs of preservatives (small arrows).

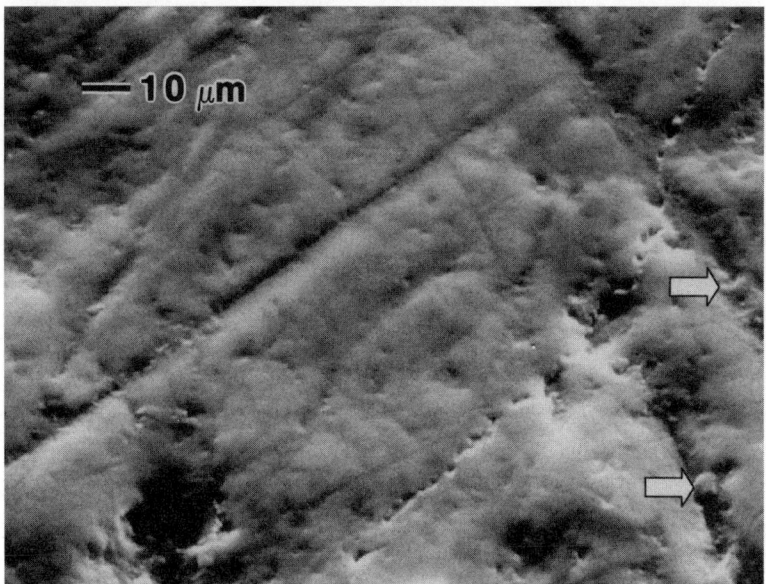

Fig. 4.2. Scanning electron micrograph of molar showing subtle preservative coating (from coastal early mission site in Florida; SMDY 46). While the micrograph may look clean at first glance, there are still tiny remnants of preservative (large arrows) and an absence of the finest detail.

in tissue paper soaked in solvent and sealed in a plastic Ziploc bag for two to three days. Solvents also varied, from acetone to alcohol to other toluene-based solvents (such as Lacquer Remover, Brush and Roller Cleaner). Still, teeth from some sites were not clean enough after *eight* cleaning sessions.

The most challenging aspect of doing multiple cleaning sessions is that once the gross levels of preservatives are removed, it is impossible to judge whether the tooth is clean enough until its cast is placed in the SEM. Even then, the preservatives were often recognizable only at higher magnifications. Sometimes, the effects would simply be unrecognizable to the untrained eye (see fig. 4.2). Clearly, if dental microwear analyses are to make use of counts of the number of features per micrograph, or measures of average feature size, the teeth must be clean, or the so-called significant differences documented through statistical analyses will be nothing but a reflection of intersite differences in tooth cleaning.

As might be expected, the cleaning problems diminished sample sizes (see table 4.1). While the study began with six incisors from Lake Jackson, for example, only four proved usable. These effects also varied from site to site. For instance, we started with 78 molars from the early mission sites of Santa Maria de Yamasee, the Santa Catalina ossuary, and San Martín de Timucua, and we finished with 41 that were usable for analysis.

Scanning Electron Microscopy and Microwear Measurements

Whenever possible, two photomicrographs (also called micrographs) were taken of each tooth. All micrographs were taken at a magnification of 500×, taking every precaution to maintain a standard working distance and to minimize stage tilt (see Gordon 1988; Pastor 1993). Incisor micrographs are from the labial (lip side) surface of the tooth near the incisal edge. Molar micrographs are from the basin side of the protocone or hypocone cusps, the so-called crushing surfaces (Phase II facets; see Kay 1977). Micrographs were scanned into a computer and then digitized using Ungar's (1994) semiautomated analysis package, Microware 3.0. The program uses a 4:1 ratio of the length to width of each feature as the cutoff for determining which features are pits and scratches. Four attributes were analyzed: measures of average pit and scratch width (in microns), percentage of pits, number of microwear features, and homogeneity of scratch orientation. The last measurement reflects whether scratch orientation is homogeneous or heterogeneous and is not dependent on tooth or micrograph orientation (see Ungar 1994). Incisor and molar individual data are presented in tables 4.2 and 4.3, respectively.

Table 4.2. Incisor microwear by individual

Site, burial	No. features	Pit width		Scratch width		Scratch orient. r[a]	%pits
		Mean	S.D.	Mean	S.D.		
Georgia late prehistoric							
Irene Mound 7	255	1.81	1.158	0.84	0.501	0.621	24.5
Irene Mound 8A	288	1.41	0.733	0.85	0.504	0.566	38.5
Irene Mound 24	270	1.64	0.944	0.80	0.604	0.656	37.8
Irene Mound 81A	366	1.63	0.865	0.78	0.550	0.478	41.0
Irene Mound 186	249	1.58	0.892	0.88	0.956	0.456	35.3
Irene Mound 220	280	1.64	0.893	0.79	0.347	0.547	41.4
Florida late prehistoric							
Lake Jackson 5	211	2.16	1.853	1.13	1.618	0.225	37.9
Lake Jackson 13	284	2.37	1.708	0.87	0.501	0.729	47.8
Lake Jackson 15	128	1.92	0.963	1.09	0.862	0.548	9.6
Lake Jackson 18	266	2.70	2.790	0.96	0.653	0.284	30.1
Florida early mission							
SM de Yamasee 44	182	2.08	1.257	0.97	0.562	0.594	31.9
Ossuary at SCDG Ind. B.	502	1.41	0.701	0.72	0.558	0.564	63.1
Ossuary at SCDG 3	179	1.76	1.005	0.86	0.763	0.683	31.3
Ossuary at SCDG 28	251	1.50	0.917	0.80	0.507	0.538	19.0
Ossuary at SCDG lab 28	239	1.62	0.873	0.85	0.995	0.431	31.8
Ossuary at SCDG 30	169	2.29	1.208	1.13	0.604	0.582	32.5
Ossuary at SCDG 32	263	2.10	1.075	0.90	0.503	0.780	43.2
Ossuary at SCDG 51	429	1.39	0.671	0.76	0.659	0.709	40.3
San Martín 91–4	179	1.97	0.839	0.95	0.412	0.719	44.1
San Martín 91–11	329	1.98	1.312	0.91	0.897	0.720	56.1
San Martín 91–12	184	1.84	0.798	1.07	0.455	0.706	39.7
San Martín 91–16	285	1.90	1.136	0.91	0.879	0.549	31.8
San Martín 91–17	280	2.60	1.887	1.09	0.940	0.634	20.5
San Martín 91–21	173	1.84	1.130	1.10	0.842	0.647	35.8
San Martín 91–24	266	2.00	0.986	0.85	0.777	0.676	35.0
San Martín 91–25	408	1.73	1.059	1.14	1.161	0.641	49.3
San Martín 91–31	156	2.67	2.320	1.11	1.348	0.713	25.7
San Martín 91–38	119	2.67	1.491	1.22	1.140	0.641	11.2
San Martín 91–39	200	2.17	0.796	1.19	0.940	0.477	27.0

a. Scratch orientation: Orientation vector length for scratches (r is a measure of the homogeneity of scratch orientation; see Ungar 1994); higher values indicate more homogeneous scratch orientation.

Table 4.3. Molar microwear by individual

Site, burial	No. features	Pit width Mean	S.D.	Scratch width Mean	S.D.	Scratch orient. r^a	%pits
Florida early prehistoric							
Mayport Mound 2	218	2.36	3.170	0.71	0.400	0.627	56.1
Mayport Mound 12	170	3.39	3.500	0.96	0.920	0.360	39.2
Mayport Mound 13	150	3.20	3.520	0.77	0.500	0.797	54.1
Mayport Mound 16	156	3.17	4.860	0.78	0.360	0.654	55.3
Mayport Mound 20	189	2.43	2.240	1.06	0.810	0.537	47.7
Mayport Mound 26	136	4.05	5.020	0.88	0.870	0.692	50.7
Mayport Mound 30b	167	4.00	6.210	0.95	0.770	0.485	40.6
Mayport Mound 37a	241	2.56	2.550	0.86	0.780	0.494	45.6
Mayport Mound 37b	298	3.40	4.840	0.78	0.595	0.527	52.3
Georgia late prehistoric							
Irene Mound 5A	387	2.33	2.030	0.77	0.350	0.476	55.0
Irene Mound 11B	593	1.77	1.595	0.67	0.366	0.557	69.0
Irene Mound 44	399	1.54	1.591	0.76	0.467	0.402	40.9
Irene Mound 62/63	731	1.33	0.906	0.62	0.495	0.676	47.3
Irene Mound 79	194	2.15	1.716	1.40	1.954	0.741	44.3
Irene Mound 151	499	1.53	1.364	0.56	0.367	0.833	42.0
Irene Mound 152	324	2.63	2.059	0.89	0.752	0.627	49.5
Irene Mound 186	480	2.39	2.305	0.81	0.426	0.523	53.5
Irene Mound 230	526	1.68	1.923	0.65	0.354	0.638	55.5
Irene Mound 238A	404	1.83	1.362	0.81	0.539	0.772	56.4
Irene Mound 247	272	3.07	4.251	1.00	0.483	0.698	31.1
Irene Mound 248	338	1.67	1.263	0.74	0.392	0.596	41.1
Irene Mound 249	284	1.90	1.219	0.93	0.654	0.325	46.0
Irene Mound 261B	206	2.01	1.342	1.10	1.520	0.603	26.9
Indian Field 1	165	2.31	1.738	1.06	0.968	0.562	50.0
Johns Mound 17	231	2.39	2.660	1.08	1.439	0.476	46.3
Johns Mound 21	199	2.21	1.619	1.13	1.223	0.656	46.8
Johns Mound 26B	137	4.12	5.940	0.97	0.520	0.606	49.1
Johns Mound 40	215	4.23	6.143	0.90	0.669	0.569	40.1
Florida late prehistoric							
Lake Jackson 1	372	1.86	1.192	0.80	0.608	0.248	47.3
Lake Jackson 5	404	2.07	1.390	0.90	0.820	0.512	51.2
Lake Jackson 7	188	3.78	4.316	1.06	0.801	0.260	34.7
Lake Jackson 10	280	2.08	1.118	0.75	0.347	0.575	53.6
Lake Jackson 15	350	2.08	1.300	0.87	0.508	0.454	41.0
Lake Jackson 18	268	2.33	2.688	0.89	0.513	0.278	45.8
Georgia early mission							
Santa Catalina 593	88	2.83	2.417	1.65	1.780	0.145	32.8
Santa Catalina 109	120	4.28	4.504	1.26	2.162	0.422	35.7
Santa Catalina 129	142	3.00	3.029	1.00	0.684	0.433	31.9
Santa Catalina 160	205	3.13	3.727	1.14	1.149	0.653	43.8
Santa Catalina 188	174	2.69	2.280	1.15	1.340	0.475	53.1
Santa Catalina 254	107	3.27	1.553	1.41	1.598	0.479	28.1
Santa Catalina 258	255	2.68	2.773	0.95	0.596	0.624	42.4
Santa Catalina 383	175	3.52	3.009	1.21	0.913	0.618	63.4
Florida early mission							
SM de Yamasee 16	160	2.81	1.97	1.52	2.328	0.575	33.1
SM de Yamasee 40	376	1.90	1.70	0.64	0.291	0.341	47.9

Site, burial	No. features	Pit width		Scratch width		Scratch orient. r[a]	%pits
		Mean	S.D.	Mean	S.D.		
SM de Yamasee 44	232	2.29	2.73	0.78	0.403	0.228	55.6
SM de Yamasee 45	141	2.71	2.03	1.22	0.898	0.177	44.2
SM de Yamasee 47	208	2.36	1.43	1.17	1.653	0.552	30.8
SM de Yamasee 48	482	1.63	1.33	0.71	0.530	0.639	59.8
SM de Yamasee 55	276	1.71	0.89	0.80	0.361	0.647	38.9
SM de Yamasee 92	220	1.93	0.96	0.92	0.557	0.497	55.5
SM de Yamasee 97	290	2.16	1.53	1.50	2.012	0.483	49.0
Ossuary at SCDG Ind. A	329	1.91	1.18	0.95	1.032	0.343	56.8
Ossuary at SCDG Ind. B	281	2.80	2.86	0.89	0.571	0.431	57.9
Ossuary at SCDG 25	272	2.24	1.92	0.81	0.586	0.270	49.3
Ossuary at SCDG 26	356	2.34	3.56	0.73	0.361	0.525	39.9
Ossuary at SCDG 28	224	1.69	1.44	0.92	0.602	0.542	40.2
Ossuary at SCDG 30	316	2.03	1.72	1.00	0.579	0.494	59.8
Ossuary at SCDG 31	229	1.76	1.21	1.08	1.769	0.533	58.3
Ossuary at SCDG 37	315	2.38	2.03	0.78	0.467	0.391	50.6
Ossuary at SCDG 45	361	1.91	1.70	0.85	0.521	0.592	59.0
Ossuary at SCDG 51	256	2.34	2.11	0.91	0.632	0.588	45.7
Ossuary at SCDG 58	258	2.39	1.68	0.82	0.480	0.505	50.4
Ossuary at SCDG 101	259	2.11	1.54	0.97	0.747	0.416	61.9
San Martín 91–3	209	2.36	1.68	1.12	1.350	0.674	44.7
San Martín 91–4	220	1.80	0.67	0.80	0.512	0.540	32.3
San Martín 91–7	221	1.73	0.95	0.95	0.789	0.694	43.4
San Martín 91–8	136	2.18	1.21	1.22	1.075	0.271	47.1
San Martín 91–11	284	1.83	0.83	0.87	0.386	0.579	47.2
San Martín 91–12	325	1.86	1.05	0.93	0.756	0.344	57.2
San Martín 91–16	250	2.14	1.48	0.88	0.942	0.397	52.6
San Martín 91–25	465	2.22	1.83	0.90	0.388	0.512	51.1
San Martín 91–31	409	1.90	1.28	0.73	0.341	0.527	41.4
San Martín 91–36	256	2.12	1.18	1.03	0.557	0.371	50.2
San Martín 91–38	354	1.92	1.38	0.82	0.648	0.694	32.2
San Martín 91–39	302	2.18	2.36	0.84	0.814	0.368	48.0
San Martín 91–42	434	1.92	2.71	0.78	0.609	0.256	42.2
San Martín 91–49	282	2.11	2.04	0.78	0.560	0.412	41.8
San Martín 91–50	499	1.93	1.73	0.73	0.421	0.237	54.1
San Martín 91–51	306	1.91	1.32	0.84	0.665	0.464	43.7
San Martín 91–53	274	2.64	2.10	1.03	0.682	0.568	40.9
San Martín 91–54	534	1.61	1.11	0.76	0.379	0.747	35.8
San Martín 91–58	414	1.42	0.89	0.75	0.437	0.556	40.3
San Martín 91–61	426	1.78	1.56	0.67	0.393	0.371	56.6
Florida late mission							
Santa Catalina Amelia 9	180	3.44	3.98	0.89	0.550	0.829	59.0
Santa Catalina Amelia 19	158	2.06	0.95	1.17	1.123	0.460	36.8
Santa Catalina Amelia 31	252	2.39	2.17	0.87	0.758	0.654	50.2
Santa Catalina Amelia 36B	129	1.64	1.10	1.01	0.905	0.516	20.2
Santa Catalina Amelia 41	95	2.55	2.28	1.51	1.520	0.353	43.5
Santa Catalina Amelia 50A	78	1.92	1.10	1.17	1.010	0.212	21.1
Santa Catalina Amelia 59B	164	3.33	7.82	0.67	0.297	0.238	53.3
Santa Catalina Amelia 93	173	2.59	2.01	1.12	1.485	0.464	54.0
Santa Catalina Amelia 99G	190	3.00	4.51	0.98	1.040	0.529	50.0

a. Scratch orientation: Orientation vector length for scratches (r is a measure of the homogeneity of scratch orientation; see Ungar 1994); higher values indicate more homogeneous scratch orientation.

Statistical Analyses

Using averages for the microwear measurements for each specimen, statistical analyses were completed for a broad comparison of late prehistoric versus early mission sites, and for more specific comparisons (e.g., late prehistoric vs. coastal and noncoastal early mission sites). In all comparisons, Lilliefors and Bartlett's tests were run to check for normal distributions and equal variances in the samples (Zar 1984). When necessary, the microwear data were either rank- or log-transformed to meet the assumptions of parametric statistics (Conover and Iman 1981; Zar 1984). The two-sample t-test was run for the simple two-part comparisons (e.g., late prehistoric vs. early mission comparisons), while single-factor ANOVA followed by Tukey's multiple comparison test were used for the three-part comparisons (e.g., late prehistoric vs. coastal and noncoastal early mission samples) (Zar 1984).

Regional and Temporal Comparisons

Prehistoric/Mission Comparisons

As can be seen from the homogeneity of scratch orientations in table 4.4, the incisors from the late prehistoric sites showed more variable scratch orientations (i.e., lower average homogeneity values) than did those from the early mission sites (see also figs. 4.3 and 4.4).

For the molars, there were two significant differences (see table 4.5). The molars from the mission sites showed significantly wider scratches than did those from the prehistoric sites. However, in contrast to the incisors, the molars from the prehistoric sites showed more *homogeneous* scratch orientations than did those from the mission sites (see figs. 4.5 and 4.6).

Table 4.4. Incisor microwear comparisons for prehistoric and mission sites (Georgia and Florida combined)

Period	N		Pit width		Scratch width		Scratch orient.[a]		% pits	
	Mean	S.E.	Mean	S.E.	Mean	S.E.	Mean	S.E.	Mean	S.E.
Late prehistoric (N=10)	260	19	1.90	0.13	0.90	0.04	0.511[b]	0.05	34.4	3.40
Early mission (N=19)	252	24	1.98	0.09	0.97	0.03	0.632	0.02	35.2	2.90

a. See table 4.3 and text for explanation.
b. Late prehistoric significantly less than early mission (p<0.014).

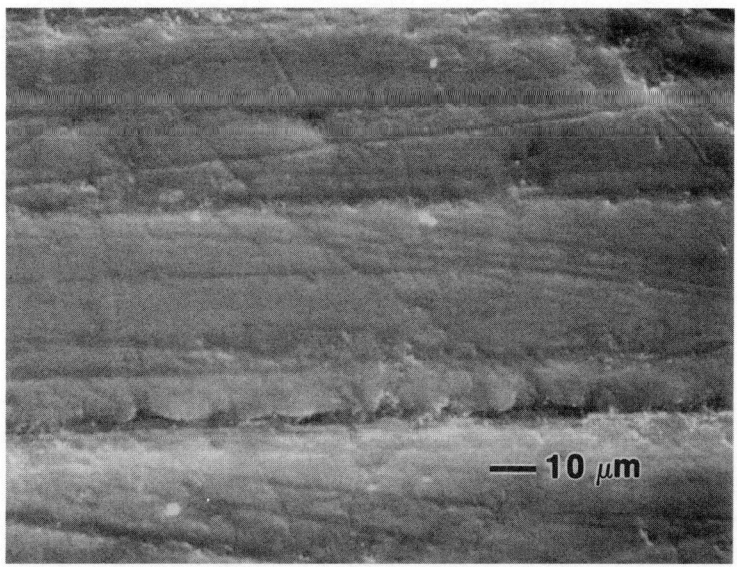

Fig. 4.3. Scanning electron micrograph of incisor from inland early mission site in Florida (SMDT 91–16). Note that most scratches are running horizontally across the image.

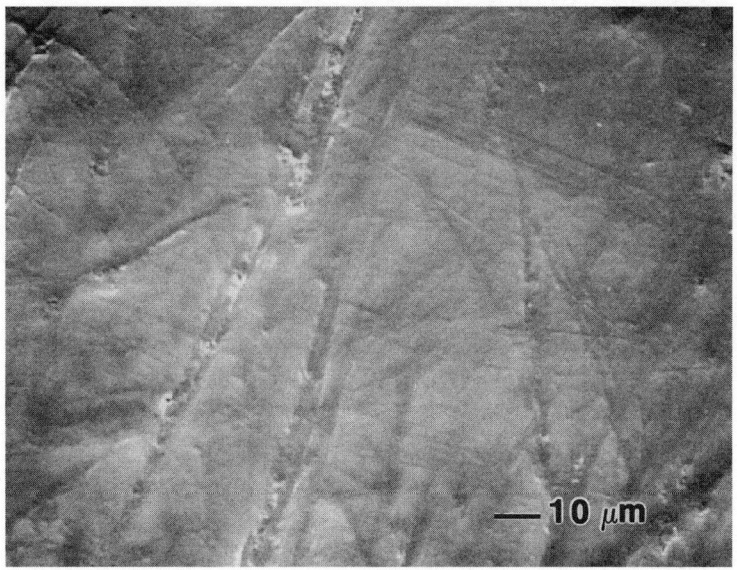

Fig. 4.4. Scanning electron micrograph of incisor from inland prehistoric site in Florida (Lake Jackson 5). Note that scratches run in multiple directions.

Table 4.5. Molar microwear comparisons for prehistoric and mission sites (Georgia and Florida combined)

Period	N		Pit width		Scratch width		Scratch orient.[a]		% pits	
	Mean	S.E.	Mean	S.E.	Mean	S.E.	Mean	S.E.	Mean	S.E.
Prehistoric (N=34)	299	24	2.50	0.10	0.88	0.03	0.550	0.03	47.2	1.40
Mission (N=58)	261	14	2.30	0.07	0.98[b]	0.03	0.470[c]	0.02	46.0	1.30

a. See table 4.3 and text for explanation.
b. Mission significantly greater than prehistoric (p<0.039).
c. Mission significantly less than prehistoric (p<0.014).

Georgia Prehistoric/Mission Comparisons

No incisor comparisons were possible for these samples. The molars showed a number of differences (see table 4.6). The prehistoric molars showed significantly more microwear than did those from the mission sites, but molars from the mission sites showed significantly wider pits and scratches than did those from the prehistoric sites.

Florida Prehistoric/Mission Comparisons

Comparisons of incisor microwear were possible in these samples, but the only significant difference involved the orientation of scratches: the prehistoric samples showed more variable scratch orientations than did the mission samples (see table 4.7). Interestingly, comparisons of pit width between samples were probably hampered by the variation in pit widths in

Table 4.6. Molar microwear comparisons for prehistoric and mission sites in Georgia

Period	N		Pit width		Scratch width		Scratch orient.[a]		% pits	
	Mean	S.E.	Mean	S.E.	Mean	S.E.	Mean	S.E.	Mean	S.E.
Prehistoric (N=19)	346[b]	37	2.30	0.20	0.89	0.05	0.600[c]	0.03	46.9	2.2
Mission (N=8)	158	20	3.20[d]	0.30	1.20[e]	0.08	0.480	0.06	41.4	4.2

a. See table 4.3 and text for explanation.
b. Prehistoric significantly greater than mission (p<0.004).
c. Prehistoric nearly significantly greater than mission (p<0.055).
d. Mission significantly greater than prehistoric (p<0.007).
e. Mission significantly greater than prehistoric (p<0.001).

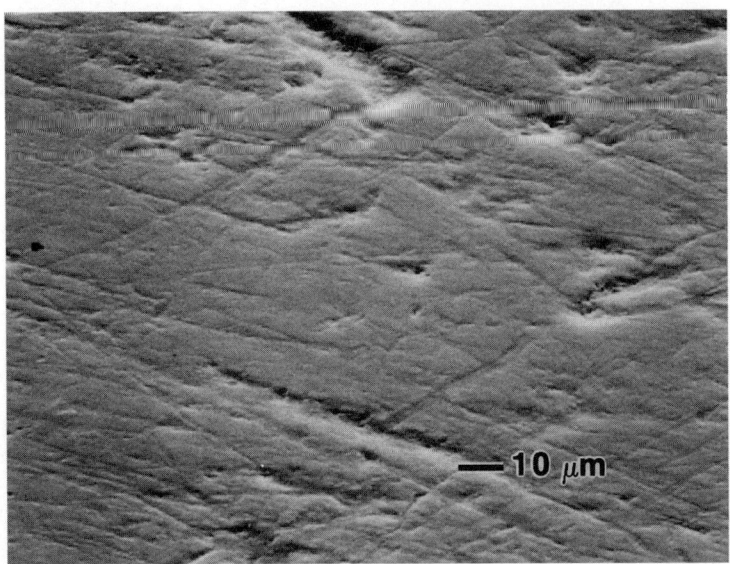

Fig. 4.5. Scanning electron micrograph of molar from inland early mission site in Florida (SMDT 91–54). Note that scratches run in multiple directions.

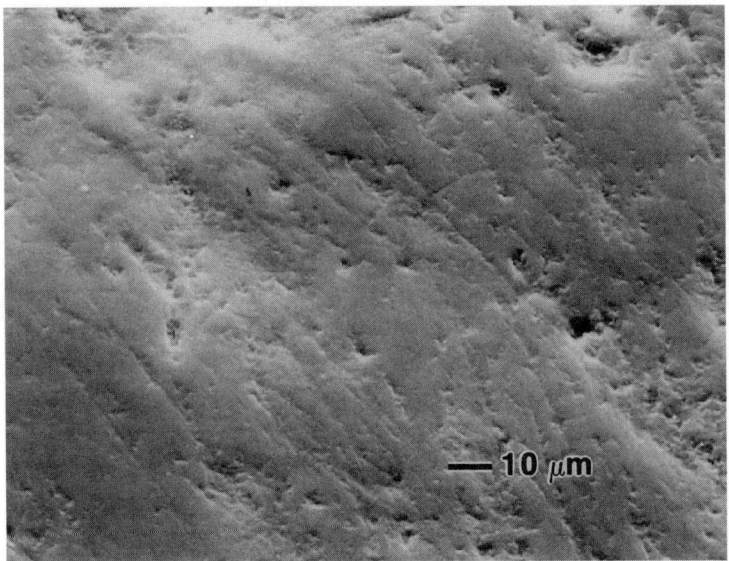

Fig. 4.6. Scanning electron micrograph of molar from inland prehistoric site in Georgia (Irene Mound 11B). Note that most scratches are running diagonally across image.

Table 4.7. Incisor microwear comparisons for prehistoric and mission sites in Florida

Period	N		Pit width		Scratch width		Scratch orient.[a]		% pits	
	Mean	S.E.	Mean	S.E.	Mean	S.E.	Mean	S.E.	Mean	S.E.
Prehistoric (N=4)	222	35	2.29	0.17	1.01	0.06	0.450[b]	0.12	31.3	8.1
Mission (N=19)	252	24	1.98	0.09	0.98	0.04	0.630	0.02	35.2	2.9

a. See table 4.3 and text for explanation.
b. Prehistoric significantly less than mission (p<0.012).

the prehistoric sample, as the standard deviations of pit widths (computed for each specimen in that sample) were significantly greater than those for the mission sample (see table 4.2).

For the molars, the only significant difference involved the measure of pit width, where the prehistoric sample showed larger pit widths than did the mission sample, despite the fact that the prehistoric sample showed larger standard deviations in pit width than did the mission sample (see tables 4.3 and 4.8).

Florida Early Prehistoric/Late Prehistoric Comparisons

No incisor comparisons were possible for these samples. For the molars, there were three significant differences. The early prehistoric sample showed significantly larger pit widths than did the late prehistoric sample but also a more homogeneous scratch orientation than in the late prehistoric sample (see table 4.9 and figs. 4.7 and 4.8). The late prehistoric sample showed significantly more microwear than did the early prehistoric sample.

Table 4.8. Molar microwear comparisons for prehistoric and mission sites in Florida

Period	N		Pit width		Scratch width		Scratch orient.[a]		% pits	
	Mean	S.E.	Mean	S.E.	Mean	S.E.	Mean	S.E.	Mean	S.E.
Prehistoric (N=15)	239	22	2.85[b]	0.19	0.87	0.03	0.500	0.04	47.7	1.7
Mission (N=50)	277	15	2.16	0.06	0.94	0.03	0.470	0.02	46.7	1.4

a. See table 4.3 and text for explanation.
b. Prehistoric significantly greater than mission (p<0.000).

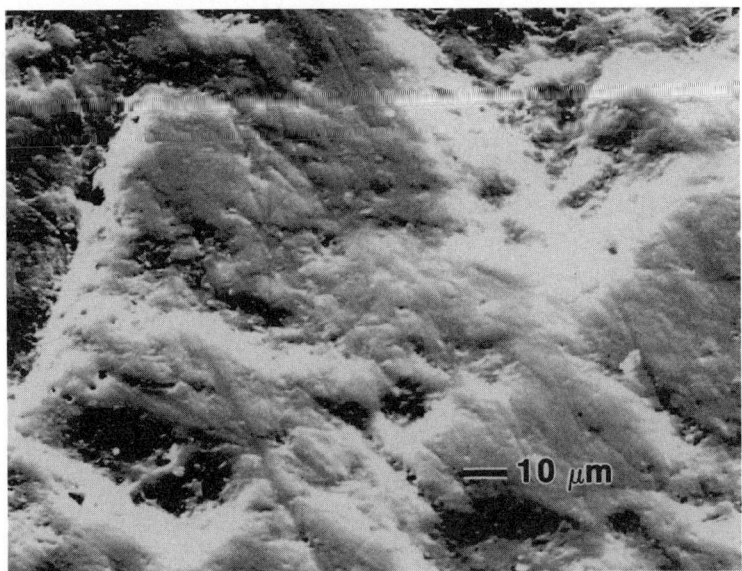

Fig. 4.7. Scanning electron micrograph of molar from coastal early prehistoric site in Florida (Mayport Mound 37B). Note preponderance of large features.

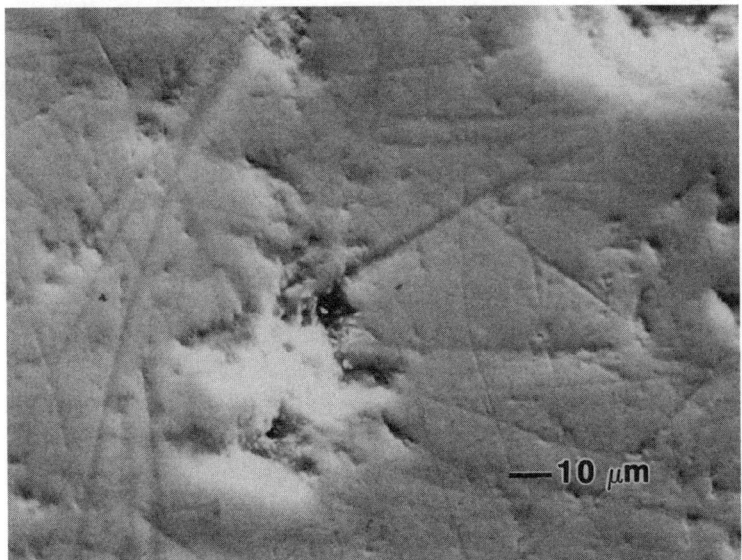

Fig. 4.8. Scanning electron micrograph of molar from inland late prehistoric site in Florida (Lake Jackson 1). Note preponderance of small features.

Table 4.9. Molar microwear comparisons for early and late prehistoric sites in Florida

Period	N		Pit width		Scratch width		Scratch orient.[a]		% pits	
	Mean	S.E.	Mean	S.E.	Mean	S.E.	Mean	S.E.	Mean	S.E.
Early prehistoric (N=9)	192	17	3.17[b]	0.21	0.86	0.04	0.580[c]	0.04	49.1	2.1
Late prehistoric (N=6)	310[d]	33	2.37	0.29	0.88	0.04	0.390	0.06	45.6	2.8

a. See table 4.3 and text for explanation.
b. Early prehistoric significantly greater than late prehistoric ($p<0.037$).
c. Early prehistoric significantly greater than late prehistoric ($p<0.021$).
d. Late prehistoric significantly greater than early prehistoric ($p<0.004$).

Florida Late Prehistoric/Mission Comparisons

The late prehistoric incisors were the only prehistoric incisors from the Florida sites that were clean enough to use. Thus, these comparisons used the exact same samples, yielding the exact same results, as in the prehistoric/mission comparisons mentioned already (see tables 4.2 and 4.7 and figs. 4.3 and 4.4).

There were no significant differences between the molars from the late prehistoric versus mission sites in Florida (see table 4.10).

Florida Late Prehistoric/Early Mission/Late Mission Comparisons

No incisor samples proved usable for the late mission period of Florida. However, the late mission molars showed significantly *less* microwear than did those from either the late prehistoric or early mission sites, while the late mission molars showed significantly wider pits than did the molars from the early mission sites (see table 4.11).

Table 4.10. Molar microwear comparisons for late prehistoric and mission sites in Florida

Period	N		Pit width		Scratch width		Scratch orient.[a]		% pits	
	Mean	S.E.	Mean	S.E.	Mean	S.E.	Mean	S.E.	Mean	S.E.
Late prehistoric (N=6)	310	33	2.37	0.29	0.88	0.04	0.390	0.06	45.6	2.8
Mission (N=50)	277	15	2.16	0.16	0.94	0.03	0.470	0.02	46.7	1.4

a. See table 4.3 and text for explanation.

Table 4.11. Molar microwear comparisons for late prehistoric, early mission, and late mission sites in Florida

Period	N		Pit width		Scratch width		Scratch orient.[a]		% pits	
	Mean	S.E.	Mean	S.E.	Mean	S.E.	Mean	S.E.	Mean	S.E.
Late prehistoric (N=6)	310	33	2.37	0.29	0.88	0.04	0.388	0.06	45.6	2.8
Early mission (N=41)	303	15	2.07	0.05	0.91	0.03	0.472	0.02	47.5	1.3
Late mission (N=9)	158[b]	17	2.50[c]	0.21	1.04	0.08	0.473	0.07	43.1	4.7

a. See table 4.3 and text for explanation.
b. Late mission significantly less than early mission (p<0.000) and late prehistoric (p<0.006).
c. Late mission significantly greater than early mission (p<0.012).

Florida Late Prehistoric/Coastal Mission/Inland Mission Comparisons

There were two significant differences in incisor microwear among the late prehistoric, coastal mission, and inland mission sites (see table 4.12). The incisors from the late prehistoric site showed significantly more variable scratch orientations (i.e., smaller measures of orientation vector length) than did those from the inland mission site. In addition, incisors from the coastal mission sites showed significantly narrower scratches than did those from the inland mission site (see figs. 4.11 and 4.12). Interestingly, the measures of pit width for the coastal mission site were also suggestive

Table 4.12. Incisor microwear comparisons for late prehistoric, coastal mission, and inland mission sites in Florida

Period	N		Pit width		Scratch width		Scratch orient.[a]		% pits	
	Mean	S.E.	Mean	S.E.	Mean	S.E.	Mean	S.E.	Mean	S.E.
Late prehistoric (N=4)	222	35	2.29[b]	0.17	1.01	0.06	0.446	0.06	31.3	8.1
Coastal mission (N=8)	276	44	1.77	0.12	0.87	0.05	0.610	0.04	36.6	4.6
Inland mission (N=11)	234	26	2.13[c]	0.11	1.05[d]	0.04	0.648[e]	0.02	34.2	3.9

a. See table 4.3 and text for explanation.
b. Late prehistoric nearly significantly greater than coastal mission (p<0.06).
c. Inland mission nearly significantly greater than coastal mission (p<0.09).
d. Inland mission significantly greater than coastal mission (p<0.018).
e. Inland mission significantly greater than late prehistoric (p<0.03).

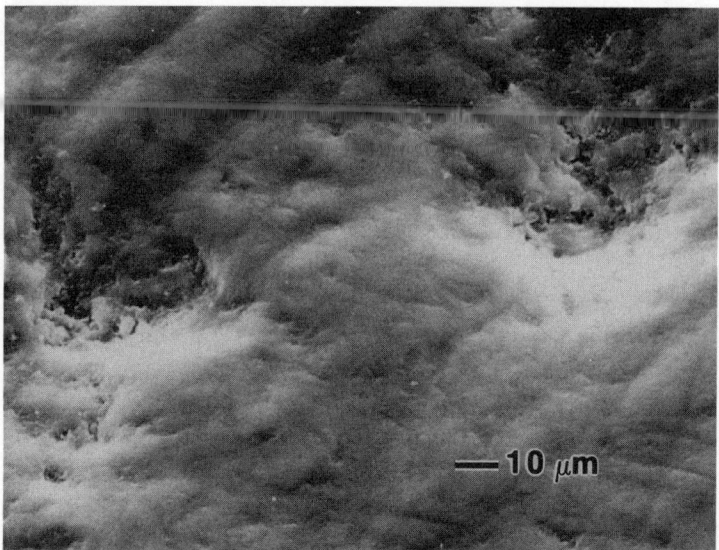

Fig. 4.9. Scanning electron micrograph of molar from coastal early mission site in Florida (Amelia Island Ossuary 26). Note presence of large pits.

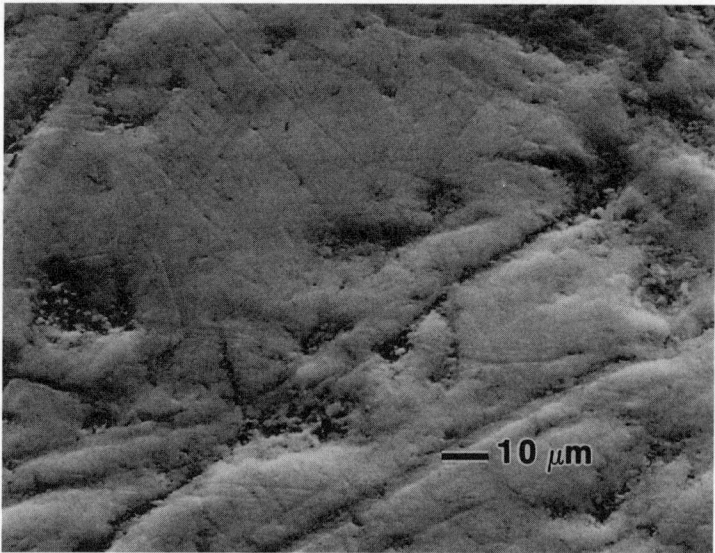

Fig. 4.10. Scanning electron micrograph of molar from inland early mission site in Florida (SMDT 91–49). Note absence of large pits and large amount of microwear.

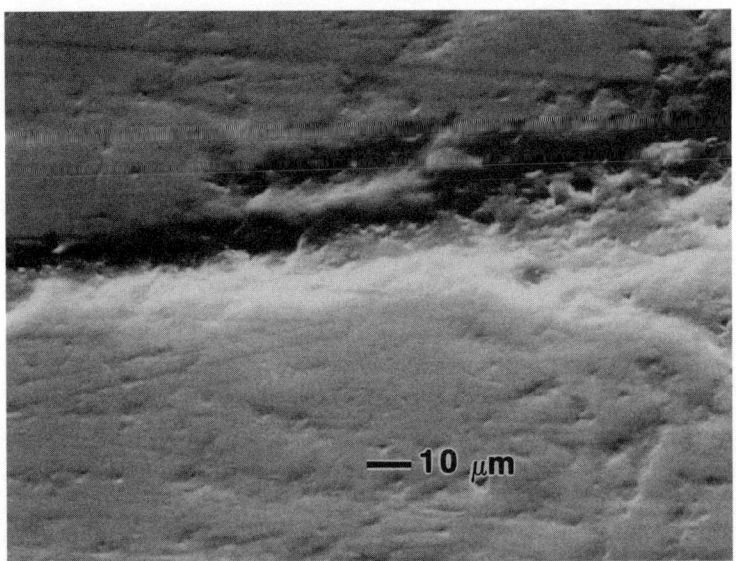

Fig. 4.11. Scanning electron micrograph of incisor from inland early mission site in Florida (SMDT 91–11).

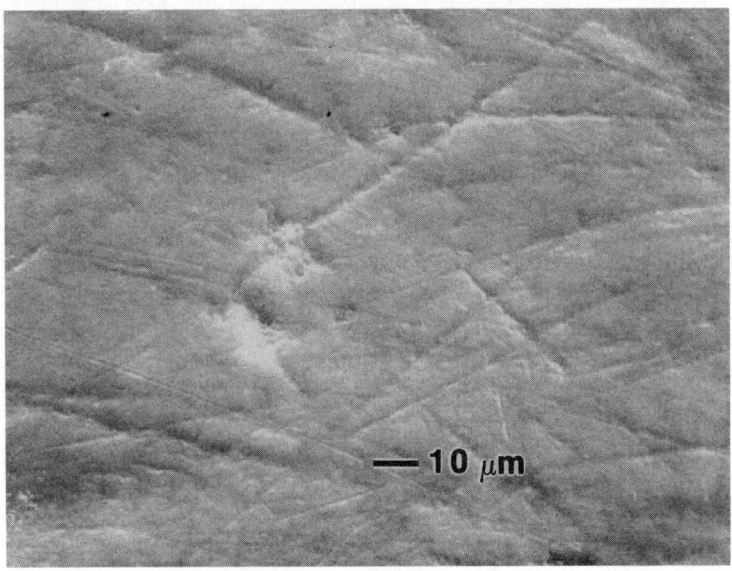

Fig. 4.12. Scanning electron micrograph of incisor from coastal early mission site in Florida (SMDY 44). Note absence of large features and preponderance of fine scratches.

Table 4.13. Molar microwear comparisons for late prehistoric, coastal mission, and inland mission sites in Florida

Period	N		Pit width		Scratch width		Scratch orient.[a]		% pits	
	Mean	S.E.	Mean	S.E.	Mean	S.E.	Mean	S.E.	Mean	S.E.
Late prehistoric (N=6)	310	33	2.37	0.29	0.88	0.04	0.388	0.06	45.6	2.8
Coastal mission (N=30)	242	16	2.28[b]	0.09	0.98	0.04	0.467	0.03	47.7	2.0
Inland mission (N=20)	330[c]	24	1.98	0.06	0.87	0.03	0.479	0.03	45.1	1.6

a. See table 4.3 and text for explanation.
b. Coastal mission significantly greater than inland mission (p<0.25).
c. Inland mission significantly greater than coastal mission (p<0.007).

of smaller sizes, although the differences were barely nonsignificant, in part due to small sample sizes (see table 4.12).

By comparison, the molars from the inland mission sites showed significantly more microwear than did those from the coastal mission sites, while the coastal mission molars showed significantly wider pits than did those from the inland mission sites (see table 4.13 and figs. 4.9 and 4.10).

Georgia Prehistoric Coastal/Inland Comparisons

No incisor comparisons were possible for these samples. However, the molars showed two significant differences. Molars from the inland prehistoric sites showed significantly more microwear and significantly smaller pits than did those from the coastal prehistoric sites (see table 4.14).

Table 4.14. Molar microwear comparisons for late prehistoric coastal and late prehistoric inland sites in Georgia

Period	N		Pit width		Scratch width		Scratch orient.[a]		% pits	
	Mean	S.E.	Mean	S.E.	Mean	S.E.	Mean	S.E.	Mean	S.E.
Late prehistoric coastal (N=5)	189	17	3.05[b]	0.46	1.03	0.04	0.574	0.03	46.5	2.0
Late prehistoric inland (N=9)	403[c]	41	1.99	0.13	0.84	0.06	0.605	0.04	47.0	2.9

a. See table 4.3 and text for explanation.
b. Prehistoric coastal significantly greater than prehistoric inland (p<0.006).
c. Prehistoric inland significantly greater than prehistoric coastal (p<0.007).

Table 4.15. Molar microwear comparisons for late prehistoric coastal and mission coastal sites in Georgia

Period	N		Pit width		Scratch width		Scratch orient [a]		% pits	
	Mean	S.E.	Mean	S.E.	Mean	S.E.	Mean	S.E.	Mean	S.E.
Late prehistoric coastal (N=5)	189	17	3.05	0.46	1.03	0.04	0.574	0.03	46.5	2.0
Mission coastal (N=9)	158	20	3.18	0.19	1.22	0.08	0.481	0.06	41.4	4.0

a. See table 4.3 and text for explanation.

Georgia Prehistoric Coastal and Early Mission Coastal Comparisons

No incisor comparisons were possible for these sites. There were no significant differences in molar microwear between these sites (see table 4.15).

Interpreting the Microwear Evidence

A plethora of recent laboratory work and field studies of nonhuman primates indicates clear differences in dental microwear between populations, and this study is no exception. What might these microwear differences mean? For a broader comparison and interpretation of our findings, we apply a three-factor ANOVA.

Three-Factor ANOVA and Molar Comparisons

With a multitude of differences for many comparisons, it is a daunting task to step through the existing results in an organized fashion. However, given the large number of comparisons (12 sets, each involving five different microwear measurements), such a task may not be necessary, as there is a possibility that some comparisons may have yielded statistically significant results by chance alone (so-called Type I errors). To alleviate this problem, and to aid in weighing interpretations of the results, a three-factor ANOVA was run, using "time period," "habitat," and "state" as factors. Unfortunately, the mission samples from Georgia were only from the early mission period, thus the multifactor ANOVA could only include a two-part analysis of time periods (prehistoric vs. mission), not a three-part analysis (prehistoric vs. early mission vs. late mission). Similarly, the incisors from the Georgia sample were only from the late prehistoric site at Irene Mound (see table 4.1). Thus, the multifactor ANOVA could only be performed on molars.

Two important points can be gleaned from the results (summarized in table 4.16). First, there are significant interactions between factors for some of the microwear measurements. One of the significant interactions, between "time period" and "state" for pit width, helps to explain some of the results of the single-factor ANOVAs. A simple comparison of molar pit width between the prehistoric and mission sites originally yielded no significant differences (see table 4.5). As indicated by the significant interaction between "time period" and "state" for pit width in table 4.16, this was because the sites in Georgia and Florida showed opposite results for that dental microwear measurement. In Georgia, the molars from the mission site showed larger pits, while in Florida, the molars from the prehistoric sites showed larger pits (compare tables 4.6 and 4.8). This is probably due to the second major point to come from the three-factor ANOVA: that is, molars from the coastal and inland sites have markedly different pit sizes and amounts of microwear, no matter what time period or state is examined. This is evident from the significant effects of "habitat" on those two variables in the three-factor ANOVA (see table 4.16). It is also evident in the results of the aforementioned comparisons of pit width for mission and prehistoric sites. If one runs a simple comparison of molar microwear measurements between coastal and inland sites, irrespective of state or time period, the teeth from the inland sites routinely show more microwear and yet smaller microwear features than do those from the coastal sites (see table 4.17; also compare figs. 4.7 and 4.9 [coastal molars] with figs. 4.5, 4.6, 4.8, and 4.10 [inland molars]).

Why, then, would the molars from the mission site in Georgia show large pits, while those from the *prehistoric* sites in Florida show large pits? We believe that the answer lies in the fact that the mission site in Georgia— Santa Catalina de Guale—was a coastal locality, and the bulk of the prehistoric teeth from Florida were also coastal (Mayport Mound). Why would the molars from the coastal sites routinely show less microwear, but larger scratches and pits, as compared with molars from inland sites? Because cooking at these sites apparently involved similar technology, and because the microwear differences bracket the transition to maize agriculture, the answer probably lies in the nature of the soil composition in the coastal and inland sites. Inland, the soils are clay, and on the coast, they are primarily sand. Finer clays are probably harder to remove from food and thus remain a constant influence on the teeth of the people at the inland sites. By contrast, sand might be easier to detect and remove and might thus be an intermittent influence on molar microwear patterns at the coastal sites.

Table 4.16. Three-factor analysis of variance of molar microwear data (all sites combined)

Three-factor ANOVA probabilities

	N	Pit width	Scratch width	Scratch orient.[a]	% pits
F-value Time period (prehistoric or mission)	9.15 (p<0.000) p<0.503	11.6 (p<0.000) p<0.322	4.63 (p<0.000) p<0.100	2.75 (p<.017) p<0.127	0.66 (p<0.682) p<0.411
Habitat (coastal or inland)	p<0.002	p<0.002	p<0.193	p<0.750	p<0.717
State (Florida or Georgia)	p<0.933	p<0.344	p<0.398	p<0.372	p<0.866
Time/habitat interaction	p<0.606	p<0.108	p<0.557	p<0.026	p<0.883
Time/state interaction	p<0.232	p<0.005	p<0.290	p<0.883	p<0.567
Habitat/state interaction	p<0.201	p<0.503	p<0.153	p<0.047	p<0.568

a. See table 4.3 and text for explanation.

Table 4.17. Molar microwear comparisons for coastal and inland sites (Florida and Georgia combined)

Period	N		Pit width		Scratch width		Scratch orient.[a]		% pits	
	Mean	S.E.	Mean	S.E.	Mean	S.E.	Mean	S.E.	Mean	S.E.
Coastal (N=52)	215	11	2.65[b]	0.11	1.00[c]	0.03	0.498	0.02	46.9	1.4
Inland (N=40)	352[d]	20	2.04	0.07	0.86	0.03	0.509	0.03	45.9	1.3

a. See table 4.3 and text for explanation.
b. Coastal significantly greater than inland (p<0.000).
c. Coastal significantly greater than inland (p<0.002).
d. Inland significantly greater than coastal (p<0.000).

Given its larger grain size, sand would tend to leave larger scratches and pits on the teeth than would clay.

The differences in molar microwear between coastal and inland sites clarify many of the other single-factor molar comparisons (in addition to the basic prehistoric/mission comparisons). For instance, when the prehistoric samples from Florida are split into early and late prehistoric sites, the bulk of the differences can again be traced to the fact that the early prehistoric site (Mayport Mound) is a coastal site while the late prehistoric site (Lake Jackson) is inland (see figs. 4.7 and 4.8). Similarly, when the prehistoric sites from Georgia are split into coastal and inland sites, the same differences are maintained, with the molars from the coastal sites showing less microwear but larger pits than the molars from the inland site.

Further support for the importance of this difference is provided by the comparisons of the Georgia prehistoric and mission coastal sites which, despite bracketing the transition between hunting-gathering and agricultural subsistence, show no significant differences in molar microwear, again probably because they are all coastal sites.

If the bulk of the molar microwear differences are related to differences in habitat, are there *any* molar microwear differences that can be related to temporal or adaptive shifts (or geographic differences) in diet? To answer this question, we need to return to the results of the three-factor ANOVA, where one other significant result remains to be discussed, namely the significant interactions between habitat and time period and habitat and state for the homogeneity of scratch orientations (see table 4.16). Recall that the single-factor ANOVAs for the basic prehistoric/mission comparisons indicated that the molars from the prehistoric sites showed more homogeneous scratch orientations than did those from the mission sites (see table 4.5).

The three-factor ANOVAs suggest that the results are not that simple. Certainly, the single-factor ANOVAs for the prehistoric and mission sites in Georgia are in agreement with the overall prehistoric/mission single factor ANOVAs (see table 4.6). However, the analyses of the Florida samples point to another difference in that the molars from the early prehistoric site (Mayport Mound) show more homogeneous scratch orientations than do those from the late prehistoric site (Lake Jackson; see table 4.9). What might cause such differences?

Unlike incisors, which habitually perform many tasks, molars are used primarily for chewing food. As a result, molars are limited in how they can move in processing certain foods. In other words, a tough diet might require more precise tooth-food-tooth movements than a less tough diet. Thus, assuming that prehistoric diets were tougher than mission diets, one might expect molars from prehistoric sites to show a more homogeneous pattern of scratches than molars from the mission sites. From this perspective, because the people at the Florida site of Lake Jackson had evidently made a shift to maize agriculture during later prehistory—and before other prehistoric populations in northern Florida (see Larsen et al., this volume)—the molars from that site might be *expected* to show unusually heterogeneous scratch orientations.

Differences in Incisor Microwear

The three-factor ANOVA was not possible for the incisors, nor were many of the single-factor ANOVAs, due to the lack of usable incisors from certain archaeological sites. Nevertheless, one consistent difference in incisor microwear that emerged from this investigation involved the homogeneity of scratch orientations: scratches on the incisors from the prehistoric sites were generally more *variably* oriented than were those from the mission sites (see figs. 4.3 and 4.4). The more variable scratch orientations on the prehistoric incisors suggest that the late prehistoric people were using their incisors for a greater variety of tasks involving the anterior dentition and perhaps for ingesting a more variable diet than were the mission people. This fits well with the stable isotopic data (see Larsen et al., this volume), but given the importance of local factors on diet variation (as evidenced by other contributions in the volume), one might reasonably ask if such broad comparisons are also masking significant differences between populations.

The number of populations for which we had usable incisors was limited to the late prehistoric sites of Lake Jackson and Irene Mound on the one hand, and the early mission sites in Florida on the other. However, no matter how the samples were subdivided, the incisors from the prehistoric

Table 4.18. Incisor microwear comparisons for Lake Jackson and Irene Mound sites

Period	N		Pit width		Scratch width		Scratch orient.[a]		% pits	
	Mean	S.E.	Mean	S.E.	Mean	S.E.	Mean	S.E.	Mean	S.E.
Lake Jackson (N=4)	222	35	2.29[b]	0.17	1.01[c]	0.06	0.446	0.12	31.3	8.1
Irene Mound (N=6)	285	17	1.60	0.05	0.82	0.02	0.554	0.03	36.4	2.5

a. See table 4.3 and text for explanation.
b. Lake Jackson significantly greater than Irene Mound (p<0.002).
c. Lake Jackson significantly greater than Irene Mound (p<0.006).

sites had more variable scratch orientations than did those from the early mission sites (compare tables 4.4, 4.7, and 4.12). Interestingly, when the Florida mission sites were split into inland and coastal sites, a difference in feature size appeared, in addition to the usual difference in scratch orientation. Specifically, incisors from the coastal mission sites showed smaller pits and scratches (see figs. 4.11 and 4.12). This is somewhat surprising given that, as mentioned, coastal molars tended to show *larger* features than did inland molars. Could the difference merely be evidence of yet another coastal versus inland difference that might cut across sites and comparisons?

At first glance, the results from the Florida sites (table 4.12) might suggest key differences between coastal and inland groups, because Lake Jackson is an inland site, and it is generally fairly similar to the inland mission site. However, two points argue against such an interpretation. First, the incisors from Lake Jackson are still different from those of the inland mission site in that they show more variably oriented scratches. Second, if the incisor samples from Irene Mound are reintroduced into the picture, it becomes clear that not all prehistoric inland sites are alike. Irene Mound and Lake Jackson are both inland sites, and yet there are significant differences in incisor microwear between them (see table 4.18). In essence, the Irene Mound incisors are virtually identical to those from the coastal *early mission* sample (compare Irene Mound in table 4.18 with coastal mission in table 4.12).

The similarities between the incisors from the Lake Jackson site and those from the inland mission site (San Martín de Timucua) may again be due to the fact that the people at Lake Jackson had a diet that was fairly similar to that of the people at the inland mission site. From that perspective, the variably oriented scratches on the Lake Jackson incisors would suggest a more variable repertoire of incisal activities in the Lake Jackson people, as compared with those from San Martín de Timucua, but the similarly sized microwear features would indicate similar abrasives in contact with the incisors. However, the incisors still leave us with a number of unanswered questions. First, in Florida, why are there differences between incisors from the inland and coastal sites, and why are those differences opposite to those shown by the molars? Also, why do the incisors from the prehistoric site in Georgia (Irene Mound) differ from those at the prehistoric site in Florida (Lake Jackson)?

The differences between incisors and molars probably relate to inter-tooth differences in function. As Ungar (1992, 1994, 1996) has repeatedly noted, incisors are generally used for the *ingestion* of food and even the preparation of nonfood items such as hides. Molars, by contrast, are usually used only for the mastication of food. If the differences in molar microwear between coastal and inland sites reflect differences in mastication, then it is entirely feasible that the incisors from the coastal and inland sites could show another pattern of differences, as the incisors could be used for an entirely distinct range of activities involving ingestion, food preparation, or activities unrelated to diet. Of course, another possibility is that larger samples would yield different results. In particular, analyses of incisors from the Georgia mission sites would be most instructive. Would incisors from the Irene Mound site be similar to those of the Georgia mission sites? Only further analyses will tell.

Conclusions

1. Simple comparisons of broadly different groups have the potential to mask many interesting differences within and between populations.

2. Local factors (e.g., coastal, terrestrial) are extremely important in interpreting microwear variation and inferring tooth use in Spanish Florida.

3. The most consistent difference in microwear is between coastal and inland sites, which may simply reflect the amount of extraneous grit in or on food in these different environments.

4. Differences in homogeneity of scratch orientation may point to dietary differences (for molars) and differences in other activities involving use of the anterior dentition (incisors).

Acknowledgments

Thanks go to David Hurst Thomas (American Museum of Natural History), Douglas Ubelaker and David Hunt (Smithsonian Institution), Jerald Milanich (Florida Museum of Natural History), and James Miller (Florida Bureau of Archaeological Research) for their permission to study and analyze the teeth under their care. The research was funded by the National Science Foundation (SBR-9305391, SBR-9601766). Thanks also go to Kristina Aldridge, Rachael Baylin, Albert Capati, Anita Lubensky, Bill Miller, Jay Mussell, Mary Silcox, and Rose Weinstein for their help in the cleaning and casting of teeth and for their assistance in the scanning electron microscopy. Peter Ungar's aid with the Microware software program is greatly appreciated.

References Cited

Bullington, J. 1991. Deciduous Dental Microwear of Prehistoric Juveniles from the Lower Illinois River Valley. *American Journal of Physical Anthropology* 84:59–73.

Conover, W. J., and R. L. Iman. 1981. Rank Transformations as a Bridge between Parametric and Nonparametric Statistics. *American Statistician* 35:124–29.

Danielson, D. R., and K. J. Reinhard. 1998. Human Dental Microwear Caused by Calcium Oxalate Phytoliths in Prehistoric Diet of the Lower Pecos Region, Texas. *American Journal of Physical Anthropology* 107:297–304.

Gordon, K. D. 1986. Dental Microwear Analysis to Detect Human Diet. *American Journal of Physical Anthropology* 69:206–7.

———. 1988. A Review of Methodology and Quantification in Dental Microwear Analysis. *Scanning Microscopy* 2:1139–47.

Grine, F. E. 1986. Dental Evidence for Dietary Differences in *Australopithecus* and *Paranthropus:* A Quantitative Analysis of Permanent Molar Microwear. *Journal of Human Evolution* 15:783–822.

Harmon, A. M., and J. C. Rose. 1988. The Role of Dental Microwear Analysis in the Reconstruction of Prehistoric Diet. In *Diet and Subsistence: Current Archaeological Perspectives,* ed. B. V. Kennedy and G. M. LeMoine, 267–72. Calgary: Archaeological Association of the University of Calgary.

Kay, R. F. 1977. The Evolution of Molar Occlusion in the Cercopithecidae and Early Catarrhines. *American Journal of Physical Anthropology* 46:327–52.

King, T., P. Andrews, and B. Boz. 1999. Effect of Taphonomic Processes on Dental Microwear. *American Journal of Physical Anthropology* 108:359–73.

Lalueza Fox, C. 1992. Dental Striation Pattern in Andamanese and Veddahs from Skull Collections of the British Museum. *Man in India* 72:377–84.

Lalueza, C., A. Pérez-Pérez, and D. Turbón. 1996. Dietary Inferences through Buccal Microwear Analysis of Middle and Upper Pleistocene Human Fossils. *American Journal of Physical Anthropology* 100:367–87.

Lucas, P. W., and M. F. Teaford. 1995. Significance of Silica in Leaves Eaten by Long-Tailed Macaques (*Macaca fascicularis*). *Folia Primatologica* 64:30–36.

Lukacs, J. R., and R. F. Pastor. 1988. Activity Induced Patterns of Dental Abrasion in Prehistoric Pakistan: Evidence from Mehrgarh and Harappa. *American Journal of Physical Anthropology* 76:377–98.

Molleson, T., and K. Jones. 1991. Dental Evidence for Dietary Changes at Abu Hureyra. *Journal of Archaeological Science* 18:525–39.

Molleson, T., K. Jones, and S. Jones. 1993. Dietary Change and the Effects of Food Preparation on Microwear Patterns in the Late Neolithic of Abu Hureyra, Northern Syria. *Journal of Human Evolution* 24:455–68.

Pastor, R. F. 1992. Dietary Adaptations and Dental Microwear in Mesolithic and Chalcolithic South Asia. *Journal of Human Ecology* 2 (special issue):215–28.

———. 1993. Dental Microwear among Prehistoric Inhabitants of the Indian Subcontinent: A Quantitative and Comparative Analysis. Ph.D. diss., University of Oregon, Eugene.

Pastor, R. F., and T. L. Johnston. 1992. Dental Microwear and Attrition. In *Human Skeletal Remains from Mahadaha: A Gangetic Mesolithic Site,* ed. K. A. R. Kennedy, 271–304. Ithaca: Cornell University Press.

Pérez-Pérez, A., J. M. Bermúdez de Castro, and J. L. Arsuaga. 1999. Nonocclusal Dental Microwear Analysis of 300,000-Year-Old *Homo heidelbergensis*. *American Journal of Physical Anthropology* 108:433–57.

Pérez-Pérez, A., C. Lalueza, and D. Turbón. 1994. Intraindividual and Intragroup Variability of Buccal Tooth Striation Pattern. *American Journal of Physical Anthropology* 94:175–87.

Puech, P.-F. 1984. A la Recherche du Menu des Premiers Hommes. *Cahiers Ligures de Prehistoire et de Protohistoire* 1:45–53.

Puech, P.-F., F. Cianfarani, and H. Albertini. 1986. Dental Microwear Features as an Indicator for Plant Food in Early Hominids: A Preliminary Study of Enamel. *Human Evolution* 1:507–15.

Radlanski, R. J. von. 1988. Scanning-Electron-Microscopic Study Concerning the Morphology of Interdental Abrasions of Human Permanent Teeth. *Anatomischer Anzeiger* 167:413–15.

Solounias, N., M. F. Teaford, and A. Walker. 1988. Interpreting the Diet of Extinct Ruminants: The Case of a Non-Browsing Giraffid. *Paleobiology* 14:287–300.

Strait, S. G. 1993. Molar Microwear in Extant Small-Bodied Faunivorous Mammals: An Analysis of Feature Density and Pit Frequency. *American Journal of Physical Anthropology* 92:63–79.

Teaford, M. F. 1988a. A Review of Dental Microwear and Diet in Modern Mammals. *Scanning Microscopy* 2:1149–66.

———. 1988b. Scanning Electron Microscope Diagnosis of Wear Patterns versus Artifacts on Fossil Teeth. *Scanning Microscopy* 2:1167–75.

———. 1991. Dental Microwear: What Can It Tell Us about Diet and Dental Function? In *Advances in Dental Anthropology,* ed. M. A. Kelley and C. S. Larsen, 341–56. New York: Wiley-Liss.

————. 1994. Dental Microwear and Dental Function. *Evolutionary Anthropology* 3:17–30.

Teaford, M. F., and M. G. Leakey. 1992. Dental Microwear and Diet in Plio-Pleistocene Cercopithecoids from Kenya. *American Journal of Physical Anthropology,* suppl. 14:160–61.

Teaford, M. F., and J. D. Lytle. 1996. Diet-Induced Changes in Rates of Human Tooth Microwear: A Case Study Involving Stone-Ground Maize. *American Journal of Physical Anthropology* 100:143–47.

Teaford, M. F., and O. J. Oyen. 1989. Live Primates and Dental Replication: New Problems and New Techniques. *American Journal of Physical Anthropology* 62:255–61.

Teaford, M. F., and J. A. Runestad. 1992. Dental Microwear and Diet in Venezuelan Primates. *American Journal of Physical Anthropology* 88:347–64.

Teaford, M. F., and A. C. Walker. 1984. Quantitative Differences in Dental Microwear between Primate Species with Different Diets and a Comment on the Presumed Diet of *Sivapithecus. American Journal of Physical Anthropology* 64:191–200.

Teaford, M. F., M. C. Maas, and E. L. Simons. 1996. Dental Microwear and Microstructure in Early Oligocene Fayum Primates: Implications for Diet. *American Journal of Physical Anthropology* 101:527–43.

Ungar, P. S. 1992. Incisor Microwear and Feeding Behavior of Four Sumatran Anthropoids. Ph.D. diss., State University of New York, Stony Brook.

————. 1994. Incisor Microwear of Sumatran Anthropoid Primates. *American Journal of Physical Anthropology* 94:339–63.

————. 1996. Dental Microwear of European Miocene Catarrhines: Evidence for Diets and Tooth Use. *Journal of Human Evolution* 31:335–66.

Ungar, P. S., and M. A. Spencer. 1999. Incisor Microwear, Diet, and Tooth Use in Three Amerindian Populations. *American Journal of Physical Anthropology* 109:387–96.

Ungar, P. S., M. F. Teaford, R. F. Pastor, and K. E. Glander. 1995. Dust Accumulation in the Canopy: Implications for the Study of Dental Microwear in Primates. *American Journal of Physical Anthropology* 97:93–99.

Walker, A. 1981. Diet and Teeth: Dietary Hypotheses and Human Evolution. *Philosophical Transactions of the Royal Society of London* 292(B):57–64.

Walker, A., H. N. Hoeck, and L. Perez. 1978. Microwear of Mammalian Teeth as an Indicator of Diet. *Science* 201:908–10.

Zar, J. H. 1984. *Biostatistical Analysis.* 2d ed. Englewood Cliffs, N.J.: Prentice-Hall.

5

Reconstructing Behavior in Spanish Florida
The Biomechanical Evidence

Christopher B. Ruff and Clark Spencer Larsen

Bones are living organs that can alter their morphology throughout life in response to changes in their environment. The mechanical environment of a bone is determined by its role in transmission of body weight and applied muscle forces. Thus, the preserved morphology of a bone provides, in part, a record of the mechanical loadings (forces) placed upon it during life, from which inferences regarding body size and behavior can be drawn.

Mechanical interpretation of biological structures is greatly facilitated if a relatively simple mechanical model of the structure can be applied. Conventional engineering beam theory (Timoshenko and Gere 1972) has been shown to model adequately the mechanical behavior of long bone diaphyses (Klenerman et al. 1967; Huiskes 1982). Under this model, cross-sectional properties of the diaphysis are used to calculate its rigidity and strength under particular kinds of mechanical loadings (Lovejoy et al. 1976). These properties include cross-sectional area of bone, proportional to compressive strength, and second moments of area, proportional to bending and torsional (twisting) rigidity and strength. Cross-sectional properties can be derived using a variety of methods. These methods have been described in detail elsewhere with more information on the properties and their engineering interpretation (Ruff and Hayes 1983; Ruff 1989, 2000a).

Biomechanical analyses of long bone diaphyses have been applied to archaeological samples with increasing frequency over the past two decades (for recent reviews see Bridges 1995; Ruff 1999, 2000a). In particular, a number of studies of pre- and protohistoric North American Native American samples have been carried out, allowing broad-based comparisons of environmental effects on bone structure (e.g., Ruff 1999). These studies include a series of previous analyses of samples from the Georgia coast (northern La Florida) to examine the effects of subsistence strategy changes and Spanish colonization (Ruff et al. 1984; Ruff and Larsen 1990; Larsen and Ruff 1994; Larsen et al. 1996).

In the current study the size of the La Florida samples is increased by more than 50 percent, to a total of 168 femora and 189 humeri, including new individuals from both the prehistoric and contact periods. In addition, non-Guale samples from La Florida are included here for the first time, making possible new types of comparisons both between and within temporal periods and different cultures. Other recently acquired information has been incorporated into the analysis: the results of recent stable isotope analyses of La Florida samples (Hutchinson et al. 1998; Larsen et al. this volume) have led to some changes in the assignment of subsamples to particular subsistence groups, and new methods of biomechanical scaling of parameters and statistical treatment of data are applied (Ruff 2000b). Results of this study both amplify and modify previous findings regarding limb bone structural characteristics, their mechanical interpretation, and behavior of native populations from La Florida. The purpose of this study is to characterize structural properties for the La Florida populations and to indicate key aspects of behavioral adaptation and strategy in a highly dynamic setting.

The Skeletal Samples

Skeletal samples included in the study are listed in table 5.1. A total of 168 femora and 189 humeri from 17 sites in Georgia and Florida was analyzed. Not including bones from the Santa Catalina ossuary, almost all of which were nonassociated, about 61 percent of the femora and humeri in the total study sample were matched—that is, they were derived from the same individuals. Thus, there is a large degree of correspondence between upper and lower limb bone sampling, although as noted later, some effects of sampling differences for the femur and humerus are evident in the results. Not including the ossuary sample, the number of individuals represented is 187. One individual in the ossuary sample had a matched humerus and femur; depending upon how many of the rest of the bones in this sample are matched, this sample could represent from 28 to 54 individuals. Thus, the total number of individuals in the entire study sample is between 215 and 241. All individuals were adult, as judged by epiphyseal closure. Approximately equal numbers of males and females were included (see subse-

Table 5.1. Skeletal samples included in the biomechanical study

Group and site	Femora	Humeri
Early prehistoric Guale		
McLeod Mound	1	0
Deptford Site	3	3
Airport	3	3
Cannons Point	0	2
Sea Island Mound	6	6
Charlie King Mound	1	1
Total	14	15
Late prehistoric Guale		
Johns Mound	5	12
Marys Mound	1	0
Irene	20	29
Martinez B	1	1
Taylor Mound	6	8
Couper Field	12	11
Total	45	61
Early mission Guale		
Pine Harbor	3	3
Santa Catalina de Guale	15	16
Total	18	19
Late mission Guale		
Santa Catalina de Santa Maria	47	48
Early mission Yamasee		
Santa Maria de Yamasee	16	19
Early mission Timucua		
Santa Catalina Ossuary	28	27
Total	168	189

quent tables for breakdowns by sex). Sex and approximate age were determined using standard osteological methods (Ubelaker 1989).

For purposes of statistical comparisons, the study sample was divided into six cultural/temporal groups (table 5.1), including three from Georgia: Early Prehistoric Guale (400 B.C.–A.D. 1000), Late Prehistoric Guale (A.D. 1000–1450), and Early Mission Guale (A.D. 1600–1680); and three from Florida (Amelia Island): Late Mission Guale (A.D. 1680–1700), Early Mission Yamasee (A.D. 1600–1680), and Early Mission Timucua (A.D. 1600–1680). For convenience in much of the following tabulation and discussion of results, they are referred to by the acronyms EPG, LPG, EMG, LMG, EMY, and EMT, respectively. These groupings were chosen for analysis because they represent distinctive subsistence strategies (e.g., the EPG group did not practice horticulture, while the LPG did), temporal periods, and/or cultural affiliations. It should be noted that some sites previously classified as "preagricultural" (Ruff et al. 1984; Ruff and Larsen 1990) (equivalent to EPG here) are now moved into the later (LPG) horticultural period based on new stable isotopic data (Hutchinson et al. 1998; Larsen et al. this volume); these include the Johns and Marys Mound sites (table 5.1). Although the degree of agriculture is not as great as in the later group, the people concerned nevertheless appear to have eaten some maize.

Well-preserved bones from either the left or right side, and in the case of some humeri from both sides, were chosen for analysis. Among humans, bilateral asymmetry is relatively small in lower limb bones but is more marked in the upper limbs (Trinkaus et al. 1994). Approximately equal numbers of right and left femora and humeri within each sex and cultural/temporal group were included. In addition, almost half of the humeral values used for the LMG and EMY groups were derived as averages of bilateral pairs. For the EPG, LPG, and EMG groups, average sex/group bilateral asymmetry in humeral properties was determined through radiographic measurement of both sides when available (Fresia et al. 1990) and used to adjust values of the other (unilateral) humeri as described previously (Ruff and Larsen 1990). We were unable to match paired humeri from nonassociated skeletons in the Santa Catalina ossuary (EMT) sample. This may reflect either our inability to do so or a mortuary practice involving selective burial of one humerus from at least some of the people interred in the ossuary pit.

Measurements

Prior to measurement, femora and humeri are first oriented according to a standardized set of anatomical axes (Ruff and Hayes 1983; Ruff and Larsen 1990). The femur is placed with the posterior edges of its condyles in contact with a measuring surface and "leveled" by raising the proximal end until the A-P (anteroposterior) midpoint of the shaft just distal to the lesser trochanter is at the same height above the measuring surface as the shaft A-P midpoint just proximal to the condyles. The coronal (M-L, mediolateral) plane of the femur is then parallel to the measuring surface. The sagittal plane of the femur is taken perpendicular to this plane through the M-L midpoints of the shaft at the same locations. The longitudinal axis of the femur is the intersection of its sagittal and coronal planes.

The humerus is oriented in essentially the same fashion, raising the distal end until the A-P midpoints of the shaft just proximal to the olecranon fossa and at the surgical neck are equidistant above the measuring surface,

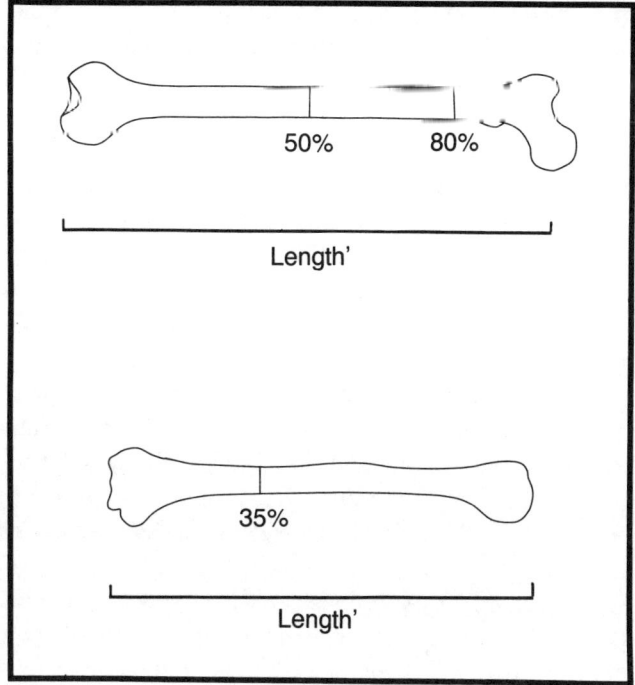

Fig. 5.1. Measurement of length' and location of cross sections in the femur (*top*) and humerus (*bottom*).

holding the trochlear-capitular long axis parallel to the surface, which now defines the coronal plane.[1] The sagittal plane is perpendicular to this through the M-L midpoints of the same shaft locations, and the longitudinal axis is again the intersection of the two planes.

Cross section locations are defined according to percentages of bone length measured parallel to the longitudinal axes of the humerus and femur. "Bone length" in the femur is the average distance between the distal ends of the condyles and the superior surface of the femoral neck (just medial to the greater trochanter), and in the humerus between the lateral lip of the trochlea and the superior surface of the humeral head. These measurements are referred to as length' to distinguish them from maximum or other length measurements. Length' of the femur averages about 6 percent less than maximum length, and length' of the humerus about 1.5 percent less than maximum length.

For this study, cross section locations were taken at 50 percent and 80 percent of length' from the distal end of the femur and at 35 percent of length' from the distal end of the humerus (fig. 5.1). For convenience these locations are referred to subsequently as femoral "midshaft" and "subtrochanteric" and humeral "mid-distal" locations, respectively. These locations were chosen because they sample biomechanically informative regions of the bones and avoid large muscle insertion crests (e.g., the insertion for the deltoid muscle in the humerus, which occurs near midshaft). Many comparative data are also available for these locations (e.g., Ruff 1987, 1999; Trinkaus et al. 1994).

Bones were sectioned transversely to their longitudinal axes at these locations using a fine-toothed bandsaw. The proximal surfaces of the sections were then photographed with a superimposed grid aligned with A-P and M-L axes, the images were developed into photographic slides, and these were projected onto a digitizer (Ruff and Hayes 1983). Subperiosteal and endosteal contours were manually traced, with x,y point coordinates of the contours input into a modified version of the program SLICE (Nagurka and Hayes 1980), which calculates biomechanical section properties.

Three section properties were considered in the present analysis: cortical area (CA), polar second moment of area (J), and the ratio of perpendicular second moments of area (I_x/I_y or I_{max}/I_{min}). CA is a measure of axial rigidity, J is a measure of average bending/torsional rigidity, and I_x/I_y and I_{max}/I_{min} are measures of A-P/M-L and maximum/minimum bending rigidity, respectively. I_x/I_y was calculated for the midshaft femur and mid-distal humerus, while I_{max}/I_{min} was calculated for the subtrochanteric femur (because this section tends to be oriented "diagonally" relative to A-P and M-L axes). Together these properties encompass the most critical aspects of cross-sectional "size" and "shape" in terms of their biomechanical consequences. As discussed later, they have been shown to vary between and within populations in response to behavioral differences, such as degree of long-distance mobility.

To derive behavioral inferences from these properties, it is also useful to factor out the effects of variation in body size, since as noted earlier, body mass itself constitutes part of the biomechanical loading placed on bones.[2] Recent theoretical and empirical allometric studies have shown that CA varies approximately with (bone length)^3, while J varies approximately with (bone length)$^{5.33}$ (Ruff et al. 1993; Ruff 1999, 2000b). This is true only if body shape—limb length relative to stature, and body breadth relative to stature—remains similar between samples (Ruff 2000b). It is not possible to test this assumption directly in the current study samples; however, it seems unlikely that body shape would have varied greatly between them, at least compared to the major differences in body shape that exist between other modern human populations (e.g., in equatorial populations versus those from higher latitudes) (Ruff 2000b). In the following tabulations of study results, both raw and body size standardized cross-sectional properties are presented, although only the size standardized values (CA_{STD} and J_{STD}) are used in statistical comparisons between groups. The latter values are also referred to as "robusticity" measures, to distinguish them from absolute strength measures (Ruff et al. 1984).

Statistical Procedures

Comparisons between groups were carried out using analyses of variance (ANOVA) followed by Tukey Multiple Comparison tests between pairs of groups. Because sex was found to be a significant factor in comparisons (see later discussion), two-way ANOVAs were carried out with both sex and cultural/temporal group included as independent variables. One-way ANOVAs of cultural/temporal groups, within sex, were also carried out; these basically confirmed the results of two-way ANOVAs. In addition, because there was some variation in age between samples (specifically, the prehistoric samples tended to be younger on average than the contact samples), age was included as a covariate; in most cases this did not affect results, but where it did, this is indicated in the tabulations. The Santa Catalina ossuary (EMT) sample could not be sexed, but appears from other indicators (especially pelvic) to be predominantly female. Because of this probable (but indeterminate) sex bias, it was not included in statistical comparisons between groups, but it is included in pooled sex tabulations of results. All statistical tests were carried out using SYSTAT for the Macintosh, version 5.2 (SYSTAT: Statistics 1992).

Analysis Results

Data summaries for each cultural/temporal grouping, by sex and pooled across sex, are shown in tables 5.2, 5.3, and 5.4 for the femoral midshaft, subtrochanteric, and humeral mid-distal section, respectively. Femoral and humeral length' are also shown in tables 5.2 and 5.4, respectively. A summary of statistical comparisons between groups is given in table 5.5.

Femoral length' shows no significant variation among cultural/temporal groups (table 5.5). Humeral length' shows significant variation, but this becomes nonsignificant when age is included as a covariate. Among females, changes in humeral and femoral length' between the two prehistoric

Table 5.2. Data summary for femoral length and midshaft femoral cross-sectional properties, by sex and cultural/temporal group

Group[a]	N	Length[1b]		CA		J		CA_STD		J_STD		I_x/I_y	
		Mean	S.E.	Mean	S.E.	Mean	S.E.	Mean	S.E.	Mean	S.E.	Mean	S.E.
Males													
EPG	6	418.3	8.8	439.7	23.0	53,336	4,549	600.9	24.8	563.6	27.2	1.333	.048
LPG	21	421.4	4.1	392.7	9.3	42,863	1,898	531.0	19.4	443.8	22.0	1.153	.040
EMG	9	420.3	7.9	400.1	13.5	47,216	2,252	546.5	31.9	501.5	37.1	1.192	.109
LMG	21	420.0	3.9	395.3	8.1	47,634	1,270	536.3	13.3	505.9	21.0	1.137	.045
EMY	8	425.9	9.8	398.5	14.5	45,803	3,317	519.6	21.3	444.2	22.7	1.110	.057
Females													
EPG	8	407.6	5.5	315.4	21.4	32,210	1,949	470.2	37.9	397.8	28.9	1.207	.068
LPG	24	400.7	5.3	301.0	11.9	29,270	2,172	468.8	15.6	381.1	18.1	1.122	.042
EMG	9	404.1	6.5	342.6	12.2	32,656	2,217	521.2	20.1	416.7	21.5	.978	.036
LMG	23	392.1	3.2	314.7	12.2	31,813	1,653	523.5	20.6	480.7	25.4	.949	.041
EMY	8	391.9	3.2	299.4	8.9	27,147	1,383	499.7	22.0	412.3	27.0	1.068	.039
Pooled sex													
EPG	14	412.2	4.9	368.7	22.8	41,264	3,604	526.2	29.4	468.8	30.0	1.261	.046
LPG	45	410.4	3.7	343.8	10.3	35,613	1,768	497.9	13.0	410.4	14.7	1.137	.029
EMG	18	412.2	5.3	371.4	11.2	39,936	2,338	533.8	18.6	459.1	23.2	1.085	.061
LMG	47	406.4	3.2	355.8	9.3	39,891	1,553	530.0	12.1	493.6	16.3	1.045	.033
EMY	16	408.9	6.6	348.9	15.2	36,475	2,969	509.7	15.0	428.2	17.5	1.089	.034
EMT	28	406.9	5.1	364.1	9.6	39,849	1,900	544.4	14.6	496.6	21.3	1.083	.040

a. EPG = early prehistoric Guale; LPG = late prehistoric Guale; EMG = early mission Guale; LMG = late mission Guale; EMY = early mission Yamasee; EMT = early mission Timucua.

b. Length[1] = biomechanical length (see text); CA = cortical area (mm^2); J = polar second moment of area (mm^4); CA_STD = (CA/Length$^{1.3}$)·10^5; J_STD = (J/Length$^{15.33}$)·10^{12}; I_x/I_y = AP/ML second moments of area.

Table 5.3. Data summary for subtrochanteric femoral cross-sectional properties, by sex and cultural/temporal group

Group[a]	N	CA[b]		J		CA_{STD}		J_{STD}		I_{max}/I_{min}	
		Mean	S.E.	Mean	S.E.	Mean	S.E.	Mean	S.E.	Mean	S.E.
Males											
EPG	6	413.1	17.7	61,066	2,901	566.9	28.0	665.8	65.3	2.186	.113
LPG	21	385.4	8.0	49,008	2,505	519.0	15.8	502.1	23.4	1.863	.053
EMG	9	416.3	15.8	55,731	3,175	564.7	26.5	589.5	45.7	1.624	.073
LMG	24	396.4	8.8	53,900	1,517	537.9	14.7	570.0	22.2	1.623	.048
EMY	8	391.9	15.5	53,998	4,855	511.0	22.1	519.6	27.4	1.555	.034
Females											
EPG	8	320.4	22.4	38,624	1,891	478.3	41.0	480.0	36.6	2.151	.122
LPG	24	295.5	10.1	33,728	2,272	462.4	15.3	445.6	21.4	2.064	.075
EMG	9	352.8	15.5	39,930	3,849	535.3	21.0	505.0	40.3	1.802	.030
LMG	23	317.2	10.6	37,531	1,789	528.4	19.0	569.8	29.5	1.760	.058
EMY	8	288.1	7.9	31,291	1,181	481.2	21.0	476.1	29.7	1.706	.051
Pooled sex											
EPG	14	360.1	19.2	48,242	3,461	516.3	28.2	559.6	42.0	2.166	.052
LPG	45	337.4	9.4	40,858	2,022	488.8	11.7	472.0	16.2	1.970	.049
EMG	18	384.6	13.2	47,831	3,087	550.0	16.8	547.3	31.3	1.713	.060
LMG	47	357.6	9.0	45,890	1,671	533.2	11.8	557.1	18.1	1.690	.042
EMY	16	340.0	15.8	42,644	3,797	496.1	15.2	497.9	20.3	1.630	.054
EMT	28	360.7	11.9	46,509	2,886	536.4	14.8	570.7	27.0	1.701	.047

a. EPG = early prehistoric Guale; LPG = late prehistoric Guale; EMG = early mission Guale; LMG = late mission Guale; EMY = early mission Yamasee; EMT = early mission Timucua.

b. CA = cortical area (mm²); J = polar second moment of area (mm⁴); CA_{STD} = $(CA/Length^{13}) \cdot 10^8$; J_{STD} = $(J/Length^{5.33}) \cdot 10^{12}$; I_{max}/I_{min} = maximum/minimum second moments of area.

Table 5.4. Data summary for humeral length and mid-distal humeral cross-sectional properties, by sex and cultural/temporal group

Group[a]	N	Length[,b]		CA		J		CA_{STD}		J_{STD}		I_x/I_y	
		Mean	S.E.	Mean	S.E.	Mean	S.E.	Mean	S.E.	Mean	S.E.	Mean	S.E.
Males													
EPG	8	309.2	6.3	215.1	14.4	14,038	1,077	736.3	63.2	769.5	85.0	.957	.043
LPG	31	319.0	2.4	202.4	5.3	12,052	508	630.3	21.2	547.3	23.3	1.018	.015
EMG	11	313.5	4.0	201.4	10.6	12,032	951	655.4	34.9	602.8	57.8	1.094	.055
LMG	24	313.6	2.7	212.0	5.1	13,710	470	690.0	18.5	686.4	29.8	1.075	.028
EMY	7	322.6	6.4	206.0	6.0	13,543	1,064	619.9	35.5	578.3	40.6	1.060	.023
Females													
EPG	7	288.3	6.0	158.0	6.1	6,999	350	669.9	48.6	557.6	52.8	1.141	.064
LPG	30	305.4	3.6	150.0	5.7	7,303	392	537.4	25.8	426.0	24.3	1.096	.021
EMG	8	301.0	5.6	154.0	7.3	6,623	587	566.0	26.8	406.2	32.6	1.125	.026
LMG	24	298.8	2.6	143.8	5.8	7,226	372	540.6	21.6	466.9	24.9	1.099	.028
EMY	12	293.4	3.2	125.4	7.2	5,849	290	496.5	26.3	415.7	24.0	1.141	.040
Pooled sex													
EPG	15	299.5	5.0	188.5	11.0	10,753	1,102	705.3	40.2	670.6	57.3	1.043	.044
LPG	61	312.3	2.3	176.6	5.1	9,717	443	584.6	17.6	487.7	18.4	1.056	.034
EMG	19	308.3	3.5	181.5	8.7	9,754	862	617.8	24.9	520.0	42.1	1.107	.034
LMG	48	306.2	2.1	177.9	6.3	10,468	558	615.3	17.8	576.6	25.0	1.087	.020
EMY	19	304.2	4.5	155.1	10.4	8,683	968	542.0	24.9	475.6	27.7	1.111	.028
EMT	27	307.6	3.4	166.2	6.2	9,318	572	569.3	16.3	501.5	19.7	1.080	.027

a. EPG = early prehistoric Guale; LPG = late prehistoric Guale; EMG = early mission Guale; LMG = late mission Guale; EMY = early mission Yamasee; EMT = early mission Timucua.

b. Length' = biomechanical length (see text); CA = cortical area (mm²); J = polar second moment of area (mm⁴); CA_{STD} = $(CA/Length^{13})·10^8$; J_{STD} = $(J/Length^{15.33})·10^{12}$; I_x/I_y = AP/ML second moments of area.

Table 5.5. Statistical comparisons between sexes and cultural/temporal groups

Bone	Property	2-way ANOVA[a]		Tukey Multiple Comparison Tests[b]
		Sex	Group	
Femur	Length'	M>F***	n.s.	
	Midshaft CA_{STD}	M>F**	n.s.	
	Midshaft J_{STD}	M>F***	**	LPG<LMG***
	Midshaft I_x/I_y	M>F***	**	EPG>LMG**, (EMG†, EMY†)
	Subtroch. CA_{STD}	M>F**	(*)	(LPG<EMG*, LMG†)
	Subtroch. J_{STD}	M>F**	**	EPG>LPG†; LPG<LMG***
	Subtroch. I_{max}/I_{min}	F>M**	***	EPG>EMG***, LMG***, EMY***; LPG>EMG**, LMG***, EMY***
Humerus	Length'	M>F***	(*)	(EPG>LPG*)
	Mid-distal CA_{STD}	M>F***	**	EPG>LPG**, (LMG†), EMY**
	Mid-distal J_{STD}	M>F***	***	EPG>LPG***, EMG**, EMY**; LPG<LMG**
	Mid-distal I_x/I_y	F>M***	n.s.	
	Mid-distal I_{max}/I_{min}	F>M***	n.s.	

a. Parentheses indicate comparisons where p>0.10 when age is included as a covariate.
b. Tukey tests between groups, controlling for sex. EPG = early prehistoric Guale; LPG = late prehistoric Guale; EMG = early mission Guale; LMG = late mission Guale; EMY = early mission Yamasee.
†p<0.10; *p<0.05; **p<0.01; ***p<0.001; n.s. = not significant.

Guale groups (EPG to LPG) are in different directions, with femora declining in length slightly and humeri increasing in length more substantially (the latter near-significant except when age is included as a covariate). This almost certainly reflects sampling differences for the two bones (see table 5.1 and earlier discussion). However, on the whole, these results indicate that differences in body size between the groups are minor.

Cross-sectional properties standardized for body size, though, show some significant differences between groups (table 5.5). In general, variation in bending/torsional robusticity (J_{STD}) is greater than variation in axial robusticity (CA_{STD}). Group differences in J_{STD}, by sex, are illustrated graphically in figures 5.2–5.4. Among males, the greatest values of either CA_{STD} or J_{STD} in every cross section are found in the EPG group. There is then a decline in the LPG group, followed by an increase to intermediate values in the two Guale mission period samples (EMG and LMG). The Yamasee mission sample (EMY) is most similar to the LPG sample.

The pattern of variation for females shows some similarities to that of males but also some differences. In the female femur, declines between EPG and LPG groups are small, and the mission period Guale groups rather

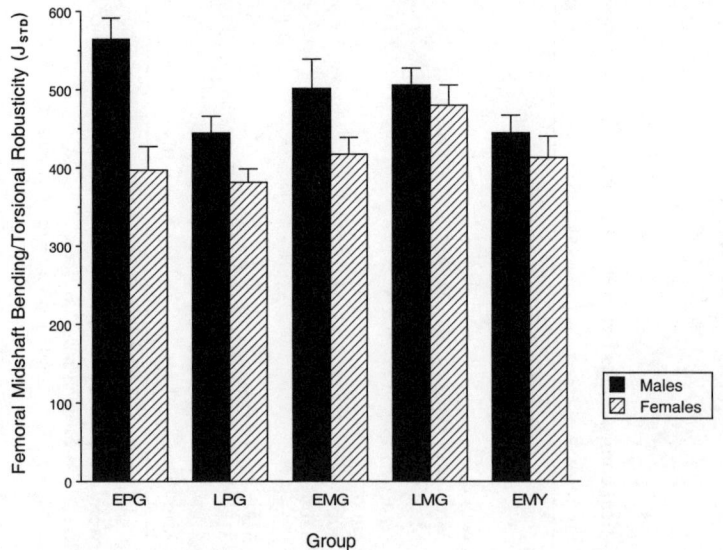

Fig. 5.2. Midshaft femoral J, standardized over body size (see table 5.2) for males and females from five cultural/temporal groups in La Florida; mean + 1 standard error. EPG = early prehistoric Guale; LPG = late prehistoric Guale; EMG = early mission Guale; LMG = late mission Guale; EMY = early mission Yamasee.

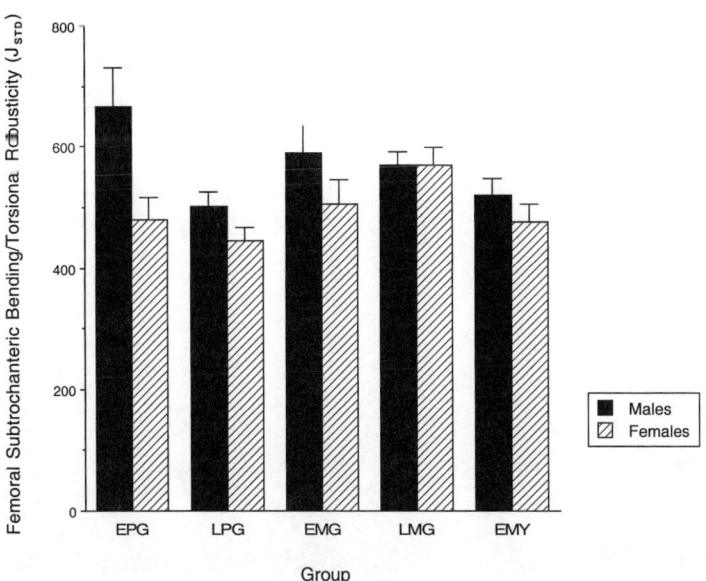

Fig. 5.3. Subtrochanteric femoral J, standardized over body size (see table 5.3) for males and females from five cultural/temporal groups in La Florida; mean + 1 standard error. See figure 5.2 for an explanation of abbreviations.

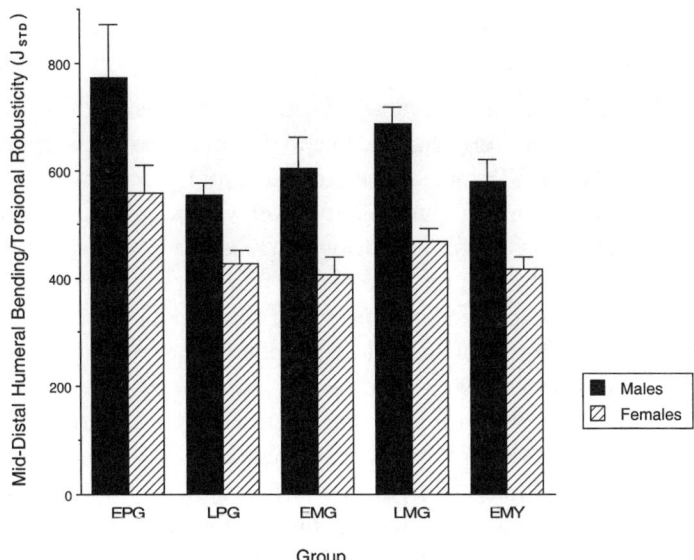

Fig. 5.4. Mid-distal humeral J, standardized over body size (see table 5.4) for males and females from five cultural/temporal groups in La Florida; mean + 1 standard error. See figure 5.2 for an explanation of abbreviations.

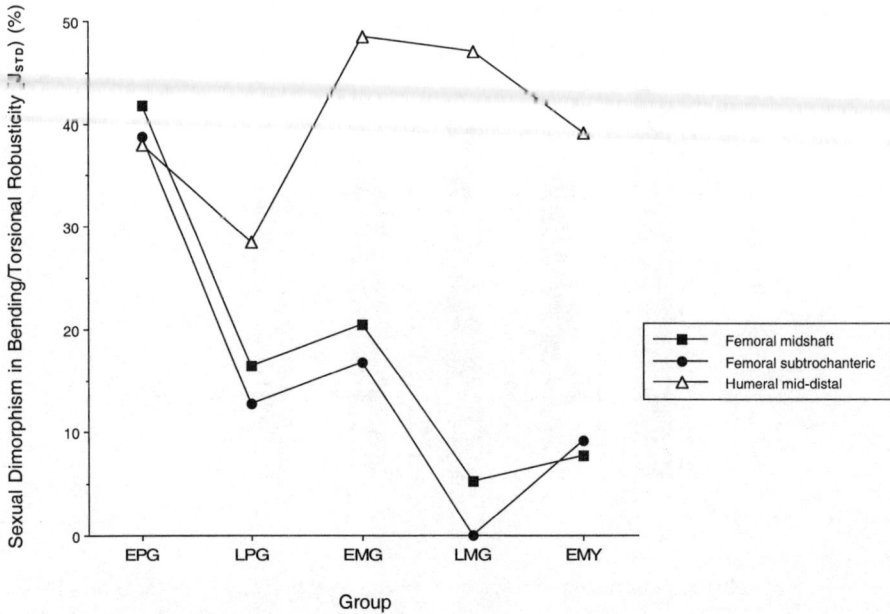

Fig. 5.5. Sexual dimorphism {[(Male – Female)/Female] × 100} in J, standardized over body size (see table 5.5) at three skeletal locations in cultural/temporal groups in La Florida. See figure 5.2 for an explanation of abbreviations.

than the EPG group are the most robust. In the humerus, the EPG group is the most robust among females, like males, and also declines greatly between EPG and LPG groups. However, humeral J_{STD} continues to decline in the EMG group among females and—even with a subsequent increase in the LMG group—remains well below the EPG group. Yamasee females are most similar to those in the LPG and EMG groups.

Because of these differences in intergroup variation among males and females, the degree of sexual dimorphism in femoral and humeral robusticity also varies between groups. Figure 5.5 plots percent sexual dimorphism in J_{STD} of the three section locations by cultural/temporal group. On the whole, males are more robust than females in all measures (table 5.5). However, sexual dimorphism in femoral J_{STD} declines greatly through time among the Guale groups, beginning at a high level in the EPG group and reaching its lowest level in the LMG group (fig. 5.5). Dimorphism in the Yamasee contact sample (EMY) is also quite low. In contrast, sexual dimorphism in humeral J_{STD} remains more constant, with no decline (and in fact, some increase) in the contact samples. The Yamasee sample is similar to the Guale contact groups. The same trends are characteristic of CA_{STD} (tables 5.2–5.4).

Another way to visualize these patterns is to plot the ratios of femoral to humeral cross-sectional properties in those individuals represented by matching pairs of bones. Both femur and humerus were analyzed for a total of 115 individuals in the sample—60 males and 55 females, not including one male in the Timucuan ossuary sample. Results must be treated with some caution, since sample sizes are small for some sex/cultural/temporal groupings (e.g., only four EPG males). However, the patterns of variation between groups in femoral midshaft/humeral mid-distal J, shown in figure 5.6, are quite consistent with those for the larger (but unmatched) samples shown in figure 5.5.[3] Males always have lower femoral/humeral ratios, probably reflecting the generally greater upper body strength of males (Bailey 1982; Jones and Round 1998). However, this difference becomes much more pronounced in the three mission samples, due to the increase in robusticity of the femur in females without a corresponding increase in their humeri (figs. 5.3, 5.4). One-way ANOVA within sex for the femoral/humeral ratio is near-significant in females ($p < 0.07$) as is the Tukey test

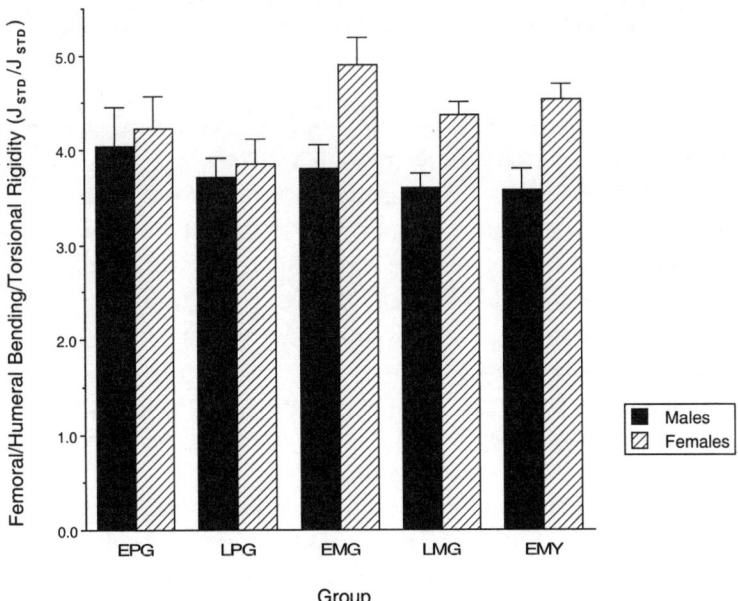

Fig. 5.6. Femoral midshaft/humeral mid-distal J for males and females from five cultural/temporal groups in La Florida; mean + 1 standard error. See figure 5.2 for an explanation of abbreviations.

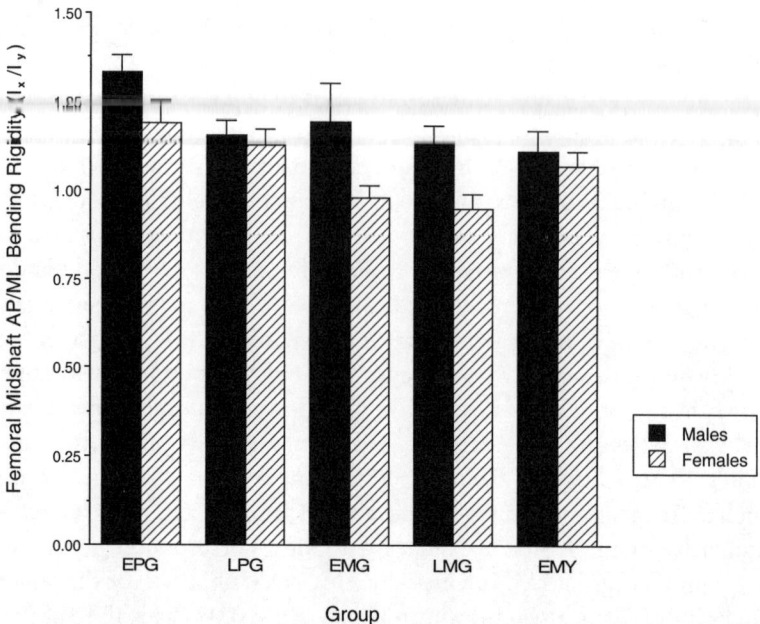

Fig. 5.7. Femoral midshaft I_x/I_y for males and females from five cultural/temporal groups in La Florida; mean + 1 standard error. See figure 5.2 for an explanation of abbreviations.

between LPG and EMG groups ($p < 0.06$); males show nonsignificant variation between groups in the ratio ($p > 0.70$).

Cross-sectional shape, as measured by ratios of perpendicular second moments of area, also shows significant variation, both between cultural/temporal groups and between the sexes (table 5.5). Group and sex-related differences in femoral midshaft I_x/I_y are highly significant ($p < 0.01$); these are illustrated graphically in figure 5.7. I_x/I_y values are greatest in the EPG group in both sexes. They subsequently decline in females through the succeeding three Guale groups; Yamasee females are most similar to LPG females. Males decline from EPG to LPG but then remain relatively constant, including the Yamasee group.

Sexual dimorphism in femoral midshaft shape varies greatly between cultural/temporal groups. This is illustrated in figure 5.8, which also places the current results within a broader comparative context. Sexual dimorphism in 12 other North American archaeological samples (Ruff 1999), arranged from highest to lowest, are plotted along with the five La Florida cultural/temporal groups. As shown previously (Ruff 1987, 1994, 1999), there is a marked decline in sexual dimorphism in femoral midshaft shape

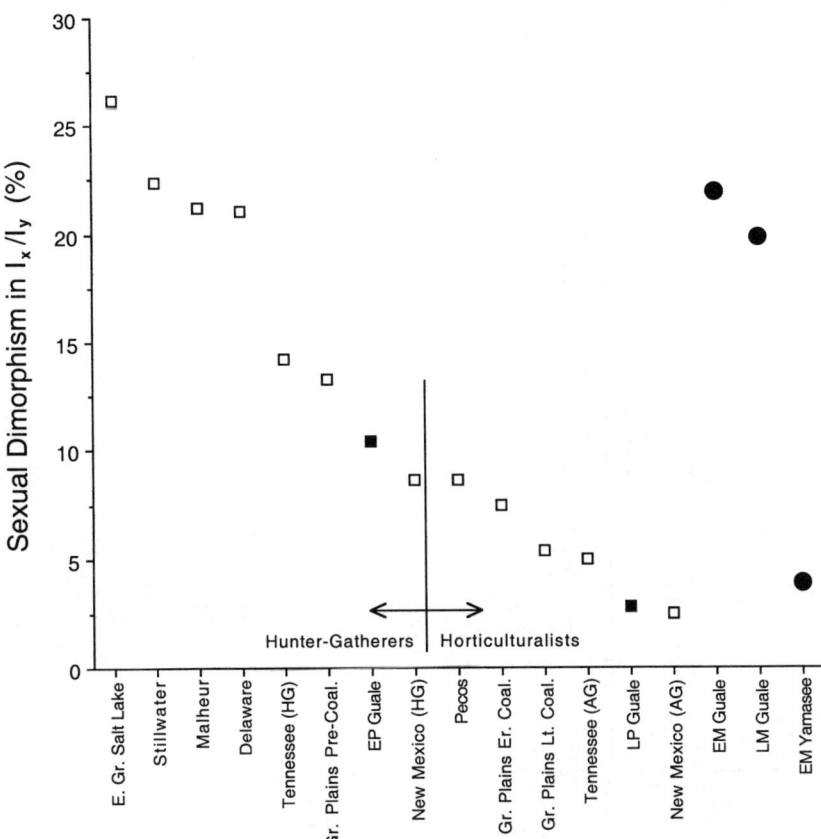

Fig. 5.8. Sexual dimorphism {[(Male – Female)/Female] × 100} in femoral midshaft I_x/I_y in five cultural/temporal groups in La Florida (filled symbols) and 12 other North American archaeological skeletal samples (open symbols). Three mission period La Florida samples are represented by larger circles. Comparative data from Ruff (1999). EP = early prehistoric; LP = late prehistoric; EM = early mission; LM = late mission; HG and AG = hunter-gatherer and agricultural, respectively, in paired samples from the same region; Coal. = coalescent; E, Er = early; L, Lt. = late.

from hunter-gatherers to horticulturalists, well illustrated in figure 5.8. The two pre-contact La Florida groups follow this same pattern, declining from EPG to LPG, and both fall within the ranges of their respective subsistence strategy categories. However, the two contact period Guale groups show a marked deviation from this pattern, with very high levels of sexual dimorphism in femoral midshaft shape, inconsistent with values for other horticultural groups (fig. 5.8). The Yamasee contact sample, though, is

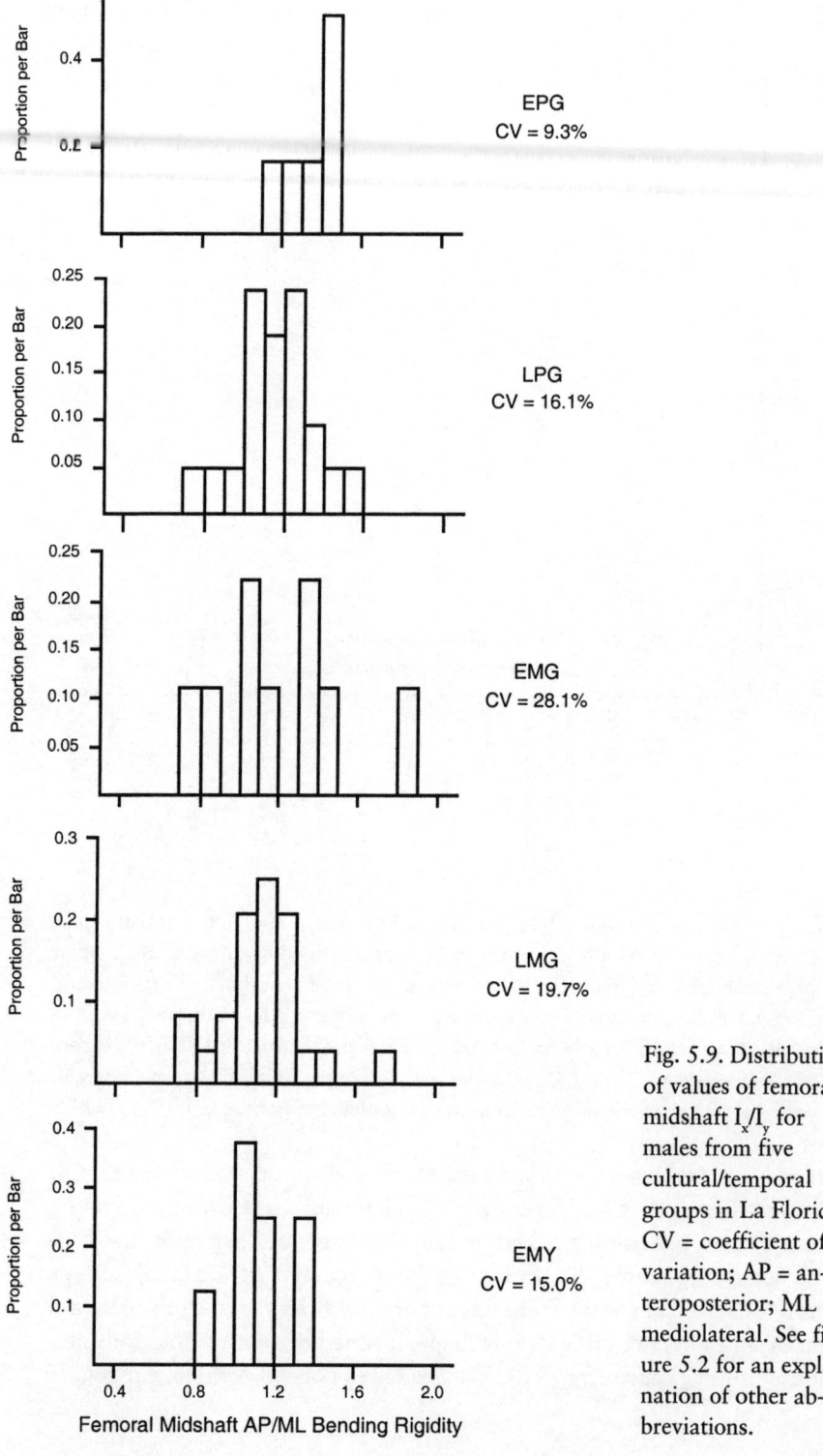

Fig. 5.9. Distribution of values of femoral midshaft I_x/I_y for males from five cultural/temporal groups in La Florida. CV = coefficient of variation; AP = anteroposterior; ML = mediolateral. See figure 5.2 for an explanation of other abbreviations.

similar in this respect to the pre-contact horticultural LPG group, with a low value.

A reason for the unusually high sexual dimorphism in femoral midshaft I_x/I_y in the EMG and LMG groups is suggested by consideration of ranges of variation within groups. It is apparent from the data summary (table 5.2) that the standard error for this property is particularly large among EMG males. A detailed consideration of data distributions for males in each of the cultural/temporal groups is shown in figure 5.9. The coefficient of variation (corrected for bias; Sokal and Rohlf 1981:59) for I_x/I_y is small in EPG males (9.3%), rises in LPG males (16.1%), and then rises dramatically in EMG males (28.1%). It then declines but remains high in LMG males. Yamasee males are similar to LPG males. It can be seen that the relatively high mean value of I_x/I_y for males in the two mission period Guale groups, particularly the EMG group (fig. 5.7), is largely due to the presence of positive outliers and greater data spread. In fact, while the majority of males in both groups fall at or below the mean for LPG males, both groups also have individuals who exceed any others in the entire study sample, including EPG males (fig. 5.9). As is further discussed later, these data indicate more variability in A-P/M-L loading of the femur among mission period Guale males than in other groups, which may be related to behavioral changes brought about by Spanish colonization. Yamasee males do

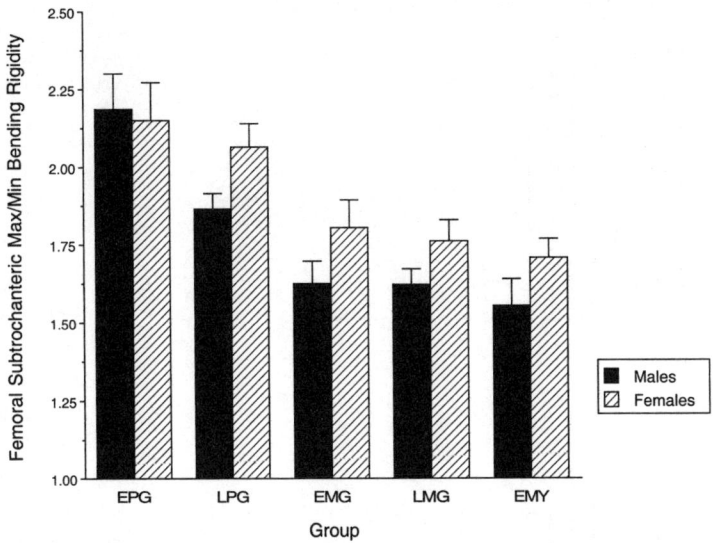

Fig. 5.10. Femoral subtrochanteric I_{max}/I_{min} for males and females from five cultural/temporal groups in La Florida. See figure 5.2 for an explanation of abbreviations.

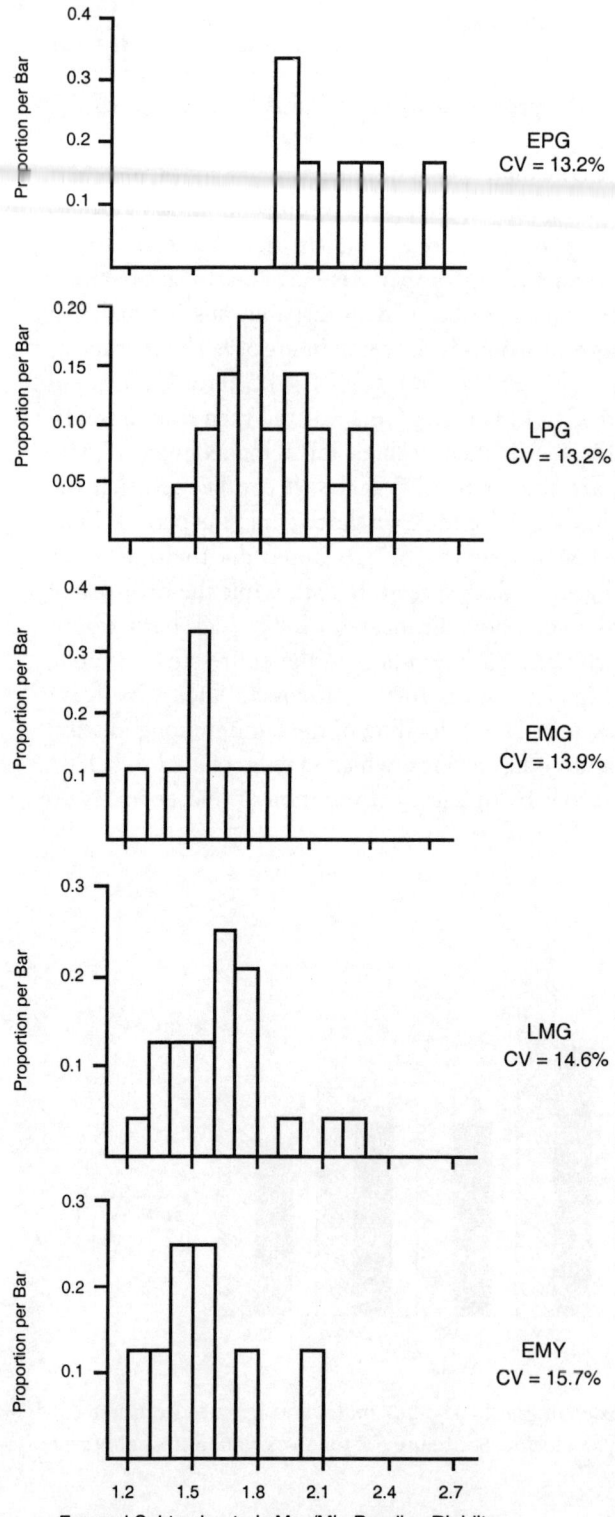

Fig. 5.11. Distribution of values of femoral midshaft I_{max}/I_{min} for males from five cultural/temporal groups in La Florida. CV = coefficient of variation; see figure 5.2 for an explanation of other abbreviations.

not show the same pattern, nor is sexual dimorphism among the Yamasee unusual for a horticultural group (figs. 5.8, 5.9), suggesting that they were not subject to the same behavioral changes as the two Guale mission groups.

Femoral subtrochanteric I_{max}/I_{min} also shows highly significant variation between cultural/temporal groups, as well as between the sexes (table 5.5). As illustrated in figure 5.10, both males and females show a similar marked decline from EPG through LPG to the mission period groups, all three of which are quite similar. On the whole females show larger I_{max}/I_{min} than males (table 5.5) and the degree of sexual dimorphism is relatively constant, except that males show slightly greater values than females in the EPG group (fig. 5.10). In broader comparative studies there is no relationship between subtrochanteric cross-sectional shape and subsistence strategy, most likely because this area of the femur, unlike the midshaft region, is most heavily influenced biomechanically by factors other than those related to behavior (i.e., rather, by intrinsic pelvic shape; Ruff 1995). As a further illustration of this difference between regions of the femur, data distributions for the same males shown for the femoral midshaft in figure 5.9 are plotted for the subtrochanteric section in figure 5.11. In contrast to

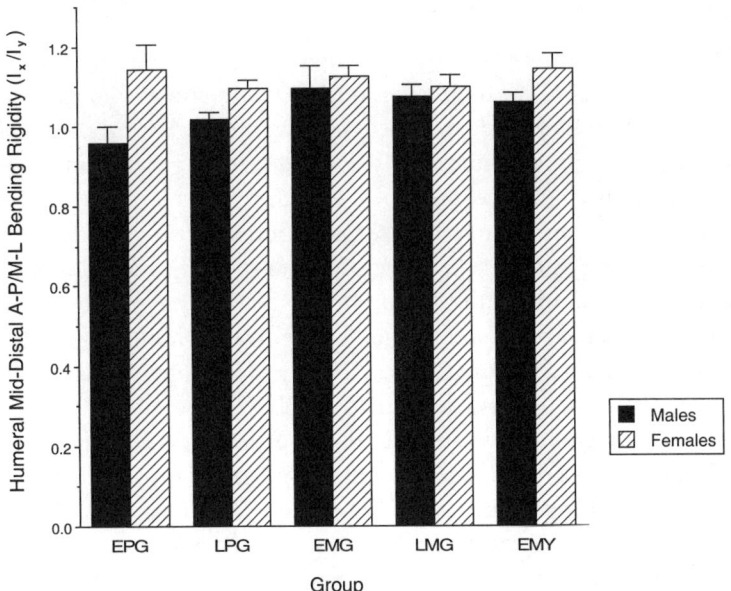

Fig. 5.12. Humeral mid-distal I_x/I_y for males and females from five cultural/temporal groups in La Florida; mean + 1 standard error. AP = anteroposterior; ML = mediolateral. See figure 5.2 for an explanation of abbreviations.

the midshaft, ranges of variation for the subtrochanteric region are similar in all cultural/temporal groups, with CVs (coefficient of variation) ranging only between 13.2 and 15.7 percent. This further highlights the specificity of mechanical loading effects in different regions of the femur, as would be expected theoretically (Ruff 1995, and see following discussion).

Cross-sectional shape of the mid-distal humerus shows no significant intergroup variation in two-way ANOVA (table 5.5). Group values for I_x/I_y, by sex, are plotted in figure 5.12. Males do show a near-significant increase in this index from the EPG through LPG to mission period groups (one-way ANOVA within sex), while females remain almost constant. Females are also greater in I_x/I_y than males in every cultural/temporal group, with the greatest degree of sexual dimorphism in the EPG group. As discussed later, the smaller values among males may be related to greater development (i.e., more proximal extension) of the flexor/extensor ridges of the distal humerus, which would tend to increase M-L second moments of area (and decrease I_x/I_y).

Discussion

Biomechanical Interpretations

These results demonstrate that there is significant variation in cross-sectional properties of the limb bones both between and within cultural/temporal groups in La Florida. Before discussing the behavioral significance of these differences, it is necessary to consider their general interpretation within a biomechanical context.

First, it is important to recognize that different cross-sectional structural properties have different meanings, depending on the nature of the property and the location of the section from which they are derived. Cortical area (CA) and the polar second moment of area (J) should reflect the *overall* level or magnitude of mechanical loading of a diaphyseal region. Second moments of area, because they reflect bending and torsional strength, are biomechanically more significant than cortical area, since the highest strains and most critical loadings in long bones occur in bending and torsion (Carter 1978; Nordin and Frankel 1980; Van Buskirk 1989). Therefore, patterns of variation in J are more critical in evaluating overall strength and robusticity and are emphasized here. When standardized by dividing by an appropriate measure of body size, structural properties should reflect the *relative* overall level of loading, factoring out differences in body size. Although the present study samples did not show statistically significant variation in body size (as assessed by bone length), it is still important to control for such differences if possible, within and between samples, in order to clarify non-body-size-related differences that should be more directly linked to behavioral differences. For example, analyses of variance between cultural/temporal groupings carried out using raw, non-standardized properties (CA and J) are nonsignificant for the femoral midshaft and humeral mid-distal locations (results not shown), while standardized properties show significant intergroup variation (table 5.5). Standardizing by a body size index also helps to control for possible biases—that is, nonrandom sampling. As shown earlier, the pattern of variation among groups in humeral and femoral lengths is slightly different, almost certainly due to sampling effects. Standardizing by powers of bone length negates these body size differences and allows trends in the upper and lower limbs to be considered together.

I_x/I_y and I_{max}/I_{min} should reflect the *types* of mechanical loadings (as opposed to overall levels) applied to a long bone during life, since they are measures of relative bending strength in different planes. I_x/I_y of the femoral midshaft is related to relative A-P bending loads in the region about the knee (from the mid-femur through the mid-tibia (Ruff 1987)). Sexual dimorphism in this index varies with subsistence economy, with the largest dimorphism in hunter-gatherers, reduced dimorphism in horticulturalists, and virtually no dimorphism in industrial societies (Ruff 1987). Because A-P bending of the knee region should increase during long-distance travel over rough terrain, greater values of midshaft femoral I_x/I_y should reflect greater long-distance mobility. The patterns observed in bone structure are consistent with ethnographic observations in which long-distance travel progressively declines in frequency among males (reducing sexual dimorphism) from hunter-gatherers through industrial societies (Ruff 1987). In contrast, cross-sectional shape of the femoral subtrochanteric region is less affected by loadings near the knee and more influenced by loadings about the hip joint, where M-L bending predominates (Ruff 1987, 1995). Thus, females almost always average greater values for subtrochanteric I_{max}/I_{min} than males, regardless of subsistence strategy, because they average greater distance between the hip joints (for obstetric reasons) and thus relatively greater M-L loading of this region (Ruff 1987). Subtrochanteric I_{max}/I_{min} is therefore *not* an index of long-distance mobility. However, it may, in part, reflect some behavioral differences. M-L loading of the hip region increases during one-legged support, as occurs during walking, and is much reduced during two-legged support. Thus, a higher frequency of relatively "static" activities in which loads are applied to the lower limb while standing on

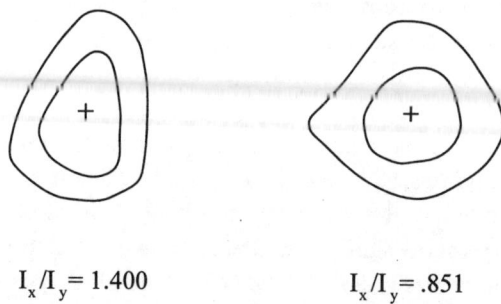

$$I_x/I_y = 1.400 \qquad\qquad I_x/I_y = .851$$

Fig. 5.13. Mid-distal humeral cross section outlines for two individuals from the Timucua ossuary (Amelia Island), demonstrating extremes in cross-sectional shape. Anterior is up, medial to the left.

both feet (e.g., during heavy lifting) would be expected to lead to reduced M-L bending of the proximal femur and a reduction in subtrochanteric I_{max}/I_{min}.

Cross-sectional shape of the humeral diaphysis is more difficult to interpret biomechanically, in part because the human upper limb is a non-locomotor organ subjected to a potentially greater variety of loadings. In addition, although the mid-distal humeral shaft is relatively round and removed from major muscle insertions such as the deltoid tuberosity, its shape may nevertheless be affected by the degree of proximal extension of the flexor and extensor ridges (partial origins of the forearm flexor and extensor muscles). Figure 5.13 shows two tracings of mid-distal humeral cross sections from the Timucuan ossuary samples, exhibiting the highest (1.400) and lowest (0.851) I_x/I_y indices in this sample. The section with the low index has obvious medial and lateral projections (particularly medial) that in the whole bone can be seen to reflect extensions of the flexor and extensor ridges, while these features are much reduced in the other bone. Flexion/extension of the shoulder and elbow, which would increase A-P bending of the humerus (and thus I_x), might often be accompanied by similar action of the forearm flexors and extensors during rigorous activity, promoting greater development of their origins on the medial and lateral margins of the humerus (and thus increases in I_y). Therefore, such activities could produce a confounding effect on mid-distal humeral cross-sectional shape, as measured by I_x/I_y. This highlights the complexity of mechanical loadings acting on the upper limb bones and the difficulty in attaching precise behavioral significance to structural variations. However, as a first approximation we have assumed here that greater similarity in cross-sectional size and shape in this region probably reflects greater similarity in use of the upper limb, even if that use is difficult to pinpoint exactly.

Differences Between and Within Cultural/Temporal Groups

Within this context, differences between the four Guale cultural/temporal groups are considered first. The Yamasee early mission group is then compared to the Guale. Finally, the pooled-sex Timucuan ossuary sample is compared to pooled-sex samples of the other groups.

Among male Guale, overall mechanical loading of both the upper and lower limbs was at a maximum in the hunter-gatherer EPG group, declined in the horticultural LPG group, and then increased again in the EMG and LMG contact groups. Among female Guale, overall lower limb loadings decreased only marginally from EPG to LPG but, as in males, increased in the two contact groups, while upper limb loadings decreased from EPG to LPG but, unlike in males, stayed low in the two contact groups. Behaviorally, these results indicate a greater change (reduction) in male locomotor activities with the transition to food production, which is consistent with ethnographic observations (see earlier discussion and Ruff 1987). Mechanical loading of the lower limb increased in both sexes after Spanish contact. This could be due to increased workload on native populations imposed by the Spanish, and/or increased relative (soft tissue) body weight brought about by greater sedentism and consumption of carbohydrates, also resulting from missionization (see Ruff and Larsen 1990; Larsen et al. 1996; Hutchinson et al. 1998). The method of body size standardizing used here relies by necessity on skeletal measurements only, so if there was a systematic increase in corpulence (body weight relative to stature) during the mission period, this would result in a systematic underestimation of body size and an overestimation of bone strength relative to body size. This explanation is consistent with the marked increase in circularity of the femoral subtrochanteric region in both sexes, which we have already argued may reflect more "static" loadings of the lower limbs, including static loads imposed by relatively greater body weight. The lack of change in the upper limb in females is also concordant, as increased relative body weight would not affect the upper limb. The greater difference in the effect of Spanish missionization on the upper and lower limbs in females may in fact argue for greater sedentism among mission females and possibly for greater relative weight gain.

Evidence from femoral midshaft shape also indicates that mission period females became generally less mobile. However, males on average did not. Mission period males also show clear evidence for greater variation in femoral midshaft shape and thus in relative long-range mobility. As discussed elsewhere (Ruff and Larsen 1990), historical records indicate that some Guale males were pressed into service by the Spanish under the repartimiento labor system and were forced into making periodic long-distance trips to St. Augustine and other locations (see also Larsen 1990). The structural data suggest that this may have affected only a portion of the male population, with other males remaining at the mission, resulting in the wide range of variation. This also produced the highly unusual (for a non-hunter-gatherer society) sexual dimorphism in mobility characteristic of these groups. Interestingly, though, sexual dimorphism in overall *level,* not type of mechanical loading of the lower limb, decreased in the mission period groups, emphasizing again the specificity of loading effects on different structural properties.[4]

The upper limb shows a different pattern of change in mission period groups, becoming more sexually dimorphic in overall robusticity but remaining unchanged in terms of cross-sectional shape from the late prehistoric group. It is possible that workload on the upper limb increased in mission period males more than in females (e.g., carrying heavy loads). The only indication of a change in type of activity (cross-sectional shape) involving the upper limb is between EPG and LPG males, perhaps related to generally greater behavioral changes occurring at the food production transition among males (Ruff 1987).

The Yamasee early mission sample is interesting in that in many respects it is more similar to the late *pre*-mission Guale group (LPG) than the mission period Guale or is intermediate between this group and the EMG group. In particular, sexual dimorphism and variation among males in long-range mobility are not increased in the Yamasee but rather fall comfortably within the range for horticultural Native Americans (including LPG). This strongly suggests that Yamasee males, unlike Guale males, were not being forced into service as long-range travelers by the Spanish, an interpretation that is consistent with historic evidence that the Yamasee were less acculturated during the mission period (see Worth 1995). In terms of overall limb bone robusticity, the Yamasee also group more closely with late pre-mission rather than mission Guale, or show intermediate values, again suggesting less behavioral modification; that is, smaller increases in workload and/or relative weight gain. One aspect in which Yamasee are most similar to the two mission period Guale groups is in femoral subtrochanteric cross-sectional shape. This appears to indicate more static loading of the lower limbs among the Yamasee, which could be associated with some behavioral changes including tasks such as heavy lifting or other activities involving two-legged support. Also, sexual dimorphism in femoral/humeral robusticity (with the humerus showing more dimorphism than the femur) is similar in the Yamasee and the two Guale mission groups. Thus, there is some evidence for alterations of behavior among the mission period Yamasee, although not to the same extent as among Guale from the same period. Interpretation of the Yamasee results would be greatly aided by more temporal depth (availability of pre- as well as post-mission Yamasee samples), so that direct assessment of the effects of contact on this culture could be carried out.

Interestingly, there is evidence from other skeletal analyses that the Yamasee were less affected by Spanish contact than the Guale. Stable isotope analysis has documented an increase in reliance on maize among native populations during the mission period as well as a general convergence in diet (Hutchinson et al. 1998; Larsen et al. this volume). However, separate analysis of the Santa Maria de Yamasee sample (n = 7) and the contemporary Santa Catalina de Guale sample (n = 22), obtained from Larsen et al., this study, indicates that both carbon and nitrogen stable isotope values differ significantly (p < 0.05, t-tests) between these samples, with the Yamasee sample lower in $\delta^{13}C$ and higher in $\delta^{15}N$. This indicates that the Yamasee relied less on maize and more on marine resources than the contemporary Guale. In fact, in a summary figure of $\delta^{13}C$ and $\delta^{15}N$ values (Hutchinson et al. 1998: fig. 7), the Yamasee would fall about midway between the Santa Catalina de Guale sample and a Georgia late prehistoric sample that was equivalent to the LPG sample in the present study, including many of the same sites. Thus, the dietary and biomechanical results are concordant, and both support the conclusion that the Yamasee were less acculturated by the Spanish than were the Guale during this period (A.D. 1600–1680).

Results for the Timucuan ossuary sample must be treated cautiously, since the exact sex composition of this sample is unknown, and sex was seen to be an important influence on biomechanical properties in the other samples. However, comparisons of pooled-sex values for this sample with the pooled-sex values for the other five groups indicate that the Timucua had robust femora—above or near the highest values for CA_{STD} and J_{STD} found in the other pooled-sex groups—while humeri were not as strong (tables 5.2–5.4). The data for the femora are particularly impressive, given that the Timucua sample is likely biased toward females, and females had smaller values of CA_{STD} and J_{STD} than males in the other samples. In terms of femoral and humeral cross-sectional shape, the EMT sample is similar to the two Guale mission groups, especially the contemporary EMG group.

Thus, in many respects the Timucua sample appears to mirror the two Guale mission samples in morphology and presumably behavior.

There is one other morphological feature of the femur that is not strictly "structural" in the sense that cross-sectional data are but that nevertheless follows an interesting pattern of variation between the La Florida cultural/temporal groups. This is the anteversion (or antetorsion) angle of the femoral neck, the degree to which the femoral head and neck project anteriorly from the coronal plane established by the femoral condyles. This angle has commonly been found to be high in Native Americans and lower in other racial groups (Stewart 1962); for example, the Pecos Pueblo sample has an average angle of 23° (Ruff and Hayes 1983), while non–Native Americans average 7–14° (Elftman 1945; Kingsley and Olmsted 1948; Hoaglund and Low 1980; Reikeras et al. 1982 and references therein). The anteversion angle of the pre-contact EPG and LPG groups in the present study averages 22.3° and 25.5°, respectively, following the Native American morphology. However, average values for the EMG and LMG groups are much lower, 15.6° and 13.8°, respectively. The EMT group is also relatively low, 15.6°, while the EMY group is intermediate, 19.1°. Thus, these patterns of variation parallel those observed in other features of the femur, in which the two Guale mission groups depart from the Guale pre-mission groups; the Timucua are similar to the Guale mission groups; and the Yamasee are intermediate between Guale pre- and post-mission.[5]

There are, in fact, low but significant ($p < 0.05$) correlations between anteversion angle, cross-sectional shape, and cross-sectional robusticity of the femur in the study sample, with rounder but more robust shafts being associated with lower angles. The precise functional significance of this finding is uncertain, although higher angles have been found in children and adolescents with various clinical abnormalities that result in reduced loading of the hip, such as poliomyelitis (Rogers 1934; Morscher 1967). Thus, an overall increase in lower limb loading, but particularly an increase in static loading (e.g., manual labor involving lifting, pushing, and carrying over short distances), may account for the changes in the femur seen in the mission period Guale and Timucua (see discussion in Larsen 1990). In any event, both the increased roundness of the femoral shaft and the reduction in anteversion angle in the mission period samples contribute to a less typically Native American morphology and a convergence with Euroamerican femoral shape (see Ruff and Hayes 1983: table 5). To the extent that this is a result of bone plasticity during growth and development, it may reflect a shift among native populations to a more Euroamerican overall behavioral pattern during the mission period.

Conclusions

Analysis of long bone structural characteristics documents significant temporal and cultural differences in behavior among native populations in La Florida. Early prehistoric hunter-gatherers from the region were robust and showed marked sexual dimorphism in behavior, in particular more long-distance traveling by males, consistent with patterns for hunter-gatherers from other regions. With the adoption of food production at about A.D. 1000, overall level of physical activity declined, and sexual dimorphism in behavior declined, the latter also consistent with trends in other regions of North America. Spanish contact had by A.D. 1600 brought major changes in behavior and possibly body form in the Guale. In general, they became more sedentary, except for a subset of the males, who were forced into making long-distance journeys. For most of the population there is evidence of an increase in relatively static work, such as tasks requiring lifting, pushing and short-distance carrying, possibly along with greater relative body weight, the latter due to increased consumption of carbohydrates. There is also evidence that Spanish contact did not affect all native populations equally. The contemporaneous Yamasee show fewer effects of missionization and in some respects are more similar to late prehistoric than to contact period Guale. This finding is also supported by comparisons of stable isotope data, which indicate that Yamasee are intermediate between pre- and post-mission Guale in terms of diet. In contrast, the Timucua appear to have been as much influenced by Spanish contact as the Guale. Overall, mission period native populations (except for the Yamasee) take on a more typically Euroamerican appearance in terms of bone structure, which may reflect more typically Euroamerican behavioral patterns. The plasticity of long bone geometry in this sense, and its sensitivity to changes in mechanical stimuli, is remarkable.

La Florida is the best studied region in the world in terms of numbers of individuals analyzed using biomechanical techniques. The size of this sample and its excellent archaeological and historic context allow comparisons between bone structural and cultural transitions that help to shed light on both processes. In this sense, it can serve as a model for similar analyses in other regions. Broader multiregional comparisons of prehistoric Native American populations have been carried out (e.g., Ruff 1999); as more data on early historic samples are gathered, it will be interesting to see how the effects of European contact documented here compare to those in other regions of the New World.

Acknowledgments

The collection of data included in this chapter was supported by the St. Catherines Island Foundation and several research grants from the National Science Foundation. We thank the various curators and their institutions for permission to study the skeletons under their care and to undertake the analyses described: David Hurst Thomas (American Museum of Natural History), Douglas Ubelaker and Donald Ortner (Smithsonian Institution), Jerald Milanich (Florida Museum of Natural History), and James Miller, Bonnie McEwan, and David Dickel (Florida Bureau of Archaeological Research).

Notes

1. This is a slight modification of the method used to orient humeri in earlier studies (Ruff and Larsen 1990), in which the trochlear-capitular axis rather than the distal shaft A-P midpoint was used in leveling. The effect on humeral position and cross-sectional properties is negligible.

2. Although human upper limb bones are not usually used for support of body mass, they have been shown to scale allometrically in a way similar to that for lower limb bones (Ruff 1999, 2000b).

3. It is not necessary to standardize cross-sectional properties by body size here, because the data are already matched for body size (i.e., ratios are intra-individual). Within sex, femoral and humeral J are isometric (in log-log regressions slopes are not significantly different from 1.0). Thus ratios should not be biased by allometric scaling effects.

4. In the study sample as a whole, measures of overall robusticity (J_{STD}) are not correlated or are only weakly correlated with measures of cross-sectional shape (I_x/I_y and I_{max}/I_{min}); the same is true between shape of the femoral midshaft and the subtrochanteric regions.

5. The cervicodiaphyseal or "neck-shaft" angle does not vary significantly between groups when differences in anteversion angle are taken into account (Trinkaus 1993).

References Cited

Bailey, S. M. 1982. Absolute and Relative Sex Differences in Body Composition. In *Sexual Dimorphism in Homo Sapiens,* ed. R. L. Hall, 363–90. New York: Praeger.

Bridges, P. S. 1995. Skeletal Biology and Behavior in Ancient Humans. *Evolutionary Anthropology* 4:112–20.

Carter, D. R. 1978. Anisotropic Analysis of Strain Rosette Information from Cortical Bone. *Journal of Biomechanics* 11:199–202.

Elftman, H. 1945. Torsion of the Lower Extremity. *American Journal of Physical Anthropology* 3:255–65.

Fresla, A., C. B. Ruff, and C. S. Laruvu. 1990. Temporal Decline in Bilateral Asymmetry of the Upper Limb on the Georgia Coast. In *The Archaeology of Mission Santa Catalina de Guale, 2: Biocultural Interpretations of a Population in Transition*, ed. C. S. Larsen, 121–32. Anthropological Papers of the American Museum of Natural History 68.

Hoaglund, F. T., and W. D. Low. 1980. Anatomy of the Femoral Neck and Head, with Comparative Data from Caucasians and Hong Kong Chinese. *Clinical Orthopaedics* 152:10–16.

Huiskes, R. 1982. On the Modelling of Long Bones in Structural Analysis. *Journal of Biomechanics* 15:65–69.

Hutchinson, D. L., C. S. Larsen, M. J. Schoeninger, and L. Norr. 1998. Regional Variation in the Pattern of Maize Adoption and Use in Florida and Georgia. *American Antiquity* 63:397–416.

Jones, D. A., and J. M. Round. 1998. Human Skeletal Muscle across the Lifespan. In *The Cambridge Encyclopedia of Human Growth and Development*, ed. S. J. Ulijaszek, F. E. Johnston, and M. A. Preece, 202–5. Cambridge: Cambridge University Press.

Kingsley, P. C., and K. L. Olmsted. 1948. A Study to Determine the Angle of Anteversion of the Neck of the Femur. *Journal of Bone and Joint Surgery* 30-A:745–51.

Klenerman, L., S.A.V. Swanson, and M.A.R. Freeman. 1967. A Method for the Clinical Estimation of the Strength of a Bone. *Proceedings of the Royal Society of Medicine* 60:10–14.

Larsen, C. S. 1990. Biological Interpretation and the Context for Contact. In *The Archaeology of Mission Santa Catalina de Guale: 2. Biocultural Interpretations of a Population in Transition*, ed. C. S. Larsen, 11–25. Anthropological Papers of the American Museum of Natural History 68.

Larsen, C. S., and C. B. Ruff. 1994. The Stresses of Conquest in Spanish Florida: Structural Adaptation and Change Before and After Conquest. In *In the Wake of Contact: Biological Responses to Conquest*, ed. C. S. Larsen and G. R. Milner, 21–34. New York: Wiley-Liss.

Larsen, C. S., C. B. Ruff, and M. C. Griffin. 1996. Implications of Changing Biomechanical and Nutritional Environments for Activity and Lifeway in the Eastern Spanish Borderlands. In *Bioarchaeology of Native American Adaptation in the Spanish Borderlands*, ed. B. J. Baker and L. Kealhofer, 95–125. Gainesville: University Press of Florida.

Lovejoy, C. O., A. H. Burstein, and K. G. Heiple. 1976. The Biomechanical Analysis of Bone Strength: A Method and Its Application to Platycnemia. *American Journal of Physical Anthropology* 44:489–506.

Morscher, E. 1967. Development and Clinical Significance of the Anteversion of the Femoral Neck. *Reconstructive Surgery and Traumatology* 9:107–25.

Nagurka, M. L., and W. C. Hayes. 1980. An Interactive Graphics Package for Calculating Cross-Sectional Properties of Complex Shapes. *Journal of Biomechanics* 13:59 61.

Nordin, M., and V. H. Frankel. 1980. Biomechanics of Whole Bones and Bone Tissue. In *Basic Biomechanics of the Skeletal System*, ed. V. H. Frankel and M. Nordin, 15–60. Philadelphia: Lea and Febiger.

Reikeras, O., A. Hoiseth, A. Reigstad, and E. Fönstlielen. 1982. Femoral Neck Angles: A Specimen Study with Special Regard to Bilateral Differences. *Acta Orthopaedica Scandinavica* 53:775–79.

Rogers, S. P. 1934. Observations on Torsion of the Femur. *Journal of Bone and Joint Surgery* 16:284–89.

Ruff, C. B. 1987. Sexual Dimorphism in Human Lower Limb Bone Structure: Relationship to Subsistence Strategy and Sexual Division of Labor. *Journal of Human Evolution* 16:391–416.

———. 1989. New Approaches to Structural Evolution of Limb Bones in Primates. *Folia Primatologica* 53:142–59.

———. 1994. Biomechanical Analysis of Northern and Southern Plains Femora: Behavioral Implications. In *Skeletal Biology in the Great Plains: A Multidisciplinary View,* ed. D. W. Owsley and R. L. Jantz, 235–45. Washington: Smithsonian Institution Press.

———. 1995. Biomechanics of the Hip and Birth in Early *Homo. American Journal of Physical Anthropology* 98:527–74.

———. 1999. Skeletal Structure and Behavioral Patterns of Prehistoric Great Basin Populations. In *Understanding Prehistoric Lifeways in Great Basin Wetlands: Bioarchaeological Reconstruction and Interpretation,* ed. B. E. Hemphill and C. S. Larsen, 290–320. Salt Lake City: University of Utah Press.

———. 2000a. Biomechanical Analyses of Archaeological Human Skeletal Samples. In *Biological Anthropology of the Human Skeleton*, ed. M. A. Katzenberg and S. R. Saunders, 71–102. New York: Wiley-Liss.

———. 2000b. Body Size, Body Shape, and Long Bone Strength in Modern Humans. *Journal of Human Evolution* 38:269–90.

Ruff, C. B., and W. C. Hayes. 1983. Cross-Sectional Geometry of Pecos Pueblo Femora and Tibiae: A Biomechanical Investigation: pt. 1. Method and General Patterns of Variation. *American Journal of Physical Anthropology* 60:359–81.

Ruff, C. B., and C. S. Larsen. 1990. Postcranial Biomechanical Adaptations to Subsistence Changes on the Georgia Coast. In *The Archaeology of Mission Santa Catalina de Guale: 2. Biocultural Interpretations of a Population in Transition*, ed. C. S. Larsen, 94–120. Anthropological Papers of the American Museum of Natural History 68.

Ruff, C. B., C. S. Larsen, and W. C. Hayes. 1984. Structural Changes in the Femur with the Transition to Agriculture on the Georgia Coast. *American Journal of Physical Anthropology* 64:125–36.

Sokal, R. R., and F. J. Rohlf. 1981. *Biometry.* New York: W. H. Freeman.

Stewart, T. D. 1962. Anterior Femoral Curvature: Its Utility for Race Identification. *Human Biology* 34:49–62.

SYSTAT: Statistics, V.E. 1992. SYSTAT, Inc., Evanston, Ill.

Timoshenko, S. P., and J. M. Gere. 1972. *Mechanics of Materials*. New York: Van Nostrand Reinhold.

Trinkaus, E. 1993. Femoral Neck-Shaft Angles of the Quafzeh-Skhul Early Modern Humans, and Activity Levels among Immature Near Eastern Middle Paleolithic Hominids. *Journal of Human Evolution* 25:393–416.

Trinkaus, E., S. E. Churchill, and C. B. Ruff. 1994. Postcranial Robusticity in *Homo*: pt. 2. Humeral Bilateral Asymmetry and Bone Plasticity. *American Journal of Physical Anthropology* 93:1–34.

Ubelaker, D. H. 1989. *Human Skeletal Remains: Excavation, Analysis, Interpretation.* 2d ed. Washington: Taraxacum.

Van Buskirk, W. C. 1989. Elementary Stress Analysis of the Femur and Tibia. In *Bone Mechanics,* ed. S. C. Cowin, 43–51. Boca Raton, Fla.: CRC Press.

Worth, J. E. 1995. *The Struggle for the Georgia Coast: An Eighteenth-Century Spanish Retrospective on Guale and Mocama.* Anthropological Papers of the American Museum of Natural History 75.

6

Patterns of Growth Disruption in La Florida

Evidence from Enamel Microstructure

Scott W. Simpson

The reconstruction of the health of past populations depends to a large degree on analyses of the hard tissues. These studies examine the frequency, distribution, and age of occurrence of pathology, providing population and demographic evidence for morbidity and mortality. Therefore, research has focused not on how healthy but on how sick a population was. Demographically, humans tend to be at an increased risk of sickness and death in their earliest years. Populations able to mitigate these stressors during this time with a resulting increase in survivorship are biologically successful. Therefore, many human biologists have attempted to reconstruct and explain the patterning of morbidity and death in the earliest years.

The last 2,000 years have seen significant changes in the subsistence patterns and social organization of Native Americans. At the beginning of that period in the southeastern United States, the Native Americans were primarily foragers (Larsen 1982), although some domesticated plants were harvested. Around A.D. 1000 or so, the economic base had a greater emphasis on agriculture, especially maize, with a concomitant change in local population densities and an increase in sedentism (Larsen 1982). During the 16th through early 18th centuries, the Spanish maintained a series of religious missions and military garrisons throughout the southeastern United States and Latin America. The well-established indigenous populations became the focus of the Spanish missionaries' activities, resulting in displacement or extinction of the local groups or their conversion to Catholicism. The displacement and deterioration of health in the Native Americans has been thoroughly documented both historically and archaeologically. The focus of this study is to document further the health changes that occurred in the native populations between approximately

A.D. 1 and 1704 due to evolutionary changes in the pre-contact subsistence base and the revolutionary changes resulting from European missionization. A review of the history of Spanish colonization and the subsequent archaeological research in the southeastern United States is provided by Larsen (this volume; and see Larsen 1990, 1993; Worth, this volume).

The approach adopted here is to examine the pattern and developmental timing of defects in dental enamel. Although innumerable studies have examined enamel surface defects, fewer earlier studies have focused on enamel microdefects or pathological striae of Retzius, also known as accentuated striae of Retzius, "Wilson Bands," or internal hypoplasia (Schour and Kronfeld 1938; Gustafson 1959; Boyde 1963; Watson et al. 1964; Johnson et al. 1965; Wilson and Schroff 1970; Rose 1977, 1979; Goodman et al. 1980; Condon 1981; Condon and Rose 1992; Rudney 1983; Goodman and Rose 1990; Wright 1990; Suga 1992). In longitudinal sections of teeth, striae of Retzius are optical phenomena seen as brown lines radiating from the dentino-enamel junction to the external surface of the tooth, best seen in the superficial portions of the crown. These striae are also visible with the scanning electron microscope (SEM) on acid-etched specimens, supporting the contention that local differences in enamel matrix mineralization exist. Normally, no differences in prism structure are visible at the Retzius lines. Along the outer margins of the longitudinal crown sections, normal Retzius striae can be seen because the prisms are offset, presenting a stair-step appearance (Gustafson 1959; Weber et al. 1974; Risnes 1986, 1990, 1998). Thus, Retzius lines have both an optical and morphological definition throughout their length. Each line represents an enamel matrix deposition growth front, or instant in time, where the ameloblasts of different ages respond concurrently and similarly to undetermined systemic phenomena. Current research suggests that about one week separates adjacent Retzius striae as calculated by counting prismatic varicosities; each line is thought to represent one day's amount of growth (Dean 1987 and citations therein; FitzGerald 1998), although it commonly spans between six and nine varicosities.

The structure of pathological striae of Retzius (PS) has been described and categorized by various authors (Schour 1936; Schour and Kronfeld 1938; Weber and Eisenmann 1971; Rose 1977, 1979; Rose et al. 1978; Whittaker and Richards 1978; Marks 1992), all of whom note irregular enamel prism microstructure as the defining characteristic. Sognnaes (1956), Wilson and Schroff (1970), and Weber and Eisenmann (1971) observed that a local thickening of the prismatic sheaths produced constriction and apparent bending of the individual enamel prisms. Whittaker

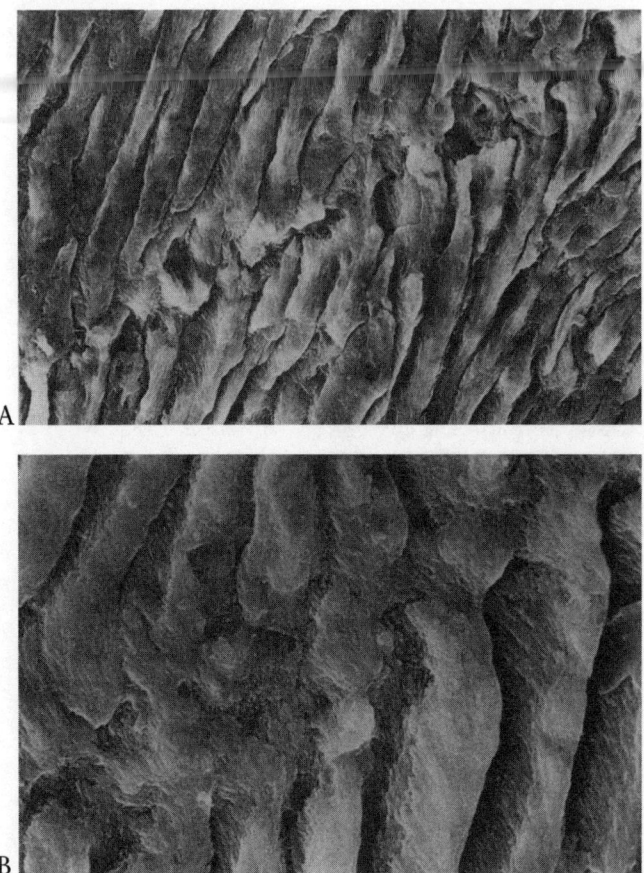

Fig. 6.1. Scanning electron micrographs of pathological enamel. A: Santa Catalina de Amelia (SM-6A1), mandibular right canine, 1200×. B: Santa Catalina de Amelia (SM-6A1), mandibular right canine, 2700×.

and Richards (1978), in an SEM study of "neonatal line" enamel structure, noted that it was a clearly defined interruption of the enamel prisms approximately 0.2 microns wide. On the postnatal side of the defect, they identified a 15- to 16-micron diffuse zone where the prisms seemed to be less tightly packed, with an increase in interprismatic substance with a total span of about 16 microns.

The definitions of pathological striae by Rose (1977, 1979) and Marks (1992) are the most useful and rely on abnormality of prism structure. Optically, the prisms appear bent, disrupted, or have a prismatic constriction due perhaps to an increase in the interprismatic substance. In extreme examples of enamel disruption, the apatite crystals lose their characteristic orientation (fig. 6.1) and crystallites from adjacent prisms become intimately associated (or "smudged" [Marks 1992]), rendering prism boundaries difficult to identify. Clearly, these latter observations can best be seen with an electron microscope. The graded range of morphology undoubtedly reflects the graded response ameloblasts have to metabolic disruption. Practically, a set of subjective morphological criteria for the identification of pathological striae can be adopted for a study and can produce internally consistent results. Different researchers may adopt different morphological criteria, or "thresholds," producing results that may differ slightly in detail but agree in principle (Rose et al. 1985; Goodman et al. 1992).

The factors producing microdefects are still unknown. Schour (1936) concluded that "neonatal lines" were due to unspecified metabolic disturbances ("neonatal trauma") occurring during birth. Subsequent studies have suggested that other factors may also produce abnormal enamel: vitamin deficiencies, toxemia during pregnancy, and a variety of viral and bacterial infections (Sheldon et al. 1945); elevated cortisol levels (Rose and Pasley 1980); crowding (Rose and Pasley 1980); hypoxia (Via et al. 1959; Grahnen et al. 1969; Johnsen et al. 1984; Brook et al. 1997); and mixed hypoxia and dehydration (Simpson 1999). Prominent striae of Retzius have also been studied in wild and extinct primates to explore patterns of seasonality and adaptation (Macho et al. 1996; Reid and Dirks 1997).

Materials and Methods

A series of mandibular canine teeth were collected from prehistoric pre-contact (pre–A.D. 1600) and post-Spanish contact (A.D. 1600–1700) archaeological sites from northern Florida (table 6.1). The prehistoric samples were divided into two groups: Florida Early Prehistoric, A.D. 0–1000 (Mayport, McKeithen, Melton, and Wacahoota mounds), and Florida Late Prehistoric, A.D. 1000–1600 (Browne Mound; Holy Spirit Church; Lake Jackson; and Goodman Mound). The post-contact sites were divided into two main categories: Florida Early Mission, A.D. 1600–1680 (Santa Maria de Yamasee [?–1683]; San Martín de Timucua [1608–1656]; San Pedro y San Pablo de Patale [1633–1647]), and Florida Late Mission, A.D. 1680–1700 (San Luis de Apalachee [1633–1704]; Santa Catalina de Amelia). An additional category, Florida Contact, Non-Mission (the ossuary at Santa Catalina de Amelia, Amelia Island) is identified here. Data for the Georgia coastal skeletal remains discussed in other chapters are not yet available.

Table 6.1. Sample composition and distribution of pathological striae

Site	Individuals (N)	No. with PS	PS per sample	% affected[a]	PS per tooth[b]	PS per pop.[c]
Early prehistoric						
Mayport Mound	7	5	9	71	1.8	1.3
McKeithen Mounds	3	2	4	67	2.0	1.3
Melton Mounds	4	2	4	50	2.0	1.0
Wacahoota Mound	1	1	1	100	1.0	1.0
Total	15	10	18	67	1.8	1.2
Late prehistoric						
Holy Spirit Church	14	2	7	14	3.5	0.5
Browne Mound	6	4	12	67	3.0	2.0
Goodman Mound	1	0	0	0	0.0	0.0
Lake Jackson	4	3	4	75	1.3	1.0
Total	25	9	23	36	2.6	0.9
Prehistoric total	40	19	41	48	2.2	1.0
Early contact (nonmission)						
Ossuary	26	14	24	54	1.7	0.9
Early mission						
Santa Maria de Yamasee	30	24	43	80	1.8	1.4
San Pedro de Patele	3	3	10	100	3.3	3.3
San Martín de Timucua	27	23	70	85	3.0	2.6
Total	60	50	123	83	2.5	2.1
Late mission						
Santa Catalina de Amelia	8	8	20	100	2.5	2.5
San Luis de Apalachee	9	6	20	67	3.3	2.2
Total	17	14	40	82	2.9	2.4
Mission total	77	64	163	83	2.5	2.1
Sample totals	143	97	228	68	2.4	1.6

a. Percentage of individuals in a sample with at least one PS.
b. Number of PS per tooth in those teeth demonstrating PS.
c. Number of PS in a sample divided by the total number of teeth in that sample; measure of population rate of morbidity.

Most of the post-contact skeletal material was recovered from a mission settlement characterized by supine burial posture with European grave goods in or adjacent to a church, although the ossuary at Amelia Island differs in pattern of interment. Although undeniably from a post-contact setting, the commingled human skeletons, which are buried in a large square pit overlying a coffin containing two individuals, antedate both the immediately adjacent Santa Maria de Yamasee and Santa Catalina de

Amelia missions (Simmons et al. 1989; Larsen 1993). The unusual burial practice of multiple individuals in various states of disassembly suggests that the remains originated from a charnel house and were relocated to this site. The population affiliation is unclear, but it has been proposed that these individuals were Timucuan and thus distinct from the subsequent Yamasee and Guale inhabitants (Larsen 1993). This sample is best described as post-contact but non-mission and is analyzed independently from the other mission samples. In population affiliation, the various samples were attributed to the Timucua, Apalachee, Yamasee, and Guale groups, each somewhat linguistically distinct although all pursuing a broadly similar pattern of sedentary agriculture and collecting. These sites are discussed more completely by Larsen (this volume).

The prehistoric sample was divided into early and late periods reflecting the change in subsistence focus that occurred around A.D. 1000. Prior to this time, native populations were primarily collector-gatherers with a limited reliance on agriculturally produced foods. After this, the local populations became increasingly dependent on a maize-based agricultural system that resulted in larger population centers and a more sedentary lifeway. The biological changes resulting from this dietary shift have been documented elsewhere (Larsen 1982, 1990, 1993).

Mandibular canines with complete labial enamel cervices were included in the study. Incompletely formed or broken teeth were omitted. Each of the enamel crowns was cleaned of dirt and calculus. Basic external dimensions were made on each tooth using needle-point calipers. Surface defect breadth and distance from the labial cervix were measured with an eyepiece micrometer on a stereomicroscope. Hypoplasias were defined as any transverse linear or pitted irregularities in the labial surface (and see Hutchinson and Larsen, this volume). Hypoplasia data are presented here to explore patterns of timing and distribution with the internal defects. Breadth and position relative to the labial cervical enamel extension were recorded for all defects. All hypoplasia data reported here are measured to the most cuspal edge of the defect.

Next, each specimen was embedded in Araldite resin (to stabilize the fragile enamel crown for cutting) and oven cured for 24 hours. Each block was sectioned along the labio-lingual plane using a Buhler Isomet low-speed sectioning saw following procedures similar to those outlined by Marks and co-workers (1996). Each face of each block was etched with 0.1N hydrochloric acid for five seconds (Wilson and Schroff 1970), rinsed with distilled water, affixed to a petrographic slide with epoxy or cyanoacrylate, and attached to a specimen holder designed to hold slide-mounted specimens and had a thin section (250–350 microns thick) re-moved. The fresh face of each section was also acid washed. Specimens were examined with a standard transmitted light microscope with magni-fications between 100 and 1000×. Internal cervical breadth and dentino-enamel junction (DEJ) height for each sectioned tooth, and DEJ position of each pathological stria, were measured with an eyepiece micrometer. PS position was measured from the dentino-enamel–cervical margin. The cuspal apex of the DEJ is the preferred measuring datum because it is the histological landmark indicating initiation of crown formation. Use of this datum was not possible due to the occlusal attrition in this sample. These sections allowed the registration of the PS with the surface defects. The remaining half of the block was also acid etched, sputter coated with 200 angstroms of gold-palladium, and examined with a JEOL 840A electron microscope in the secondary electron mode. Each specimen was examined at a range of magnifications. Photographic montages of the mandibular canines were made at 40× and the position of each PS was recorded. Patho-logical striae were also examined at higher magnification (< 5000×) to examine their ultrastructure.

In addition to the study of pathological striae, normal mandibular ca-nine developmental anatomy was studied. In unworn or slightly worn specimens, the number, position, and regional density of the striae of Retzius were recorded. These data also allowed the calculation of the du-ration of crown formation necessary to develop a chronology of the disrup-tive events.

These archaeological specimens showed evidence of diagenesis. The sediments of the coastal southeastern United States are rather acidic, caus-ing deterioration and destruction of the dentin and discoloration and de-mineralization of the enamel crown. Most of the changes were evident on the external enamel surface, but specimens missing the dentin also showed changes in the enamel color and opacity passing outward from the DEJ. The surface discolorations commonly penetrate the surface about 0.5 mil-limeters and in some cases the entire thickness of enamel. Thin enamel, especially in the cervical margins, was often completely discolored, limiting observations in this area. Changes in mineral composition were also evi-dent on the acid-etched specimens with the SEM. The preferential erosion of the enamel in the diagenetic areas highlighting the normal and abnormal striae of Retzius suggest that changes in the mineralogical composition of these regions occurred. Some highly modified teeth were omitted from the analysis due to difficulties in observing their microstructure.

Results

Subsample Comparisons of Pathological Striae

In the final analysis, 143 individuals were represented by the permanent mandibular canine (LC) (table 6.1). The sample of teeth ranged from complete unworn crowns with little root to individuals with substantial attrition. Only teeth with a complete labial cervical enamel margin were included in the analysis.

Examination of the samples included evaluation of aspects of the following subgroupings: early prehistoric, late prehistoric, early mission, late mission, pre-contact combined, and post-contact combined. These observations focus on the following aspects of the mandibular canines: crown breadth; crown height measured along the DEJ; frequency of teeth with at least one PS; mean location of the pathological striae; number of PS per afflicted tooth; and number of PS per tooth within the population. Crown dimensions provide information about the comparability of the samples and give insight into the range of population differences in prismatic geometry (Simpson 1996). Crown size varies between populations, and similarity in size in these samples is indirect evidence of biological similarity. More important, it demonstrates that the geometrical and developmental similarity of the samples allows direct comparison. Crown height also provided indirect evidence for occlusal age of the samples.

Complete Sample (All Periods Combined)

In the complete sample of mandibular canines, 68 percent (97 of 143 teeth) had at least one pathological stria (table 6.1). The mean affliction rate for the entire sample is 1.6 PS per tooth (228 PS on 143 teeth examined). Individuals exhibiting pathological striae in their mandibular canine had, on average, a frequency of 2.4 PS per afflicted tooth (228 PS recorded in 97 teeth). Mean position of the pathological striae in the sample is 5.87 mm (table 6.2) from the cervical margin or slightly more than half of the distance between the cervix and the DEJ cusp (10.63 ± 1.90 mm in unworn teeth).

Florida Prehistoric

The early and late prehistoric groups from Florida have virtually identical cervical breadths (table 6.2). The crown heights of the prehistoric groups are notably, but not statistically, different. The crown of the early group is about 0.75 mm, or 8 percent, taller than the later group, suggesting that the

Table 6.2. Summary descriptive mandibular canine metrics: DEJ height and cervical breadth (total sample, teeth without pathological striae, teeth with pathological striae)

	Florida prehistoric			Early contact		Florida mission	
	Early	Late	Total	Ossuary	Early	Late	Total
DEJ height Total sample	9.78±2.08 (15)	9.03±1.39 (25)	9.31±1.70 (40)	8.74±1.47 (26)	9.29±1.67 (60)	9.75±1.46 (17)	9.39±1.63 (77)
DEJ height Teeth without PS	10.04±3.16 (5)	8.91±1.36 (16)	9.18±1.90 (21)	8.35±1.67 (12)	8.84±2.08 (10)	8.17±1.38 (3)	8.69±1.91 (13)
DEJ height Teeth with PS	9.65±1.50 (10)	9.23±1.50 (9)	9.46±1.47 (19)	9.06±1.24 (14)	9.42±1.59 (50)	9.09±1.27 (14)	9.57±1.55 (64)
Cervical breadth[a] Total	7.23±0.70 (13)	7.21±0.52 (21)	7.22±0.58 (34)	7.10±0.55 (25)	7.29±0.61 (48)	7.18±0.69 (16)	7.27±0.63 (65)
Cervical breadth Teeth without PS	7.53±0.81 (5)	7.25±0.38 (14)	7.32±0.52 (19)	7.06±0.40 (11)	7.44±0.68 (9)	6.97±0.50 (3)	7.31±0.66 (12)
Cervical breadth Teeth with PS	7.09±0.64 (7)	7.14±0.75 (7)	7.12±0.67 (14)	7.13±0.66 (14)	7.28±0.61 (41)	7.23±0.74 (13)	7.27±0.64 (54)
Location Absolute[b]	6.32±1.91 (18)	5.63±1.44 (23)	5.93±1.67 (41)	5.75±1.68 (24)	5.82±2.05 (123)	6.04±2.00 (40)	5.87±2.03 (163)
Location Relative[c]	0.96±0.25 (13)	0.70±0.12 (13)	0.83±0.23 (26)	0.80±0.26 (24)	0.76±0.27 (96)	0.80±0.25 (37)	0.77±0.26 (133)

a. Cervical breadth is measured on the longitudinally sectioned teeth between the most cervical extensions of the unbroken labial and lingual surfaces. Not all specimens had a complete cervical breadth.
b. Mean location of all of the PS for that subsample in millimeters as measured from the midlabial cervical margin.
c. Relative position of each PS, calculated by dividing its absolute position by the cervical breadth of that tooth.

age profiles of the two groups are not identical and perhaps reflecting differences in their underlying demographic structure. Crown height differences between the various groups may have implications for the distribution of pathological striae and are discussed later. Two-thirds of the early prehistoric sample and about one-third of the late sample (36%) have PS, although there is a great variance between the individual sites (table 6.1). The mean number of PS per afflicted individual in the early prehistoric is 1.8. The later group shows a much higher number of PS per afflicted tooth (2.6 PS). The late prehistoric Holy Spirit site is unique and is discussed later. The number of PS per tooth is similar between the early (1.2 PS) and the late samples (0.9 PS). The mean location of the PS measured from the cervix differs, although not statistically, by about 7 percent of the mean unworn crown height between the two subsamples (fig. 6.2; table 6.2). The earlier group has an earlier mean age of occurrence of enamel disruptions

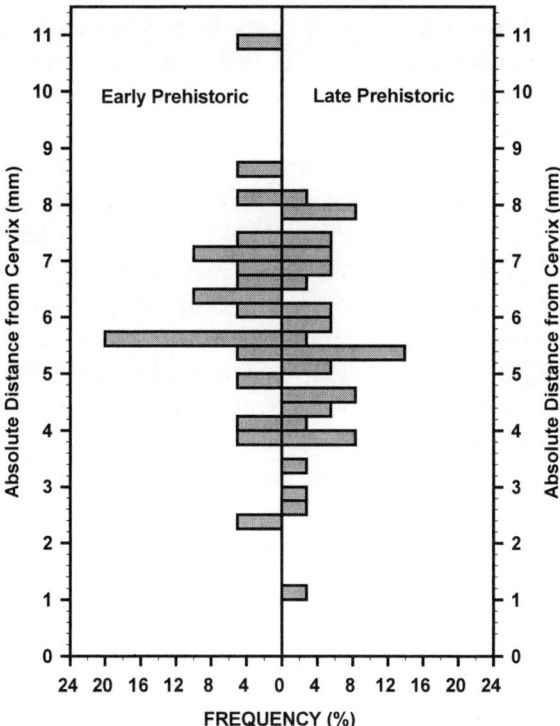

Fig. 6.2. Distribution of pathological striae in early prehistoric (A.D. 0–1000) and late prehistoric (A.D. 1000–1600) mandibular canines. All measurements in millimeters from the midlabial cervical margin.

(greater distance from the cervical enamel margin) than the later groups. Differences in normalized position of the PS (PS location/cervical breadth) are significantly different (table 6.2), indicating that there are differences in the distribution of the pathological striae with a greater frequency of PS in the more cuspal, or earlier forming, portion of the crown in the early prehistoric sample.

Holy Spirit stands out from the other late prehistoric period sites (and the entire sample) in having a low frequency of individuals with PS, 14 percent (2 of 14 individuals, table 6.1). This produced a low population rate of affliction (0.5 PS per tooth). The inclusion of the Holy Spirit sample in the late prehistoric period undoubtedly lowered the entire late prehistoric rates of affliction, both in terms of number of individuals with PS and PS per tooth values. The number of PS per individual is higher (3.5 PS per afflicted tooth) than for any other group in the study. Overall, fewer individuals were getting sick, although those who did had systemic growth disruptions more often than did contemporary and later groups. A possible contributing factor is the location of the Holy Spirit site. Unlike the contemporary Browne Mound site, the Holy Spirit site was located inland from the coast and has a more negative mean $\delta^{13}C$ than the other Florida late prehistoric sites, indicating a reduced dietary reliance on maize. However, the Lake Jackson material was also recovered in a noncoastal setting, yet it had less negative $\delta^{13}C$ values (Larsen et al., this volume), a high individual frequency of affliction (75% of individuals have PS), and a lower individual rate of morbidity (1.3 PS per individual). Unlike the Holy Spirit site, the Lake Jackson site was within the Mississippian sphere of influence, demonstrating a dense sedentary population with an emphasis on maize agriculture, both of which contributed to the high morbidity rate seen in these individuals. However, with sample sizes this small, detailed intergroup differences should be examined cautiously.

Overall, the greatest differences between these two prehistoric samples are the frequency of affliction (67% vs. 36%) and the number of morbid events per affected individual (1.8 vs. 2.6).

Santa Catalina de Amelia Ossuary

The ossuary from Santa Catalina de Amelia stands out from all other groups in terms of morbid events. This single pit feature contained the remains of at least 59 individuals, with a preponderance of females (Simmons et al. 1989; Larsen 1993). Buried beneath the commingled bones were the remains of a coffin, indisputable evidence of European influence. However, as already indicated, the unusual nature of interment suggests that the remains were collected from charnel houses and were not part of a mission population. In this case, this early group perhaps dates from the time of contact, and the individuals represented in the ossuary may represent a pericontact but not a resettled population, thus having a unique mixture of prehistoric adaptations although buried in a post-contact setting. This material is characterized as a post-contact, non-mission sample. Similar samples could possibly be the 16th-century southeastern United States sites at Pine Harbor and Tatham Mound, which are traditional aboriginal burial and habitation sites that include European artifacts. The ossuary collection has a relatively low frequency of affliction (54% of the sample) and a concomitant low population frequency of PS per tooth (0.9 PS for all teeth; see table 6.1). The individual rate of affliction is 1.7 PS/canine, which is lower than in the late prehistoric and mission samples and most closely approximates the early prehistoric sample. The ossuary sample also has the shortest mean crown height (table 6.2), perhaps indicating the greatest survivorship of any of the subgroups.

Florida Mission (Excluding Ossuary)

The mission samples were also divided into early and late groups to explore the possibility of trends in health changes under Spanish domination. As in the pre-contact group, the cervical breadth of the sample teeth is identical. Mean crown heights differ slightly, but insignificantly, with the early mission group having somewhat shorter crowns (table 6.2). The early sample has a frequency of individuals with PS identical to that in the later sample (83% vs. 82%), which is an increase from the previous periods. The early mission collection also has a slightly lower frequency of PS per afflicted canine (2.5) than the later group (2.9). Overall, the early and late mission samples demonstrate similar rates of metabolic disruption. Individual rates of PS show that each individual had, on average, 2–3 disruptive events ranging from a low in the Santa Maria de Yamasee (1.8 PS/individual) to a high in the San Luis de Apalachee and Patale sites (3.3 PS/individual). The early mission sample shows a similar, but slightly lower, population rate to the later group (2.1 PS early mission vs. 2.4 PS late mission). Population rates are the same in both the early and late mission samples (2.5 PS/individual early mission and 2.9 PS/individual late mission). The mean position of the PS measured from the cervix does not differ significantly; however, the shape of the distribution does (fig. 6.3). The early mission period is platykurtic and unskewed whereas the late mission is skewed to the left, with a high proportion of PS being clustered in the cuspal, or earlier forming, half of the enamel crown. This difference is also seen in the median values (early mission 5.82 mm; late mission 6.64 mm), which represent about six months' difference in developmental age (see later discussion). Although minor differences in crown height may contribute to the final mean location, it appears that this alone cannot account for the variation in PS distribution.

Although the contemporary Santa Maria de Yamasee (SMDY) and San Martín de Timucua sites share a similar population rate of affliction (80% SMDY, 85% San Martín), they are quite different in their patterns of population morbidity, representing the extremes in the early mission samples (SMDY 1.4 PS/tooth, San Martín 2.6 PS/tooth). The high rates of individual and population morbidity at the San Martín de Timucua site are understandable given the history of the site. The San Martín de Timucua mission was an important site along the Camino Real, the primary land

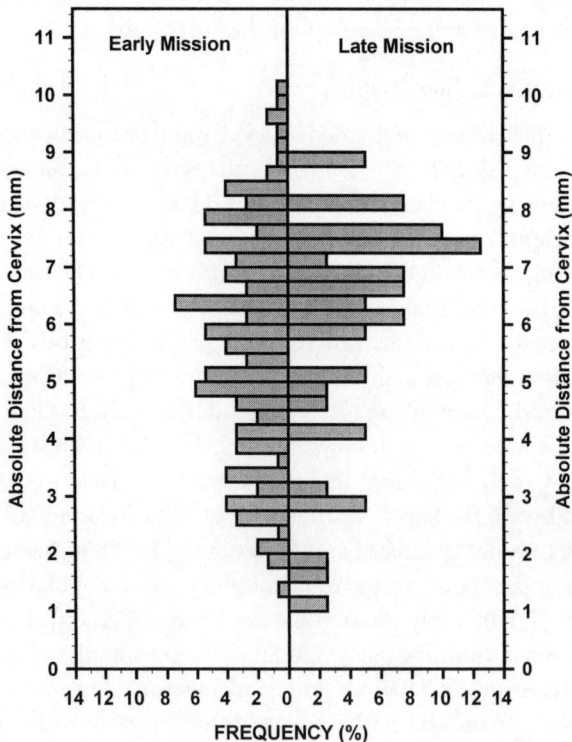

Fig. 6.3. Distribution of pathological striae in early mission (A.D. 1600–1680) and late mission (A.D. 1680–1700) mandibular canines. All measurements in millimeters from the midlabial cervical margin.

route between the inland Florida missions and St. Augustine, and people there may have "suffered some of the worst abuses and excesses of the colonial system" (Worth, pers. comm.). In addition, several instances of massive population loss (up to 50%) have been documented at that site. The resulting recruitment of males for repartimiento led to a reduced capacity of the missions to farm their fields, which in turn meant a low carrying capacity yielding little salable surplus corn and further exacerbating the dietary insufficiencies (Worth, this volume). All of this undoubtedly contributed to the high rates of morbidity at this site.

Overall, except for the early Santa Maria de Yamasee sample, the mission samples are highly similar with a high frequency of affliction, multiple disruptive events per individual, and a high population frequency of PS.

Comparison of Prehistoric and Mission Groups

The prehistoric and mission samples have virtually identical crown dimensions (table 6.2). This suggests that both samples have similar, and thus comparable, canine metrics and developmental geometry. The percentage of individuals with PS is much higher in the mission groups than in the prehistoric groups (83% vs. 48%; table 6.1). The mean number of PS per afflicted individual for the two groups is similar (prehistoric 2.2 PS/tooth, mission 2.5 PS/tooth). The two time-successive groups differ markedly in the population rate of PS per tooth, with the mission samples having a greater absolute frequency (prehistoric 1.0 PS/tooth, mission 2.1 PS/tooth). The mean position of the enamel defects is the same in both groups (table 6.2; fig. 6.4).

As noted, there are characteristic differences in crown height among the groups. There is a strong positive relationship between crown height and position of the PS, the groups with taller crowns having a more cuspal mean position of PS (fig. 6.5). This suggests that attrition has some impact on the final mean distribution of PS position. Crown height (attrition or age) must be controlled, or at least acknowledged, before differences in PS position or frequency of hypoplasia affliction (Simpson et al. 1990) can be ascribed to differences in adaptation.

Additional information about the samples can be derived from observations of crown height. Except for the early Florida prehistoric group, the teeth that demonstrate pathological striae have taller crowns than those without PS. Age and attrition are highly correlated, allowing height to be used as a rough guide to the age composition of the samples. Individuals with pathological striae have slightly taller crowns (9.47 ± 1.49 mm) than individuals without microstructural evidence of disruption (8.83 ± 1.84

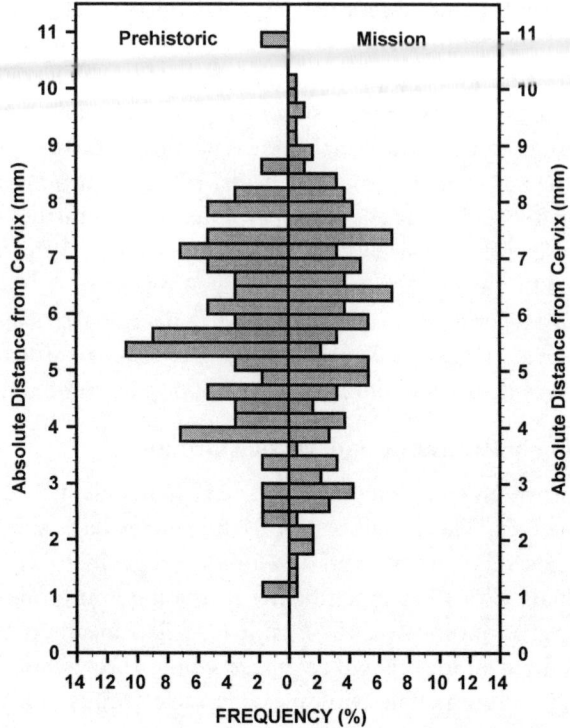

Fig. 6.4. Distribution of pathological striae in prehistoric (A.D. 1–1600) and mission (A.D. 1600–1700) mandibular canines. All measurements in millimeters from the midlabial cervical margin.

mm; table 6.2). Individuals who have pathological enamel tend to have taller crowns, or an earlier age at death. As demonstrated elsewhere for the Georgia mission populations, there is a relationship between crown size and age at death (Simpson et al. 1990). Those individuals who bear evidence of higher rates of morbidity and growth disruptions early in life may be predisposed to greater subsequent health problems, resulting in an earlier age at death. Although it may be suggested that disruption at an earlier age (during the first year) has a greater impact on survivorship than do later events, this cannot be fully tested by these data.

There is a secular trend in the pathology across the four major groups in terms of frequency of affliction and population numbers of PS per tooth (fig. 6.6). The late mission sample is notably less healthy than the early prehistoric group by having greater population (frequency of affliction and population rate of affliction) and individual (number of PS per afflicted

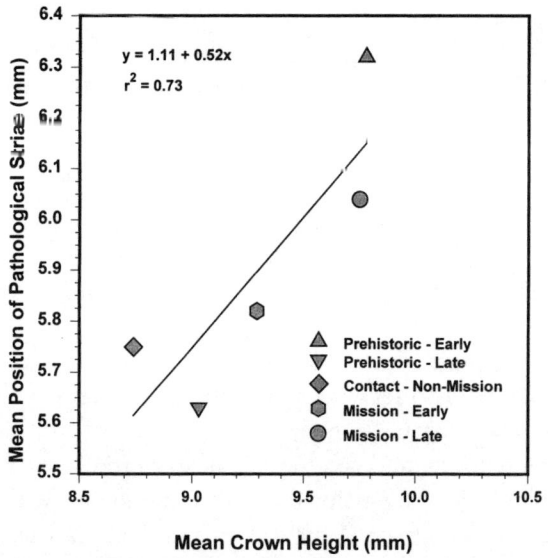

Fig. 6.5. Bivariate comparison of sample mean crown height with sample mean position of pathological striae (PS). There is a strong positive relationship between these two variables, indicating that population age composition can effect summary measures of PS position.

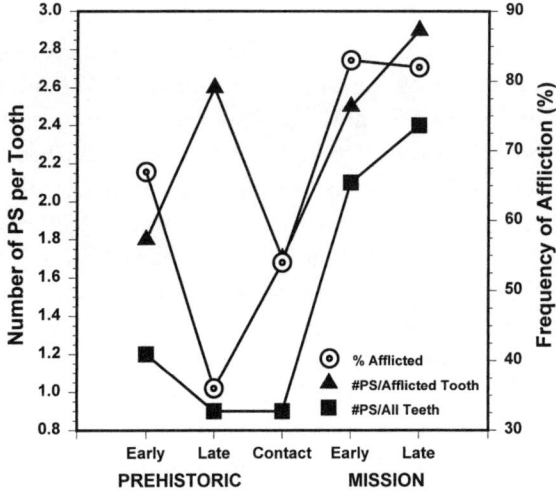

Fig. 6.6. Secular trends in population and individual rates of pathological striae (PS). Circles represent the frequency of individuals in a subsample that demonstrate PS. Filled triangles represent the subsample frequency of PS per tooth of those individuals that have a PS. Filled squares represent the subsample frequency of PS per tooth of all the teeth combined. Note that both the maximal values of population affliction and population frequency of PS per tooth show a marked trend with the highest values in the mission samples. Individual rate of PS per tooth also demonstrates an increase through time, although the late prehistoric sample has a very high individual rate.

individual) morbidity rates. A similar pattern was also found in the prevalence of anemia-related porotic hyperostosis, enamel hypoplasia (Hutchinson and Larsen 1990), nonspecific infection (Larsen and Hutchinson 1992), and declining quality of life and diet (Hann 1986; Larsen 1990; Schoeninger et al. 1990; Larsen and Hutchinson 1992)—especially marked at the time of Spanish conquest. The PS data indicate that a significantly greater percentage of each successive population was subjected to a severe disruptive event. However, the number of morbid events producing pathological striae per afflicted individual does not change across time (fig. 6.6). Those individuals who do get severely ill tend to experience multiple events independent of their cultural context.

Overall, the patterns and frequencies of appearance of pathological striae in the prehistoric and mission teeth corresponds well with the historical, archaeological, and trace element data of a marked decline in health due to change and disruption of the Native American societies.

Linking the Position of Pathological Striae and Surface Defects

Surface defects were also recorded for these samples prior to sectioning. A sample of 115 individuals from the five subsets was examined and a total of 180 surface defects in 81 teeth (70% affliction rate) was observed. The individual rate was 2.2 defects per affected tooth and the population rate was 1.6 defects per tooth for all canines combined. The mean location of the surface defects is 3.55 mm from the enamel cervical margin. These values are broadly similar to data previously published (Larsen and Hutchinson 1992). Interestingly, these values are almost identical to those for the pathological striae (population frequency: PS 68%, surface defects 70%; individual rate of affliction: PS 2.3, surface defects 2.2; population rate of affliction: PS 1.6, surface defects 1.6), although the location of the defects and their underlying causes are very different (see later discussion). Subsample comparisons of surface defects are not examined here and the hypoplasia data are included to highlight similarities to and differences from pathological striae in appearance and distribution.

It is necessary to link the internal and external surface defects of the canine crown. The Retzius lines seen in longitudinal section of the crown span the thickness of enamel from the DEJ to the external surface and are the successive growth fronts of enamel matrix deposition. Perikymata are the external manifestation of the Retzius lines. The Retzius striae course radially outward from the DEJ and curve toward the cusp. The lines are nonparallel, reflecting the decrease in enamel thickness from cusp to cervix. In teeth with enamel of a regular thickness (e.g., chimpanzee canines), the Retzius lines are parallel. Because these striae provide direct evidence about the nature and timing of crown formation, they can be used to describe the absolute and relative rates of crown extension along the DEJ, and they link the surface and microstructural defects into a single, internally consistent distribution, allowing their direct comparison.

This external location of the surface defect can be translated into the position along the DEJ, and a direct calculation of the time of the insult can be made. On a series of teeth, the course of the striae of Retzius were followed from the DEJ to the external surfaces and their termini were measured from the enamel cervix. The following function is useful in translating the DEJ origin of the Retzius striae (measured from the labial enamel cervix) to its point of intersection along the external surface of the crown for the labial surface of the mandibular canines in this sample (fig. 6.7, top):

equation 1: $y_{EXT} = 0.058 + (x_{DEJ} * 0.887) + (x_{DEJ}^2 * 0.082)$

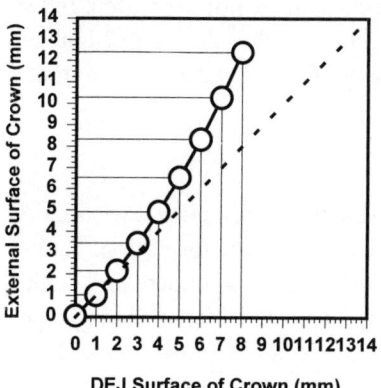

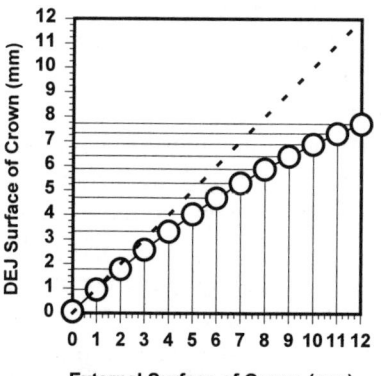

Fig. 6.7. Illustration of the nonlinear functions used to register the two termini (DEJ and external surface) of the striae of Retzius in the mandibular canine. Top: Estimated position of Retzius line terminus on the external surface when its position along the midlabial DEJ is known using the function: $y_{EXT} = 0.058 + (x_{DEJ} * 0.887) + (x_{DEJ}^2 * 0.082)$. Bottom: Estimated position of the Retzius line terminus along the midlabial DEJ when its position along the external surface is known using the function: $y_{DEJ} = 0.062 + (x_{EXT} * 0.902) - (x_{EXT}^2 * 0.022)$.

164 | Scott W. Simpson

where x_{DEJ} equals the distance from the labial cervix to the striae of Retzius along the DEJ and y_{EXT} equals the position along the intersection of the Retzius line with the external surface of the crown, also measured from the cervix. In a series of mandibular canines, the difference between calculated and measured external position did not differ by more than 6 percent. This function is not applicable in this sample when the DEJ values are much greater than about 8.00 mm because enamel formed earlier than that has no external counterpart.

The complementary function translating positions on the external surface into a location along the DEJ (fig. 6.7, bottom) is:

equation 2: $y_{DEJ} = 0.062 + (x_{EXT} * 0.902) - (x_{EXT}^2 * 0.022)$

where y_{DEJ} is equal to the DEJ position of the Retzius line and x_{EXT} equals the position along the outer surface of the crown. This is useful for calculating the developmental timing and duration of surface defects.

These functions are significantly nonlinear, indicating that a simple linear model based on radiographic standards does not accurately reflect enamel crown growth (cf. Goodman and Rose 1990; Berti and Mahaney 1992) (fig. 6.7) and produces nonrepresentative schedules of growth disruption.

Timing of Growth Disruptions

In this study, a combination of radiographic and histologic data were used to estimate the timing and duration of canine crown formation. Radiographs from over 300 contemporary children were examined, and canine crown completion age was calculated from both cumulative frequency analyses and mean ages of attainment (Simpson and Kunos 1998). Histologic estimates of crown formation duration were made by counting developmental increments (Retzius lines and prismatic varicosities) in complete crowns. Using these different media, a more accurate schedule of canine crown formation necessary for determining the timing of microstructural and surface enamel defects can be created.

The radiographic approach was to examine radiographs from over 300 children from both a modern pediatric dental clinic and the longitudinal Bolton-Brush collection (Simpson and Kunos 1998). Canine crown completion was determined to be 60–65 months (fig. 6.8). Histologically, the number of striae of Retzius were counted from the cusp to the cervix in complete specimens using both SEM and LM. Of the specimens observed here, seven daily increments (prismatic varicosities) were identified between adjacent striae of Retzius (Dean 1987). This suggests that each stria

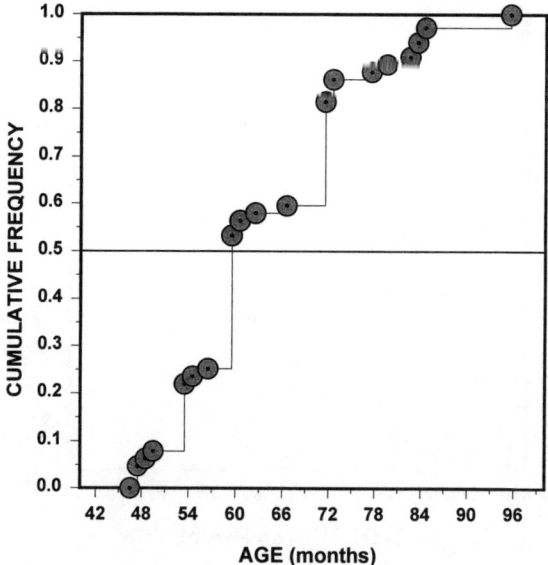

Fig. 6.8. Cumulative distribution of absolute time of mandibular canine crown formation (n = 67). Data derived from the Bolton-Brush Growth Study and the Case Western Reserve University Pediatric Dental Clinic (from Simpson and Kunos 1998).

of Retzius represents one week's duration of growth. Based on this assumption, crown formation duration was calculated to last approximately 57–60 months. Calculation of crown formation duration histologically provides a similar period of growth to both the radiographic study (Simpson and Kunos 1998) and other histologic estimates (Reid et al. 1998). The canine crown initiates formation after birth but before the sixth month, providing a crown completion age of 63–66 months. This is substantially shorter than the 78 months often used by other researchers (Goodman et al. 1992).

The number and density of striae of Retzius were measured along the length of the DEJ in teeth with unworn or slightly worn crowns. The striae were counted in 10 percent increments of the crown and plotted (fig. 6.9). The density varies markedly along the length of the DEJ, increasing as the cervix is approached. Each stria is considered an equal increment in time. Together, this provides a schedule of crown elongation from cusp to cervix. The radiographic and histologic data indicate that mandibular canine crown formation is approximately 57–60 months and can be added to the

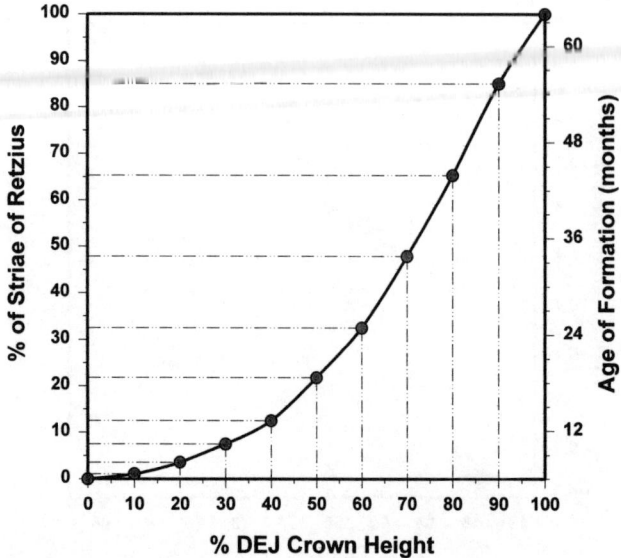

Fig. 6.9. Comparison of Retzius line density, crown position, and period of crown formation. This figure allows direct calculation of the age of formation of crown enamel of the La Florida sample. For example, about 22 percent of the total number of Retzius lines are found in the cuspal 50 percent of the crown. An absolute age of formation of the cuspal half of the enamel crown is about 18–21 months (Simpson 1999).

plot, producing an internally consistent schedule of formation that allows calculation of age of disruption from crown position.

Based on the density and number of developmental striae observed here, the rate of DEJ elongation is initially rapid and slows as the middle third of the crown is reached (fig. 6.9). Formation of the cuspal 40 percent of the DEJ height takes approximately 10–15 percent of the total period needed to form the entire crown. Approximately 35 percent of the DEJ crown height is formed before any of the external surface enamel is formed (the "hidden increments" of Bromage and Dean 1985) and identifiable hypoplastic bands cannot be formed during this stage (Hillson 1986). This period lasts from a postnatal age of six months (the commonly accepted time of mandibular canine crown initiation) to 15–18 months and is difficult to sample for hypoplasia (Skinner and Goodman 1992).

A substantial difference exists between the mean values of the PS and surface defects measured from the cervical margin (PS: 5.87 mm; surface defects: 3.55 mm). These measures are not comparable because the posi-

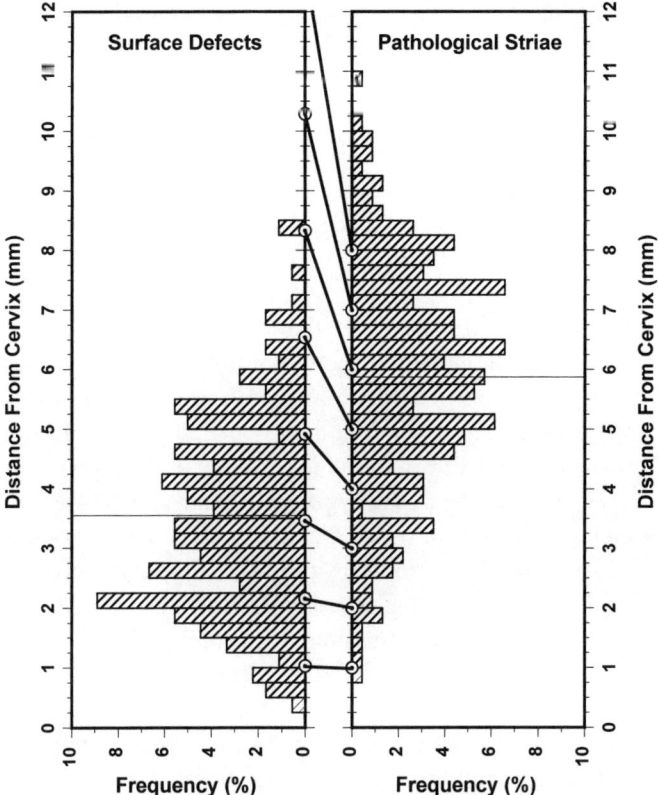

Fig. 6.10. Comparison of the distribution of pathological striae (PS) and surface defects. All measurements in millimeters from the midlabial cervix. Surface defects are measured along the outer surface of the enamel. PS are measured along the DEJ. Connecting the two distributions are registration lines (using the functions given with fig. 6.7) that link the two types of defects into a single chronological sequence. Surface defects: mean (S.D.) = 3.55 (1.64), n = 115 individuals, 180 surface defects. Pathological striae: mean (S.D.) = 5.87 (1.93), n = 143 individuals, 223 PS. The means values for each distribution are plotted.

tions of the PS are measured along the DEJ and the surface defects are measured along the external surface of the crown (fig. 6.10). The mean position of PS is 5.87 mm from the cervix along the DEJ, which translates into a position for the PS of about 8.09 mm (using equation 1) along the outer surface of crown, substantially earlier chronologically than the surface defects. The mean external position of surface defects is 3.55 mm, which converts to a position of about 2.99 mm (equation 2) from the cervix along the DEJ. Goodman and Armelagos (1985) noted that hypoplasias are nonrandomly distributed throughout the crown and that most are located in the cervical two thirds of the crown (midcoronal and cervical thirds) (fig. 6.10). In the canine, the two-thirds position on the outside of the crown corresponds to a spot about half of the distance between the cervix and the cusp along the DEJ.

Next, the mean time of occurrence of the PS and surface defects can be calculated. PS peak at about the age of 18–19 months, and the middle 50 percent were formed between the ages of 12 and 30 months. The peak for surface defects is located at about 36 months, with a range for the middle 50 percent spanning the ages of 26 to 54 months. Fifty percent of the PS are located in the cuspal half of the crown (>5.8 mm), whereas *less than 2 percent of the surface defects* are found in enamel forming at the same time. About 75 percent of the PS are found in portions of the crown where only approximately one-quarter of the hypoplastic bands are located. Although many hypoplastic areas have an associated PS, the reverse is not necessarily true. The chronological distributions of the two types of defects are very different, undoubtedly sampling different phenomena occurring according to different chronological schedules. It is clear that pathological striae and surface defects are not simply a graded response to a common homeostatic disruption.

Not all of the samples show a similar pattern of mean distribution of the PS. The early preagricultural prehistoric group shows a chronologically earlier (greater distance from the cervix) absolute and relative mean location of PS, with the later agricultural prehistoric and post-contact groups having an older age of mean appearance. This is estimated to be four to five months later in time. This has implications for the epidemiology of growth disruptions in these groups (see later discussion).

As already noted, the cuspal portion of the crown includes only a small percentage of the surface defects. Although the cuspal third represents a major portion of the crown's external surface, the amount of time it takes to form the enamel between the cusp tip and the two-thirds boundary is only 12 months (aged ~6–18 months). Additionally, not all of the enamel formed at this time contributes to the external surface of the tooth. The non-occlusal enamel that does contribute to the cuspal third of the external surface is formed over a short period, lasting less than six months. Thus, this surface presents fewer hypoplasias because of its short period of development and, by extension, risk. In addition, the acute angle of intersection of the striae of Retzius with the external surface (Hillson and Bond 1997) results in shallow and broad hypoplasias with indistinct margins, making them difficult to discern. By comparison, the cervical 20 percent of the DEJ crown height accounts for about one-third of the duration it takes to form the canine crown and contains about 35 percent of the surface defects and only 5 percent of the PS. This raises two points: first, observations of enamel hypoplasia are restricted to between 15 and 54 months and with a variable ability to recognize the defects across this range; and second, each increment of external crown height does not represent a similar duration of time. As such, PS can provide information about the health status of an individual in the earliest years that is not possible from observation of hypoplasia. Studies of hypoplastic breadth must acknowledge that prismatic geometry is a significant contributing factor to detect breadth throughout the crown and that events of similar breadths but different crown locations do not represent a similar duration (Hillson and Bond 1997). Thus, prismatic geometry of the canine crown provides some insight into the timing and distribution of enamel surface defects. Finally, schedules of growth disruption that rely on a linear model of crown formation assuming a linear relationship between crown height and time need to be reconsidered.

Discussion

Pathological striae of Retzius are not unambiguous structures (Schour 1936; Wilson and Schroff 1970; Rose et al. 1985; Goodman et al. 1992). They present a graded degree of severity ranging from prismatic bending and increased interprismatic space to marked crystal disorganization with complete loss of prismatic structure (Gustafson 1959; Weber and Eisenmann 1971; Weber et al. 1974; Whittaker and Richards 1978; Rose 1979; Marks 1992). This reflects a graded response to homeostatic imbalance (Cook 1981; Rudney 1983). The PS identified here are narrow bands of prismatic irregularity (~10–15 microns) with reasonably discrete boundaries similar to the many published descriptions (Wilson and Schroff 1970; Weber and Eisenmann 1971; Rose 1977, 1979; Rose et al. 1985; Whittaker and Richards 1978; Marks 1992). With a daily rate of enamel formation of approximately 3.5–4 microns (Risnes 1986), this represents about four days. Following the insult, the normal prismatic structure is generally regained, although some residual changes in the ameloblastic function can occur, sometimes resulting in a temporary disruption in the matrix mineralization (fig. 6.11) (Gustafson 1959; Suga 1992). Further research into the relationship between patterns of prismatic disruption and mineralization irregularities is necessary.

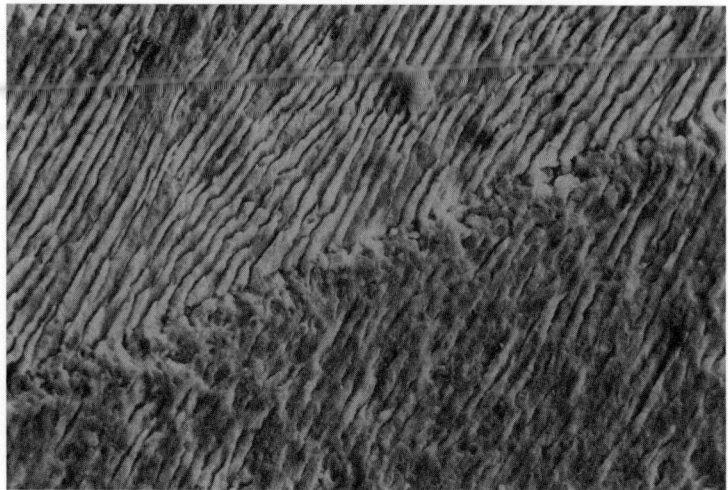

Fig. 6.11. Scanning electron micrograph of pathological enamel showing differences in enamel structure and texture prior to (bottom of micrograph) and after (top of micrograph) a pathological stria. Note the change in the character of the mineralized enamel following the disruption. This specimen was acid etched with 0.1N HCl for five seconds prior to gold-palladium sputter coating. Santa Catalina de Amelia (SM-6A1), mandibular right canine, 350×.

Although pathological striae may be found throughout the crown, their distribution is not random in this sample. The modal distribution of the PS is due in part to two phenomena: one is a sampling problem and the other a consequence of the enamel structure. This sample ranges in age from young individuals with unworn completed crowns to individuals exhibiting significant attrition. Consequently, the older the sample, the fewer apical, or early formed, PS (and also surface defects [Simpson et al. 1990]) will be seen. Thus, the sample age composition (reflected by wear) produces the attenuated distribution of PS in the earliest years and is biased against these observations. As shown earlier, there is a strong positive relationship between crown height and mean position of PS (fig. 6.5). In the samples analyzed here, the mean DEJ height is 9.25 mm, which is about 87 percent of the mean crown height of unworn specimens. Enamel formed in the first 6–8 months (ages 12–14 months) of crown formation are, on average, lost in the sample. The more the tooth has been eroded, the faster the rate of "time" lost as a consequence of the increasing density of developmental increments. Fortunately, both the prehistoric and post-contact samples have similar crown heights, allowing their direct comparison.

Developmental enamel geometry may also contribute to the modal distribution of PS. The elongation of the DEJ initiating at the cusp slows markedly as the cervix is approached, and this is indicated by the angle of intersection between the DEJ and the Retzius line (Shellis 1984). The absolute duration of time per unit height of crown differs with position such that each unit has a different potential risk of disruption. This may partially explain the different positional distribution of PS found in the canine by Condon and Rose (1992).

Potentially, pathological striae can be identified throughout the entire period of crown formation. Practically, however, it becomes difficult to identify PS in the cervical quarter of the tooth for two reasons. First, when the cervical enamel thins to less than about 0.5 mm, the striae become very prominent and PS identification difficult due to normal prismatic bending and offset. Especially apparent in the cervix are prominent, not necessarily pathological, striae of Retzius "cluster bands" associated with the more prevalent cervical hypoplasia (Goodman et al. 1992). This makes distinguishing prominent striae from pathological striae very difficult. Second, in this sample, diagenetic discoloration preferentially apparent in the cervix also makes observation of PS in this region difficult. Together, these factors may contribute to the underrepresentation of PS in the cervix (Goodman and Rose 1990; Skinner and Goodman 1992). Although the recommendations of Goodman and Rose (1990:93) that "Wilson bands not be recorded in the terminal 1 to 2 mm of the labial enamel of the permanent canines" are not supported here, their statement is understandable. Thus, not all regions of the enamel crown are equal in their ability to demonstrate prismatic defects.

Hypoplasias, on the other hand, are readily identifiable on the labial surfaces of teeth. They are not characterized by gross structural changes in enamel matrix but are identified by a transversely oriented surface depression or pitting resulting from a localized reduction in enamel matrix deposition. As noted previously, they are nonrandomly distributed (Goodman and Armelagos 1985; Goodman and Rose 1990), being most commonly located in the midcoronal and cervical portions of the crown and infrequently found in the cuspal third of the tooth. Enamel hypoplasia can be broad, being millimeters in breadth, and specimens in this study have hypoplastic bands spanning over 60 perikymata. Boundaries between adjacent hypoplasias can be indistinct, and multiple disruptive events may be identified as a single chronic episode, thus having a low chronological resolution. By contrast, pathological striae are narrow, discrete, and capable of providing a more precise chronological assignment of amelogenic disruption. Hypoplasias have been identified to result from a wide variety of stressors including dietary disruption, trauma, bacterial and viral infection, psychological stress, and febrile diseases (Goodman and Rose 1990).

Although cluster bands, or collections of prominent Retzius striae, are found in association with some surface defects (especially those more cervically located), their prismatic microstructure is not necessarily abnormal and cannot be considered PS. In this study, surface defects and PS do not necessarily co-occur. However, when surface defects and PS are found together, the PS are most often found at the "leading edge," or time of onset, of the hypoplastic events (Suckling and Purdell-Lewis 1982), although they may also be found within the trough of the hypoplasia or at the "trailing edge." Similar results have been discussed by others (Rose 1977; Condon 1981; Goodman and Rose 1990; Wright 1990). The appearance of pathological striae at the leading edge of a hypoplasia coincides with the onset of a metabolic insult.

To review, hypoplasias and pathological striae have both a different microstructural appearance and a different pattern of timing. Pathological striae are narrow disruptions in the normal structure of the enamel prisms and are most commonly found in enamel formed between 12 and 30 months. Hypoplasias involve thinning in the enamel crown over an area that can be quite broad; lack changes in the prismatic structure; and are most commonly found in enamel formed after 25 months. This suggests that the etiology differs between the two (Wright 1990). Hypoplastic defects have been attributed to a wide variety of phenomena and are best described as nonspecific indicators of metabolic disruption. The proximate factors producing pathological striae are unclear; however, their form, breadth, and timing suggest some possibilities. First, pathological striae are short events, probably generally less than four days, with a rapid return to normally formed enamel (although residual changes in the quality of mineralization may occur; see fig. 6.11). This suggests a brief and acute metabolic disruption. Second, the enamel microstructure is disorganized due to irregularities in enamel matrix formation. The hydroxyapatite crystals form on a temporary matrix of hydrophobic amelogenins and acidic non-amelogenin proteins (Doi et al. 1984; Warshawsky et al. 1981; Warshawsky 1985; Deutsch 1989; Robinson et al. 1989; Nanci et al. 1996), which act as crystallite-spacing and mineral-diffusing elements and provide a template for crystal formation. Normal enamel structure requires the enamel protein structure to produce oriented crystal growth (Simmer and Fincham 1995).

A common health problem in a number of traditional societies involves disorders producing diarrhea, which are most prevalent during the first two years of life (Gordon et al. 1963). Many bouts of infant diarrhea have a rapid and acute onset and diminish over the course of a couple of days. As with many transitory gastrointestinal bacterial or viral diseases, the first indication of disease is an acute onset indicated by vomiting and diarrhea, both contributing to dehydration. During systemic dehydration, fluid is recruited from the interstitial to the plasma spaces (Connor and Gibson 1988). These fluid losses are accompanied by loss of electrolytes, which are crucial for maintaining normal cellular homeostasis. Continued fluid shortage leads to movement of fluids from the intracellular to the extracellular spaces, leading to severe cell dysfunction (Connor and Gibson 1988). This dysfunction at the cellular level can include disruption of normal enamel matrix formation. Water is a necessary component in the normal formation, function, and structure of enamel-forming proteins. Acute systemic dehydration may ultimately modify enamel protein structure adversely, leading to a disruption of enamel crystallite orientation. This may explain the common co-occurrence of surface defects and pathological striae at the time of onset and less frequently later during the defects span. Surface and prismatic defects co-occur not because they are graded responses to a common health problem but rather because the onset of disease is generally accompanied by a wide variety of severe and transitory homeostatic imbalances, including dehydration and fevers. Infant weanling diarrhea reaches its highest frequency and severity in the first year and becomes less common and severe by the end of the second year (Herring et al. 1998). The incorporation of nonmaternal foods and drink into the infant diet with its increased risk of infection tends to occur in the latter half of the first year with a slow transition lasting two or more years. It is not the end of nursing that is most stressful to the child; rather it is the introduction of novel foods and their pathogenic load that can cause multiple health problems. The acute dehydration produced by weanling diarrhea associated with this change in diet is a serious health problem. In nonwestern societies it remains one of the primary causes of infant death, with mortality rates as high as 40 percent (Gordon et al. 1963).

An additional consequence of acute dehydration is the resulting systemic electrolyte imbalance that this produces. This disrupts the normal ionic concentration across the cell membrane, altering intracellular fluid volume regulation. In reversible cell injury, hydropic swelling occurs, producing significant changes in the endoplasmic reticulum, cell membrane, mitochondria, and nucleus. In ameloblasts, this has the potential of disrupting the matrix-synthesizing organelles and matrix secreting Tomes process, the normal structure of which is crucial to the normal deposition of the rod and interrod matrices on which the crystallites form.

What factors can produce this weanling diarrhea? A number of diseases associated with unsanitary conditions can produce severe dehydration via diarrhea. Cholera results in potentially fatal dehydration via the production of copious amounts of watery diarrhea, potentially exceeding 1 liter per hour (Connor and Gibson 1988). The onset of disease is rapid and acute and can result in hypovolemic shock and death within a day of initial symptom presentation, and the duration is short. Fevers are not associated with the earlier stages of cholera. The cholera bacillus (*Vibrio cholerae*) passes to the individual through contaminated water or foods prepared with contaminated water. The bacilli pass into the small intestine and propagate, and the enterotoxins cause "a massive outpouring of water and electrolytes" (Connor and Gibson 1988:367). Normal gastric acidity is an effective barrier to infection, although factors reducing acidity (vomiting, dietary inhibition) result in individuals with a greater susceptibility to infection. A host of other common infectious agents produce diarrhea during their course, including *Salmonella enteritidis, Vibrio parahaemolycticus, Escherichia coli, Campylobacter* sp., and *Shigellosis* spp. This latter dysentery-producing organism is virulent, especially in areas of poor hygiene, and the course of the disease initiates with often severe bouts of diarrhea. Clostridial diseases causing food poisoning (notably *Clostridium perfrigens*) are also rapid-onset, short-duration diseases and produce both diarrhea and vomiting. Viral gastroenteritis produced by rotaviruses has been identified as a self-limiting, although acute, cause of diarrheal disorders afflicting children less than two years of age (Rubin and Farber 1988). All of these tend to last a short time—two to five days—with a cessation of the primary symptoms and absence of chronic infection, although the rotaviruses may cause impaired intestinal absorption for up to two months following exposure (Rubin and Farber 1988). Thus, these enteropathies should produce a distinctive signature in the developing enamel.

Researchers have identified that febrile diseases are often associated with hypoplastic enamel defects (Goodman and Rose 1990). The lack of a strong correspondence between pathological striae and surface enamel defects may be due to their differential expression in homeostatic imbalances. Febrile diseases often last for extended periods (>1 week), whereas prismatic disruption bears evidence of a shorter duration, suggesting that systemic fevers are not a primary cause of abnormal enamel microstructure.

In sum, it is hypothesized here that pathological striae are a result of severe dehydration including a marked electrolyte imbalance consequent to weanling diarrhea during the transition to an extramaternal diet and the presence of novel and density-dependent diseases.

The Spanish missionaries caused a major upheaval of the social and economic lives of the Native American populations, which reduced the quality of their health. These changes included population displacement, increased demands for labor, novel infectious diseases, an altered dietary base, and local increases in population density with a concomitant reduction in sanitary quality. This scenario provided the opportunity for diarrheal diseases to increase their prevalence in a population overworked and subject to dietary compromise, resulting in higher rates of morbidity and mortality.

Analyses of pathological striae of Retzius provide a sensitive technique for distinguishing population differences and their chronology in extrinsic stressors. Retzius striae have a very different distribution, duration, microstructure, and possible etiology from surface defects. Thus, schedules of metabolic insult derived from the two media are not synonymous. The two may be used to create a single picture of adaptation but they cannot be combined as different aspects of the same process. Further integrative research by historians, archaeologists, and biological anthropologists is necessary to explore more fully these differences observed in the Native American populations in the southeastern United States.

Acknowledgments

I thank Clark Spencer Larsen for inviting me to participate in archaeological fieldwork in coastal Georgia and Florida and in presenting the research in this book. Marianne Reeves helped to catalogue and prepare specimens and collect data used in this analysis. Michael Decker provided some useful suggestions. This research was funded by a grant from the National Science Foundation (SBR-9305391). Additional funding was supplied by a Case Western Reserve University Research Initiation Grant. Thanks are especially extended to the curators and institutions who granted permission to study the dentitions under their care and to undertake the analyses described in this chapter: David Hurst Thomas (American Museum of Natural History), Jerald Milanich (Florida Museum of Natural History), and

Bonnie McEwan, David Dickel, and James Miller (Florida Bureau of Archaeological Research).

References Cited

Berti, P. R., and M. C. Mahaney. 1992. Quantification of the Confidence Intervals for Linear Enamel Hypoplasia Chronologies. *Journal of Paleopathology* 2:19–30

Boyde, A. 1963. Estimation of Age at Death of Young Human Skeletal Remains from Incremental Lines in the Dental Enamel. Paper, Third International Meeting in Forensic Immunology, Medicine, Pathology, and Toxicology, London, England.

Bromage, T., and M. C. Dean. 1985. Re-evaluation of the Age at Death of Plio-Pleistocene Fossil Hominids. *Nature* 317:525–27.

Brook, A. H., J. M. Fearne, and J. M. Smith. 1997. Environmental Causes of Enamel Defects. In *Dental Enamel,* ed. D. J. Chadwick and G. Cardew, 212–22. Chichester: John Wiley and Sons.

Condon, K. W. 1981. Correspondence of Developmental Enamel Defects between the Mandibular Canine and the First Premolar. M.A. thesis, University of Arkansas, Fayetteville.

Condon, K. W., and J. C. Rose. 1992. Intertooth and Intratooth Variability in the Occurrence of Developmental Enamel Defects. *Journal of Paleopathology* 2:61–77.

Connor, D. H., and D. W. Gibson. 1988. Infectious and Parasitic Diseases. In *Pathology,* ed. E. Rubin and J. L. Farber, 326–451. Philadelphia: J. B. Lippincott.

Cook, D. C. 1981. Mortality, Age-Structure, and Status in the Interpretation of Stress Indicators in Prehistoric Skeletons: A Dental Example from the Lower Illinois Valley. In *The Archaeology of Death,* ed. R. Chapman, I. Kinnes, and K. Randsborg, 133–44. Cambridge: Cambridge University Press.

Dean, M. C. 1987. Growth Layers and Incremental Markings in Hard Tissues: A Review of the Literature and Some Preliminary Observations about Enamel Structure in *Paranthropus. Journal of Human Evolution* 16:157–72.

Deutsch, D. 1989. Structure and Function of Enamel Gene Products. *Anatomical Record* 224:189–210.

Doi, Y., E. D. Eanes, H. Shimokawa, and J. D. Termine. 1984. Inhibition of Seeded Growth of Enamel Apatite Crystals by Amelogenin and Enamelin Proteins *in vitro. Journal of Dental Research* 63:98–105.

FitzGerald, C. M. 1998. Do Enamel Microstructures Have Regular Time Dependency? Conclusions from the Literature and Large-Scale Study. *Journal of Human Evolution* 35:371–86.

Goodman, A. H., and G. J. Armelagos. 1985. Factors Affecting the Distribution of

Enamel Hypoplasias within the Human Permanent Dentition. *American Journal of Physical Anthropology* 68:479–93.

Goodman, A. H., and J. C. Rose. 1990. Assessment of Systemic Physiological Perturbations from Dental Enamel Hypoplasias and Associated Histological Structures. *Yearbook of Physical Anthropology* 33:59–110.

Goodman, A. H., G. J. Armelagos, and J. C. Rose. 1980. Enamel Hypoplasias as Indicators of Stress in Three Prehistoric Populations from Illinois. *Human Biology* 52:515–28.

Goodman, A. H., D. L. Martin, C. P. Klein, M. S. Peele, N. A. Cruse, L. R. McEwan, A. Saeed, and B. M. Robinson. 1992. Cluster Bands, Wilson Bands and Pit Patches: Histological and Enamel Surface Indicators of Stress in the Black Mesa Anasazi Population. *Journal of Paleopathology* 2:115–27.

Gordon, J. E., I. D. Chitkara, and J. B. Wyon. 1963. Weaning Diarrhea. *American Journal of Medical Science* 245:345.

Grahnen, H., S. Sjolin, T. Arwill, and B. O. Magnusson. 1969. Neonatal Asphyxia and Mineralisation Defects of the Primary Teeth: pt. 1. Clinical Investigation. *Caries Research* 3:301–7.

Gustafson, A.-G. 1959. *A Morphologic Investigation of Certain Variations in the Structure and Mineralization of Human Dental Enamel.* Malmö, Sweden: Odontologisk Tidskrift.

Hann, J. H. 1986. Demographic Patterns and Changes in Mid-Seventeenth Century Timucua and Apalachee. *Florida Historical Quarterly* 64:371–92.

Herring, D. A., S. A. Saunders, and M. A. Katzenberg. 1998. Investigating the Weaning Process in Past Populations. *American Journal of Physical Anthropology* 105:425–39.

Hillson, S. 1986. *Teeth.* Cambridge: Cambridge University Press.

Hillson, S., and S. Bond. 1997. Relationship of Enamel Hypoplasia to the Pattern of Tooth Crown Growth: A Discussion. *American Journal of Physical Anthropology* 104:89–103.

Hutchinson, D. L., and C. S. Larsen. 1990. Stress and Lifeway Change: The Evidence from Enamel Hypoplasias. In *The Archaeology of Mission Santa Catalina de Guale: 2. Interpretations of a Population in Transition*, ed. C. S. Larsen, 50–65. Anthropological Papers of the American Museum of Natural History 68.

Johnsen, D., C. Krejci, M. Hack, and A. Fanaroff. 1984. Distribution of Enamel Defects and the Association with Respiratory Distress in Very Low Birthweight Infants. *Journal of Dental Research* 63:59–64.

Johnson, N. P., A. O. Watson, and M. Massler. 1965. Tooth Ring Analysis in Mongolism. *Australian Dental Journal* 10:282–86.

Larsen, C. S. 1982. *The Anthropology of St. Catherines Island: 3. Prehistoric Human Biological Adaptation.* Anthropological Papers of the American Museum of Natural History 57, pt. 3.

178 | Scott W. Simpson

———. 1990. Biological Interpretation and the Context for Contact. In *The Archaeology of Mission Santa Catalina de Guale*: 2. *Interpretations of a Population in Transition*, ed. C. S. Larsen, 11–25. Anthropological Papers of the American Museum of Natural History 68.

———. 1993. On the Frontier of Contact: Mission Bioarchaeology in La Florida. In *The Spanish Missions of La Florida*, ed. B. G. McEwan, 322–56. Gainesville: University Press of Florida.

Larsen, C. S., and D. L. Hutchinson. 1992. Dental Evidence for Physiological Disruption: Biocultural Interpretations from Eastern Spanish Borderlands, U.S.A. *Journal of Paleopathology* 2:151–69.

Macho, G. A., D. J. Reid, M. G. Leakey, N. Jablonski, and A. D. Beynon. 1996. Climatic Effects on Dental Development of *Theropithecus oswaldi* from Koobi Foora and Olorgesailie. *Journal of Human Evolution* 30:57–70.

Marks, M. K. 1992. Developmental Dental Enamel Defects: An SEM Analysis. *Journal of Paleopathology* 2:79–90.

Marks, M. K., J. C. Rose, and W. D. Davenport Jr. 1996. Thin Section Procedure for Enamel Histology. *American Journal of Physical Anthropology* 99:493–98.

Nanci, A., J. Hashimoto, S. Zalzal, and C. E. Smith. 1996. Transient Accumulation of Proteins Interrod and Rod Enamel Growth Sites. *Advances in Dental Research* 10:135–49.

Reid, D. J., and W. Dirks. 1997. Histological Reconstruction of Dental Development and Its Relationship to Periodic Stress in the Awash Baboons. *American Journal of Physical Anthropology* Supp. 24:195–96.

Reid, D. J., A. D. Beynon and F. V. Ramirez Rozzi. 1998. Histological Reconstruction of Dental Development in Four Individuals from a Medieval Site in Picardie, France. *Journal of Human Evolution* 35:463–77.

Risnes, S. 1986. Enamel Apposition Rate and the Prism Periodicity in Human Teeth. *Scandinavian Journal of Dental Research* 94:394–404.

———. 1990. Structural Characteristics of Staircase-Type Retzius Lines in Human Dental Enamel Analyzed by Scanning Electron Microscopy. *Anatomical Record* 226:135–46.

———. 1998. Growth Tracks in Enamel. *Journal of Human Evolution* 35:331–50.

Robinson, C., J. Kirkham, N. J. Stonehouse, and R. C. Shore. 1989. Control of Crystal Growth During Enamel Maturation. *Connective Tissue Research* 22:139–45.

Robinson, C., S. J. Brookes, J. Kirkham, W. A. Bonass, and W. C. Shore. 1996. Crystal Growth in Dental Enamel: The Role of Amelogenins and Albumins. *Advances in Dental Research* 10:173–80.

Rose, J. C. 1977. Defective Enamel Histology of Teeth from Illinois. *American Journal of Physical Anthropology* 46:439–46.

———. 1979. Morphological Variation of Enamel Prisms within Abnormal Striae of Retzius. *Human Biology* 51:139–51.

Rose, J. C., and J. N. Pasley. 1980. Stress and Dental Development: An Experimental Paleopathological Model. *American Journal of Physical Anthropology* 52:272.

Rose, J. C., G. J. Armelagos, and J. W. Lallo. 1978. Histological Enamel Indicators of Childhood Stress in Prehistoric Skeletal Samples. *American Journal of Physical Anthropology* 49:511–16.

Rose, J. C., K. W. Condon, and A. H. Goodman. 1985. Diet and Dentition: Developmental Disturbances. In *The Analysis of Prehistoric Diets,* ed. R. I. Gilbert and J .H. Meilke, 281–305. Orlando: Academic Press.

Rubin, E., and J. L. Farber. 1988. The Gastrointestinal Tract. In *Pathology,* ed. E. Rubin and J. L. Farber, 628–721. Philadelphia: J. B. Lippincott.

Rudney, J. D. 1983. Dental Indicators of Growth Disturbance in a Series of Ancient Lower Nubian Populations: Changes over Time. *American Journal of Physical Anthropology* 60:463–70.

Schoeninger, M. J., N. J. van der Merwe, K. Moore, J. Lee-Thorp, and C. S. Larsen. 1990. Decrease in Dietary Quality between the Prehistoric and Contact Periods. In *The Archaeology of Mission Santa Catalina de Guale: 2. Interpretations of a Population in Transition,* ed. C. S. Larsen, 78–93. Anthropological Papers of the American Museum of Natural History 68.

Schour, I. 1936. The Neonatal Line in the Enamel and Dentin of the Human Deciduous Teeth and First Permanent Molar. *Journal of the American Dental Association* 23:1946–55.

Schour, I., and R. Kronfeld. 1938. Tooth Ring Analysis: pt. 4. Neonatal Dental Hypoplasia: Analysis of the Teeth of an Infant with Injury of the Brain at Birth. *Archives of Pathology* 26:471–90.

Schour, I., and H. G. Poncher. 1937. Rate of Apposition of Enamel and Dentin, Measured by the Effect of Acute Fluorosis. *American Journal of Diseases of Children* 54:757–76.

Sheldon, M., B. G. Bibby, and B. Bales. 1945. The Relationship between Microscopic Enamel Defects and Infantile Debility. *Journal of Dental Research* 24:109–16.

Shellis, R. P. 1984. Variations in Growth of the Enamel Crown in Human Teeth and a Possible Relationship between Growth and Enamel Structure. *Archives of Oral Biology* 29:697–705.

Simmer, J. P., and A. G. Fincham. 1995. Molecular Mechanisms of Dental Enamel Formation. *Critical Reviews in Oral Biology and Medicine* 62:84–108.

Simmons, S., C. S. Larsen, and K. F. Russell. 1989 Demographic Interpretations from Ossuary Remains during the Late Contact Period in Northern Spanish Florida. Paper, annual meeting of the American Association of Physical Anthropologists, San Diego, Calif.

Simpson, S. W. 1996. Variation in the Prismatic Geometry of Incisor and Canine Enamel. Paper, Evolution of Enamel Workshop, Paris, France.

———. 1999. Reconstructing Patterns of Growth Disruption from Enamel Microstructure. In *Human Growth in the Past: Studies from Bones and Teeth,* ed. R. Hoppa and C. FitzGerald, 241–63. Cambridge: Cambridge University Press.

Simpson, S. W., and C. A. Kunos. 1998. A Radiographic Study of the Development of the Human Mandibular Dentition. *Journal of Human Evolution* 35:479–505.

Simpson, S. W., D. L. Hutchinson, and C. S. Larsen. 1990. Coping with Stress: Tooth Size, Dental Defects, and Age-at-Death. In *The Archaeology of Mission Santa Catalina de Guale*: 2. *Interpretations of a Population in Transition*, ed. C. S. Larsen, 66–77. Anthropological Papers of the American Museum of Natural History 68.

Skinner, M. F., and A. H. Goodman. 1992. Anthropological Uses of Developmental Defects of Enamel. In *The Skeletal Biology of Past Peoples: Research and Methods*, ed. S. A. Saunders and M. A. Katzenberg, 153–74. New York: Wiley-Liss.

Sognnaes, R. F. 1956. Histological Evidence of Developmental Lesions in Teeth Originating from Paleolithic, Prehistoric and Ancient Man. *American Journal of Pathology* 32:547–77.

Suckling, G., and D. J. Purdell-Lewis. 1982. The Pattern of Mineralization of Traumatically-Induced Developmental Defects of Sheep Enamel Assessed by Microhardness and Microradiography. *Journal of Dental Research* 61:1211–16.

Suga, S. 1992. Hypoplasia and Hypomineralization of Teeth Enamel. *Journal of Paleopathology* 2:269–92.

Via, W. F., W. K. Elwood, and J. Bebin. 1959. The Effect of Maternal Hypoxia upon Fetal Dental Enamel. *Henry Ford Hospital Medical Bulletin* 7:94–101.

Warshawsky, H. 1985. Ultrastructural Studies on Amelogenesis. In *The Chemistry and Biology of Mineralized Tissues*, ed. M. J. Glimcher and J. B. Lian, 33–44. New York: Gordon and Breach.

Warshawsky, H., K. Josephsen, A. Thylstrup, and O. Fejerskov. 1981. The Development of Enamel Structure in Rat Incisors as Compared to the Teeth of Monkey and Man. *Anatomical Record* 200:371–99.

Watson, A., M. Massler, and M. Perlstein. 1964. Tooth Ring Analysis of Cerebral Palsy. *American Journal of Dentistry* 107:370–84.

Weber, D. F., and D. R. Eisenmann. 1971. Microscopy of the Neonatal Line in Developing Human Enamel. *American Journal of Anatomy* 132:375–92.

Weber, D. F., D. R. Eisenmann, and P. L. Glick. 1974. Light and Electron Microscope Studies of Retzius Lines in Human Cervical Enamel. *American Journal of Anatomy* 141:91–104.

Whittaker, D. K., and D. Richards. 1978. Scanning Electron Micrography of the Neonatal Line in Human Enamel. *Archives of Oral Biology* 23:45–50.

Wilson, D. F., and F. R. Schroff. 1970. The Nature of the Striae of Retzius as Seen with the Optical Microscope. *Australian Dental Journal* 15:162–71.

Wright, L. E. 1990. Stresses of Contact: A Study of Wilson Bands and Enamel Hypoplasias in the Maya of Lamanai. *American Journal of Human Biology* 2:25–35.

7

Enamel Hypoplasia and Stress in La Florida

Dale L. Hutchinson and Clark Spencer Larsen

For the past two decades, there has been an enormous effort directed at investigating the consequences of European colonization for native populations inhabiting the New World at the time of contact. In addition to verifying Spanish and French observations of various aspects of the lives of the indigenous inhabitants, or delineating the broad patterns of contact and the consequences shared by many indigenous populations, researchers have also directed their efforts at clarifying regional variations in the contact experience, especially as it relates to the impact on health and lifestyle of native peoples.

The European colonization of La Florida in the 17th century was built around an extensive mission system in northern Florida and Atlantic coastal Georgia (Bolton 1921; Geiger 1937; Gannon 1983; Worth 1998, this volume). The chain of missions that stretched east to west across the northern panhandle of Florida and from south to north on the Georgia coast provided thoroughfares along which flowed the goods and services of the indigenous populations participating in the repartimiento in one direction and various imported European products and personnel in the other (Hann 1986, 1988, 1996; McEwan 1993; Bushnell 1994). Maize was an especially important indigenous product with a lengthy history of cultivation for many native groups in Spanish Florida (Hann 1988; Larsen et al., this volume).

The disruptive effects of Spanish missionization and colonization in the southeastern United States materialized as massive indigenous population movements and indigenous social and biological degradation (Larsen 1990; Worth 1995). We have previously documented the biological consequences of the colonial process in the coastal Georgia province of Guale (Hutchinson and Larsen 1988, 1990; Ruff and Larsen 1990; Schoeninger et al. 1990; Simpson et al. 1990; Larsen et al. 1990, 1991, 1992a; Larsen and Hutchinson 1992; Larsen and Harn 1994; Larsen and Ruff 1994; Hutchinson et al. 1998). The focus of this study is to enlarge the scope of our previous research by incorporating a large sample of human remains from the Franciscan mission chain of northern Florida. These missions encompass a more diverse region culturally, ecologically, and temporally than those of the Georgia coast, and they serve both to enrich our current perspectives on biocultural change in La Florida and to help us formulate and test new hypotheses regarding the multifaceted effects of colonization on health and lifestyle.

Negative biological effects of the colonial experience are interpreted in this study through the analysis of enamel growth arrests known as enamel hypoplasias. Hypoplasias are surface features of tooth enamel characterized by deficiency in enamel thickness. They occur in a variety of forms ranging from pits to linear furrows (Hillson 1996; Hillson and Bond 1997). Most hypoplasias we have observed in dentitions from the southeastern United States have been of the linear furrow type. Dental enamel does not remodel during life, and therefore enamel hypoplasias represent a permanent profile of disruptions during normal growth and development in the childhood years between approximately birth and 10 years (Goodman 1989; Dobney and Goodman 1991).

A variety of causal factors have been linked with the disruption of enamel growth and the formation of enamel hypoplasias in laboratory experiments (Kreshover and Clough 1953a, 1953b; Kreshover 1944; Suckling et al. 1983, 1986; Suckling and Thurley 1984), and a number of clinical associations have been made between hypoplastic defects and infectious diseases, malnutrition, or both (Pindborg 1970; Cuttress and Suckling 1982). Thus, following Kreshover (1960), many considered them to be a nonspecific indicator of metabolic stress arising from nutritional or disease insult or both. In Spanish Florida, native populations were exposed to a variety of stressors that could have caused the formation of enamel defects, such as poor diets, especially those focused on maize, infectious diseases, labor demands, and poor living conditions.

For this study, we first present our earlier analysis of enamel hypoplasias for populations inhabiting Atlantic coastal Georgia and adjacent inland areas. We then discuss populations from northern Florida in order to present a general picture of stress in La Florida and to make chronological comparisons between the earlier missions in the north and those which were established later in the south.

Materials and Methods

Our previous research was focused on 310 individuals from 17 populations inhabiting the Georgia coast and adjacent inland localities and represent the Guale cultural group (Hutchinson and Larsen 1988, 1990, 1995; Larsen and Hutchinson 1992). The individuals were grouped into three chronological periods: early prehistoric (400 B.C.–A.D. 1000), late prehistoric (A.D. 1000–A.D. 1550), and early mission (A.D. 1600–A.D. 1680) (table 7.1). We have reconsidered the temporal placement and dietary focus of these populations since our earlier studies and have therefore placed four skeletal series (Johns Mound, Marys Mound, and Southend Mounds I and II) into the late prehistoric period. Our reconsideration is based on stable isotope reconstruction of the diet of these populations, which shows isotopic signatures indicative of the increased maize consumption that is more common for late prehistoric groups (Hutchinson et al. 1998).

In our study of northern Florida populations, 262 individuals from 17 skeletal series were examined for enamel hypoplasias (table 7.1). The individuals were grouped into four chronological periods: Early Prehistoric (A.D. 0–1000), Late Prehistoric (A.D. 1200–1600), Early Mission (A.D. 1600–1680), and Late Mission (A.D. 1680–1700). They represent populations inhabiting coastal and inland localities from four cultural groups: Guale, Timucua, Apalachee, and Yamasee. Individual sites and skeletal series are discussed in more detail in Larsen (this volume).

Our methods followed those previously established in earlier studies (Hutchinson and Larsen 1988, 1990, 1995; Larsen and Hutchinson 1992). Permanent maxillary and mandibular incisors and canines were examined. Teeth were selected from the left side of the dentition if possible, with right teeth substituted in the case of missing left teeth. If necessary, teeth were cleaned of surface debris with acetone prior to observation. Observation of individual teeth was made using a dissecting microscope at a power of approximately 10×. Two observations were made on each tooth: defect presence and location on the tooth crown; and width of the defect, measured from the superior to inferior margins. Measurement of the defect locations and widths was accomplished using a micrometer mounted in the microscope eyepiece. All measurements are in millimeters.

In all, 2,097 teeth representing 772 individuals from 34 populations in Georgia and northern Florida were assessed for enamel hypoplasias (table 7.2). Four types of information were analyzed for this study: (1) percentage of individuals affected by at least one hypoplasia on at least one tooth, (2) frequency of teeth affected by at least one hypoplasia, (3) frequency of

Table 7.1. Samples used for hypoplasia analysis

Site	Group	N[a]
Georgia early prehistoric		
Cunningham Mound C	Guale	2
Cunningham Mound D	Guale	2
Cunningham Mound E	Guale	1
McLeod Mound	Guale	11
Seaside Mound I	Guale	8
Seaside Mound II	Guale	5
Airport site	Guale	19
Deptford site	Guale	10
Cannons Point sites	Guale	6
Sea Island Mound	Guale	17
Charlie King Mound	Guale	17
Florida early prehistoric		
Melton Mound A	Timucua	1
Melton Mound 3	Timucua	2
Mayport Mound	Timucua	11
Wacahoota	Timucua	1
McKeithen Mound C	Timucua	5
Cross Creek	Timucua	1
Georgia late prehistoric		
Marys Mound	Guale	2
Johns Mound	Guale	28
South End Mound I	Guale	1
South End Mound II	Guale	12
Irene Mound	Guale	140
Florida late prehistoric		
Goodman Mound	Timucua	2
Holy Spirit	Timucua	17
Browne Mound	Timucua	10
Leslie Mound	Timucua	1
Lake Jackson	Apalachee	10
Georgia early mission		
Santa Catalina de Guale	Guale	229
Florida early mission		
San Pedro de Patale	Apalachee	15
Santa Maria de Yamasee	Yamasee	40
San Martín de Timucua	Timucua	24
Ossuary at Santa Catalina de Santa Maria	Timucua	39
Florida late mission		
Santa Catalina de Amelia	Guale	64
San Luis de Apalachee	Apalachee	19

a. Number of individuals represented by at least one tooth in the dentition.

Table 7.2. Distribution of dental elements

Tooth	Early prehistoric	Late prehistoric	Early mission	Late mission	Total
			Georgia		
	(N=98)[a]	(N=183)	(N=229)	—	(N=510)
Max. I1	38	80	77	—	195
Max. I2	35	80	77	—	192
Max. C	45	103	128	—	276
Mand. I1	30	75	84	—	189
Mand. I2	43	91	90	—	224
Mand. C	57	119	138	—	314
Total	248	548	594	—	1,390
			Florida		
	(N=21)	(N=40)	(N=118)	(N=83)	(N=262)
Max. I1	6	8	38	51	103
Max. I2	5	7	36	52	100
Max. C	15	11	62	56	144
Mand. I1	4	6	29	49	88
Mand. I2	7	13	39	57	116
Mand. C	15	26	54	61	156
Total	52	71	258	326	707

a. Number of individuals represented by at least one tooth in the dentition.

hypoplasias per tooth type (expressed as mean values), and (4) width of each hypoplasia from superior to inferior margin of enamel defects (expressed as mean values).

Results

There was little difference in the percentage of Georgia individuals affected by at least one hypoplasia on at least one tooth when comparing the different groups (table 7.3). Individuals were affected equally during the early prehistoric and early mission periods (88%). Only 2 percent fewer (86%) individuals were affected during the late prehistoric. None of the differences is statistically significant (chi-square; $p \leq 0.05$). Comparison of individual tooth types affected by at least one hypoplasia shows that a higher frequency of affected teeth occurs during the early prehistoric period (table 7.4).

Mean frequency of hypoplasias in the Georgia populations is slightly higher for the early prehistoric populations when examined by tooth type. For four of six tooth types (maxillary central and lateral incisors, maxillary canine and mandibular canine), the mean frequency is higher for the early

Table 7.3. Percentage of individuals affected by hypoplasia

Early prehistoric		Late prehistoric		Early mission		Late mission		Total
				Georgia				
(N=98)[a]		(N=183)		(N=229)		—		(N=510)
%	N[b]	%	N	%	N			
88	86	86	157	88	202	—		445
				Florida				
(N=21)		(N=40)		(N=118)		(N=83)		(N=262)
%	N	%	N	%	N	%	N	
76	16	58	23	50	57	59	49	145
				Difference[c]				
(N=119)		(N=223)		(N=347)				(N=689)
%	N	%	N	%	N			
-12	102	-28	180	-38	259	—		541

a. Number of individuals represented by at least one tooth in the dentition.
b. Number of individuals affected by at least one enamel hypoplasia.
c. Difference = Florida – Georgia.

prehistoric groups, with higher mean frequencies exhibited for one tooth (maxillary lateral incisor) from the late prehistoric, and one tooth (mandibular central incisor) for the mission group (table 7.5). Mean width of hypoplasias is generally greater for the late prehistoric and mission groups, although mean width was greatest for the early prehistoric groups for the mandibular lateral incisor (table 7.6).

In order to compare the differences in hypoplasia width between the Georgia periods statistically, statistical (t-test) comparisons and distribution plots were assembled for several period comparisons, all for the mandibular canine. Comparisons are made by using mirror image dot density plots that plot data points using raw values and actual frequencies along the central axis with a normal curve plotted above the data points. Box plots are placed at the exterior side of each series in order to illustrate outliers in the data, plotted as asterisks and circles. Comparison of the early prehistoric and late prehistoric periods (table 7.6) shows a dramatic difference in mean width that is statistically significant (t-test; $p \leq 0.01$)(fig. 7.1). Comparison of the late prehistoric with the early mission sample (table 7.6) showed similar mean values with statistically significant differ-

Table 7.4. Percentage of teeth affected by hypoplasia

Tooth	Early prehistoric		Late prehistoric		Early mission		Late mission		Total
					Georgia				
	(N=98)[a]		(N=183)		(N=229)		—		(N=510)
	%	N[b]	%	N	%	N	%	N	
Max. I1	76	38	71	80	71	77	—		195
Max. I2	94	35	68	80	74	77	—		192
Max. C	89	45	74	103	78	128	—		276
Mand. I1	53	30	44	75	43	84	—		189
Mand. I2	74	43	56	91	52	90	—		224
Mand. C	95	57	78	119	87	138	—		314
Total		248		548		594	—		1,390
					Florida				
	(N=21)		(N=40)		(N=118)		(N=83)		(N=262)
Max. I1	50	6	75	8	42	38	35	51	103
Max. I2	40	5	43	7	22	36	21	52	100
Max. C	67	15	55	11	40	62	32	56	144
Mand. I1	0	4	0	6	7	29	18	49	88
Mand. I2	14	7	31	13	13	39	18	57	116
Mand. C	60	15	58	26	44	54	48	61	156
Total		52		71		258		326	707

a. Number of individuals represented by at least one tooth in the dentition.
b. Number of teeth examined (hypoplastic + nonhypoplastic).

ences (t-test; p ≤ 0.05; see fig. 7.2). Late mission populations have smaller mean width values than the early mission populations by only 0.2 mm. Examination of the early mission distribution shows that the difference between the median (.50) and the mean (.73) is extremely high and the early mission sample had several more outliers than the late prehistoric sample (fig. 7.2). Comparison of the temporal extremes, early prehistoric and late mission (table 7.6), shows the same distinct mean width values as for the early and late prehistoric. The difference between the early prehistoric and early mission populations is statistically significant (t-test; p ≤ 0.01; see fig. 7.3).

The percentages of northern Florida individuals affected by at least one hypoplasia on at least one tooth (table 7.3) show that the most individuals were affected during the early prehistoric (76%) and late mission (59%) periods, although the late prehistoric (58%) and early mission (50%) frequencies were not substantially different from the late mission period fre-

Table 7.5. Mean hypoplasia frequency

Tooth	Early prehistoric		Late prehistoric		Early mission		Late mission		Total
					Georgia				
	(N=98)[a]		(N=183)		(N=229)		—		(N=510)
	%	N[b]	%	N	%	N	%	N	
Max. I1	2.41	38	2.26	80	2.38	77	—		195
Max. I2	2.36	35	2.22	80	2.09	77	—		192
Max. C	2.43	45	2.18	103	2.29	128	—		276
Mand. I1	1.94	30	1.70	75	2.08	84	—		189
Mand. I2	1.59	43	2.08	91	1.96	90	—		224
Mand. C	3.13	57	2.41	119	2.42	138	—		314
Total		248		548		594	—		1,390
					Florida				
	(N=21)		(N=40)		(N=118)		(N=83)		(N=262)
Max. I1	1.33	6	1.33	8	1.63	38	1.56	51	103
Max. I2	1.00	5	1.33	7	2.13	36	1.55	52	100
Max. C	2.10	15	1.67	11	2.00	62	1.78	56	144
Mand. I1	0.00	4	0.00	6	1.00	29	1.33	49	88
Mand. I2	1.00	7	1.00	13	1.20	39	1.60	57	116
Mand. C	3.67	15	2.00	26	1.67	54	1.76	61	156
Total		52		71		258		326	707
					Difference[c]				
	(N=119)		(N=223)		(N=347)		—		(N=689)
Max. I1	-1.08	44	-0.93	88	-0.75	115	—		247
Max. I2	-1.36	40	-0.89	87	0.04	113	—		240
Max. C	-0.33	60	-0.51	114	-0.29	190	—		364
Mand. I1	-1.94	34	-1.70	81	-1.08	113	—		228
Mand. I2	-0.59	50	-1.08	104	-0.76	129	—		283
Mand. C	0.54	72	-0.41	145	-0.75	192	—		409
Total		300		619		852	—		1,771

a. Number of individuals represented by at least one tooth in the dentition.
b. Number of teeth examined (hypoplastic + nonhypoplastic).
c. Difference = Florida – Georgia.

quencies. None of the differences was statistically significant (chi-square; p ≤ 0.05). Comparison of individual tooth types affected by at least one hypoplasia shows that in general a higher frequency of affected teeth occurs during the early and late prehistoric periods rather than the early and late mission periods (table 7.4). The exception is the mandibular central incisor, which expressed hypoplasias for only individuals in the early and late mission samples.

Table 7.6. Mean hypoplasia width

Tooth	Early prehistoric		Late prehistoric		Early mission		Late mission		Total
	Georgia								
	(N=98)[a]		(N=183)		(N=229)		—		(N=510)
	%	N[b]	%	N	%	N	%	N	
Max. I1	0.58	38	0.65	80	0.58	77	—		195
Max. I2	0.49	35	0.58	80	0.70	77	—		192
Max. C	0.57	45	0.63	103	0.73	128	—		276
Mand. I1	0.51	30	0.55	75	0.41	84	—		189
Mand. I2	0.51	43	0.50	91	0.46	90	—		224
Mand. C	0.50	57	0.72	119	0.73	138	—		314
Total		248		548		594	—		1,390
	Florida								
	(N=21)		(N=40)		(N=118)		(N=83)		(N=262)
Max. I1	0.70	6	0.73	8	0.59	38	0.46	51	103
Max. I2	0.40	5	0.68	7	0.39	36	0.43	52	100
Max. C	0.62	15	0.60	11	0.60	62	0.43	56	144
Mand. I1	0.00	4	0.00	6	1.05	29	0.48	49	88
Mand. I2	0.20	7	0.85	13	0.77	39	0.40	57	116
Mand. C	0.74	15	0.65	26	0.87	54	0.58	61	156
Total		52		71		258		326	707
	Difference[c]								
	(N=119)		(N=223)		(N=347)		—		(N=689)
Max. I1	0.12	44	0.08	88	0.01	115	—		247
Max. I2	-0.09	40	0.10	87	-0.31	113	—		240
Max. C	0.05	60	-0.03	114	-0.13	190	—		364
Mand. I1	-0.51	34	-0.55	81	0.64	113	—		228
Mand. I2	-0.31	50	0.35	104	0.31	129	—		283
Mand. C	0.24	72	-0.07	145	0.14	192	—		409
Total		300		619		852	—		1,771

a. Number of individuals represented by at least one tooth in the dentition.
b. Number of teeth examined (hypoplastic + nonhypoplastic).
c. Difference = Florida – Georgia.

Neither mean frequency of hypoplasias nor mean width of hypoplasias shows a consistent pattern when examined by tooth type. For two of six tooth types (maxillary canine and mandibular canine), the mean frequency is higher for the prehistoric groups, with higher mean frequencies exhibited for three teeth (maxillary central and lateral incisors and mandibular lateral incisor) of mission groups (table 7.5). Mean width of hypoplasias is generally greater for the prehistoric groups, although there are no man-

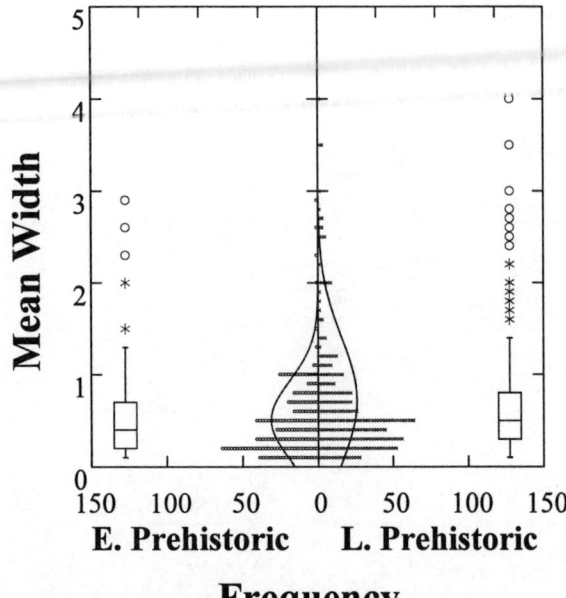

Frequency

Fig. 7.1. Comparison of mean hypoplasia width for Georgia early prehistoric and Georgia late prehistoric. The y axis shows the mean width of hypoplasia (in mm) and the x axis shows the actual frequency of hypoplasia for each 0.1 mm width category. Overlying the actual frequency is a normal distribution plot line running vertically. A box plot is presented on either side of the actual frequency and the normal distribution plot line. The central horizontal line within the box represents the median value. The bottom and top of the box ("hinges") mark the first and third quantiles, respectively. The median splits the sample in half, and the first and third quantiles split the remaining halves in half again. Thus, the central 50 percent of the values fall within the range of the box. The upper and lower vertical lines extending from the top and bottom of the box ("whiskers") mark the H-spread (= 1.5 × absolute value of the difference between the hinges). The asterisks (*) mark the values falling outside the lower and upper inner fences. For example, the lower inner fence represents the product of 1.5 × median-lower hinge. The circles (o) mark the values falling outside the lower and upper outer fences. For example, the lower outer fence is a product of 3 × median-lower hinge. The asterisks and circles are considered outliers in the data samples.

dibular central incisors for the prehistoric which allow comparison (table 7.6). Mean hypoplastic width for two teeth—the mandibular central incisor and canine—are greatest in the early mission groups. More important, one consistent pattern emerges—late mission teeth often exhibit hypoplasias of lesser width than in any other period.

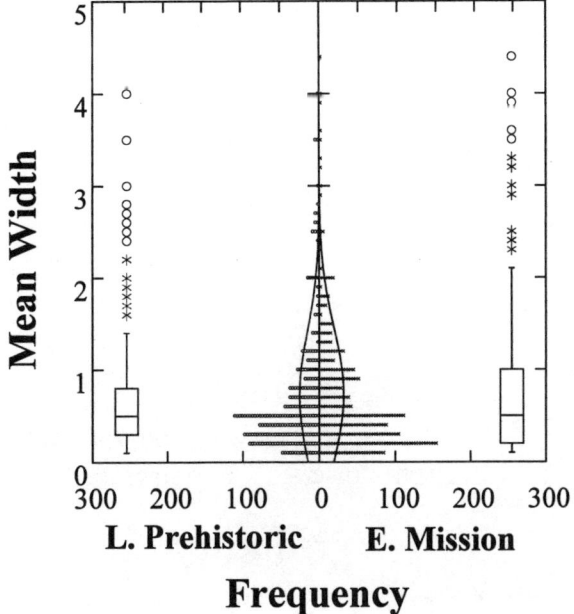

Fig. 7.2. Comparison of mean hypoplasia width for Georgia late prehistoric and Georgia early mission. See figure 7.1 for an explanation of the symbols and statistical graphics.

In order to compare the differences in hypoplasia width between the periods statistically, t-test comparisons and distribution plots were assembled for several period comparisons, all for the mandibular canine. Comparisons were made in the same fashion as for the Georgia series, by using mirror image dot density plots. Comparison of the early prehistoric and late prehistoric periods shows similar mean width values with no statistically significant difference (t-test; $p \leq 0.05$; see fig. 7.4). Comparison of the temporal extremes, early prehistoric and late mission, shows more distinct mean width values, but they are not statistically significant (t-test; $p \leq 0.05$; see fig. 7.5). However, comparison of the two mission period samples—early mission and late mission—revealed disparate mean values with statistically significant differences (t-test; $p \leq 0.05$) (fig. 7.6). That is, the late mission populations have smaller mean width values than the early mission populations. Examination of the distribution and the difference between the median (0.50) and the mean (0.87) shows that extremely high values are present in the early mission sample.

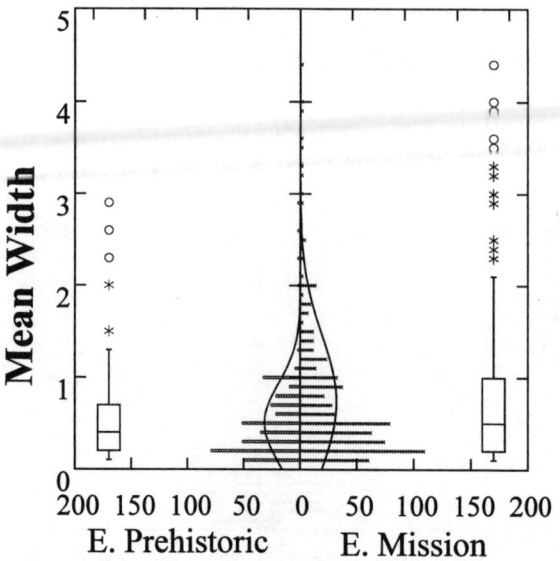

Fig. 7.3. Comparison of mean hypoplasia width for Georgia early prehistoric and Georgia early mission. See figure 7.1 for an explanation of the symbols and statistical graphics.

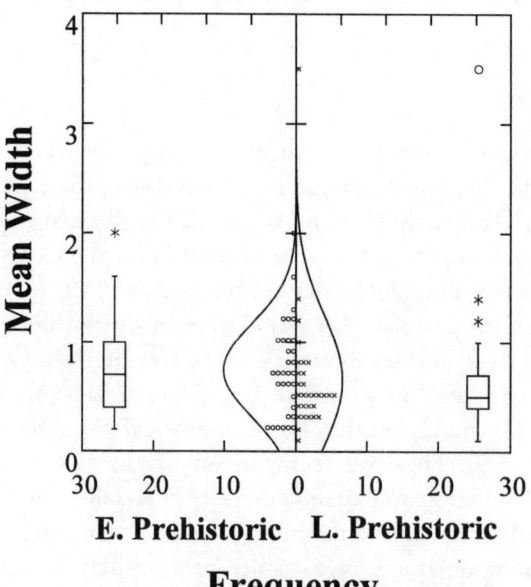

Fig. 7.4. Comparison of mean hypoplasia width for Florida early prehistoric and Florida late prehistoric. See figure 7.1 for an explanation of the symbols and statistical graphics.

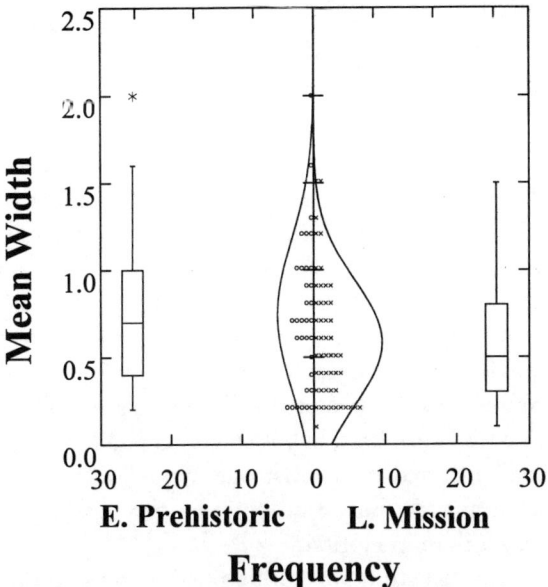

Fig. 7.5. Comparison of mean hypoplasia width for Florida early prehistoric and Florida late mission. See figure 7.1 for an explanation of the symbols and statistical graphics.

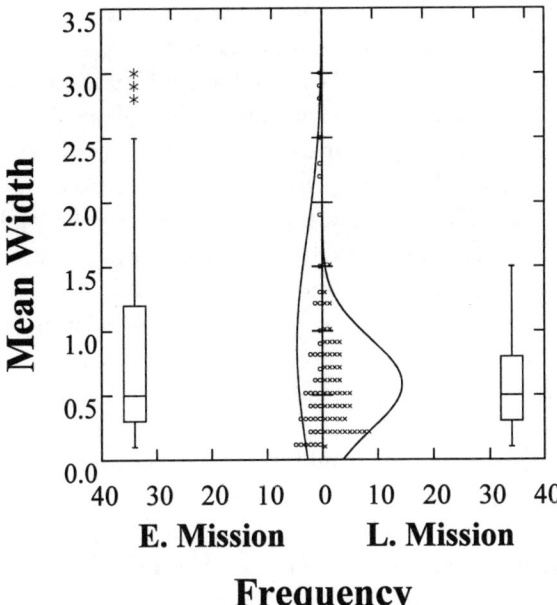

Fig. 7.6. Comparison of mean hypoplasia width for Florida early mission and Florida late mission. See figure 7.1 for an explanation of the symbols and statistical graphics.

Discussion

The following primary results emerge from our analysis and comparison of these populations. First, frequency of enamel defects (percentage of individuals affected) is greater in the Georgia groups than in the Florida groups. Second, width of hypoplasias is often highest for the late prehistoric and early mission Georgia groups, whereas Florida hypoplasia width is often greatest for the late prehistoric groups. Third, while mean width of enamel defects is greatest for about half the tooth types for Florida and half of the tooth types for Georgia in each period, mean frequency of defects per tooth type is almost always greatest for the Florida populations in every period (tables 7.5 and 7.6). Last, in both Georgia and Florida, the percentage of individuals affected by at least one hypoplasia is greatest for the earliest and latest groups, but in all periods there are more individuals affected in Georgia than in Florida.

In order to place the study of Florida mission populations within the broader regional context of Spanish Florida, it is necessary to examine the patterns elucidated in our previous study of populations inhabiting the Georgia coast (Hutchinson and Larsen 1988, 1990, 1995; Larsen and Hutchinson 1992). When the northern Florida hypoplasia data are incorporated with previous data from our study of enamel defects in the region of Spanish Florida, they form a sample based on 772 individuals from 34 skeletal series (table 7.1), based on 1,390 teeth from Guale and 707 teeth from the other mission settings. The individuals examined represent populations that inhabited coastal and inland localities occupied by four cultural groups: Guale, Timucua, Apalachee, and Yamasee. They can additionally be grouped into four chronological periods: early prehistoric, late prehistoric, early mission, and late mission; the specific chronological placement varies depending on the region (table 7.1).

Our regional analysis of stable isotope diet information indicates that the transition to increased reliance on maize agriculture differed in chronology and in geography for populations inhabiting Georgia and Florida (Hutchinson et al. 1998; Larsen et al., this volume). Unlike in Georgia, many populations in Florida exhibit little evidence for maize consumption prior to European contact. However, following contact with Europeans there was a convergence of diet to increased maize consumption, with all populations consuming maize, regardless of location. Prehistoric variation was due largely to the exploitation of different ecological areas proximal to settlements, although cultural differences undoubtedly contributed some of the variation. Some sites, such as Lake Jackson in Florida and Irene

Mound in Georgia, exhibit the mound and plaza configurations commonly associated with Mississippian groups after A.D. 1000 (Hutchinson et al. 1998), but many others lack any evidence of a Mississippian affiliation.

There are reasons to expect differences between the mission populations of Georgia and Florida in aspects of health and disease. Santa Catalina de Guale on St. Catherines Island, Georgia, is the earliest of the missions examined in this study. The experience of the Spanish in exploiting resources in the region undoubtedly increased through time. As well, the island location of Santa Catalina de Guale likely contributed to differences in the mission experience relative to that in the later inland missions in northern Florida. For instance, fresh water may have been more difficult to obtain on the islands, but regular transport and exchange of goods and supplies was facilitated by the seaboard location. Long-distance labor exploitation of native groups may have varied between island and inland locations, and pre-contact experience with maize agriculture varied between the two broad ecological zones (Hutchinson et al. 1998; Larsen et al., this volume).

Three areas of inquiry can be addressed by a broad comparative examination of populations inhabiting Florida and Georgia: (1) differences between Georgia and Florida populations for number of individuals affected by at least one hypoplasia, (2) differences between Georgia and Florida populations for hypoplasia widths, and (3) general conclusions about the impact of the missionization process on the life and health of the indigenous inhabitants. In many studies worldwide, the number of individuals affected by enamel defects has been interpreted as one measure of metabolic stress in a population. However, in populations exhibiting roughly equal numbers of individuals affected by hypoplasia, percentage of individuals affected offers limited information regarding the differences in stress widths. For example, when the number of individuals affected in the Florida skeletal series is compared to the number of individuals affected from the Georgia coast, we can easily see that more individuals are affected on the Georgia coast than in Florida (fig. 7.7). However, the distribution offers little information regarding the quality of stress events in the Georgia coastal populations, where there is only a 2 percent difference across three periods.

Interestingly, Simpson (this volume) finds that the percentage of individuals affected by at least one pathological stria is reduced in the late prehistoric Florida sample (36%) as compared to the early prehistoric Florida sample (67%). This is the same pattern exhibited for percentage of individuals affected by at least one enamel hypoplasia in prehistoric Flor-

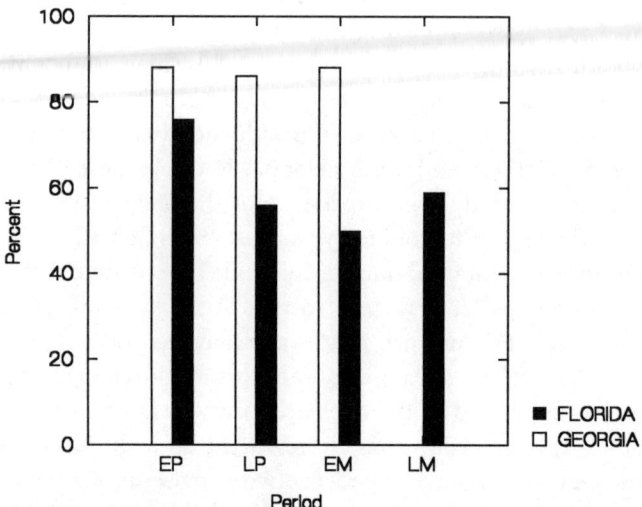

Fig. 7.7. Comparison of percentage of individuals affected by at least one hypoplasia, Georgia and Florida. EP = early prehistoric, LP = late prehistoric, EM = early mission, LM = late mission (available Florida only).

ida. However, percentage of individuals affected by at least one pathological stria increases dramatically in the early mission (83%) and late mission (82%) Florida samples. This is a different pattern than that exhibited by enamel hypoplasia. Individuals affected by at least one hypoplasia decrease in the early mission (50%) Florida sample and increase only slightly in the late mission (59%) Florida sample. As Simpson (this volume) points out, clearly pathological striae and enamel hypoplasias provide different kinds of information and potentially have different etiologies.

Measures of hypoplasia frequency and width offer another possibility of addressing the differences in metabolic stress. They are undoubtedly related because wider hypoplasias are likely correlated with lower hypoplasia frequencies. In other words, more of the available tooth crown is occupied by a wide hypoplasia and it leaves less tooth crown for additional hypoplastic defects. The *meaning* of hypoplasia width has been actively debated in recent years. Two predominant interpretations have emerged: widths indicate either *severity* of metabolic insult or *duration* of metabolic insult (Blakey and Armelagos 1985; Hutchinson and Larsen 1988; Ensor and Irish 1995) or some unknown combination. Recently, Hillson and Bond (1997) have presented a third interpretation: that hypoplasia width is directly correlated to the location of the defect on the tooth crown. We

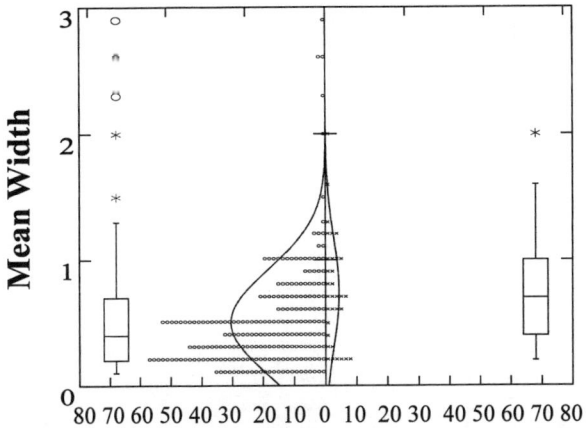

Georgia E. Prehistoric   Florida E. Prehistoric

Frequency

Fig. 7.8. Comparison of mean hypoplasia width for Georgia early prehistoric and Florida early prehistoric. See figure 7.1 for an explanation of the symbols and statistical graphics.

believe that hypoplasia width serves as an indicator of stress differences between human populations and provides different information than the frequency of affected individuals.

Comparison of the early prehistoric series from Florida with the early prehistoric series from coastal Georgia indicates a discrepancy between two measures of hypoplasia, namely percentage of individuals affected and width of hypoplasia (figs. 7.7–7.8). The higher percentage of individuals affected from the Georgia coast (88%) as compared to Florida (76%) provides little qualitative information and in fact is not statistically significant. However, there is a significant difference in hypoplasia width measures; the Florida early prehistoric series has a mean width of hypoplasias for the mandibular canine 0.24 mm greater than the Georgia coastal series, a statistically significant difference (t-test; p ≤ 0.01). Clearly, percentage of individuals affected and width of hypoplasia yield different information.

In a previous study of Guale from Georgia and north Florida missions, we concluded that mean hypoplasia width declined in the late mission period or, viewed another way, that significant differences are present when comparing mean hypoplasia width between early mission Guale and late mission Guale (Larsen and Hutchinson 1992; Larsen et al. 1992a).

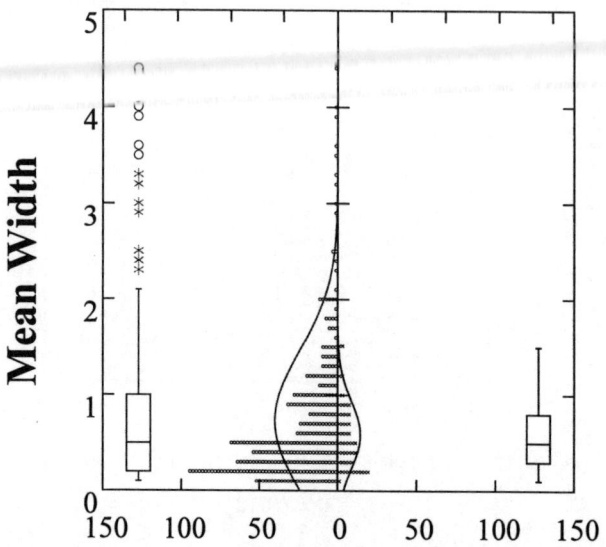

Fig. 7.9. Comparison of mean hypoplasia width for Georgia early mission and Florida late mission. See figure 7.1 for an explanation of the symbols and statistical graphics.

Even with new data and additional tribes sampled in the present study, that distinction remains (fig. 7.9). The difference is statistically significant (t-test; $p \leq 0.05$). Although there is a significant difference in hypoplasia width between early mission and late mission populations in Florida, there is not a significant difference in mean hypoplasia width between early mission populations in Florida and early mission populations in Georgia, despite the numerous outliers in both populations (fig. 7.10).

There are several possible explanations for the greater frequency and width of hypoplasias in the prehistoric groups, especially the late prehistoric groups in both Florida and Georgia, as compared to the mission groups. Certainly, populations foraging are likely subjected to seasonal shortages, and the relatively smaller but more numerous hypoplasias for early prehistoric groups in both Georgia and Florida may indicate such seasonal shortages. We previously noted that the enamel hypoplasia data suggest that the transition from a lifeway based on foraging to one based at least in part on maize agriculture occasioned relatively greater metabolic

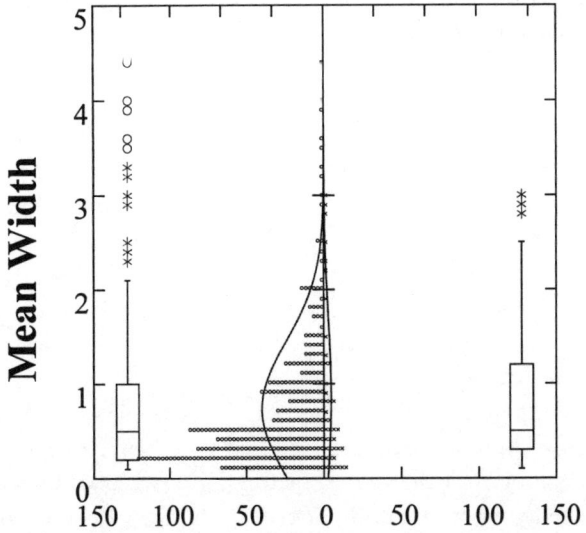

Fig. 7.10. Comparison of mean hypoplasia width for Georgia early mission and Florida early mission. See figure 7.1 for an explanation of the symbols and statistical graphics.

stress than did the transition in lifeway associated with the arrival of Europeans and the establishment of mission centers (Larsen and Hutchinson 1992). A second explanation is that late prehistoric populations were under increased stress for other reasons, such as intrapopulation conflict, scarce resources, and internal strife.

There are several alternative explanations for the decrease in (or decrease in size of) hypoplasia width during the late mission period. First, it is possible that the contact experience placed significantly greater stresses on the Native American populations initially contacted by the Spaniards and placed within a mission environment than on later mission populations. Such an explanation inherently contains an associated increase in adaptive success. Ethnohistoric accounts that report increased labor demands and increases in other skeletal lesions, such as porotic hyperostosis (Larsen et al. 1992a), do not support a hypothesis of adaptive success and decreased stress. Surprisingly, all other biological indicators of stress argue for a continued decline in health during the late mission period. Simpson (this volume) also finds that the percentage of individuals exhibiting pathological striae remains the same for the late mission groups.

A second explanation is that the regional differences, which include differences in ecological variability and resource availability between Florida and Georgia, contribute to lower values for the late mission sample. Two things argue against this interpretation. First, most of the late mission sample is from Amelia Island, Florida, and therefore the environmental and resource constraints are extremely similar to those for coastal Georgia. Second, early prehistoric series from Florida exhibit wider hypoplasias than in the Georgia coastal series, necessitating explanation of an ecological/resource condition negatively affecting the early series but positively affecting the late series.

A third explanation for the decrease in hypoplasia width is that there may be some kind of sampling bias that could explain the decline in late mission hypoplasia values. Two factors argue against this as an explanation for the hypoplasia width patterns. First, the values are similar for the early mission series in Georgia and Florida—both series exhibit wider hypoplasias and have numerous outliers. Second, the addition of new data into the late mission sample did not alter our previous observations of a decrease in late mission hypoplasia width.

The importance of approaching cultural and biological change as a complex regional phenomenon was clearly demonstrated in our study of dietary change in La Florida (Hutchinson et al. 1998). Our dietary reconstruction of many of the same populations included in that analysis showed clear regional differences in diet prior to Spanish contact, especially between the coastal and interior localities but also between the modern states of Florida and Georgia. Our analysis of metabolic stress in the Florida and Georgia individuals shows important similarities as well as important differences.

In summary, interpreting the health of Native Americans following European contact is a complex issue, and multiple factors need to be considered, including geographic location, ecology, social and political organization, diet, and other behavioral variables. Variation in these factors between regions such as we see in Florida and Georgia can influence native responses to European colonization. Most important, we see similar regional variation in the enamel growth response to general metabolic stress as we saw for diet—there are real differences between populations inhabiting Georgia and Florida. The enamel hypoplasia data make it clear that the early process of indigenous and foreign population integration was neither simple nor uniform.

Acknowledgments

This project is a contribution to the La Florida Bioarchaeology Project. Bioarchaeological fieldwork on St. Catherines Island and Amelia Island was facilitated through the cooperative projects with David Hurst Thomas, Kenneth Hardin, Jerald Milanich, Rebecca Saunders, and Bonnie McEwan. Krusheska Quiros assisted in the cataloguing and specimen preparation for this analysis. For editing and other useful suggestions during this project, we thank Lorraine Aragon, Katherine Russell, and Scott Simpson. Collection of data from the Georgia skeletal series was supported by a fellowship from the American Museum of Natural History Graduate Research Participation Program. Collection of data from the Florida skeletal series was funded by the Edward John Noble Foundation, Dr. and Mrs. George H. Dorion, and the National Science Foundation (grant awards SBR-9305391, BNS-8406773, and BNS-8703848). We thank the following curators and their institutions for permission to study the teeth under their care and to undertake the analyses described in this chapter: David Hurst Thomas (American Museum of Natural History), Jerald Milanich (Florida Museum of Natural History), Douglas Ubelaker and Donald Ortner (Smithsonian Institution), and Bonnie McEwan, David Dickel, and James Miller (Florida Bureau of Archaeological Research).

References Cited

Blakey, M., and G. J. Armelagos. 1985. Deciduous Enamel Defects in Prehistoric Americans from Dickson Mounds: Prenatal and Postnatal Stress. *American Journal of Physical Anthropology* 66:371–80.

Bolton, H. E. 1921. *The Spanish Borderlands: A Chronicle of Old Florida and the Southwest.* New Haven: Yale University Press.

Bullen, A. K. 1963. *Physical Anthropology of the Goodman Mound.* Contributions of the Florida State Museum, Social Sciences 10:61–71.

Bushnell, A. T. 1986. *Santa Maria in the Written Record.* Florida State Museum Department of Anthropology Miscellaneous Project Report Series 21.

———. 1994. *Situado and Sabana: Spain's Support System for the Presidio and Mission Provinces of Florida.* Anthropological Papers of the American Museum of Natural History 74.

Caldwell, J., and C. McCann. 1941. *Irene Mound Site, Chatham County, Georgia.* Athens: University of Georgia Press.

Cuttress, T. W., and G. W. Suckling. 1982. The Assessment of Non-Carious Defects of the Enamel. *International Dental Journal* 32:119–22.

Dobney, K., and A. H. Goodman. 1991. Epidemiological Studies of Dental Enamel Hypoplasias in Mexico and Bradford: Their Relevance to Archaeological Skeletal Studies. In *Health in Past Societies: Biocultural Interpretations of Human Skeletal Remains in Archaeological Contexts*, ed. H. Bush and M. Zvelebil, 81–100. British Archaeological Reports International Series 567.

Ensor, B. E., and J. D. Irish. 1995. Hypoplastic Area Method for Analyzing Dental Enamel Hypoplasia. *American Journal of Physical Anthropology* 98:507–17.

Gannon, M. V. 1983. *The Cross in the Sand: The Early Catholic Church in Florida 1513–1870*. Gainesville: University Presses of Florida.

Geiger, M. 1937. *The Franciscan Conquest of Florida (1573–1618)*. Studies in Hispanic-American History 1. Washington: Catholic University of America.

Goodman, A. H. 1989. Dental Enamel Hypoplasias in Prehistoric Populations. *Advances in Dental Research* 3:265–71.

Hann, J. H. 1986. Demographic Patterns and Changes in Mid-Seventeenth Century Timucua and Apalachee. *Florida Historical Quarterly* 64:371–92.

———. 1988. *Apalachee: The Land Between the Rivers*. Gainesville: University Presses of Florida.

———. 1990. Summary Guide to Spanish Florida Missions and *Visitas*, with Churches in the Sixteenth and Seventeenth Centuries. *Americas* 56:417–513.

———. 1996. *A History of the Timucua Indians and Missions*. Gainesville: University Press of Florida.

Hillson, S. 1996. *Dental Anthropology*. Cambridge: Cambridge University Press.

Hillson, S., and S. Bond. 1997. Relationship of Enamel Hypoplasia to the Pattern of Tooth Crown Growth: A Discussion. *American Journal of Physical Anthropology* 104:89–104.

Hoshower, L. M. 1992. Bioanthropological Analysis of a Seventeenth-Century Native American Spanish Mission Population: Biocultural Impacts on the Northern Utina. Ph.D. diss., University of Florida, Gainesville.

Hoshower, L. M., and J. T. Milanich. 1993. Excavations in the Fig Springs Mission Burial Area. In *The Spanish Missions of La Florida*, ed. B. G. McEwan, 217–43. Gainesville: University Press of Florida.

Hulse, F. S. 1941. The People Who Lived at Irene: Physical Anthropology. In *Irene Mound Site, Chatham County, Georgia*, ed. J. Caldwell and C. McCann, 57–68. Athens: University of Georgia Press.

Hutchinson, D. L., and C. S. Larsen. 1988. Determination of Stress Episode Duration from Linear Enamel Hypoplasias: A Case Study from St. Catherines Island, Georgia. *Human Biology* 60:93–110.

———. 1990. Stress and Lifeway Change: The Evidence from Enamel Hypoplasias. In *The Archaeology of Mission Santa Catalina de Guale: 2. Biocultural Interpretations of a Population in Transition*, ed. C. S. Larsen, 50–65. Anthropological Papers of the American Museum of Natural History 68.

———. 1995. Physiological Stress in the Prehistoric Stillwater Marsh: Evidence of Enamel Defects. In *Bioarchaeology of the Stillwater Marsh: Prehistoric Human Adaptation in the Western Great Basin*, ed. C. S. Larsen and R. L. Kelly, 81–95. Anthropological Papers of the American Museum of Natural History 77.

Hutchinson, D. L., and L. Norr. 1994. Late Prehistoric and Historic Diet in Gulf Coast Florida. In *In the Wake of Contact: Biological Responses to Conquest*, ed. C. S. Larsen and G. R. Milner, 81–95. New York: Wiley-Liss

Hutchinson, D. L., C. S. Larsen, and I. Choi. 1997. Stressed to the Max? Physiological Perturbation in the Krapina Neandertals. *Current Anthropology* 38:904–14.

Hutchinson, D. L., C. S. Larsen, M. J. Schoeninger, and L. Norr. 1998. Regional Variation in the Pattern of Maize Adoption and Use in Florida and Georgia. *American Antiquity* 63:397–416.

Jackson, R. H. 1985. Demographic Change in Northwestern New Spain. *Americas* 41:462–79.

Jones, B.C. 1982. Southern Cult Manifestations at the Lake Jackson Site, Leon County, Florida: Salvage Excavation of Mound 3. *Midcontinental Journal of Archaeology* 7:3–44.

Jones, B. C., R. Storey, and R. Widmer. 1991. The Patale Cemetery: Evidence Concerning the Apalachee Mission Mortuary Complex. In *San Pedro y San Pablo de Patale: A Seventeenth-Century Spanish Mission in Leon County, Florida*, ed. B. C. Jones, J. Hann, and J. F. Scarry, 109–146. Florida Archaeology 5.

Kreshover, S. J. 1944. The Pathogenesis of Enamel Hypoplasia: An Experimental Study. *Journal of Dental Research* 23:231–39.

———. 1960. Metabolic Disturbances in Tooth Formation. *Annals of the New York Academy of Sciences* 85:161–67.

Kreshover, S. J., and O. W. Clough. 1953a. Prenatal Influences on Tooth Development: pt. 1. Alloxan Diabetes in Rats. *Journal of Dental Research* 32:246–61.

———. 1953b. Prenatal Influences on Tooth Development: pt. 2. Artificially Induced Fever in Rats. *Journal of Dental Research* 32:565–72.

Larsen, C. S. 1982. *The Anthropology of St. Catherines Island: 3. Prehistoric Human Biological Adaptation.* Anthropological Papers of the American Museum of Natural History 57, pt. 3.

———. 1993. On the Frontier of Contact: Mission Bioarchaeology in La Florida. In *The Spanish Missions of La Florida*, ed. B. G. McEwan, 322–456. Gainesville: University Press of Florida.

———. 1996. Unpublished data on file at Research Laboratories of Archaeology, University of North Carolina, Chapel Hill.

Larsen, C. S. (ed.). 1990. *The Archaeology of Mission Santa Catalina de Guale: 2. Biocultural Interpretations of a Population in Transition.* Anthropological Papers of the American Museum of Natural History 68.

Larsen, C. S., and D. E. Harn. 1994. Health in Transition: Disease and Nutrition in the Georgia Bight. In *Paleonutrition: The Diet and Health of Prehistoric Americans*, ed. K. D. Sobolik, 222–34. Southern Illinois University Center for Archaeological Investigations Occasional Paper 22.

Larsen, C. S., and D. L. Hutchinson. 1992. Dental Evidence for Physiological Disruption: Biocultural Interpretations from the Eastern Spanish Borderlands,

U.S.A. In *Recent Contributions to the Study of Enamel Developmental Defects,* ed. A. H. Goodman and L. L. Capasso, 151–69. Journal of Paleopath ology Monographic Publications 2.

Larsen, C. S., and C. B. Ruff. 1994. The Stresses of Conquest in Spanish Florida: Structural Adaptation and Change Before and After Contact. In *In the Wake of Contact: Biological Responses to Conquest,* ed. C. S. Larsen and G. R. Milner, 21–34. New York: Wiley-Liss.

Larsen, C. S., R. Shavit, and M. C. Griffin. 1991. Dental Caries Evidence for Dietary Change: An Archaeological Context. In *Advances in Dental Anthropology,* ed. M. A. Kelley and C. S. Larsen, 179–202. New York: Wiley-Liss.

Larsen, C. S., C. B. Ruff, M. J. Schoeninger, and D. L. Hutchinson. 1992a. Population Decline and Extinction in La Florida. In *Disease and Demography in the Americas: Changing Patterns Before and After 1492,* ed. J. W. Verano and D. H. Ubelaker, 81–95. Washington: Smithsonian Institution Press.

Larsen, C. S., M. J. Schoeninger, D. L. Hutchinson, K. F. Russell, and C. B. Ruff. 1990. Beyond Demographic Collapse: Biological Adaptation and Change in Native Populations of La Florida. In *Columbian Consequences: 2. Archaeological and Historical Perspectives on the Spanish Borderlands East,* ed. D. H. Thomas, 409–28. Washington: Smithsonian Institution Press.

Larsen, C. S., M. J. Schoeninger, N. J. van der Merwe, K. M. Moore, and J. A. Lee-Thorpe. 1992b. Carbon and Nitrogen Stable Isotope Signatures of Human Dietary Change in the Georgia Bight. *American Journal of Physical Anthropology* 89:197–214.

Larsen, C. S., A. W. Crosby, M. C. Griffin, D. L. Hutchinson, C. B. Ruff, K. F. Russell, M. J. Schoeninger, L. E. Sering, S. W. Simpson, J. L. Takács, and M. F. Teaford. N.d. A Biohistory of Health and Behavior in the Georgia Bight: The Agricultural Transition and the Impact of European Contact. In *The Backbone of History: Health and Nutrition in the Western Hemisphere,* ed. R. H. Steckel and J. C. Rose. New York: Cambridge University Press. In press.

Marrinan, R. A. 1993. Archaeological Investigations at Mission Patale, 1984–1991. In *The Spanish Missions of La Florida,* ed. B. G. McEwan, 244–94. Gainesville: University Press of Florida.

McEwan, B. G. 1993. Hispanic Life on the Seventeenth-Century Florida Frontier. In *The Spanish Missions of La Florida,* ed. B. G. McEwan, 295–321. Gainesville: University Press of Florida.

Milanich, J. T. 1978. Two Cades Pond Sites in North-Central Florida: The Occupational Nexus as a Mode of Settlement. *Florida Anthropologist* 31:151–75.

———. 1994. *Archaeology of Precolumbian Florida.* Gainesville: University Press of Florida.

Milanich, J. T., A. Cordell, V. Knight, and B. Sigler-Lavelle. 1984. *McKeithen Weeden Island: The Culture of Northern Florida, A.D. 200–900.* Orlando: Academic Press.

Pindborg, J. J. 1970. *Pathology of the Dental Hard Tissues*. Philadelphia: W. B. Saunders.

Recourt, P. 1975. Final Notes on the Goodman Mound. *Florida Anthropologist* 28:85 95.

Ruff, C. B., and C. S. Larsen. 1990. Postcranial Biomechanical Adaptations to Subsistence Strategy Changes on the Georgia Coast. In *The Archaeology of Mission Santa Catalina de Guale*: 2. *Biocultural Interpretations of a Population in Transition*, ed. C. S. Larsen, 94–120. Anthropological Papers of the American Museum of Natural History 68.

Saunders, R. 1988. *Excavations at 8NA41: Two Mission Period Sites on Amelia Island, Florida*. Florida State Museum Department of Anthropology Miscellaneous Project Report Series 35.

Schoeninger, M. J., N. J. van der Merwe, K. Moore, J. Lee-Thorpe, and C. S. Larsen. 1990. Decrease in Diet Quality between the Prehistoric and Contact Periods. In *The Archaeology of Mission Santa Catalina de Guale*: 2. *Biocultural Interpretations of a Population in Transition*, ed. C. S. Larsen, 78–94. Anthropological Papers of the American Museum of Natural History 68.

Sears, W. H. 1959. *Two Weeden Island Period Burial Mounds, Florida: The W. H. Browne Mound, Duval County; the MacKenzie Mound, Marion County*. Contributions of the Florida State Museum Social Sciences 5.

Shapiro, G., and B. G. McEwan. 1992. *Archaeology at San Luis*: pt. 1. *The Apalachee Council House*. Florida Archaeology 6.

Simmons, S., C. S. Larsen, and K. F. Russell. 1989. Demographic Interpretations from Ossuary Remains in Northern Spanish Florida. *American Journal of Physical Anthropology* 78:302.

Simpson, S. W., D. L. Hutchinson, and C. S. Larsen. 1990. Coping with Stress: Tooth Size, Dental Defects, and Age-at-Death. In *The Archaeology of Mission Santa Catalina de Guale*: 2. *Biocultural Interpretations of a Population in Transition*, ed. C. S. Larsen, 66–77. Anthropological Papers of the American Museum of Natural History 68.

Smith, S. D. 1971. A Reinterpretation of the Cades Pond Archaeological Period. M.A. thesis, University of Florida, Gainesville.

Suckling, G. W., and D. C. Thurley. 1984. Developmental Defects of Enamel: Factors Influencing Their Macroscopic Appearance. In *Tooth Enamel IV*, ed. R. W. Fearnhead and S. Suga, 357–62. Amsterdam: Elsevier.

Suckling, G. W., D. C. Elliot, and D. C. Thurley. 1983. The Production of Developmental Defects of Enamel in the Incisor Teeth of Penned Sheep Resulting from Induced Parasitism. *Archives of Oral Biology* 28:393–99.

———. 1986. The Macroscopic Appearance and Associated Histological Changes in the Enamel Organ of Hypoplastic Lesions of Sheep Incisor Teeth Resulting from Induced Parasitism. *Archives of Oral Biology* 31:427–39.

Thomas, D. H. 1987. *The Archaeology of Mission Santa Catalina de Guale*: 1.

Search and Discovery. Anthropological Papers of the American Museum of Natural History 63, pt. 2.

Weisman, B. R. 1992. *Excavations on the Franciscan Frontier: Archaeology at the Fig Springs Mission.* Gainesville: University Press of Florida.

———. 1993. Archaeology of the Fig Springs Mission, Ichetucknee Springs State Park. In *The Spanish Missions of La Florida,* ed. B. G. McEwan, 165–92. Gainesville: University Press of Florida.

Wilson, R. L. 1965. *Excavations at the Mayport Mound, Florida.* Contributions of the Florida State Museum, Social Sciences, 13.

Worth, J. E. 1995. *The Struggle for the Georgia Coast: An Eighteenth-Century Spanish Retrospective on Guale and Mocama.* Anthropological Papers of the American Museum of Natural History 75.

———. 1998. *The Timucuan Chiefdoms of Spanish Florida.* 2 vols. Gainesville: University Press of Florida.

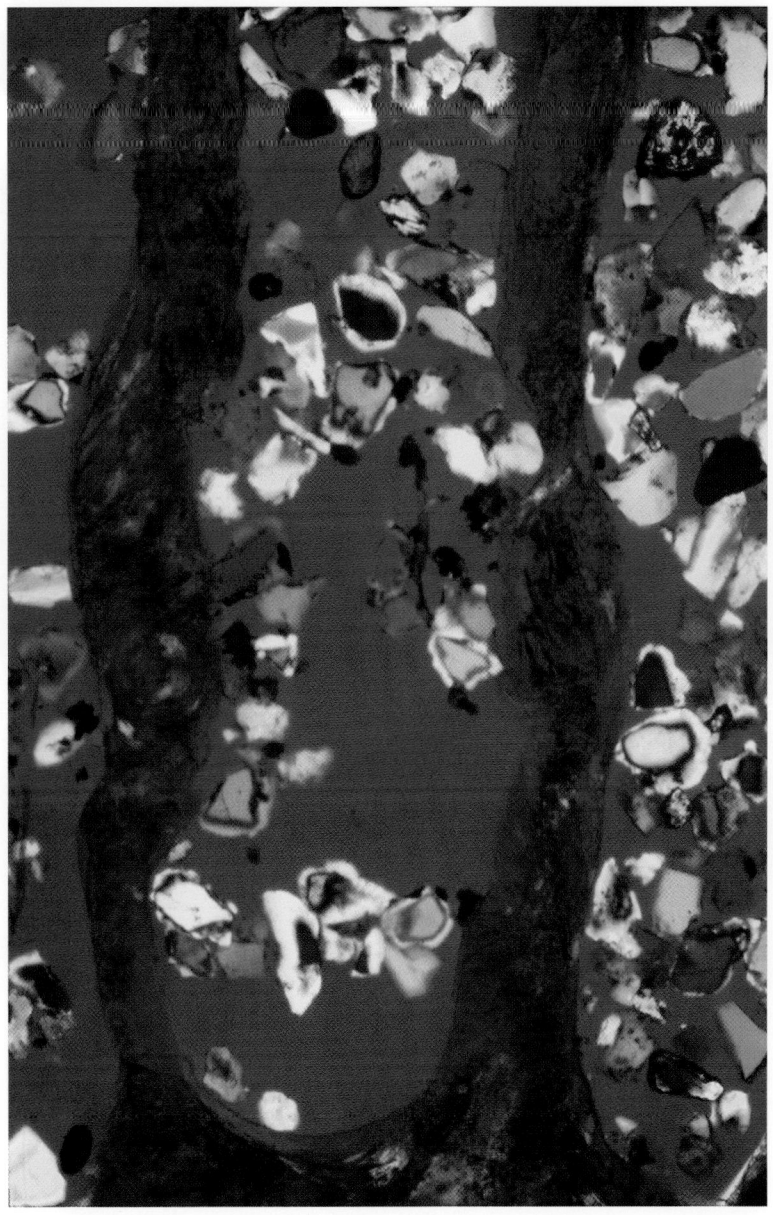

Note: The four color plates are microscopic views of thin-ground sections using polarized light and hilfsobject red 1st order (quartz) as compensator. Thickness of ground sections 70 microns and magnification 70×.

Plate I, 1. Individual 1, Santa Maria de Yamasee 106. Frontal section through the frontal bone (sample a). Parallel bone trabeculae in the newly built bone formation indicate the hair-on-end phenomenon of chronic anemia. There are sand crystals in the modules of the red bone marrow.

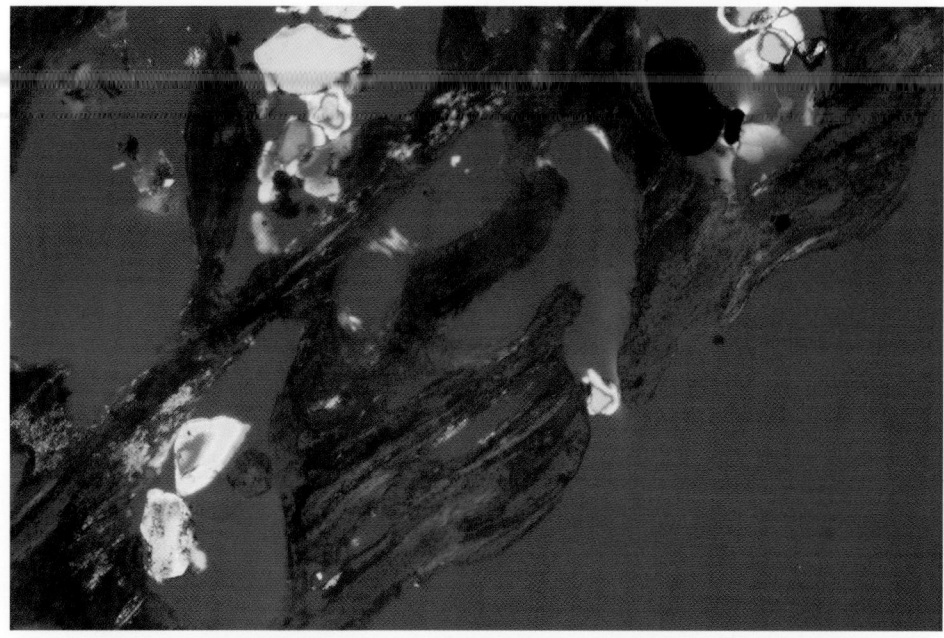

Plate I, 2. Individual 2, Santa Maria de Yamasee 110. Sagittal section through the left parietal bone (sample a). Newly built bone formation on the original endocranial surface represents a healed hemorrhagic reaction. There are sand crystals in the modules of the red bone marrow.

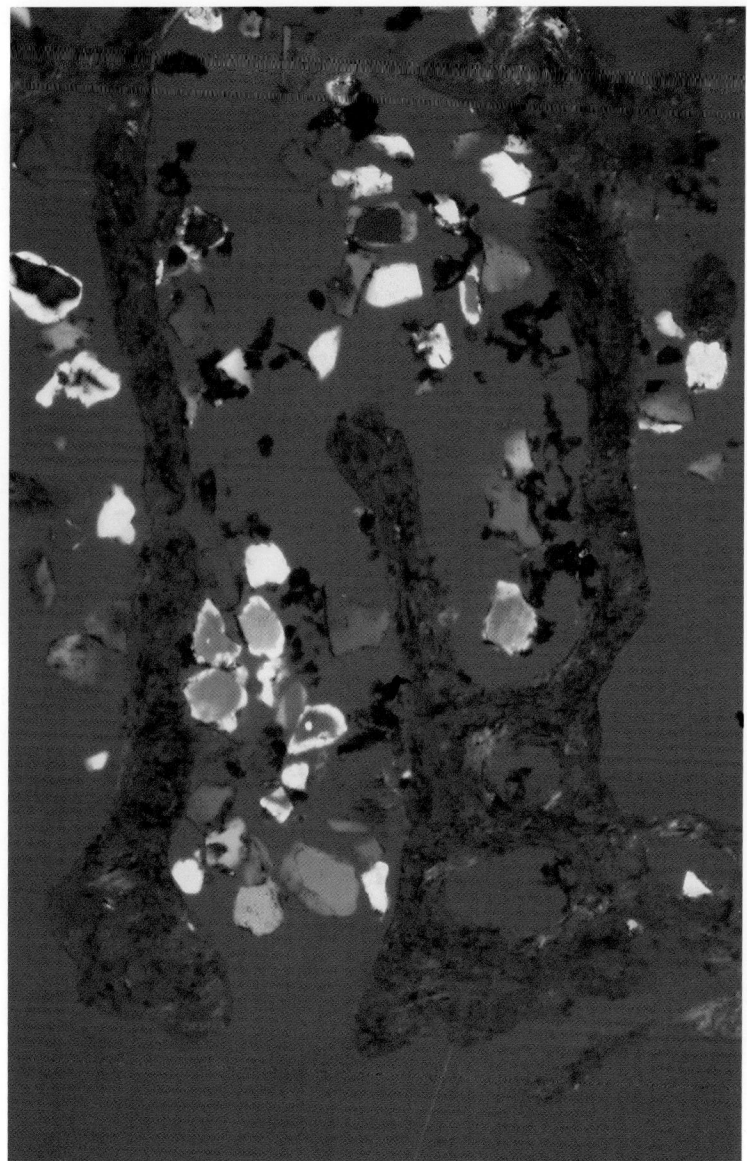

Plate I, 3. Individual 2, Santa Maria de Yamasee 110. Sagittal section through the left orbital roof (sample b). Parallel bone trabeculae in the newly built bone formation indicate the hair-on-end phenomenon of chronic anemia. There are sand crystals in the modules of the red bone marrow.

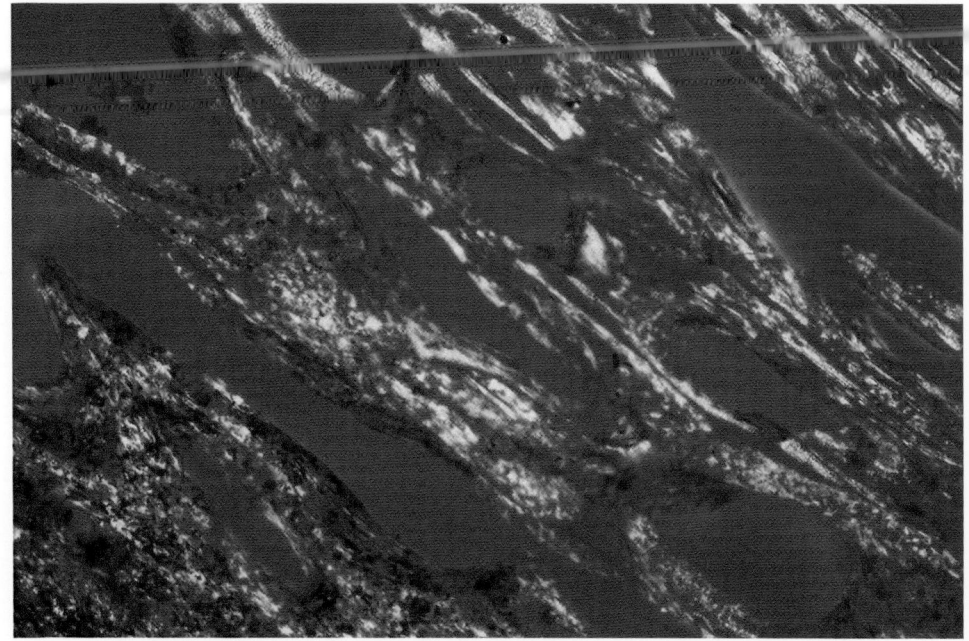

Plate I. 4. Individual 4, ossuary at Santa Catalina de Santa Maria 44. Frontal section thtough the left parietal (sample a). Diploë demonstrating sclerotic changes of unknown causes.

niques—which facilitate reliable differential diagnoses. The purpose of this research is to demonstrate different causes of porotic hyperostosis and cribra orbitalia in a small sample of crania from mission period La Florida, underscoring the importance of microscopic analysis in disease diagnosis.

Previous Findings: Macroscopic Investigation

Larsen and Sering (2000) and Schmidt (1993) visually examined pre-contact and contact-era crania from the region of La Florida inhabited by Guale, Yamasee, and coastal Timucua (table 8.1). Larsen and Sering (2000) found a distinctive temporal change in frequency of porotic hyperostosis/cribra orbitalia. Unlike in a number of other investigations, especially from the American Southwest (e.g., El-Najjar et al. 1976), there was no change in frequency during the pre-contact period in comparison of prehistoric foragers and prehistoric farmers (table 8.2). In fact, there was a slight decline in frequency from the earlier to the later period. For both prehistoric periods, porotic hyperostosis and cribra orbitalia were found to occur in fewer than 10 percent of skulls examined. Larsen and Sering (2000) attributed the low frequency of cranial lesions to adequate intake of dietary iron owing to high consumption of seafood by native populations throughout the period. Maize is deficient in iron owing to the presence of phytate. Clinical evidence reveals that when maize is consumed with fish, iron status is greatly improved (Layrisse et al. 1968).

The mission period crania show a striking increase in frequency of porotic hyperostosis and cribra orbitalia (table 8.2). For the protohistoric and early mission sample (ossuary at Santa Catalina, Santa Catalina de Guale, Santa Maria de Yamasee), there was a substantial increase in frequency relative to the prehistoric farmers, a trend that continued in the late mission period (Santa Catalina de Santa Maria). The most profound increase occurred for juveniles. In the late mission sample from Amelia Island, Florida, 73.3 percent of juveniles had cribra orbitalia and 50.0 percent had porotic hyperostosis (table 8.2). The reasons for the increase represent a complex interplay of dietary changes and alterations in living circumstances. There is a shift to include more maize and less marine foods in diet, as indicated by stable isotope evidence (Larsen et al., this volume). In addition to dietary changes, there was a decline in quality of living circumstances brought about by population relocation, aggregation of people in mission centers, poor hygienic conditions, and generally deteriorating circumstances (Larsen 1990). Moreover, evidence of decrease in quality of drinking water is suggested by the shift from use of streams to water from

8

Disease in Spanish Florida

Microscopy of Porotic Hyperostosis and Cribra Orbitalia

Michael Schultz, Clark Spencer Larsen, and Kerstin Kreutz

Porotic hyperostosis and cribra orbitalia are pathological features affecting the vault and orbital roof areas of the human skull. These features refer to porous, sieve-like lesions on the outer (and sometimes inner) surfaces of the major flat bones of the skull vault (especially parietals and occipital) and roof areas of the eye orbits. The features have been found in archaeological skeletons from around the world (Stuart-Macadam 1992; Larsen 1997), but they are especially common in prehistoric and historic-era Native Americans from the American Southwest and Mesoamerica (El-Najjar et al. 1976; Stodder 1994; Wright and Chew 1999). Many American researchers contend that these changes are due primarily to anemia, especially iron deficiency anemia (El-Najjar et al. 1976; Taylor 1985; Ubelaker 1992; Wright and Chew 1999). Others have shown, however, that these features are also caused by inflammatory processes on the skull (e.g., osteitis; Schultz 1986, 1990, 1993) or scalp (Schultz 1993), hemorrhagic (bleeding) processes on the external cranial surface (e.g., scurvy; Wadsworth 1992; Schultz et al. 1998), or other diseases (e.g., tumors or rickets; Schultz 1993; Schultz and Merbs 1995; Carli-Thiele 1996; Kreutz 1997).

Evidence indicates, therefore, that porotic hyperostosis and cribra orbitalia are not characteristic of a particular disease. Rather, they are a descriptive morphological feature affecting the cranium. It is important to examine carefully these changes in order to obtain reliable disease diagnosis or to identify more precisely the factors causing the pathological condition. Macroscopic inspection or radiological investigation alone are not sufficient for diagnosis, because the hyperostotic and porotic newly built bone formations caused by different diseases are similar in appearance. Thus, a variety of techniques should be used—especially microscopic tech-

Table 8.1. Skeletal samples and mortuary localities

Site	N[a]
Early prehistoric	
Cunningham Mound C	2
Cunningham Mound D	2
McLeod Mound	5
Seaside Mound I	5
Seaside Mound II	4
Evelyn Plantation	1
Airport site	18
Deptford (nonmound)	17
Cannons Point	5
Cedar Grove, Mound B	1
Sea Island Mound	11
Johns Mound	26
Marys Mound	4
Charlie King Mound	1
Cedar Grove Mound C	4
South End Mound II	10
Late prehistoric	
North End Mound	1
Low Mound, Shell Bluff	1
Townsend Mound	1
Deptford Mound	2
Norman Mound	16
Kent Mound	19
Lewis Creek, Mound III	1
Lewis Creek, misc.	3
Lewis Creek, Mound E	1
Seven Mile Bend	10
Oatland Mound	2
Irene Mound	187
Grove's Creek	1
South End Mound I	13
Little Pine Island	9
Red Bird Creek Mound	1
Couper Field	23
Taylor Mound	16
Indian Field	8
Taylor Mound/Martinez B	1
Protohistoric/early mission	
Ossuary, Santa Catalina	53
Santa Catalina de Guale	32
Santa Maria de Yamasee	48
Late mission	
Santa Catalina de Santa Maria	92

a. N=number of individuals with at least one orbit and/or vault element complete enough for observation; see Larsen, this volume, for references to specific archaeological sites. For purposes of analysis, Johns Mound, Marys Mound, and South End Mound II are included in Georgia early prehistoric.

Table 8.2. Cribra orbitalia and porotic hyperostosis frequency

	EP[a] % (n)[b]	LP % (n)	EM % (n)	LM % (n)	Significant change[c]
Cribra orbitalia					
Total[d]	5.7 (104)	3.1 (287)	14.0 (121)	22.9 (70)	none
Juvenile[e]	38.5 (13)	6.1 (33)	21.7 (23)	73.3 (15)	EP/LP, LP/EM
Porotic hyperostosis					
Total	0.0 (113)	3.3 (308)	15.8 (133)	21.1 (90)	none
Juvenile	0.0 (13)	0.0 (33)	20.0 (25)	50.0 (18)	EM/LM

a. EP, Early Prehistoric; LP, Late Prehistoric; EM, Early Mission; LM, Late Mission.
b. Percent of orbits/vaults affected; n=total number of orbits/vaults examined (pathological + nonpathological).
c. Statistically significant change (chi-square: $p \pm 0.05$, two-tailed).
d. Juveniles, unsexed adults, adult females, and adult males combined.
e. Individuals less than 10 years old.

shallow wells that are easily contaminated by parasites (e.g., St. Catherines Island; see also Larsen, this volume). It is in these kinds of circumstances that we would expect to see an increase in the types of disease and nutritional stress that Schultz and others (references already given) have found to cause porotic hyperostosis and cribra orbitalia.

The Skeletons and Microscopic Analysis

For the present study, two skulls from Santa Maria de Yamasee (individuals 106 and 110) and two skulls from the ossuary adjacent to Santa Catalina de Santa Maria (individuals SE59 and 44) on Amelia Island, Florida, were examined by macroscopic, endoscopic, radiological, light microscopic (polarization, microradiography), and scanning electron microscopic techniques at M. Schultz's laboratory at the University of Göttingen. The two individuals from the ossuary near the Santa Catalina mission are from a mass of disarticulated remains lying on top of the remains of two fully articulated adult males contained within a wooden box. The wooden box had been constructed with a series of iron spikes. The presence of historic-era artifacts indicates a clear post-contact association of these remains. The non-Christian style of burial indicates, however, that the remains likely predate the period of full missionization. Prior to the mission period, Amelia Island was occupied by Timucua Indians, and it is likely that the remains are Timucuan (Larsen 1993, this volume).

The Santa Maria de Yamasee individuals are from a cemetery located inside a church structure. The remains are from Yamasee Indians who lived at the site prior to A.D. 1683 (Larsen 1993, this volume). Previous research revealed that 28.3 percent (of 53 crania) from the ossuary and 28.2 percent (of 71 crania) from Santa Maria de Yamasee had porotic hyperostosis and/ or cribra orbitalia (Schmidt 1993; Larsen and Sering 2000, unpublished).

Following preliminary documentation of individual crania (photography, detailed drawings, and measurement), bone samples were removed from each of the four skulls for microscopic analysis. The pathological alterations were registered according to Schultz's (1988a) criteria (and see later discussion). The analysis involves four individuals.

Individual 1, Santa Maria de Yamasee 106. Samples include (a) a large piece of the frontal bone; (b) a small piece from the roof of the right orbit for light microscopy; and (c) a small piece of the frontal bone for scanning electron microscopy.

Individual 2, Santa Maria de Yamasee 110. Samples include (a) a large piece of frontal and left parietal bone (sagittal section); (b) a small piece from the roof of the eye orbit for light microscopy; and (c) a small piece of right parietal bone for scanning electron microscopy.

Individual 3, ossuary near Santa Catalina de Santa Maria SE59. Samples include (a) a large piece (sagittal section) from the right parietal and (b) a small piece from the roof of the right orbit for light microscopy.

Individual 4, ossuary near Santa Catalina de Santa Maria 44. Samples include (a) a large piece (frontal section) from the left parietal; (b) a small piece from the roof of the left orbit for light microscopy; and (c) a small piece of the left parietal bone for scanning electron microscopy.

In order to identify diseases that caused porotic hyperostosis and cribra orbitalia (see Schultz 1993; Schultz and Merbs 1995; Carli-Thiele 1996; Kreutz 1997), thin-ground sections for microscopic analysis were made using the technique described by Schultz (1988b) and Schultz and Drommer (1983). In brief, the sections are produced in the following manner. First, each small sample was extracted with a hand-held jeweler's saw, placed in a dichloromethane solvent, and then air-dried. Next, samples were placed in a clear epoxy resin hardener and placed in an enclosed vacuum for six to seven hours for extraction of gas bubbles. The samples in the hardener matrix were then allowed to harden at room temperature for three days, followed by curing at 30°C in an oven for about two and a half weeks. The individual bone sections were initially cut with a rotary diamond saw and then mounted on glass slides. The mounted slides were again attached to the diamond saw and each section was cut to about 50 and 70 microns in thickness. Last, prior to the attachment of the slide covers, the sections were manually polished with fine-grained sandpaper.

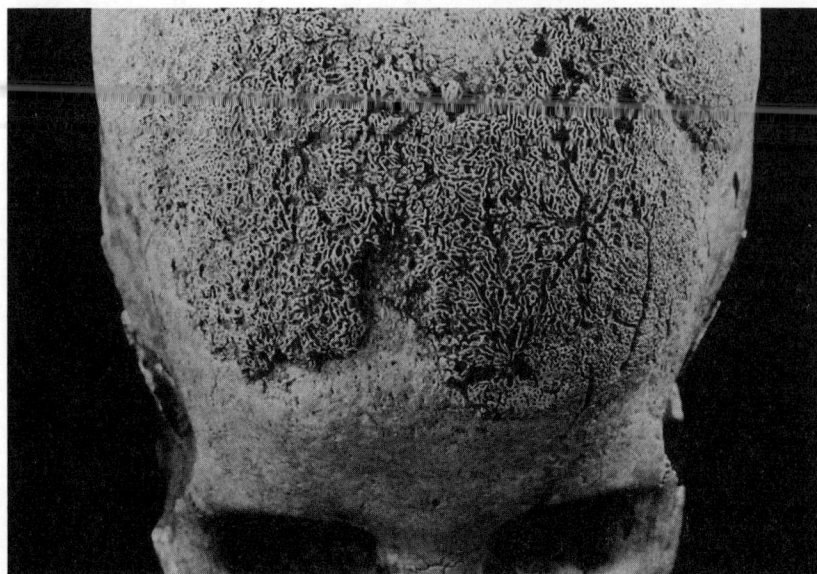

Fig. 8.1. Individual 1, Santa Maria de Yamasee 106. External surface of the skull vault showing extensive porotic hyperostosis. The bone formations represent severe chronic anemia.

The ground sections were investigated microscopically in plane and polarized transmission light using a hilfsobject red 1st order (quartz) as a compensator.

Results

Bones of three skulls (individuals 1–3) are abnormally thick and porotic to varying degrees. The fourth skull (individual 4) showed no significantly thickened bone in its vault. Radiological examination of the four skulls confirmed these observations. Additionally, the x-ray photographs of child 106 from Santa Maria de Yamasee reveal a typical hair-on-end phenomenon showing numerous parallel lines of opacity, a characteristic feature of chronic anemia (Ortner and Putschar 1985). The examination of thinground sections viewed in plane and polarized light yields results that not only allow a diagnosis of disease but also provide important information about preservation quality and postmortem destruction (Schultz 1997). For the present investigation, in particular, light microscopic analysis demonstrated that the bone samples contained many minute sand crystals, which reflect the burial of the skeletons in sandy soil. These sand crystals had also slightly eroded the original surfaces of the bones. The erosive effects of the sand crystals are shown in the scanning electron microscopic analysis. Owing to the degree of erosion, scanning electron microscopy was generally inconclusive in disease diagnosis.

Following are our observations of the four individuals:

Individual 1, Santa Maria de Yamasee 106

This skull of a 9–12-year-old child is almost completely preserved. However, the occipital bone and the temporal bones were damaged by postmortem soil pressure. The cranium was consolidated in situ with polyvinyl acetate, so that the damaged region of the skull is still present but deformed postmortem. The shape of the skull indicates that there was a slight skull deformation that had occurred while the individual was alive. Skull morphology is greatly altered owing to the development of a huge newly built bone formation (extensive porotic hyperostosis), involving the upper frontal bone, most of both parietals (fig. 8.1), and a small region of the right side of the occipital. The surface of this formation is more or less regularly porotic. A series of small hole-like breaks were caused postmortem, and confirmed by scanning electron microscopy. The skull vault is thick (13 mm in the frontal region), with the pathological bone formation measuring 7 mm in places. The porotic formation touches the left and extends slightly over the right temporal line. The ectocranial sutures of the skull vault are almost completely fused owing to the pathological processes. Only the lambdoidal suture is still partly visible. The pathological bone formation is distinctly thinner in the area of the sagittal suture and clearly enlarged in the midregions of both parietals. These enlargements result in a saddle-like impression on the external skull surface in the region of the occipital half of the sagittal suture.

There are no pathological changes on the internal surfaces of the skull vault. However, the endocranial sutures of the skull vault are fused, which normally does not occur until later in life. The orbital roofs are characterized by classic cribra orbitalia (degree II/III). There are porotic formations and very short blood vessel impressions on the bone surfaces of the orbital roofs. The bottoms of the orbits also show a slightly porotic surface. The palatine and the alveolar processes of both maxillae are porotic.

The microscopic analysis of the large sample taken from the skull vault demonstrates that the new bone formation is built of parallel, relatively long and gracile bone trabeculae situated at right angles to the original surface of the external lamina of the skull vault. These trabeculae, which are only preserved as residue in the region of the newly built bone formation, are enlarged in the vertical plane. They are responsible for the radiologically observed hair-on-end phenomenon (plate I, 1). In life, this pattern would have been created by the presence of highly enlarged modules of the red blood marrow. Because these modules are not closed by any bony formations at the external surface of the skull vault, the bone looks highly porotic from the outside. The original diploë—the area of bone between the internal and external surfaces of the skull vault—has a more or less normal morphology. All features are characteristic of a florid chronic anemia (Schultz 1988a).

Microscopic examination of the roof of the right orbit yields interesting insights into the character of cribra orbitalia for this individual. The orbital bone surface was partly absorbed in life. The bony trabeculae, which are relatively gracile and slightly elongated, show a parallel orientation in the central region of the section. This morphology indicates that the modules of the red bone marrow are relatively enlarged. Although somewhat hidden by postmortem diagenesis, the enlarged features are not visible macroscopically. All abnormal or pathological features are associated with chronic anemia.

Individual 2, Santa Maria de Yamasee 110

The skull of this four- to six-year-old child is incompletely preserved. The occipital region and the base of the skull with the exception of the left temporal bone are missing owing to postmortem diagenesis. There is no significant evidence that the skull was deformed in life. On the external bone surfaces, we observed two features, each caused by a different disease. First, on the right frontal bone, approximately 45 mm posterior to the orbital margin and 33 mm anterior to the coronal suture, there are relatively deep blood vessel impressions. These impressions are arranged in a star-shaped configuration measuring 20 mm by 23 mm. Scanning electron microscopic examination indicates that this lesion represents the scar of a process that occurred during the life of the individual, probably involving soft tissue between the external surface of the skull vault and the scalp. Second, on the left parietal, there is a small coarse porotic area measuring 15 mm by 18 mm situated close to the region of the lambdoidal suture approximately 10 mm above asterion (point where the temporal, parietal, and occipital bones meet). Because there is postmortem bone loss in the occipital region of the left parietal bone, it is probable that the area of pathological bone was originally larger. The skull vault is not thickened in this porotic area. The corresponding region on the right parietal bone was not preserved. This lesion is a vestige of chronic anemia.

Fig. 8.2. Individual 2, Santa Maria de Yamasee 110. Internal surface of the skull vault showing porotic hyperostosis. The newly built bone formation represents severe hemorrhagic (e.g., pachymeningeosis haemorrhagica interna) or hemorrhagic-inflammatory process of the meninges.

In addition to these changes, there are some other porotic changes on the external surface of the skull. The left temporal squama, the greater wing of the left sphenoid, and the adjoining part of the left parietal have an irregular porotic appearance. The corresponding bones of the right side were not preserved. Both temporal lines in the region of the frontal bone and their adjoining regions look strikingly porotic. The porotic area extends for at least 20 mm along this part of the temporal lines. In this region, the temporal lines are also slightly thickened. All of these changes are slightly more clearly expressed on the left side of the skull. The region around the anterior bony aperture of the nose, the interior walls of the nasal cavity, and the external surfaces of both zygomatic bones are also remarkably porotic. The interior walls of the nasal cavity possess impressions of short blood vessels.

The internal surface of the skull vault has severe porotic hyperostosis (fig. 8.2). The changes start in the frontal bone, parallel to the frontal crest, with an extension of approximately 20 mm on each side and spreading to both parietals with an extension of 50 mm to 60 mm. The occipital is not affected. The surface of this newly built bone formation is coarsely porotic and shows several postmortem breaks. The thickness of the skull vault,

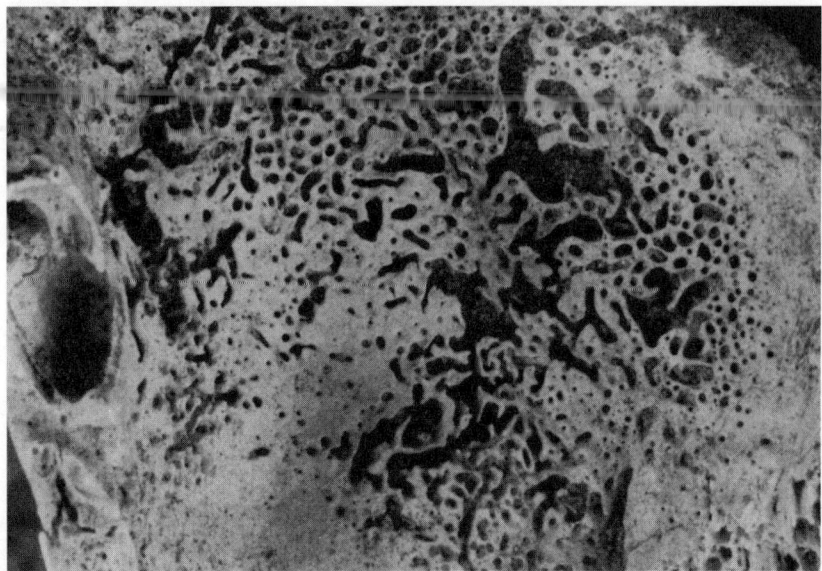

Fig. 8.3. Individual 2, Santa Maria de Yamasee 110. Roof of the left orbit showing cribra orbitalia. The newly built bone formation represents severe chronic anemia.

including the porotic formation, measures 8 mm in the left parietal region parallel to the sagittal suture. The newly built formation alone measures 3 mm. The orbital roofs are characterized by pronounced cribra orbitalia (degree III/IV), which show a coarse porotic appearance with small irregular gaps scattered over the area; the orbits are also thickened (fig. 8.3). The bottoms of the eye orbits show a more or less coarsely porotic surface. The palatine and the alveolar processes of both maxillae are slightly porotic.

Microscopic investigation of this hyperostotic skull vault detects a rare pathological condition that is difficult to interpret. The internal surface and the diploë of the skull bones are unaffected by metaplastic processes. Thus, the thickening of the skull vault is restricted to the endocranial (internal bone surface) region. The modules of the red bone marrow in the original diploë are relatively uniform and enlarged in the transverse level. The overwhelming majority of the bony trabeculae of the diploë is relatively gracile. The morphology of the newly built bone formation consisting of woven bone shows a design that is frequently associated with bony remodeled hemorrhagic processes, such as an epidural hematoma (bleeding) (plate I, 2). Because the original internal surface of the skull bones is almost completely absorbed by some pathological process, the newly built spongy bone is directly connected with the original diploë.

Microscopic examination of the roof of the left orbit presents a characteristic case of cribra orbitalia caused by long-lasting chronic anemia (plate I, 3). The orbital lamina is virtually missing premortem. The bony trabeculae, which are not very gracile, show a parallel orientation and the modules of the red bone marrow are significantly enlarged. These structures are reminiscent of the aforementioned hair-on-end phenomenon seen in skull vaults of individuals with chronic anemia.

Individual 3, Ossuary near Santa Catalina de Santa Maria SE59

Robust and unusually heavy, this skull of a subadult or young adult male is well preserved. Some major parts of the center of the skull base are missing. The skull was deformed in life in the frontal and occipital region in a style frequently seen in Mesoamerica and the American Southeast. The external surfaces of the occipital squama and the occipital halves of both parietal bones are slightly porotic and bulging (fig. 8.4). The internal surface of the skull vault is severely eroded by postmortem destruction. However, small areas of intact bone are characterized by fine porosity. The skull

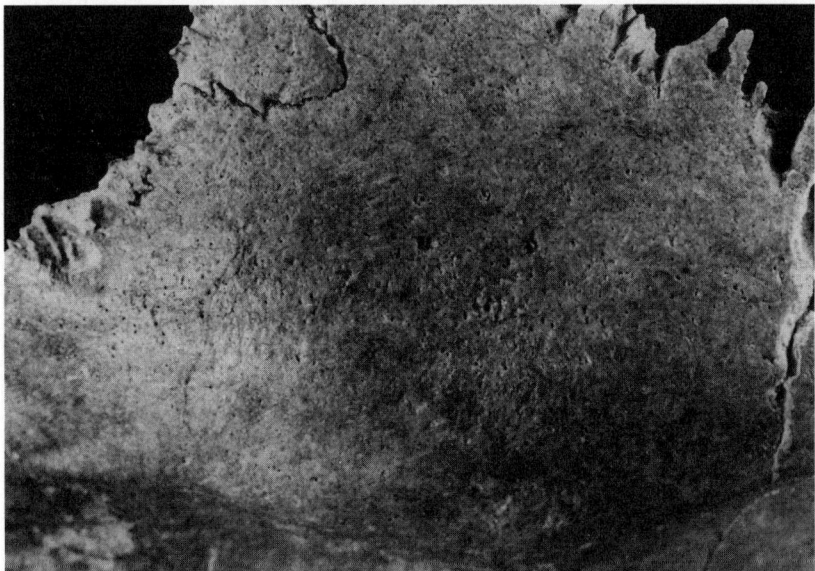

Fig. 8.4. Individual 3, ossuary at Santa Catalina de Santa Maria SE59. The external surface of the occipital squama shows porotic hyperostosis. The slightly porotic surface, which is also slightly bulging (scars), is reminiscent of a healed inflammatory process of the scalp and the bones of the skull vault; these are even normal structures.

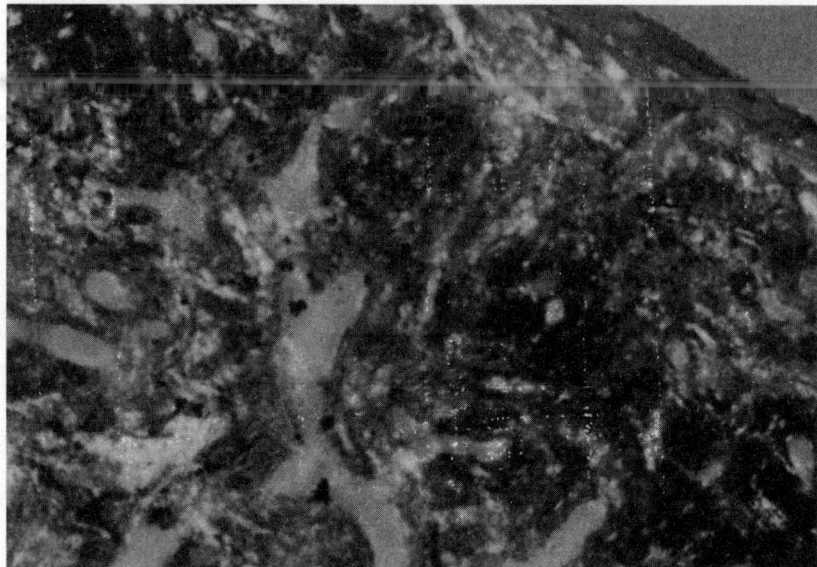

Fig. 8.5. Individual 3, ossuary at Santa Catalina de Santa Maria SE59. Sagittal section through the right parietal (sample a). Condensed diploë shows coarse sclerotic changes.

vault is significantly thickened. At its thickest region—located in the center of the right parietal—the skull vault measures 13 mm. The surfaces of both middle cranial fossae are slightly bulging. The left cranial fossa also shows some small plugs, which can be interpreted as the product of an inflammatory process involving the meninges. Cribra orbitalia (degree III) is present in both orbital roofs, which are incompletely preserved.

Microscopic examination of a large sample taken from the occipital region of the right parietal bone shows that the external and internal surfaces of the bone are not altered by any pathological process. Similarly, scanning electron microscopy of a small sample taken from the right parietal revealed no pathological changes. On the other hand, observation of ground sections viewed in polarized light shows that the diploë between the external and internal surfaces is greatly enlarged and the modules of the red bone marrow are rarefied and irregularly shaped. The bony trabeculae are thickened and partly dilated. Thus, the diploë partly has a coarse sclerotic character (fig. 8.5). All these changes make for a probable diagnosis that the skull vault, particularly the diploë, was affected by a process that healed by building up condensed (i.e., sclerotic) structures. These changes also explain the high weight of the skull.

Analysis of the ground sections taken from the right orbital roof verified not only postmortem destruction but also relatively well developed cribra orbitalia caused by anemia. The presence of anemia for this person during life is indicated by the slightly enlarged modules of bone marrow for red blood cells and the parallel orientation of some of the bony trabeculae.

Individual 4, Ossuary near Santa Catalina de Santa Maria 44

From this gracile, relatively thin-walled skull (4–5 mm thick) of a four- to seven-year-old child, only the calotte is preserved. There is a slight occipital flattening similar to the degree of artificial deformation that can be seen in Anasazi juveniles from the American Southwest. The external surface of the occipital halves of both parietals is characterized by a fine, irregular porosity. The internal surface of the skull vault shows slightly enlarged digital impressions and also fine porosity. Both orbital roofs have cribra orbitalia characterized by an irregular, relatively fine porosity (fig. 8.6).

The results of the light microscopic and scanning electron microscopic examinations demonstrate that the changes in the skull vault are similar to the alterations seen in individual SE59 from the ossuary. Thus, the diploë has partly started to acquire a coarse sclerotic character (plate I, 4). The

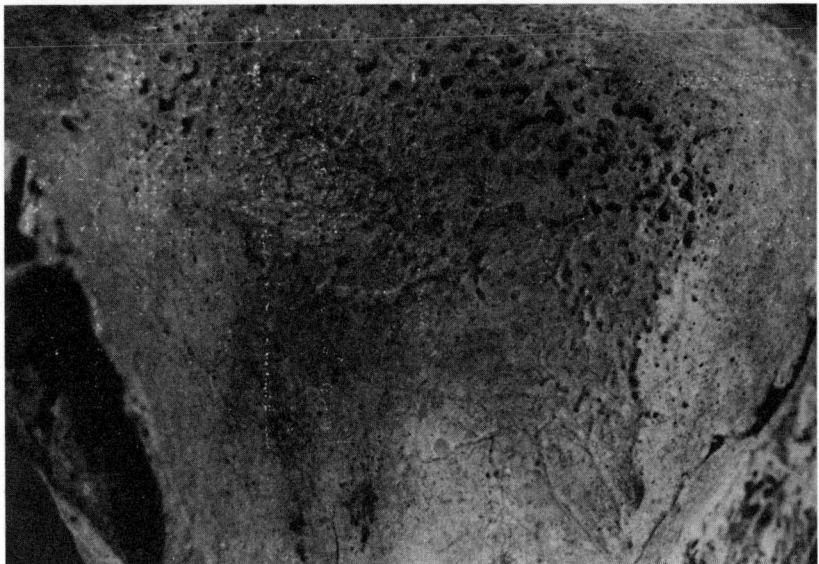

Fig. 8.6. Individual 4, ossuary at Santa Catalina de Santa Maria 44. Roof of the left orbit showing cribra orbitalia. Porotic structures mainly represent postmortem destruction and also some vestiges of chronic anemia.

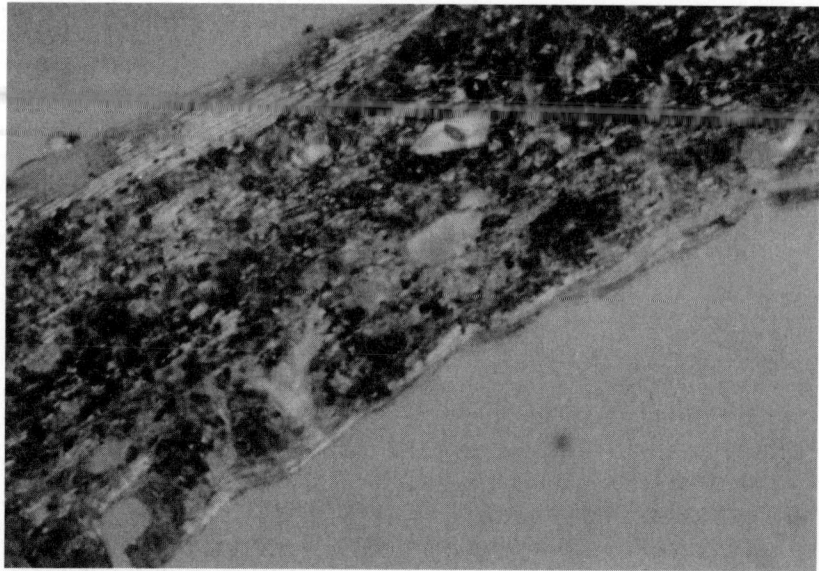

Fig. 8.7. Individual 4, ossuary at Santa Catalina de Santa Maria 44. Sagittal section through the left orbital roof (sample b). The bone changes are postmortem, not related to pathology.

cause for this change is unknown. Alterations macroscopically observed on the external surface of the skull vault and in the orbital roofs appear to be of postmortem origin (fig. 8.7).

Discussion and Conclusions

The results of the microscopic examinations are striking. In individual 1 (Santa Maria de Yamasee 106), the enormous porotic hyperostosis of the external skull vault and the hair-on-end phenomenon are classic characteristics of florid chronic anemia. (Indeed, this is one of the most extreme examples of porotic hyperostosis that we have seen from around the world.) Other interpretations, such as a large hematoma on the skull vault (caused by scurvy) or a meningeoma, can be excluded by the results of our macroscopic and microscopic investigation. Additionally, cribra orbitalia was also caused by this anemic process. The reason the child suffered from anemia is unclear. However, there are some possible explanations, including parasitic disease (Reinhard 1992; Larsen and Sering 2000; Larsen, this volume); chronic malnutrition, such as chronic deficiency of the amino acid tryptophan (Schultz 1982); or chronic iron deficiency due to iron-poor diets (El-Najjar et al. 1976). At this point, a more detailed diagnosis is not possible (cf. Garn 1992). The endocranial fusion of the sutures of the skull vault is probably due to the pathological process caused by the chronic anemia.

For individual 2 (Santa Maria de Yamasee 110), the causes of the various changes we observed are difficult to determine. There is reliable evidence of anemia in the skull vault and the orbital roofs, but the morphology characteristic of chronic anemia is not expressed as in individual 1. The other porotic structures diagnosed in several regions of the skull (cf. Ortner 1999), particularly in the visceral cranium and the star-shaped configuration of blood vessels on the external lamina of the skull, which can be a residue of an external subperiosteal hematoma, indicate the strong possibility of severe chronic scurvy (vitamin C deficiency). The well expressed hemorrhagic process on the internal lamina of the skull vault probably represents an epidural hematoma (bleeding) due to scurvy. As a rule, microscopic analysis of an epidural hematoma yields characteristic results—the original internal surface of the skull vault is microscopically visible below the newly built spongy bone representing the hemorrhage. Only in extensive bleeding can the internal lamina be partly absorbed due to the endocranial pressure of the hematoma (Schultz 1993), which is certainly the case for this child's skull. However—and this is important for differential diagnoses—the porotic formation can also represent pachymeningeosis haemorrhagica interna, which is not induced only by extensive bleeding. This diagnosis is unlikely because of the constellation of the various morphological features presented. In any case, the changes are well organized, such as those associated with an advanced healing phase. Inflammatory processes, such as what might cause the porotic alterations on the external surfaces of this skull, are implausible. We note, however, that the changes in the interior walls of the nasal cavity are probably caused by an inflammatory process, such as nonspecific granulomatous rhinitis.

For individual 3 (ossuary SE59), the slightly porotic and bulging surface (scars) is reminiscent of a healed inflammatory process of the scalp and the bones of the skull vault. It is possible that these are normal structures. If so, this means that the external skull morphology is not affected by pathology. However, the results of the microscopic analysis demonstrate that there are sclerotic structures of the diploë that resemble structures found in an early neolithic individual from Aiterhofen, Germany, who suffered from an inflammatory process of the skull vault (Schultz 1986). Thus the pathological structures could only be detected reliably by microscopy.

For individual 4 (ossuary 44), the diploë when viewed microscopically shows a partly coarse sclerotic character. The cause for this change is unknown. No other pathological changes could be diagnosed. It is important to note that the changes in the orbital roofs, diagnosed macroscopically without doubt as cribra orbitalia caused by anemia, are microscopically diagnosed as postmortem changes or pseudopathology (cf. Wells 1967; Schultz 1986). Thus this is an excellent example to demonstrate that the histological examination can differentiate between normal and pathological features in archaeological skeletal remains.

Summary

Four skulls from Spanish Florida showing macroscopically the morphological features of porotic hyperostosis of the skull vault and cribra orbitalia were examined by macroscopic, endoscopic, radiological, light microscopic (polarization) and scanning electron microscopic techniques. Previous studies interpreted the widespread pattern of porotic hyperostosis and cribra orbitalia in the mission period to reflect anemia brought about by poor living conditions, such as parasitism and water contamination (Larsen and Sering 2000). The results of the microscopic analysis demonstrate that porotic hyperostosis and cribra orbitalia can be caused by different diseases, not only by anemia, and that postmortem destruction can simulate pathological conditions like cribra orbitalia. These findings are important for future research on the epidemiology of ancient diseases and emphasize the necessity of microscopic research in paleopathology. The macroscopic and, in particular, the microscopic investigation of these four individuals from Spanish Florida graphically demonstrate that native people who lived during the contact period suffered from malnutrition and infectious diseases.

Acknowledgments

We acknowledge the generous support of the University of Florida in the excavation of skeletal remains from the Mission Santa Maria de Yamasee and the ossuary at Santa Catalina on Amelia Island, Florida. The fieldwork was undertaken in cooperation with Jerald Milanich and Rebecca Saunders of the Florida Museum of Natural History. We thank the following curators and their institutions for permission to study the skeletons and to undertake the analyses described in this chapter: Jerald Milanich (Florida Museum of Natural History), Douglas Ubelaker (Smithsonian Institution), David Hally (University of Georgia), David Hurst Thomas (American Museum of Natural History), and Bonnie McEwan, David Dickel, and

James Miller (Florida Bureau of Archaeological Research). For technical
assistance (preparation of ground sections, scanning electron microscopy),
the authors thank M. Brandt and I. Hettwer-Steeger, Zentrum Anatomie,
University of Gottingen. Study of these remains was made possible by
funding from the National Science Foundation (to C. S. Larsen) and the
University of Göttingen (to M. Schultz). A grant from the University Research Council at the University of North Carolina funded the reproduc-
tion of the four color plates.

References Cited

Carli-Thiele, P. 1996. Spuren von Mangelerkrankungen an steinzeitlichen
  Kinderskeleten. In Fortschritte in der Paläopathologie und Osteoarchäologie 1,
  ed. by M. Schultz, 13–267. Göttingen: Verlag Erich Goltze.
El-Najjar, M. Y., D. J. Ryan, C. G. Turner II, and B. Lozoff. 1976. The Etiology of
  Porotic Hyperostosis among the Prehistoric and Historic Anasazi Indians of
  the Southwestern United States. American Journal of Physical Anthropology
  44:477–87.
Garn, S. M. 1992. The Iron-Deficiency Anemias and Their Skeletal Manifesta-
  tions. In Diet, Demography, and Disease: Changing Perspectives on Anemia,
  ed. P. Stuart-Macadam and S. Kent, 33–61. New York: Aldine de Gruyter.
Kreutz, K. 1997. Ätiologie und Epidemiologie von Erkrankungen des Kindesalters
  bei der Bajuwarischen Population von Straubing (Niederbayern). In Beiträge
  zur Paläopathologie 1, 2, ed. M. Schultz, 1:1–161, plates 1–30, 2:1–273.
  Göttingen: Cuvillier Verlag.
Larsen, C. S. 1993. On the Frontier of Contact: Mission Bioarchaeology in La
  Florida. In The Spanish Missions of La Florida, ed. B. G. McEwan, 322–56.
  Gainesville: University Press of Florida.
———. 1997. Bioarchaeology: Interpreting Behavior from the Human Skeleton.
  Cambridge: Cambridge University Press.
Larsen, C. S. (ed.). 1990. The Archaeology of Mission Santa Catalina de Guale: 2.
  Biocultural Interpretations of a Population in Transition. Anthropological Pa-
  pers of the American Museum of Natural History 68.
Larsen, C. S., and L. E. Sering. 2000. Inferring Iron Deficiency Anemia from Hu-
  man Skeletal Remains: The Case of the Georgia Bight. In Bioarchaeological
  Studies of Life in the Age of Agriculture, ed. P. M. Lambert, 116–33. Tusca-
  loosa: University of Alabama Press.
Layrisse, M., C. Martínez-Torres, and M. Roche. 1968. Effect of Interaction of
  Various Foods on Iron Absorption. American Journal of Clinical Nutrition
  21:1175–83.
Ortner, D. J. 1999. Scurvy: Its Skeletal Manifestations and Prevalence in North
  and South American Skeletal Samples. American Journal of Physical Anthropology suppl. 28:216.

Ortner, D. J., and W.G.J. Putschar. 1985. *Identification of Pathological Conditions in Human Skeletal Remains.* Washington: Smithsonian Institution Press.

Reinhard, K. J. 1992. Patterns of Diet, Parasitism and Anemia in Prehistoric West North America. In *Diet, Demography, and Disease: Changing Perspectives on Anemia,* ed. P. Stuart-Macadam and S. Kent, 219–58. New York: Aldine de Gruyter.

Schmidt, C. W. 1993. Paleodemographic Analysis of the Santa Catalina de Guale de Santa Maria Ossuary. M.A. thesis, Purdue University, West Lafayette.

Schultz, M. 1982. Umwelt und Krankheit des vor- und frühgeschichtlichen Menschen. In *Kindlers Enzyklopädie: Der Mensch 2,* ed. H. Wendt and N. Loacker, 259–312. Munich: Kindler Verlag.

———. 1986. Die mikroskopische Untersuchung prähistorischer Skeletfunde: Anwendung und Aussagemöglichkeiten der differentialdiagnostischen Untersuchung in der Paläopathologie. In *Archäologie und Museum,* ed. Amt für Museen und Archäologie BL & Anthropologisches Forschungsinstitut Aesch, 6:7–140. Liestal: Amt für Museen und Archäologie.

———. 1988a. Paläopathologische Diagnostik. In *Anthropologie: Handbuch der Vergleichenden Biologie des Menschen 1, Wesen und Methoden der Anthropologie 1,* ed. R. Knussmann, 480–96. Stuttgart and New York: Fischer Verlag.

———. 1988b. Methoden der Licht-und Elektronenmikroskopie. In *Anthropologie: Handbuch der Vergleichenden Biologie des Menschen 1, Wesen und Methoden der Anthropologie 1,* ed. R. Knussmann, 698–730. Stuttgart and New York: Fischer Verlag.

———. 1990. Erkrankungen des Kindesalters bei der Frühbronzezeitlichen Population vom Ikiztepe (Türkei). In *Gedenkschrift für Jürgen Driehaus,* ed. F. M. Andraschko and W.-R. Teegen, 83–90. Mainz: Verlag Philipp von Zabern.

———. 1993. Spuren unspezifischer Entzündungen an prähistorischen und historischen Schädeln: Ein Beitrag zur Paläopathologie (Vestiges of non-specific inflammations in prehistoric and historic skulls: A contribution to paleopathology). *Anthropologische Beiträge* 4A:84, 4B:plate 51. Aesch: Anthropologisches Forschungsinstitut Aesch and Anthropologische Gesellschaft Basel.

———. 1997. Microscopic Investigation of Excavated Skeletal Remains: A Contribution to Paleopathology and Forensic Medicine. In *Forensic Taphonomy: The Postmortem Fate of Human Remains,* ed. W. D. Haglund and M. H. Sorg, 201–22. Boca Raton: CRC Press.

Schultz, M., and R. Drommer. 1983. Möglichkeiten der Präparateherstellung aus dem Gesichtsschädelbereich für die makroskopische und mikroskopische Untersuchung unter Verwendung neuer Kunststofftechniken. In *Experimentelle Mund-Kiefer-Gesichtschirurgie. Mikrochirurgische Eingriffe,* ed. W. Hoppe, 95–97. New York: Thieme-Verlag.

Schultz, M., and C. F. Merbs. 1995. What Does Porotic Hyperostosis Mean? Results of Microscopic Investigations in Pre-Columbian Skulls from the North American Southwest. *Paleopathology Newsletter* 94, suppl., 5.

Schultz, M., T. H. Schmidt-Schultz, and K. Kreutz. 1998. Ergebnisse der paläo-pathologischen Untersuchung an den frühbronzezeitlichen Kinderskeleten von Jelsovce (Slowakische Republik). In Mensch und Umwelt in der Bronzezeit Europas (Man and environment in European Bronze Age), ed. B. Hänsel, 77–90. Kiel: Oetker-Voges Verlag.

Stodder, A.L.W. 1994. Bioarchaeological Investigations of Protohistoric Pueblo Health and Demography. In In the Wake of Contact: Biological Responses to Conquest, ed. C. S. Larsen and G. R. Milner, 97–107. New York: Wiley-Liss.

Stuart-Macadam, P. 1992. Anemia in Past Human Populations. In Diet, Demography, and Disease: Changing Perspectives on Anemia, ed. P. Stuart-Macadam and S. Kent, 151–70. New York: Aldine de Gruyter.

Taylor, M. G. 1985. The Paleopathology of a Southern Sinagua Population from Oak Creek Pueblo, Arizona. In Health and Disease in the Prehistoric Southwest, ed. C. F. Merbs and R. J. Miller, 115–18. Arizona State University Anthropological Research Papers 34.

Ubelaker, D. H. 1992. Porotic Hyperostosis in Prehistoric Ecuador. In Diet, Demography, and Disease: Changing Perspectives on Anemia, ed. P. Stuart-Macadam and S. Kent, 201–17. New York: Aldine de Gruyter.

Wadsworth, G. R. 1992. Physiological, Pathological, and Dietary Influences on the Hemoglobin Level. In Diet, Demography, and Disease: Changing Perspectives on Anemia, ed. P. Stuart-Macadam and S. Kent, 63–104. New York: Aldine de Gruyter.

Wells, C. 1967. Pseudopathology. In Diseases in Antiquity, ed. D. R. Brothwell and A. T. Sandison, 5–19. Springfield, Ill.: Charles C. Thomas.

Wright, L. E., and F. Chew. 1999. Porotic Hyperostosis and Paleoepidemiology: A Forensic Perspective on Anemia among the Ancient Maya. American Anthropologist 110:924–39.

9

Biological Relationships and Population History of Native Peoples in Spanish Florida and the American Southeast

Mark C. Griffin, Patricia M. Lambert, and Elizabeth Monahan Driscoll

This study was conducted in order to estimate population distances between Native American skeletal samples from the southeastern United States and to place Guale in particular in the larger landscape of biological distance and population history in this region. Previous research (Griffin 1989, 1993; Griffin and Nelson 1996) using dental and cranial nonmetric traits has placed some of these samples in a local perspective. This study takes a broader regional perspective, examining population samples from North Carolina, Tennessee, Georgia, and Florida. These additional samples represent a diverse cross section of cultural and linguistic groups from the southeastern United States.

In order to assess population affinity, biological distances are calculated using dental and cranial morphological data. Previous studies have demonstrated that this combined approach of including more than one source of data provides complementary rather than redundant results (Corruccini 1974; Trinkaus 1978; Kennedy 1981; Molto 1983; Hanihara 1992; Griffin 1993). The two sets of traits were chosen because of their demonstrated usefulness in describing population relationships. Dental morphology—more specifically, the number, configuration, and size of cusps and other surface features of teeth—has been shown to be highly correlated with genetic ancestry below the level of reproductive population and often to the level of family group (Scott and Turner 1997). Cranial morphology, specifically the presence, number, and placement of ossicles, foramina, and other features of the skull, has similarly been shown to be highly correlated with genetic ancestry (Hauser and De Stefano 1989). Biological distance, in the sense used here, refers to a statistical expression of morphological similarity between populations that is derived from genetically controlled traito.

Dental and cranial nonmetric traits have been extensively used to assess population affinity and patterns of microevolution (Saunders and Popovich 1978; Pietrusewsky 1981, 1984; Greene 1982; Turner 1986a, 1986b, 1987a, 1987b, 1990; Dodo 1987; Sofaer et al. 1986; Katayama 1988; Haeussler et al. 1989; Nichol 1989, 1990; Ishida 1990; Sciulli 1990; Townsend et al. 1990; Lukacs and Hemphill 1991; Dodo et al. 1992; Ishida and Dodo 1993; Scott and Turner 1997). Recent research using both types of nonmetric traits has focused on population microdifferentiation. That is, nonmetric traits in recent research have been used to differentiate between local populations rather than between large, aggregate, geographically defined populations (e.g., between groups of Native Americans rather than between Native Americans and Europeans). The present study is also focused on population microdifferentiation.

Materials

Skeletal samples from 13 archaeological sites used for this study all derive from the southeastern United States. The geographic locations of the sites are indicated in figure 9.1, and the population samples are summarized in table 9.1. Culturally, the population samples included here represent a diverse cross section of the protohistoric Southeast spanning a period from around A.D. 1200 to 1700. In broad geographic terms, they can be divided into three physiographic areas: coastal plain, piedmont, and ridge and valley.

Three of the coastal samples have been archaeologically and ethnographically identified as Guale. These samples come from the geographic area described by David Thomas as La Florida (Thomas 1987). The Guale skeletal samples examined here were recovered from three sites: (1) Irene Mound in Chatham County, Georgia (9Ch1), (2) Santa Catalina de Guale (9Li274) on St. Catherines Island, Georgia (hereafter referred to as Santa Catalina), and (3) Santa Catalina de Guale de Santa Maria (8Na41) on Amelia Island, Florida (hereafter referred to as Santa Maria).

The first of the Guale sites, Irene Mound, is located in coastal Georgia near the Savannah River mouth. This prehistoric site was occupied from around A.D. 1150 to 1450 (Caldwell and McCann 1941). The second Guale site, Santa Catalina, is located on St. Catherines Island, Georgia, and represents the first of a series of Spanish missions. The mission was occupied from A.D. 1608 to 1680. The third Guale site, Santa Maria, is

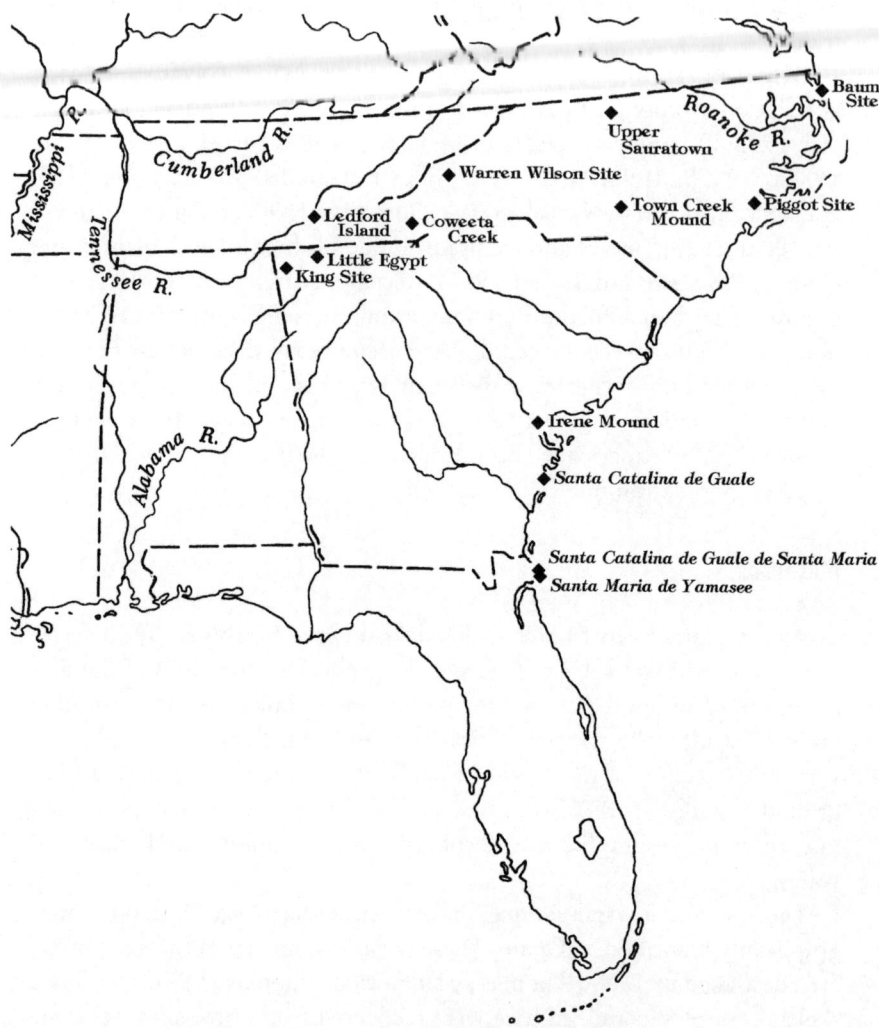

Fig. 9.1. Geographic locations of population samples for biodistance study.

located on Amelia Island, Florida, and represents the last in this same series of Spanish missions. This mission was occupied from A.D. 1686 to 1702. Ethnographic records indicate that the Guale inhabitants of the Santa Catalina and the Santa Maria missions were descendant populations from the pre-contact Guale of Irene Mound.

A fourth sample from the coastal plain area is from the Spanish mission of Santa Maria de Yamasee (8Na41d) on Amelia Island, Florida. This skel-

Table 9.1. Summary of population samples

Site	N	Temporal period A.D.	References
Guale			
Irene Mound (9Ch1)	248	1150–1550	Caldwell and McCann 1941; Hulse 1941; Larsen 1982; Anderson 1990
Santa Catalina de Guale (9Li274)	431	1608–1680	Thomas 1987; Larsen 1990; Larsen et al. 1990
Santa Catalina de Guale de Santa Maria (8Na41)	112	1686–1702	Saunders 1988; Larsen 1991
Yamasee			
Santa Maria de Yamasee (8Na41d)	105	1675–1683	Saunders 1988
Lamar/Dallas/Mouse Creek			
Ledford Island (16By13)	456	1400–1600	Lewis and Kneberg 1946; Boyd 1984; Sullivan 1986
King site (9Fl5)	213	1500–1650	Blakely 1988; Hally 1975a, b
Little Egypt (9Mu102)	65	1350–1500	Hally 1979
Carolina Algonquian			
Baum, Burial 1 (31Ck9)	55	1315±70	Phelps 1980a, b
Baum, Burial 5 (31Ck9)	33	1315±70	Phelps 1980a, b
Baum, Burial 7 (31Ck9)	27	1425±70	Phelps 1980a, b
Piggot site (31Cr14)	40	1230±65	Phelps 1980a, b
Pisgah			
Warren Wilson site (31Bn29)	61	1200–1400	Dickens 1976
Pee Dee			
Town Creek Mound (31Mg2,3)	216	1200–1400	Ward and Davis 1999
Qualla			
Coweeta Creek (31Ma34)	105	1620–1650	Dickens 1978
Siouan			
Upper Saura Town (31Sk1a)	103	1670–1710	Ward and Davis 1999

etal sample, tentatively identified as Yamasee (Bushnell 1986; Saunders 1988), was recovered immediately south of the Santa Catalina de Guale de Santa Maria cemetery on Amelia Island. The population sample is referred to here as Santa Maria de Yamasee. The Yamasee, like the Guale, were refugees from northern Georgia and lower South Carolina and are considered inland relatives of the coastal Guale (Mooney 1969). Although it is clear that the Yamasee were probably close linguistic and cultural relatives of the Guale, the biological affinity of these two groups is unclear.

The final two coastal plain samples derive from the Late Woodland Baum (31Ck9) and Piggot (31Cr14) prehistoric Carolina Algonquian sites. Prior to European contact, the North Carolina coastal region was occupied by two distinct cultures, the Carolina Algonquians of the Tidewater zone and the Tuscarora of the Inner Coastal Plain (Phelps 1983). Two local phases have been established for these Late Woodland cultures of the North Coastal region: Colington is the phase name given the Algonquian culture of the Tidewater zone, and Cashie is applied to the territory of the Tuscarora, Meherrin, and Nottaway in the interior Coastal Plain (Phelps 1983). Current radiocarbon dates for the Colington phase range from A.D. 860 ± 85 to 1315 ± 70 (Phelps 1977). The North Carolina population samples used here are all from the Colington phase Algonquian cultural tradition. Three of the Algonquian population samples included in this study were recovered from the Baum site. The Baum site, located in coastal North Carolina, covers at least five acres and contains a Middle Woodland period component (300 B.C.–A.D. 800) and a Late Woodland component (A.D. 800–1650). Five ossuary-type burials have been recovered from the Baum site in excavations from 1972 to 1983. All five ossuaries have been found overlying the Middle Woodland component, indicating a Late Woodland, Colington phase affiliation. A radiocarbon date for the Burial 1 ossuary of A.D. 1315 ± 70 confirms this association (Phelps 1980b). The remaining ossuary sample was recovered from the Piggot site (31Cr14). The Piggot site is located in Carteret County, North Carolina, near the southern boundary of the traditional Algonquian distribution (Phelps 1980a). The site has been radiocarbon dated to A.D. 1230 ± 65. The pattern of deposition in the ossuary suggests that it is associated with the Colington phase (Truesdell 1995).

The population samples from the Piedmont include Town Creek Mound (31Mg2 and 3) and Upper Saura Town (31Sk1a), both located in North Carolina. Town Creek is a late prehistoric Pee Dee phase palisaded mound and village dating to about A.D. 1200 to 1400 (Ward and Davis 1999). The site is located on the southern piedmont near the confluence of the Pee Dee and Little rivers. The so-called Pee Dee people who occupied this site had cultural traditions distinct from those observed at more northerly pied mont settlements. According to Coe (1995), physical traits (e.g., nose form and stature), the practice of fronto-occipital cranial deformation, ceramic styles, and mound construction link Town Creek biologically and cultur- ally more closely with South Appalachian Mississippian traditions better known at sites like Irene Mound than to northern Siouan villages like Up- per Saura Town. Upper Saura Town, the second piedmont sample included here, is a historic Siouan village dating to the latter part of the 17th century. The site is located along the Dan River on the northern piedmont, well outside the sphere of Mississippian cultural influence (Ward and Davis 1999).

The population samples from the ridge and valley area include Warren Wilson (31Bn29) and Coweeta Creek (31Ma34) in North Carolina; Led- ford Island (16By13) in Tennessee; and the King (9Fl5) and Little Egypt (9Mu102) sites in Georgia. The Warren Wilson site is a Pisgah phase pali- saded proto-Cherokee village dating to about A.D. 1200 to 1400. The site is located on the Swannanoa River east of Asheville, North Carolina. Co- weeta Creek is an early Qualla phase Cherokee village dating to the early 17th century. According to Ward and Davis (1999), the prehistoric moun- tain villages in this area were part of the South Appalachian Mississippian cultural tradition.

The remaining three sites, Ledford Island, King, and Little Egypt are all from the Lamar/Dallas/Mouse Creek traditions. The Mouse Creek phase site of Ledford Island was a large Mississippian town located in the Hi- wassee River of eastern Tennessee on an island of the same name. The site of Ledford Island was likely inhabited from around A.D. 1400 to 1600. The final two sites, the King and Little Egypt sites, are from the Late Mississip- pian Lamar cultures. The King site is an early historic town located in northwest Georgia in the floodplain of the Coosa River, approximately 20 miles west of the city of Rome, Georgia. The site was occupied in the 16th century for less than 50 years. According to Crowder (1988), the cultural affiliation of the King site has been archaeologically identified as Creek. The Little Egypt site is located on the south side of the Coosawattee River, approximately 35 miles northeast of Rome, Georgia. The predominant occupation of Little Egypt was during the Late Mississippian period, from A.D. 1350 to 1500. According to Hally (1980), Little Egypt was probably the center for the paramount chiefdom of Coosa.

Previous Studies: Guale

Previous examination of the Guale samples included here (Griffin 1989, 1993; Griffin and Nelson 1996) indicate a number of interesting relationships. Univariate and multivariate analyses demonstrated that the Guale samples in the present study are particularly diverse in terms of expression of dental and cranial nonmetric traits. However, despite the diversity demonstrated by statistically significant differences in frequencies in a large number of cranial and dental traits, the Guale samples from Santa Catalina and Santa Maria were consistently placed close to one another in multivariate analyses (figs. 9.2, 9.3, and 9.4). This result supports the contention that Santa Maria is a descendant population from that of Santa Catalina. The sample from Santa Maria de Yamasee was consistently placed close to the Santa Maria sample in multivariate analyses. This outcome may suggest a close biological affiliation between these two populations. The relationship between the Santa Catalina sample and the Santa Maria de Yamasee sample was less clear but may also suggest a biological affiliation between the two groups. The ethnographic record indicates that the Guale and Yamasee were distinct groups (Bushnell 1986; Mooney 1969). However, evidence presented in this analysis may suggest a closer affinity than the ethnographic record indicates. It may be that historically the Guale and Yamasee were distinguished solely by geographic location and not by cultural, linguistic, or biological differences.

The Santa Catalina population has been identified as the descendants of the prehistoric inhabitants of Irene Mound. The degree of dissimilarity suggested by univariate and multivariate analyses casts some doubt on this relationship. Separate multivariate analyses of dental and cranial nonmetric traits in the Griffin (1993) study consistently placed this sample relatively far from the other Guale samples and closer to the inland sample from Ledford Island. This result is especially notable with regard to the placement of the other Guale samples quite far from the Ledford Island sample and distinct from the Irene Mound sample. These results do not necessarily indicate a biological relationship between the population samples from Irene Mound and Ledford Island, but they do call into question the putative relationship between the inhabitants of Irene Mound and the historic Guale.

The degree of dissimilarity observed between the Irene Mound sample and the other Guale samples cannot be adequately explained by random genetic drift. Other mechanisms must be invoked to explain this difference. This is not to suggest that inhabitants of Irene Mound migrated from Ten-

Dental Samples

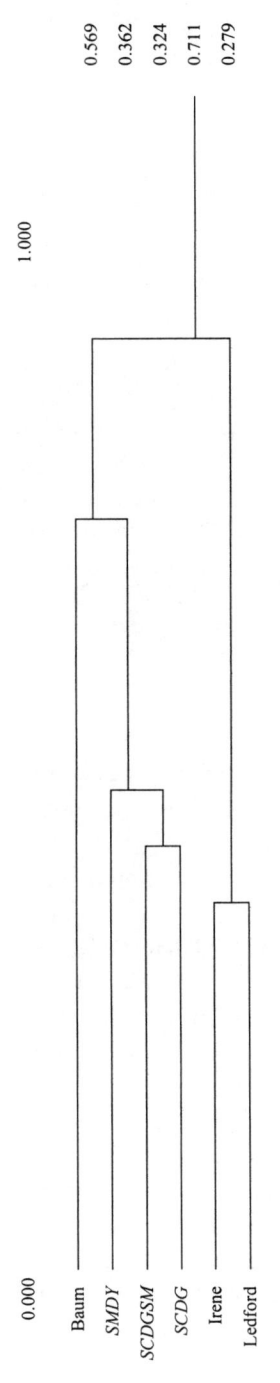

0.000   1.000

Baum ———————————————— 0.569

SMDY ———————————————— 0.362

SCDGSM ——————————————— 0.324

SCDG ———————————————— 0.711

Irene ———————————————— 0.279

Ledford

Cranial Samples

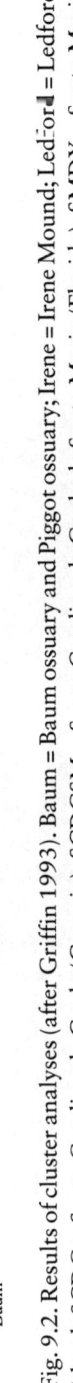

0.000   1.000

SMDY ———————————————— 0.392

Irene ———————————————— 0.269

SCDGSM ——————————————— 0.361

Ledford ——————————————— 0.510

Baum

Fig. 9.2. Results of cluster analyses (after Griffin 1993). Baum = Baum ossuary and Piggot ossuary; Irene = Irene Mound; Ledford = Ledford Island; SCDG = Santa Catalina de Guale (Georgia); SCDGSM = Santa Catalina de Guale de Santa Maria (Florida); SMDY = Santa Maria de Yamasee.

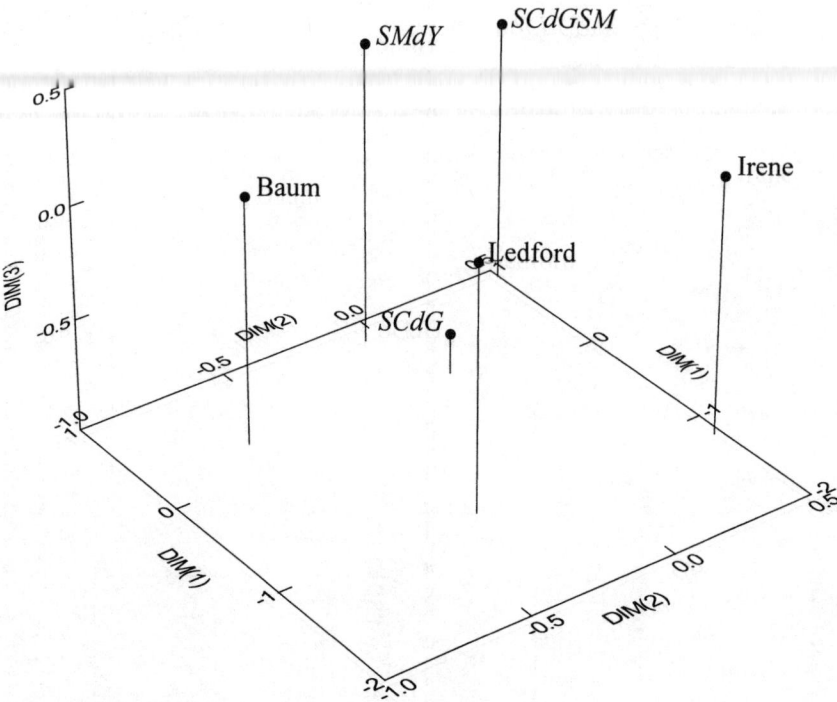

Fig. 9.3. Results of multidimensional scaling analysis of southeastern U.S. dental samples, sites as identified for figure 9.2 (after Griffin 1993).

nessee. It does, however, cast some doubt on the contention that the Irene Mound sample and the later Guale samples are a continuous population.

It has been inferred from the ethnographic record that the Guale were a derivative group from the inland Creek (Spencer and Jennings 1977). That the Guale sample from Irene Mound and the population sample from Ledford Island are quite similar in terms of dental and cranial morphology suggests a close biological connection between these groups. While the results of multivariate analyses of dental morphology consistently placed the Irene Mound and Ledford samples close to one another, the results obtained from analysis of cranial morphology were less consistent. The somewhat equivocal results of the cranial analyses with regard to the placement of Irene Mound and Ledford Island samples may suggest a less straightforward relationship than that suggested by analyses of dental nonmetric traits. It should also be noted that the term Guale was used interchangeably by Spanish explorers to mean a geographic location and a

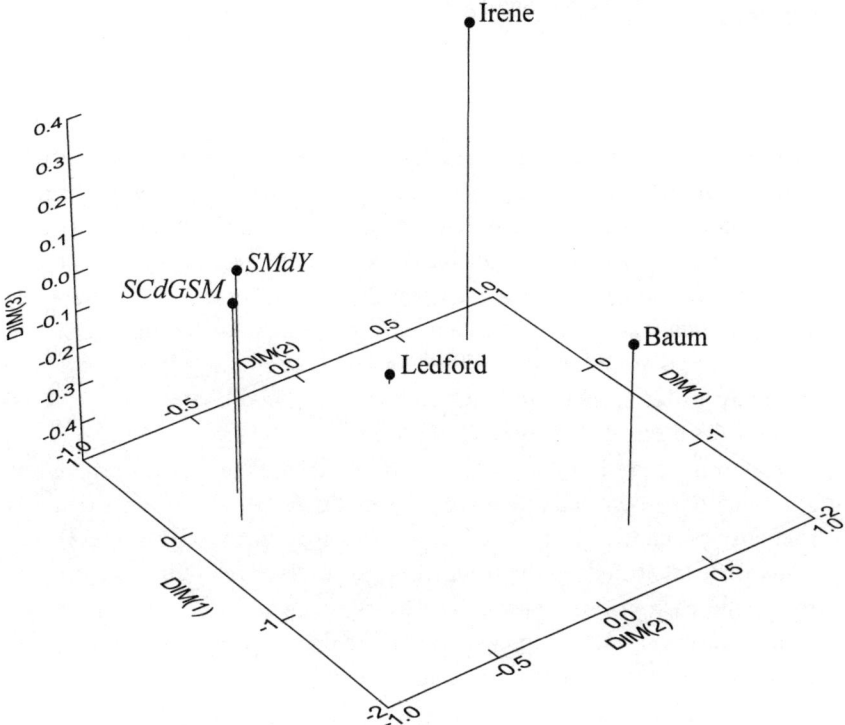

Fig. 9.4. Results of multidimensional scaling analysis of southeastern U.S. cranial samples, sites as identified for figure 9.2 (after Griffin 1993).

cultural/linguistic group (Jones 1978). Therefore, referring to a group as Guale may have connoted geographic location and not necessarily linguistic, cultural, or biological affiliation. It may also be the case that while the Guale represented a distinct linguistic and cultural group, they did not represent a distinct biological one.

If the historic Guale populations of the Georgia coast derive from the late prehistoric Irene Mound population, quite substantial population changes must have occurred. If this is the case, extensive gene flow from other populations was likely involved because of the relatively brief time interval between the occupation of Irene Mound and that of Santa Catalina de Guale (~100 years). Given the particularly unstable political and social conditions among the Guale after European contact and the extensive period of missionization of the native inhabitants, aggregation of local populations could have precipitated such gene flow.

Methods

Dental Traits

Morphological observations were made on 100 dental crown and root variables using the standardized Arizona State University dental anthropology system (Turner et al. 1991). This system consists of a wide range of dental morphological variables, including multitooth expression of a single trait and traits involving a single pair of antimeres. This information facilitates the identification of the most variable tooth or site for trait expression. The ASU system has proven particularly useful for distinguishing between local populations as well as larger regional series (Scott and Dahlberg 1982; Turner 1985). Most of the traits in this study are observed using ordinal scales with several grades.

Previous research on population samples from the southeastern United States has demonstrated that 35 traits from the ASU system are particularly useful for population distance studies in this area (Griffin 1989, 1993). The traits were identified on the basis of intra-observer reliability, wear sensitivity, and ease of observation. The traits consist of 35 dental nonmetric traits and two cranial nonmetric traits. The dental nonmetric traits used in the present study are summarized in table 9.2.

Cranial Traits

Morphological observations were made on 25 nonmetric cranial traits described by Berry and Berry (1967) and Hauser and De Stefano (1989). Numerous nonmetric cranial traits have been described in the literature, but these descriptions generally lack information on the reliability of specific traits in describing and comparing populations. This creates a situation in which the researcher must rely to a large degree on precedents set by other workers or on personal preference.

The traits selected for this study were chosen on the basis of three criteria: (1) reliability of scoring and observation, (2) demonstrated ability to discriminate populations, and (3) low intercorrelation with sex and age. The 25 traits included in this study are listed in table 9.3. The traits used here were observed recording presence or absence of the trait. No ordinal scales are used because these tend to be highly subjective (see Kennedy 1981).

Dental nonmetric traits were scored along a continuum of expression in each population sample using the methodology provided by Turner and others (1991). Cranial nonmetric traits were recorded as present or absent, with present representing any degree of trait expression. The dental

Table 9.2. Dental morphological traits

Trait	Teeth observed	References
Winging	upper central incisors	Enoki and Dahlberg 1958; Dahlberg 1963; Scott 1973
Shoveling	upper incisors	Hrdlička 1920; Dahlberg 1956, 1963; Moorrees 1957; Scott 1973
Curvature	upper central incisors	Nichol et al. 1984
Double-shoveling	upper central incisors	Dahlberg 1956; Turner 1967
Interruption groove	upper lateral incisors	Turner 1967
Tuberculum dentale	upper lateral incisors	Scott 1973; Turner et al. 1991
Canine mesial ridge	upper canines	Morris 1975; Turner et al. 1991
Canine distal accessory ridge	upper canines	Turner 1967; Scott 1973, 1980
Premolar mesial and distal accessory cusps	upper premolars	Turner 1967
Tri-cusped premolars	upper premolars	Turner et al. 1991
Distosagittal ridge	upper premolars	Morris et al. 1978
Metacone	upper 3rd molars	Turner et al. 1991
Hypocone	upper 1st and 2nd molars	Larson 1970, 1978; Scott 1973; Turner et al. 1991
Metaconule	upper 1st and 2nd molars	Harris 1977; Harris and Bailit 1980
Carabelli's trait	upper 1st and 2nd molars	Dahlberg 1956, 1963; Scott 1973, 1980
Parastyle	upper 3rd molar	Katich 1975; Turner et al. 1991
Enamel extensions	upper 1st and 2nd molars	Pedersen 1949
Premolar root number	upper premolar 3	Turner 1967, 1981
Molar root number	upper 2nd molars	Turner 1967
Radical number	all teeth	Turner 1967
Peg-shaped incisor	upper lateral incisor	Turner et al. 1991
Peg-shaped molar	upper 3rd molar	Turner et al. 1991
Odontome	premolars	Pedersen 1949; Alexandersen 1970
First lower premolar lingual cusp variation	lower 1st premolars	Pedersen 1949; Kraus and Furr 1953; Scott 1973
Second lower premolar lingual cusp variation	lower 2nd premolars	Pedersen 1949; Kraus and Furr 1953; Scott 1973
Anterior fovea	lower 1st molar	Hrdlička 1924; Turner et al. 1991
Groove pattern	lower 1st and 2nd molars	Gregory 1916; Hellman 1929; Jørgensen 1955

(continued)

Table 9.2—*Continued*

Trait	Teeth observed	References
Cusp number	lower 1st and 2nd molars	Gregory 1916; Hellman 1929; Turner 1967
Deflecting wrinkle	lower 1st molars	Weidenreich 1937; Scott and Dahlberg 1982; Turner et al. 1991
Distal trigonid crest	lower 1st molars	Hrdlička 1924
Protostylid	lower 1st and 2nd molars	Dahlberg 1956, 1963; Turner 1967; Scott 1973
Cusp 5	lower 1st and 2nd molars	Turner 1970; Scott and Dahlberg 1982; Turner et al. 1991
Cusp 6	lower 1st and 2nd molars	Turner 1970; Scott 1973; Scott and Dahlberg 1982; Turner et al. 1991
Cusp 7	lower 1st and 2nd molars	Turner 1970; Turner et al. 1991
Canine root number	lower canines	Turner 1967
Tomes' root	lower 1st premolar	Tomes 1923; Turner et al. 1991
First molar root number	lower 1st molar	Turner 1967; Turner et al. 1991
Second molar root number	lower 2nd molar	Turner 1967; Turner et al. 1991
Torsomolar angle	lower 3rd molar	Neiberger 1978; Turner et al. 1991
Palatine torus	palate	Miller and Roth 1940; Turner et al. 1991
Mandibular torus	mandible	Johnson et al. 1965; Morris 1970

Table 9.3. Cranial morphological traits

Trait	References
Ossicle at lambda	Bennett 1965; Berry and Berry 1967; Molto 1983
Lambdoid ossicles	Bennett 1965; Berry and Berry 1967; Herzog 1968
Ossicle at asterion	Berry and Berry 1967; Suchey 1975; Molto 1983
Parietal notch bone	Oetteking 1930; Berry and Berry 1967; Ossenberg 1969
Epipteric bone	Wood-Jones 1930a, b, c; Berry and Berry 1967; Molto 1983
Bregmatic bone	Wood-Jones 1930a, b, c; Berry and Berry 1967
Coronal ossicle	Wood-Jones 1930a, b, c ; Sublett 1966; Berry and Berry 1967
Metopism	Limson 1924; Bolk 1931; Tørgersen 1951
Fronto-temporal articulation	Collins 1926, 1930; Ossenberg 1969
Supraorbital foramen	Le Double 1903; Berry and Berry 1967; Ossenberg 1969; Korey 1970
Frontal notch	Wood-Jones 1930a, b, c; Berry and Berry 1967
Auditory torus	Wood-Jones 1930a, b, c; Berry and Berry 1967
Foramen of Huschke	Anderson 1962; Berry and Berry 1967; Molto 1983
Condylar facet double	Anderson 1962; Berry and Berry 1967; Kennedy 1981
Precondylar tubercle	Inglemark 1947; Berry and Berry 1967
Foramen ovale	Wood-Jones 1930a, b, c; Berry and Berry 1967
Foramen spinosum	Berry and Berry 1967; Korey 1970; Suchey 1975
Accessory lesser palatine foramen	Berry and Berry 1967
Palatine torus	Suzuki and Sakai 1960; Turner et al. 1991
Maxillary torus	Berry and Berry 1967
Parietal foramen	Berry and Berry 1967; Ossenberg 1969; Molto 1983
Posterior condylar canal patent	Boyd 1930; Berry and Berry 1967; Ossenberg 1969; Korey 1970
Mastoid foramen exsutural	Berry and Berry 1967
Anterior condylar canal double	Berry and Berry 1967; Korey 1970; Ossenberg 1969; Molto 1983
Zygomatico-facial foramen	Berry and Berry 1967; Molto 1983
Accessory infraorbital foramen	Berry and Berry 1967

nonmetric traits were dichotomized for the statistical analyses involving angular transformations using the criteria suggested by Turner (1987a). Dental and cranial morphological trait frequencies are presented in appendices 9.A and 9.B.

Trait Intercorrelation

With the large number of genetic and nongenetic factors influencing the expression of nonmetric traits, the number of traits that are statistically correlated is expected to be low. Research has shown this presumption to be generally false (Suzuki and Sakai 1960; DeVilliers 1968; Buikstra 1972; Corruccini 1974; Ossenberg 1976; Molto 1983). Molto (1983) attributes the higher than expected frequencies of correlations to four major factors: nonmetric traits (1) are often alternative expressions of a single underlying variable, (2) often have a common regional or embryological origin, (3) can be affected by similar developmental phenomena, and (4) may be affected by the shared interaction of some combination of the foregoing. Given these factors, frequencies of nonmetric traits are expected to show a considerable number of positive correlations. Arguably, nonmetric traits offer redundant information in the real population.

Many authors have simply assumed a priori that correlations between frequency of expression for nonmetric traits are nonexistent (Berry and Berry 1967; Benfer 1970; Spence 1971; Berry 1972). In part, this decision was based on studies of *Mus musculus* (Truslove 1961) and *Homo sapiens* (Berry and Berry 1967; Kellock and Parsons 1970a; Corruccini 1974). Other researchers have suggested significant correlation between classes of traits (Suzuki and Sakai 1960; DeVilliers 1968; Ossenberg 1976). That is, traits that have similar developmental pathways (e.g., hypostotic, hyperstotic, oral tori, basicranial foramina) will have similar degrees of expression in an individual. However for the most part, as Corruccini (1974) has pointed out, the nature of such correlations often differs randomly from group to group.

The question here is not whether nonmetric traits are correlated. Some very clearly are. The real issue is what to do with those that are significantly correlated. Many approaches have been used to deal with this issue. Kennedy (1981) reasoned that because correlations are usually "random" when compared between populations, they could be ignored. Sjøvold (1977) has taken a similar approach, claiming that the pattern of low correlation will not cause serious distortion of the results. Buikstra (1972) has taken a reductionist approach by simply eliminating traits until the matrix was free of all significant correlations. Ossenberg (1976) has taken yet a different approach by amalgamating significantly intercorrelated matrices of common traits as a single trait. A reductionist approach approximating Molto's (1983) is adopted here. Traits that have significant correlations and clear etiological connections are eliminated from the analyses of population distance.

Many authors have recommended the use of the phi coefficient rather than other coefficients to detect the correlations between nonmetric traits in place (Benfer 1970; Sjøvold 1977; Molto 1983). Another related statistic, Tau-b (Goodman and Kruskal 1954, 1959, 1963), is used here because many of the traits are not exclusively dichotomous, as required for phi correlation analysis. Tau-b, like phi, gives a close approximation to the chi-square distribution and therefore is more sensitive to this task than are other coefficients of association (Thomas 1986). Correlation coefficients were calculated for both classes of traits in this study.

The statistics commonly used to analyze nonmetric trait variation do not take into account the existence of intertrait correlations and depend on the assumption that the traits used are not statistically correlated (Kennedy 1981). For this reason the dental and cranial traits chosen for this analysis were tested separately in pair-wise combinations via two-way contingency tables and Tau-b correlation coefficients. These analyses were performed in order to detect statistically significant and strong intertrait correlations.

A number of strong correlations were observed between traits in this study. Without exception, these correlations result from the nature of the traits. That is, in each case either the traits involved occur on multiple teeth (i.e., field effects) or the traits are different manifestations of the same complex. An example of the latter would be central incisor curvature and central incisor double-shoveling. By definition, these traits vary inversely. Therefore, they are strongly negatively correlated. Two of the traits showing a strong association with each other are central incisor shoveling and lateral incisor shoveling. The traits eliminated from the analysis because of intercorrelation are central incisor curvature, upper first molar hypocone, upper second molar metaconule, lower second molar cusp number, lower first molar cusp five, lower first molar cusp six, and mastoid foramen exsutural.

Population Distance

The objective of this study is to estimate biological distances among a time-successive series of Guale samples and place them in a context with other culturally and linguistically distinct Native American groups. A number of different statistical procedures are employed to compare these groups. Among these procedures are estimations of mean measures of divergence (Green and Suchey 1976; Sofaer et al. 1986), cluster analysis (Aldenderfer and Blashfield 1984), and multidimensional scaling (Kruskal and Wish 1978).

Assessment of biological distance is best achieved by expressing the degree of dissimilarity between populations with a single numerical value, rather than trying to evaluate relationships on a trait by trait basis using univariate statistics (Cybulski 1975; Molto 1983). The single numerical value is calculated using multivariate statistics and is derived from the sum of the squared differences between corresponding variates of two population samples (Smith 1972). When the populations are similar, the coefficient value should be small, and when the populations are dissimilar, it should be large. Dissimilarity in population studies is equated with biological distance. The distance for population models is usually defined in terms of Euclidean distance. In other words, populations are plotted relative to one another in terms of their values for a given set of variables. Euclidean distance is the distance between the plotted positions. In the simplest case, one could describe two populations in terms of two variables, X and Y. Plotting the populations two-dimensionally and measuring the distance between the two points on the graph gives one the Euclidean distance between the populations. As more variables are added, calculation of Euclidean distance becomes more complex and requires the use of distance coefficients.

Most of the distance coefficients used for nonmetric morphological data are based on C.A.B. Smith's mean measure of divergence (Grewal 1962). This statistic uses an angular transformation of the original trait frequencies for each population sample being compared. The angular transformation stabilizes the variance so that sampling error does not distort the estimation of distance. This is necessary with dichotomous traits because the variance of the *sample* proportion is a function of the *population* proportion (Sjøvold 1977; Molto 1983). The mathematical foundation of the Mean Measure of Divergence as an appropriate distance measure using nonmetric data has been substantiated by Sjøvold (1977). This is the most widely utilized statistic for estimating population distance for nonmetric data (Sjøvold 1977; Molto 1983). However, use of the mean measure of divergence without corrective statistics on small population sample sizes has been cautioned against (Green and Suchey 1976; Sjøvold 1977). There are a number of transformations currently used to remove the effects of small sample size (Anscombe 1948; Freeman and Tukey 1950). The usefulness of each technique is dependent on how quickly and effectively they stabilize the variance (Molto 1983). The transformation devised by Smith (in Grewal 1962) has been widely used (Pietrusewsky 1969, 1971; Jantz 1970; Kellock and Parsons 1970a, b; Buikstra 1972; Lane and Sublett 1972; Corruccini 1974; Cybulski 1972; Finnegan 1972; Rightmire 1972; Birkby 1973; Berry 1974; Gaherty 1974; McWilliams 1974). Green and Suchey (1976) have demonstrated that this transformation produces inflated variances for small sample sizes combined with small trait frequencies. Thus the variance is not adequately stabilized and tests of significance between samples are unreliable.

Other researchers have proposed the use of alternate transformations (Green and Suchey 1976; De Souza and Houghton 1977; Sjøvold 1977). The best are those of Freeman and Tukey (1950) and Anscombe (1948) According to Molto (1983), there is little empirical difference between the two transformations. However, the Freeman and Tukey transformation is slightly more efficient at stabilizing the variance of very small proportions, which are common in archaeological samples (Green and Suchey 1976; Sjøvold 1977).

The mean measures of divergence for this study were calculated using the Freeman and Tukey transformation and the method suggested by Green and Suchey (1976). The angular transformation for each trait was carried out using the formula suggested by Freeman and Tukey (1950). The standard deviation of the mean measures of divergence was calculated using the method suggested by Sofaer and others (1986). A mean measure of divergence equal to or greater than twice its standard deviation is considered to be statistically significant at the $p < 0.05$ level (Molto 1983). When two samples have identical frequencies of each variant or sample sizes are small, the mean measure of divergence assumes a negative value (Turner and Bird 1981). As Constandse-Westermann (1972:3) points out, "lack of significance usually does point to a close association of populations." However, nonsignificant distance does not necessarily mean that the samples being compared are drawn from the same population (Constandse-Westermann 1972; Hiernaux 1972; Rightmire 1972; Sjøvold 1977). It is equally misleading to interpret statistically significant distances as indicating samples from different populations. As Grüneberg (1952, 1963) has noted, distances between populations may increase at a constant rate over generations due to random genetic drift.

Taxonomic Statistics

Interpreting biological relationships from a large matrix of distance coefficients can be quite a confusing task. In order to make interpretation easier, two related taxonomic statistical techniques have traditionally been employed (Lukacs and Hemphill 1991; Molto 1983). These two techniques are cluster analysis and multidimensional scaling. Both of these procedures express biological dissimilarity in terms of Euclidean distance (Molto 1983).

Affinity of the groups is assessed using cluster analysis, a metric approach leading to the establishment of clusters of similar groups (Aldenderfer and Blashfield 1984; Anderberg 1973; Blashfield 1976; Everitt

1974). The object of the analysis is: given a sample of n objects, each of which has a score on p variables, devise a scheme for grouping the objects into classes so that similar ones are in the same class. The objects here are the population samples and the scores are the arcsine transformed trait frequencies. The method must be completely numerical and, unlike in discriminant function analyses, the number of classes is not known.

There are several hierarchical methods available for cluster analysis. These methods operate on a distance matrix to construct a dendrogram that illustrates the relationships among the population samples. Agglomerative hierarchical methods in cluster analysis start with the calculation of the distances of each individual to all other individuals. Groups are then formed by a process of agglomeration. All objects start by being alone in groups of one. Close groups are then gradually merged until finally all individuals are in a single group. Of the methods available, Ward's minimum variance provides the most accurate results for the type of data used here (Blashfield 1976; Molto 1983). This method is designed to generate clusters so that the variance within clusters is minimal (Ward 1963). The procedure uses an error sum of squares function that computes the sum of squares of the distance from each point to its parent cluster. At each step, it combines those two clusters, which results in the least increase in the within-group sum of squares objective function. A cluster formed by this method can, therefore, be defined as a group of entities such that the error sum of squares among the members of each cluster is minimal (Blashfield 1976).

The next procedure used to illustrate population distances is multidimensional scaling (Tørgersen 1952; Kruskal and Wish 1978; Schiffman et al. 1981). Multidimensional scaling is a technique that attempts to position objects in space according to distance measures rather than classifying them as in cluster analysis. The objects in this case are again the population samples, and the distances used are the standardized mean measures of divergence derived with the Freeman-Tukey transformation and using the method of Sofaer and others (1986). A point is usually specified in terms of its coordinate location in reference to a set of axes. An axis defines a direction of movement and the number of axes defines the dimensionality of the space. The reference axes are assumed to be at right angles to each other and can be referred to as a Cartesian coordinate system (Molto 1983).

The procedure for multidimensional scaling is iterative and the groups are moved around within a space of specified dimensionality in order to find a monotone function expressing the original distances and the distances in the configuration. The fit between the two distances and a monotone function is expressed as a measure referred to as "stress" (Kruskal 1964a, b). The stress is computed as the square root of the sum of the squared deviations of the distances in the configuration space from the monotone function divided by the sum of the squares in the configuration space (Kruskal 1964a, b). This statistic has a theoretical range from 0 to 1 with the larger the value the weaker the fit of the data to a given configuration. After a series of iterations has produced a configuration of minimal stress in some number of dimensions, the procedure is terminated. Generally, increasing the number of dimensions improves the fit of the data to a configuration. However, beyond three dimensions, interpretation becomes problematic.

In multidimensional scaling, the position of the objects in space can be described in one dimension (if the objects fall on a line), in two dimensions (if the objects lie on a plane), in three dimensions (if the objects can be represented by points in space), or in a higher number of dimensions (in which case an immediate geometrical representation is not possible). In this study, the representations are in three dimensions because interpretation of more dimensions is problematic at best.

Results

Biological distance is most easily evaluated by expressing the degree of divergence between the populations with a single numerical value rather than by trying to evaluate relationships on a trait by trait basis using univariate statistics (Cybulski 1975; Molto 1983). The single numerical value chosen for this analysis is the mean measure of divergence based on the method of Green and Suchey (1976) and standardized mean measures of divergence using the method of Sofaer and others (1986).

Standardized mean measures of divergence were calculated by dividing each mean measure of divergence by its standard deviation. The standardized mean measures of divergence are more appropriate for comparison of distances among groups of populations with greatly varying sample sizes (Sofaer et al. 1986). In order to be considered statistically significant at the $p < 0.05$ level, the mean measure of divergence must be at least twice its standard deviation. An examination of the distance matrices for the dental and cranial traits (tables 9.4 and 9.5) reveals that the vast majority of the mean measures of divergence are statistically significant. Two notable and consistent exceptions to this are the comparisons of Santa Maria with Santa Maria de Yamasee and Town Creek with Upper Saura Town. Both dental and cranial morphological measures of divergence for these comparisons are quite small and with one exception are not statistically significant.

As one can see, it is impossible to assess simultaneously the relationships among large numbers of population samples from a matrix of distance coefficients. In order to make interpretation easier, two related taxonomic statistical techniques were used: cluster analysis and multidimensional scaling.

Cluster Analysis

For the first multivariate method, arcsine transformed trait frequencies were used as input for a cluster analysis program (Cluster, SYSTAT Inc., Wilkinson 1988a). This program is designed to construct dendrograms in Euclidean space based on Ward's Minimum Variance method (Ward 1963). The results of cluster analyses are reported in figure 9.5. Examination of cluster analyses derived independently from the dental and cranial traits reveals some differences in results.

In the dental analysis, the eleven population samples form four distinct clusters. Some of these clusters are somewhat unexpected. According to ethnographic accounts, the Irene Mound, Santa Catalina, and Santa Maria population samples represent part of a temporally successive and biologically continuous series. Cluster analysis suggests, however, that the Irene Mound sample is biologically more similar to the population samples from Ledford Island and the King site than to the other Guale samples. In fact, this cluster separates as a distinct isolate from the other eight sites at a higher level than even the Carolina Algonquian samples. The results of cluster analysis also suggest that the Santa Maria and Santa Maria de Yamasee samples are biologically similar. However, the results of this analysis do not indicate such a close relationship between Santa Catalina and Santa Maria. Two notable isolates from the other clusters are the Baum sample and the Town Creek–Upper Saura Town cluster. The Algonquian are archaeologically and ethnographically identified as quite separate from the other southeastern U.S. populations examined here. This analysis reflects that separation. Some have speculated that the Guale of Irene Mound and the inhabitants of Town Creek are biologically affiliated (Coe 1995). This analysis does not confirm that relationship.

The clusters produced by the cranial analysis are slightly different from those produced by the dental traits. In this analysis, Irene Mound does not separate from the other Guale samples as in the dental analysis. Instead a close cluster is formed by Irene Mound and Santa Maria. The Santa Maria and Santa Maria de Yamasee samples are separated by two hierarchical

Table 9.4. Mean measures of divergence, cranial samples

	Irene	SCdGSM	SMdY	Baum	Ledford	U. Saura Town	Town Creek	Warren Wilson
Irene	—	0.04193	0.07725	0.15449	0.08102	0.22426	0.19217	0.29136
SCdGSM	3.38009	—	0.04364	0.09825	0.04275	0.19716	0.14840	0.22026
SMdY	3.24833	1.77934	—	0.15589	0.05047	0.39893	0.31170	0.40970
Baum	13.69704	8.13507	6.64755	—	0.20261	0.28868	0.28466	0.31375
Ledford	4.46042	2.25475	1.66520	11.35671	—	0.46151	0.25455	0.44014
U. Saura Town	8.54383	7.32912	10.50533	11.11083	14.24488	—	0.06067	0.04525
Town Creek	14.91720	10.87424	12.47359	22.62514	13.14351	2.17251	—	0.04082
Warren Wilson	12.61187	9.23929	11.66509	13.75196	14.91050	1.20289	1.66757	—

Note: Mean measures of divergence above diagonal (Green and Suchey 1976), standardized mean measures of divergence below diagonal (Schaer et al. 1986).

Table 9.5. Mean measures of divergence, dental samples

	Irene	SCdG	SCdGSM	SmdY	Baum	Ledford	King	Little Egypt	Coweeta Creek	U. Saura Town	Town Creek
Irene	—	0.11228	0.18057	0.19898	0.31603	0.04826	0.03475	0.16008	0.05196	0.10575	0.20653
SCDG	14.43324	—	0.06330	0.09839	0.16060	0.11460	0.09557	0.03995	0.03638	0.08318	0.15561
SCDGSM	12.10184	4.57742	—	0.04278	0.12991	0.23015	0.23119	0.16367	0.07159	0.16606	0.25132
SMDY	12.83859	6.86477	1.99151	—	0.11897	0.21463	0.26445	0.11715	0.07018	0.13877	0.21698
Baum	9.78760	5.13672	3.42878	3.08025	—	0.20130	0.35235	0.25701	0.20186	0.24332	0.27652
Ledford	4.92674	13.26569	14.61100	13.04322	6.09860	—	0.04462	0.09926	0.08787	0.20840	0.28299
King	2.72717	8.26442	12.35684	13.61961	9.84655	3.23763	—	0.07062	0.09795	0.14760	0.26312
Little Egypt	4.90792	1.27115	4.27929	2.98623	4.67250	2.94672	1.92750	—	0.03570	0.14928	0.21868
Coweeta Creek	3.55730	2.69237	3.46452	3.31042	5.33413	5.68262	5.32419	0.93773	—	0.03088	0.08084
U. Saura Town	6.33256	5.31141	7.37429	5.97279	6.11322	11.85859	7.20889	3.71976	1.37398	—	-0.02018
Town Creek	18.27998	15.27574	14.52446	12.14013	7.96241	23.26790	17.42754	6.27282	4.72243	-1.04934	—

Note: Mean measures of divergence above diagonal (Green and Suchey 1976), standardized mean measures of divergence below diagonal (Sofaer et al. 1986).

Cluster Analysis, Dental Samples

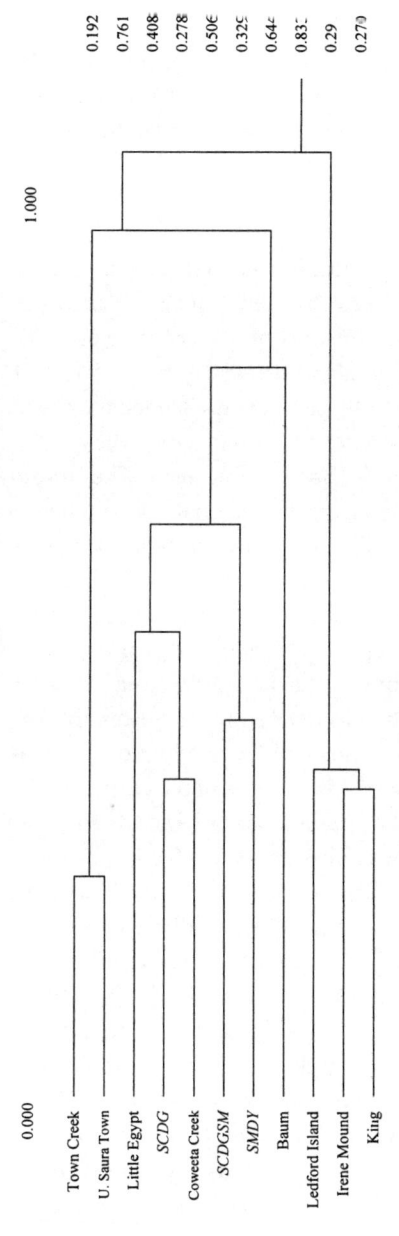

Town Creek	0.192
U. Saura Town	0.761
Little Egypt	0.408
SCDG	0.278
Coweeta Creek	0.506
SCDGSM	0.325
SMDY	0.644
Baum	0.831
Ledford Island	0.29
Irene Mound	0.270
King	

0.000   1.000

Cluster Analysis, Cranial Samples

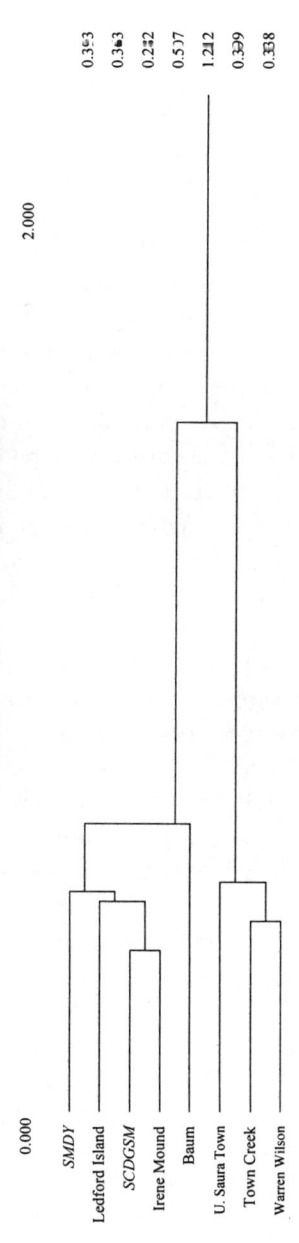

SMDY	0.363
Ledford Island	0.363
SCDGSM	0.242
Irene Mound	0.537
Baum	1.212
U. Saura Town	0.399
Town Creek	0.338
Warren Wilson	

0.000   2.000

Fig. 9.5. Results of cluster analysis.

levels rather than clustered together. The Baum site is still separated into a unique isolate in the cranial analysis. A widely divergent cluster is formed by the sites of Upper Saura Town, Town Creek, and Warren Wilson. These are slightly different relationships from those suggested by the dental analysis. The Baum sample and the other three North Carolina samples reflect much the same relationship as indicated by the dental analysis. However, the relationships between the Guale samples and the sample from Ledford Island appear more complicated.

Multidimensional Scaling

For the second multivariate technique, multidimensional scaling, arcsine transformed trait frequencies were utilized in a mean measure of divergence analysis. The standardized mean measures of divergence were used as input for a multidimensional scaling analysis (MDS-Guttman, SYSTAT Inc., Wilkinson 1988a). Guttman's (1968) coefficient of alienation was used. Each analysis was stopped when a level of stress in fitting the coordinate points to the monotonic function dropped below zero. The output from this program results in a table of three-dimensional coordinates in Euclidean space for each sample. These coordinates are then plotted in three-dimensional space, giving a representation of the relative distances between populations (Plot, SYGRAPH, Wilkinson 1988b). The results of multidimensional scaling analyses are reported in figures 9.6 and 9.7.

The results of multidimensional scaling of the dental trait frequencies in many ways correspond with the conclusions derived from cluster analysis of the dental traits. The same close placement of Irene Mound, the King site, and Ledford Island are indicated here. Likewise as in the cluster analysis, a close relationship between Santa Catalina, Santa Maria, and Santa Maria de Yamasee is suggested. Two notable differences from the cluster analysis are the cluster of Upper Saura Town, Little Egypt, and Coweeta Creek and the isolation of Town Creek well away from all the other sites.

The results of multidimensional scaling derived from the cranial traits also in many ways correspond with the conclusions derived from cluster analysis of the cranial traits. The close relationship between Santa Maria and Santa Maria de Yamasee is more clearly defined here. A similar relationship between Ledford Island and Irene Mound is also more clearly defined here. As in all of the previous analyses, the Baum samples are clearly demarcated from the rest of the samples. Slightly different from the cluster analysis, a close relationship is suggested between Upper Saura Town and Warren Wilson, while Town Creek appears as a relative isolate.

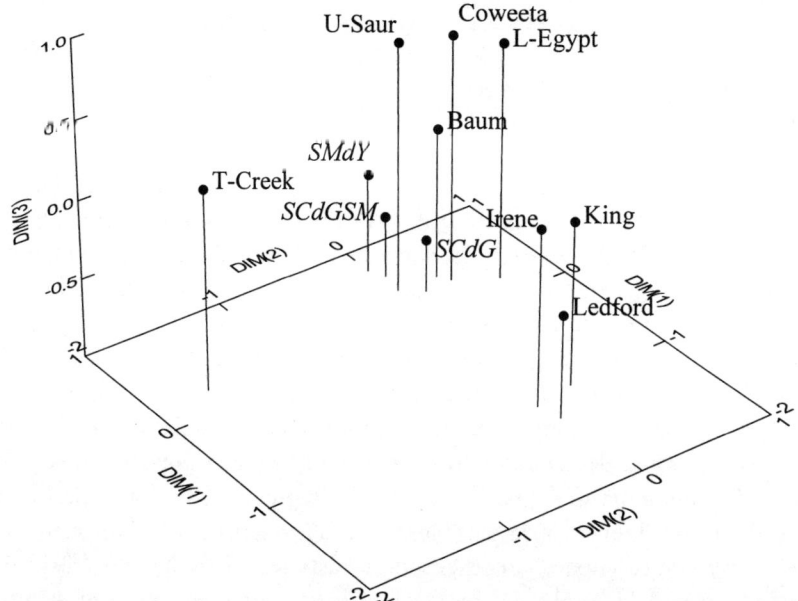

Fig. 9.6. Results of multidimensional scaling analysis of dental samples. Baum = Baum ossuary and Piggot ossuary; Coweeta = Coweeta Creek; Irene = Irene Mound; King = King site; Ledford = Ledford Island; L-Egypt = Little Egypt; SCDG = Santa Catalina de Guale (Georgia); SCDGSM = Santa Catalina de Guale de Santa Maria (Florida); SMDY = Santa Maria de Yamasee; T-Creek = Town Creek; U-Saur = Upper Saura Town; .

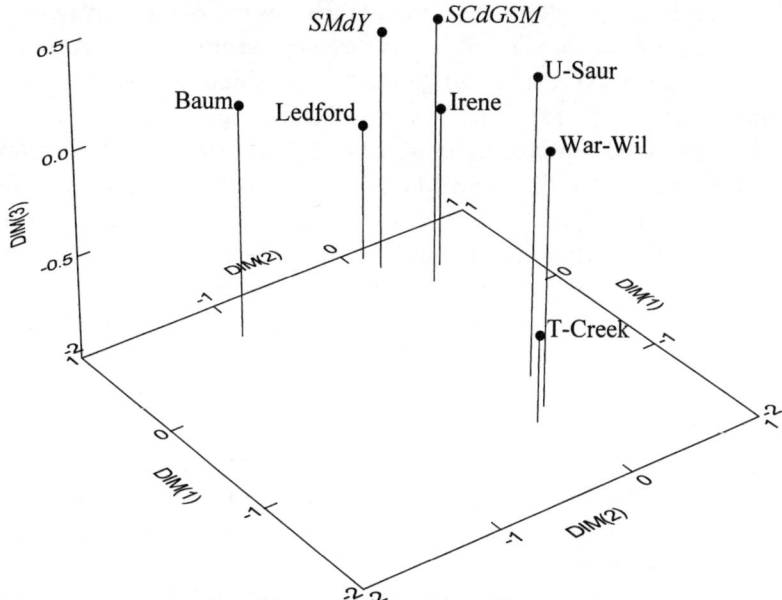

Fig. 9.7. Results of multidimensional scaling analysis of cranial samples from seven sites identified for figure 9.6, plus War-Wil = Warren Wilson.

Discussion

The results of this study can be discussed in relation to at least two specific issues: (1) the likely biological relationships between the three Guale samples, and (2) the biological affinity of the Guale to other groups from the Southeast. With regard to the suggested relationship among the Guale samples, ethnographic sources indicate that the samples included here represent a continuous series of populations. According to independent analyses of distance estimates generated from dental and cranial traits, the Guale samples do not represent a continuous population.

Specifically, the assertion that the Santa Maria population represents the migrants and descendants from the Santa Catalina population is supported by all of the analyses. The degree of dissimilarity between the Santa Catalina and Santa Maria samples, although statistically significant, is relatively small compared to other sample distances. This degree of dissimilarity can best be explained by genetic drift. This interpretation is supported by the comparatively smaller sample size observed at Santa Maria, which represents the temporally later sample.

An explanation for the significant differences between Santa Catalina and Santa Maria may be inferred from the differing degrees of diversity observed within each sample. The Santa Catalina sample exhibits a great deal more variability in terms of trait expression than that observed for the Santa Maria sample. Because Santa Catalina was one of the early missions in the area and may have been characterized by the mixture of diverse gene pools, one might expect that this sample would exhibit a wide range of trait variability. Given that (1) in terms of biological distance the Santa Catalina and Santa Maria samples are quite close, (2) the Santa Catalina sample temporally preceded the Santa Maria sample, and (3) the population of Santa Maria most likely derived from that of Santa Catalina, the evidence suggests a population "bottleneck" between the two temporal periods. That is, the gene pool was sharply restricted between the temporal period of Santa Catalina and that of Santa Maria. Considering the volatile social circumstances at the time, many possible explanations for such a bottleneck exist (e.g., warfare, circumscription, differential mortality, and migration).

Separate analyses consistently placed the Irene Mound sample relatively far from the other Guale samples and closer to the samples from the Lamar/Dallas/Mouse Creek cultures. This degree of dissimilarity is not likely due to the action of random genetic drift alone. This result casts some doubt on the contention that the Irene Mound sample and the later Guale samples are a continuous population. The explanation may be that the Irene Mound sample was more closely affiliated with prehistoric inland groups rather than with the later Guale from Santa Catalina and Santa Maria. Because populations in this geographic area were in a state of political and social flux between the temporal period of Irene Mound and that of the later Guale samples, this interpretation is plausible. It should also be noted that the term *Guale* was used interchangeably as a geographic location and a cultural/linguistic group (Jones 1978). Therefore, referring to a group as Guale may have connoted geographic location and not necessarily linguistic, cultural, or biological affiliation.

As noted, the Spanish called the location Guale as well as using this name for a cultural group. The sample from Santa Catalina likely represents an aggregate population. If this is the case, one would hardly expect the prehistoric Irene Mound inhabitants to be similar to the population sample from Santa Catalina. This is further complicated by the probability that because it was a ceremonial center, Irene Mound likely was also an aggregate population. Regardless of which interpretation one chooses, it is clear from the results presented here that the prehistoric Guale from Irene Mound were significantly dissimilar in terms of dental and cranial morphology from the historic Guale of both Santa Catalina and Santa Maria.

If the historic Guale populations of the Georgia coast derive from the late prehistoric Irene Mound population, quite substantial population changes must have occurred. If this is the case, extensive gene flow from other populations was likely involved because of the relatively brief time interval between the occupation of Irene Mound and that of Santa Catalina (less than 100 years).

In regard to the suggested relationships for the Guale and non-Guale samples, with the exception of the Irene Mound sample, the coastal La Florida samples appear fairly distinct from the inland samples from North Carolina, Georgia, and Tennessee. This is especially true for the North Carolina piedmont and ridge and valley samples. Considering the samples one at a time, the population sample from Santa Maria de Yamasee was consistently placed close to the Santa Maria sample in multivariate analyses. This outcome may suggest a close biological affiliation between these two populations. The relationship between the Santa Catalina sample and the Santa Maria de Yamasee sample was less clear but may also suggest a biological affiliation between the two groups.

It is unexpected that the Santa Maria and Santa Maria de Yamasee population samples consistently placed close together in a population distance analysis. The ethnographic record is unclear as to the cultural and linguistic affiliation of the Guale and Yamasee. However, these two groups are usually considered distinct groups (Mooney 1969; Bushnell 1986). Evidence presented in this analysis may suggest a closer affinity than the ethnographic record indicates. It may be that historically the Guale and Yamasee were distinguished solely by geographic location and not by cultural, linguistic, or biological differences.

A consistent result for all of the analyses is the close association of the Irene Mound sample with the inland samples from Ledford Island and the King site. This does not necessarily imply a biological connection between these groups; however, the small standardized mean measures of divergence are notable. The distinct similarity between these samples is in sharp contrast to the consistent dissimilarity with the historic Guale.

Another consistent result for all the analyses is the marked dissimilarity between the Guale samples and the samples from the piedmont. Not only do these samples consistently cluster separately in the cluster and multidimensional scaling analyses but the standardized mean measures of divergence are some of the highest of all the comparisons. This is especially true for the Town Creek sample. This result does not support the proposal of biological affinity between Town Creek and coastal populations of La Florida.

In all analyses, the Carolina Algonquian samples from the Baum and Piggot sites are consistently identified as a distinct isolate from the other southeastern United States samples. This outcome is not unexpected considering the ethnographic identification of the Algonquian as a group with origins far to the north and unlike many of their geographically close neighbors in the Southeast.

Conclusions

The results of this study support the earlier contention that the Native American inhabitants of the Georgia and Florida coasts do not necessarily represent a biologically continuous series of populations. As might be expected, the analyses suggest a complex series of relationships among these populations.

Univariate and multivariate analyses indicate that the Guale population samples examined here are particularly diverse in terms of expression of dental and cranial nonmetric traits. This diversity cannot be fully explained in terms of in situ genetic drift. These results contradict, in part, earlier assumptions of population relationships on the Georgia coast. Given the unstable political and social conditions among the Guale after

European contact and the extensive period of missionization of the native inhabitants, aggregation of local populations could have precipitated such gene flow.

There are at least two alternative hypotheses that the results of this study could support. The first possibility is that the pre-contact Guale of the Georgia coast and the post-contact Guale of the Georgia and Florida coasts represent a single temporally and biologically continuous population. If this were indeed the case, the results of this study should have indicated a homogeneous population over all of the temporal periods with few significant differences in frequency for the dental and cranial nonmetric traits. Likewise, if the population samples in this study represented a temporally continuous population, it would be expected that the biological distances between the Guale samples would be small in comparison to distances from other non-Guale groups. In this case, comparison with the non-Guale population samples should reveal a significant difference in trait frequencies and in biological distance. It would be expected that the differences would be greater for those groups geographically more distant from the Guale (e.g., Algonquian and inland groups) than for the closer populations (e.g., Yamasee), which have a greater opportunity for gene flow.

The second possibility is that the results of this study could have indicated a heterogeneous population with differing degrees of diversity between the temporal periods. This being the case, large biological distances between the Guale samples would suggest the presence of discontinuous populations. The possibilities for such an apparent lack of continuity include: (1) high levels of genetic drift occurred between generations of an in situ population, (2) significant amounts of gene flow from other populations altered the composition of the gene pool, or (3) the samples actually represent genetically different populations rather than a series of related populations. Any one of these processes or a combination of them could cause significant changes in composition of the gene pool between temporal periods.

The results of this study support the later alternative. The Guale samples examined here represent a diverse series of population samples in terms of both dental and cranial morphology. Although biological continuity may be argued for the post-contact Guale from Santa Catalina and Santa Maria, the same argument does not seem to hold true for the relationship between the pre-contact Irene Mound sample and the post-contact Guale groups. The marked similarity between the inland population sample from Ledford Island and the Guale sample from Irene Mound may suggest a biological connection between these populations. According to ethno-graphic sources, the Guale are a derivative group from the Creek (Spencer and Jennings 1977). The similarity between the Ledford Island and Irene Mound samples may therefore reflect the retention of ancestral Muskogean traits in both samples. This contention cannot be fully ex-plored without further comparative studies of other Muskogean groups.

References Cited

Aldenderfer, M. S., and R. K. Blashfield. 1984. *Cluster Analysis.* Sage University Paper Series on Quantitative Applications in the Social Sciences. Beverly Hills, Calif.: Sage Publications.

Alexandersen, V. 1970. Tandmorfologisk Variation hos Eskimoer og Andre Mongoloide Populationer. *Tandlaegbladet* 74:587–602.

Anderberg, M. R. 1973. *Cluster Analysis for Applications.* New York: Academic Press.

Anderson, D. G. 1990. Political Change in Chiefdom Societies: Cycling in the Late Prehistoric Southeastern United States. Ph.D. diss., University of Michigan, Ann Arbor.

Anderson, J. E. 1962. The Development of the Tympanic Plate. *National Museums of Canada, Bulletin,* ser. 57, 180:143–215.

Anscombe, F. J. 1948. The Transformation of Poisson, Binomial, and Negative-Binomial data. *Biometrika* 35:246–54.

Benfer, R. A. 1970. Associations among Cranial Traits. *American Journal of Physical Anthropology* 32:463.

Bennett, K. A. 1965. The Etiology and Genetics of Wormian Bones. *American Journal of Physical Anthropology* 23:255–60.

Berry, A. C. 1972. The Use of Minor Skeletal Variants in Human Populations Studies. Ph.D. diss., University of London.

———. 1974. The Use of Nonmetrical Variations of the Cranium in the Study of Scandanavian Population Movements. *American Journal of Physical Anthro-pology* 40:345–58.

Berry, A. C., and R. J. Berry. 1967. Epigenetic Variation in the Human Cranium. *Journal of Anatomy* 101:361–79.

Birkby, W. H. 1973. Discontinuous Non-metric Traits of the Skull as Population Markers in the Prehistoric Southwest. Ph.D. diss., University of Arizona, Tuc-son.

Blakely, R. L. (ed.). 1988. *The King Site: Continuity and Contact in Sixteenth-Century Georgia.* Athens: University of Georgia Press.

Blashfield, R. K. 1976. Mixture Model Tests of Cluster Analysis: Accuracy of Four Agglomerative Hierarchical Models. *Psychological Bulletin* 83(3):377–88.

Bolk, L. 1931. On Metopism. *American Journal of Anatomy* 22:27–47.

Boyd, D. C. M. 1984. A Biological Investigation of Skeletal Remains from the Mouse Creek Phase and a Comparison with Two Late Mississippian Skeletal Populations from Middle and East Tennessee. M.A. thesis, University of Tennessee, Knoxville.

Boyd, G. I. 1930. The Emissary Foramina of the Cranium in Man and the Anthropoids. *Journal of Anatomy* 65:108–21.

Buikstra, J. E. 1972. Hopewell in the Lower Illinois River Valley: A Regional Approach to the Study of Biological Variability and Mortuary Activity. Ph.D. diss., University of Chicago.

Bushnell, A. T. 1986. *Santa Maria in the Written Record.* Miscellaneous Project Report 21, Florida State Museum, Department of Anthropology, Gainesville.

Caldwell, J., and C. McCann. 1941. *Irene Mound Site, Chatham County, Georgia.* Athens: University of Georgia Press.

Coe, J. L. (ed.). 1995. *Town Creek Indian Mound.* Chapel Hill: University of North Carolina Press.

Collins, H. B., Jr. 1926. The Temporo-Frontal Articulation in Man. *American Journal of Physical Anthropology* 9:343–48.

———. 1930. Notes on the Pterion. *American Journal of Physical Anthropology* 14:41–44.

Constandse-Westermann, T. S. 1972. *Coefficients of Biological Distance.* Amsterdam: Oosterhout N.B.

Corruccini, R. S. 1974. An Examination of the Meaning of Cranial Discrete Traits for Human Skeletal Biological Studies. *American Journal of Physical Anthropology* 40:425–46.

Crowder, L. E. 1988. Cultural Affiliations of the King Site. In *The King Site: Continuity and Contact in Sixteenth-Century Georgia,* ed. R. L. Blakely, 47–59. Athens: University of Georgia Press.

Cybulski, J. S. 1972. Skeletal Variability in British Columbia Coastal Populations. A Descriptive and Comparative Assessment of Cranial Morphology. Ph.D. diss., University of Toronto.

———. 1975. *Skeletal Variability in British Columbia Coastal Populations: A Descriptive and Comparative Assessment of Cranial Morphology.* Archaeological Survey of Canada, National Museum of Man, Mercury Series, 30.

Dahlberg, A. A. 1956. *Materials for the Establishment of Standards for Classification of Tooth Characters, Attributes and Techniques in Morphological Studies of the Dentition.* Chicago: Department of Anthropology, University of Chicago.

———. 1963. Analysis of the American Indian Dentition. In *Dental Anthropology,* ed. Donald R. Brothwell, 147–77. New York: Pergamon Press.

De Souza, P., and P. Houghton. 1977. The Mean Measure of Divergence and the Use of Non-Metric Data in the Estimation of Biological Distances. *Journal of Archaeological Science* 4:163–69.

258 | Mark C. Griffin, Patricia M. Lambert, and Elizabeth Monahan Driscoll

DeVilliers, H. 1968. *The Skull of the South African Negro.* Johannesburg: Witwatersrand University Press.

Dickens, R. S., Jr. 1976. *Cherokee Prehistory: The Pisgah Phase in the Appalachian Summit Region.* Knoxville: University of Tennessee Press.

———. 1978. Mississippian Settlement Patterns in the Appalachian Summit Area: The Pisgah and Qualla Phases. In *Mississippian Settlement Patterns,* ed. Bruce D. Smith, 115–39. New York: Academic Press.

Dodo, Y. 1987. Supraorbital Foramen and Hypoglossal Canal Bridging: The Two Most Suggestive Nonmetric Cranial Traits in Discriminating Major Racial Groupings of Man. *Journal of the Anthropological Society of Nippon* 95:19–35.

Dodo, Y., H. Ishida, and N. Saitou. 1992. Population History of Japan: A Cranial Nonmetric Approach. In *The Evolution and Dispersal of Modern Humans in Asia,* ed. T. Akazawa, K. Aoki, and T. Kmura. Tokyo: Hokusensha.

Enoki, K., and A. A. Dahlberg. 1958. Rotated Maxillary Central Incisors. *Orthodontic Journal of Japan* 17:157.

Everitt, B. S. 1974. *Cluster Analysis.* London: Halstead Press.

Finnegan, M. J. 1972. Population Definition on the Northwest Coast by Analysis of Discrete Character Variation. Ph.D. diss., University of Colorado, Boulder.

Freeman, M. F., and J. W. Tukey. 1950. Transformations Related to the Angular and Square Root. *Annals of Mathematical Statistics* 21:607–11.

Gaherty, G. G. 1974. Discrete Traits, Cranial Measurements, and Nonbiological Data in Africa. *American Journal of Physical Anthropology* 40:136.

Goodman, L. A., and W. H. Kruskal. 1954. Measures of Association for Cross Classifications. *Journal of the American Statistical Association* 49:732–64.

———. 1959. Measures of Association for Cross Classifications, pt. 2: Further Discussion and References. *Journal of the American Statistical Association* 54:123–63.

———. 1963. Measures of Association for Cross Classifications, pt. 3: Approximate Sampling Theory. *Journal of the American Statistical Association* 58:310–64.

Green, R. F., and J. M. Suchey. 1976. The Use of Inverse Sign Transformations in the Analysis of Non-Metric Cranial Data. *American Journal of Physical Anthropology* 45:61–68.

Greene, D. L. 1982. Discrete Dental Variations and Biological Distances of Nubian Populations. *American Journal of Physical Anthropology* 58:75–79.

Gregory, W. K. 1916. Studies on the Evolution of the Primates. Part I: The Cope-Osborn "Theory of trituberculy" and the Ancestral Molar Patterns of the Primates. Part II: Phylogeny of Recent and Extinct Anthropoids, with Special Reference to the Origin of Man. *Bulletin of the American Museum of Natural History* 35:239–355.

Grewal, M. S. 1962. The Rate of Divergence of Sublines in the C57BL Strain of Mice. *Genetical Research* 3:226–37.

Griffin, M. C. 1989. Dental Variation of Native Populations from Northern Spanish Florida. M.A. thesis, Northern Illinois University, DeKalb.

——. 1993. Morphological Variation of the Late Precontact and Contact Period Guale. Ph.D. diss., Purdue University, West Lafayette, Ind.

Griffin, M. C., and A. M. Nelson. 1996. Adult and Deciduous Dental Morphology in Four U.S. Amerindian Population Samples: A Comparative Study. *American Journal of Physical Anthropology* suppl. 22:175.

Grüneberg, H. 1952. Genetical Studies on the Skeleton of the Mouse, pt. 4: Quasi-Continuous Variations. *Journal of Genetics* 51:95–114.

——. 1963. *The Pathology of Development: A Study of Inherited Skeletal Disorders in Animals.* New York: John Wiley and Sons.

Guttman, L. A. 1968. A General Nonmetric Technique for Finding the Smallest Co-ordinate Space for a Configuration of Points. *Psychometrika* 33:469–506.

Hally, D. J. 1975a. Archaeological Investigations of the King Site, Floyd County, Georgia. Manuscript on file, Department of Anthropology, University of Georgia, Athens.

——. 1975b. The King Site and Its Investigation. *Southeastern Archaeological Conference Bulletin* 18:48–54.

——. 1979. *Archaeological Investigation of the Little Egypt Site (9Mu102), Murray County, Georgia, 1969 Season.* University of Georgia, Laboratory of Archaeology Series, report 18.

——. 1980. Archaeological Investigation of the Little Egypt Site (9MU102), Murray County, Georgia, 1970–1972. Report submitted to the Heritage Conservation and Recreation Service, U.S. Dept. of the Interior.

Hanihara, T. 1992. Dental and Cranial Affinities among Populations of East Asia and the Pacific: The Populations in East Asia, IV. *American Journal of Physical Anthropology* 88:163–82.

Harris, E. F. 1977. Anthropologic and Genetic Aspects of the Dental Morphology of Solomon Islanders, Melanesia. Ph.D. diss., Arizona State University, Tempe.

Harris, E. F. and H. L. Bailit. 1980. The Metaconule: A Morphologic and Familial Analysis of a Molar Cusp in Humans. *American Journal of Physical Anthropology* 53:349–58.

Haeussler, A. M., J. D. Irish, D. H. Morris, and C. G. Turner II. 1989. Morphological and Metrical Comparison of San and Central Sotho Dentitions from Southern Africa. *American Journal of Physical Anthropology* 78:115–22.

Hauser, G., and G. F. De Stefano. 1989. *Epigenetic Variants of the Human Skull.* Stuttgart: E. Schweizerbart'sche Verlagsbuchhandlung (Nägele u. Obermiller).

Hellman, M. 1929. Racial Characters in Human Dentition, pt. 1: A Racial Distribution of the *Dryopithecus* Pattern and its Modifications in the Lower Molar Teeth of Man. *Proceedings of the American Philosophical Society* 67:157–74.

Herzog, K. P. 1968. Associations between Discontinuous Cranial Traits. *American Journal of Physical Anthropology* 29:397–404.

Hiernaux, J. 1972. The Analyses of Multivariate Biological Distances between

Human Populations: Principles and Applications to Sub-Saharan Africa. In *The Assessment of Population Affinities in Man,* ed. J. Weiner and J. Huizinga, 96–114. Oxford: Clarendon Press.

Hrdlička, A. 1920. Shovel-Shaped teeth. *American Journal of Physical Anthropology* 3:429–65.

———. 1924. New Data on the Teeth of Early Man and Certain Fossil European Apes. *American Journal of Physical Anthropology* 7(1):109–32.

Hulse, F. S. 1941. The People Who Lived at Irene: Physical Anthropology. In *Irene Mound Site, Chatham County, Georgia,* ed. J. Caldwell and C. McCann, 57–68. Athens: University of Georgia Press.

Inglemark, B. E. 1947. Über das Craniovertebrale Grenzgebiet beim Menschen. *Acta Anatomica,* supplement 6, vol. 6.

Ishida, H. 1990. Cranial Morphology of Several Ethnic Groups from the Amur Basin and Sakhalin. *Journal of the Anthropological Society of Nippon* 98:137–48.

Ishida, H., and Y. Dodo. 1993. Nonmetric Cranial Variation and the Populational Affinities of the Pacific Peoples. *American Journal of Physical Anthropology* 90:49–57.

Jantz, R. L. 1970. Change and Variation in Skeletal Populations of Arikara Indians. Ph.D. diss., University of Kansas, Lawrence.

Johnson, C. C., R. J. Gorlin, and V. E. Anderson. 1965. Torus Mandibularis: A Genetic Study. *American Journal of Human Genetics* 17:433–42.

Jones, G. D. 1978. The Ethnohistory of the Guale Coast through 1684. In *The Anthropology of St. Catherines Island*: 1. *Natural and Cultural History,* by D. H. Thomas, G. D. Jones, R. S. Durham, and C. S. Larsen, 178–210. Anthropological Papers of the American Museum of Natural History 55:178–210.

Jørgensen, K. D. 1955. The *Dryopithecus* Pattern in Recent Danes and Dutchmen. *Journal of Dental Research* 34(2):195–208.

Katayama, K. 1988. A Comparison of the Incidence of Non-Metric Cranial Variants in Several Polynesian Populations. *Journal of the Anthropological Society of Nippon* 96:357–69.

Katich, J. F. 1975. Parastyle Variation in Hawaiian Maxillary Molars. *American Journal of Physical Anthropology* 42:310.

Kellock, W. L., and P. A. Parsons. 1970a. Variations of Minor Nonmetrical Skeletal Variants in Australian Aborigines. *American Journal of Physical Anthropology* 32:409–21.

———. 1970b. A Comparison of the Incidence of Nonmetrical Cranial Variants in Australian Aborigines with Those of Melanesia and Polynesia. *American Journal of Physical Anthropology* 33:235–39.

Kennedy, B. 1981. *Marriage Patterns in an Archaic Population: A Study of Skeletal Remains from Port au Choix, Newfoundland.* Archaeological Survey of Canada, National Museum of Man, Mercury Series, paper 104.

Korey, K. A. 1970. Characteristics of the Distributions of Non-metric Variants of the Skull. M.A. thesis, University of Chicago.

Kraus, B. S., and M. L. Furr. 1953. Lower First Premolars, pt. 1: A Definition and Classification of Discrete Morphologic Traits. *Journal of Dental Research* 33:554–64.

Kruskal, J. B. 1964a. Multidimensional Scaling by Optimizing Goodness of Fit to a Nonmetric Hypothesis. *Psychometrika* 29:1–27.

———. 1964b. Nonmetric Multidimensional Scaling: A Numerical Method. *Psychometrika* 29:115–29.

Kruskal, J. B., and M. Wish. 1978. *Multidimensional Scaling.* University Paper Series on Quantitative Applications in the Social Sciences, 07–011. Beverly Hills, Calif.: Sage Publications.

Lane, R. A., and A. J. Sublett. 1972. Osteology of Social Organization: Residence Pattern. *American Antiquity* 37:186–201.

Larsen, C. S. 1982. *The Anthropology of St. Catherines Island: 3. Prehistoric Human Biological Adaptation.* Anthropological Papers of the American Museum of Natural History 57, pt. 3.

———. 1990. Biocultural Interpretation and the Context for Contact. *The Archaeology of Mission Santa Catalina de Guale: 2. Biocultural Interpretations of a Population in Transition,* ed. C. S. Larsen, 11–24. Anthropological Papers of the American Museum of Natural History 68.

———. 1991. On the Frontier of Contact: Mission Bioarchaeology in *La Florida. Florida Anthropologist* 44:268–84.

Larsen, C. S., M. J. Schoeninger, D. L. Hutchinson, K. F. Russell, and C. B. Ruff. 1990. Beyond Demographic Collapse: Biological Adaptation and Change in Native Populations of *La Florida.* In *Columbian Consequences, 2: Archaeological and Historical Perspectives on the Spanish Borderlands East,* ed. D. H. Thomas, 409–28. Washington: Smithsonian Institution Press.

Larson, M. A. 1970. Maxillary Molar Classification. Unpublished manuscript.

———. 1978. Dental Morphology of the Gran Quivira Indians. M.A. thesis, Arizona State University, Tempe.

Le Double, A. F. 1903. *Traite des Variations des Os du Crane de l'Homme et de Leur Signification au Point de Vue de l'Anthropologie Zoologique.* Paris: Vigot.

Lewis, T.M.N., and M. Kneberg. 1946. *Hiwassee Island: An Archaeological Account of Four Tennessee Indian Peoples.* Knoxville: University of Tennessee Press.

———. 1955. *The First Tennesseans: An Interpretation of Tennessee Prehistory.* Knoxville: Department of Anthropology Papers, University of Tennessee.

Limson, M. 1924. Metopism as Found in Filipino Skulls. *American Journal of Physical Anthropology* 7:317–24.

Lukacs, J. R., and B. E. Hemphill. 1991. The Dental Anthropology of Prehistoric Baluchistan: A Morphometric Approach to the Peopling of South Asia. In *Ad-*

vances in Dental Anthropology, ed. M. A. Kelley and C. S. Larsen, 77–120. New York: Wiley-Liss.

McWilliams, K. R. 1974. Gran Quivira Pueblo and Biological Distance in the U.S. Southwest. Ph.D. diss., Arizona State University, Tempe.

Miller, S. C., and H. Roth. 1940. Torus Palatinus, a Statistical Study. *Journal of the American Dental Association* 27:1950–57.

Molto, J. E. 1983. *Biological Relationships of Southern Ontario Woodland Peoples: The Evidence of Discontinuous Cranial Morphology.* National Museums of Canada, Archaeological Survey of Canada, Paper 117.

Mooney, J. 1969. The Yamassee. In *Handbook of American Indians North of Mexico*, ed. F. W. Hodge, 986–87. Smithsonian Institution, Bureau of American Ethnology, Bulletin 30.

Moorrees, C.F.A. 1957. *The Aleut Dentition.* Cambridge: Harvard University Press.

Morris, D. H. 1975. Bushmen Maxillary Canine Polymorphism. *South African Journal of Science* 71:333–35.

Morris, D. H., A. A. Dahlberg, and S. Glasstone-Hughes. 1978. The Uto-Aztecan Premolar: The Anthropology of a Dental Trait. In *Development, Function, and Evolution of the Teeth*, ed. P. M. Butler and K. A. Joysey, 69–79. London: Academic Press.

Morris, N. T. 1970. The Occurrence of the Mandibular Torus at Gran Quivira. M.A. thesis, Arizona State University, Tempe.

Neiberger, E. J. 1978. Incidence of Torsiversion in Mandibular Third Molars. *Journal of Dental Research* 57:209–12.

Nichol, C. R. 1989. Complex Segregation Analysis of Dental Morphological Variants. *American Journal of Physical Anthropology* 78:37–60.

———. 1990. Dental Genetics and Biological Relationships of the Pima Indians of Arizona. Ph.D. diss., Arizona State University, Tempe.

Nichol, C. R., C. G. Turner II, and A. A. Dahlberg. 1984. Variation in the Convexity of the Human Maxillary Incisor Labial Surface. *American Journal of Physical Anthropology* 63:361–70.

Oetteking, B. 1930. *Craniology of the North Pacific Coast.* American Museum of Natural History Memoirs 15:1–391.

Ossenberg, N. S. 1969. Discontinuous Morphological Variation in the Human Cranium. Ph.D. diss., University of Toronto.

———. 1976. Within and Between Race Distances in Population Studies Based on Discrete Traits of the Human Skull. *American Journal of Physical Anthropology* 45:701–16.

Pedersen, P. O. 1949. *The East Greenland Eskimo Dentition.* Meddelelser om Gronland 142:1–256.

Phelps, D. S. 1977. Recent Archaeological Research in Northeastern North Carolina. *Eastern States Archaeological Federation Bulletin* 35–36:19–20.

————. 1980a. Carolina Algonkian Ossuaries. Paper presented, Southeastern Archaeological Conference, New Orleans, La.

————. 1980b. Archaeological Salvage of an Ossuary at the Baum Site. Report on file, Archaeology Laboratory, East Carolina University, Greenville.

————. 1983. Archaeology of the North Carolina Coast and Coastal Plain: Problems and Hypotheses. In *The Prehistory of North Carolina: An Archaeological Symposium*, ed. M. A. Mathis and J. J. Crow, 1–51. Raleigh: North Carolina Division of Archives and History, Department of Cultural Resources, State of North Carolina.

Pietrusewsky, M. 1969. The Physical Anthropology of Early Tongan Populations: A Study of Bones and Teeth and an Assessment of Their Biological Affinities Based on Cranial Comparisons with Eight Other Pacific Populations. Ph.D. diss., University of Toronto.

————. 1971. Application of Distance Statistics to Anthroposcopic Data and a Comparison of Results with Those Obtained by Using Discrete Traits of the Skull. *Archaeology and Physical Anthropology in Oceania* 4:21–33.

————. 1981. Cranial Variation in Early Metal Age Thailand and Southeast Asia Studied by Multivariate Procedures. *Homo* 32:1–26.

————. 1984. *Metric and Nonmetric Cranial Variation in Australian Aboriginal Populations Compared with Populations from the Pacific and Asia*. Occasional Papers in Human Biology 3. Canberra: Australian Institute of Aboriginal Studies.

Rightmire, G. P. 1972. Cranial Measurements and Discrete Traits Compared in Distance Studies of African Negro Skulls. *Human Biology* 44:263–76.

Saunders, R. 1988. *Excavations at 8NA41: Two Mission Period Sites on Amelia Island, Florida*. Miscellaneous Project Report Series 35. Gainesville: Florida State Museum, Department of Anthropology.

Saunders, S. R., and F. Popovich. 1978. A Family Study of Two Skeletal Variants: Atlas Bridging and Clinoid Bridging. *American Journal of Physical Anthropology* 49:193–204.

Schiffman, S. S., M. L. Reynolds, and F. W. Young. 1981. *Introduction to Multidimensional Scaling*. New York: Academic Press.

Sciulli, P. W. 1990. Cranial Metric and Discrete Trait Variation and Biological Differentiation in the Terminal Late Archaic of Ohio: The Duff Site Cemetery. *American Journal of Physical Anthropology* 82:19–29.

Scott, G. R. 1973. Dental Morphology: A Genetic Study of American White Families and Variation in Living Southwest Indians. Ph.D. diss., Arizona State University, Tempe.

————. 1980. Population Variation of Carabelli's Trait. *Human Biology* 49:453–69.

Scott, G. R., and A. A. Dahlberg. 1982. Microdifferentiation in Tooth Morphology among Indians of the American Southwest. In *Teeth: Form, Function and Evolution*, ed. B. Kurten, 259–91. New York: Columbia University Press.

Scott, G. R., and C. G. Turner II. 1997. *The Anthropology of Modern Human Teeth: Dental Morphology and Its Variation in Recent Human Populations.* Cambridge: Cambridge University Press.

Sjøvold, T. 1973. The Occurrence of Minor Nonmetrical Variants in the Skeleton and Their Quantitative Treatment for Population Comparisons. *Homo* 24:204–33.

———. 1977. Non-Metrical Divergence between Skeletal Populations: The Theoretical Foundation and Biological Importance of C. A. B. Smith's Mean Measure of Divergence. *Ossa* 4 (suppl. 1):1–133.

Smith, C.A.B. 1972. Review of T. S. Constandse-Westermann: *Coefficients of Biological Distance. Annals of Human Genetics* 36:241–45.

Sofaer, J. A., P. Smith, and E. Kaye. 1986. Affinities between Contemporary and Skeletal Jewish and Non-Jewish Groups Based on Tooth Morphology. *American Journal of Physical Anthropology* 70:265–75.

Spence, M. W. 1971. Skeletal Morphology and Social Organization in Teotihuacán, Mexico. Ph.D. diss., Southern Illinois University, Carbondale.

Spencer, R. F., and J. D. Jennings. 1977. *The Native Americans: Ethnology and Backgrounds of the North American Indians.* New York: Harper and Row.

Sublett, A. J. 1966. Seneca Physical Type and Changes through Time. Ph.D. diss., State University of New York at Buffalo.

Suchey, J. M. 1975. Biological Distance of Prehistoric Central California Populations Derived from Non-metric Traits of the Cranium. Ph.D. diss., University of California, Riverside.

Sullivan, L. P. 1986. The Late Mississippian Village: Community and Society of the Mouse Creek Phase in Southeastern Tennessee. Ph.D. diss., University of Wisconsin, Milwaukee.

Suzuki, M., and T. Sakai. 1960. A Familial Study of Torus Palatinus and Torus Mandibularis. *American Journal of Physical Anthropology* 18:263–72.

Thomas, D. H. 1986. *Refiguring Anthropology: First Principles of Probability and Statistics.* 2d ed. Prospect Heights, Ill.: Waveland Press.

———. 1987. *The Archaeology of Mission Santa Catalina de Guale: 1. Search and Discovery.* Anthropological Papers of the American Museum of Natural History 63, pt. 2.

Tomes, C. S. 1923. *A Manual of Dental Anatomy, Human and Comparative.* 8th ed. London: J. and A. Churchill.

Tørgersen, J. 1951. The Developmental Genetics and Evolutionary Meaning of the Metopic Suture. *American Journal of Physical Anthropology* 9:193–210.

Torgersen, W. S. 1952. Multidimensional Scaling, pt. 1: Theory and Method. *Psychometrika* 17:401–19.

Townsend, G., H. Yamada, and P. Smith. 1990. Expression of the Entoconulid (Sixth Cusp) on Mandibular Molar Teeth of an Australian Aboriginal Population. *American Journal of Physical Anthropology* 82:267–74.

Trinkaus, E. 1978. Bilateral Asymmetry of Human Skeletal Nonmetric Traits. *American Journal of Physical Anthropology* 49:315–18.

Truesdell, S. W. 1995. Paleopathological and Paleodemographical Analysis of the Piggot Ossuary (31Cr14) Carteret County, North Carolina. M.A. thesis, Wake Forest University, Winston-Salem, North Carolina.

Truslove, G. M. 1961. Genetic Studies on the Skeleton of the Mouse XXX: A Search for Correlations between Some Minor Variants. *Genetical Research* 2:431–38.

Turner, C. G. II. 1967. Dental Genetics and Microevolution in Prehistoric and Living Koniag Eskimo. *Journal of Dental Research* 46(5) suppl.:911–17.

———. 1970. New Classifications on Non-Metrical Dental Variation: Cusps 6 and 7. Paper presented, American Association of Physical Anthropologists, Washington, D.C.

———. 1981. Root Number Determination in Maxillary First Premolars for Modern Human Populations. *American Journal of Physical Anthropology* 54:619–36.

———. 1985. The Dental Search for Native American Origins. In *Out of Asia: Peopling the Americas and the Pacific,* ed. R. Kirk and E. Szathmáry, 31–78. Canberra: Journal of Pacific History, Australian National University.

———. 1986a. Dentochronological Separation Estimates for Pacific Rim Populations. *Science* 232:1140–42.

———. 1986b. The First Americans: The Dental Evidence. *National Geographic Research* 2:37–46.

———. 1987a. Late Pleistocene and Holocene Population History of East Asia based on Dental Variation. *American Journal of Physical Anthropology* 73:305–21.

———. 1987b. Telltale Teeth. *Natural History* 96(1):6–10.

———. 1990. Major Features of Sundadonty and Sinodonty, Including Suggestions about East Asian Microevolution, Population History, and Late Pleistocene Relationships with Australian Aboriginals. *American Journal of Physical Anthropology* 82:295–318.

Turner, C. G., and J. Bird. 1981. Dentition of Chilean Paleo-Indians and the Peopling of the Americas. *Science* 212:1053–55.

Turner, C. G. II, R. Scott, and C. Nichol. 1991. Scoring Procedures for Key Morphological Traits of the Permanent Dentition: Arizona State University Dental Anthropology System. In *Advances in Dental Anthropology,* ed. M. A. Kelley and C. S. Larsen, 13–31. New York: Wiley-Liss.

Ward, H. T., and R. P. S. Davis, Jr. 1999. *Time Before History: The Archaeology of North Carolina.* Chapel Hill: University of North Carolina Press.

Ward, J. H. 1963. Hierarchical Grouping to Optimize an Objective Function. *Journal of the American Statistical Association* 58:236–44.

Weidenreich, F. 1937. *The Dentition of* Sinanthropus pekinensis: *A Comparative*

Odontography of the Hominids. Palaeontologia Sinica (ser. D) (whole ser. 101).

Wilkinson, L. 1988a. *SYSTAT: The System for Statistics.* Evanston, Ill.: SYSTAT.

———. 1988b. *SYGRAPH.* Evanston, Ill.: SYSTAT.

Wood-Jones, F. 1930a. The Non-Metrical Morphological Characters of the Skull as Criteria for Racial Diagnosis, pt. 1: General Discussion of the Morphological Characters Employed in Racial Diagnosis. *Journal of Anatomy* 65:179–95.

———. 1930b. The Non-Metrical Morphological Characters of the Skull as Criteria for Racial Diagnosis, pt. 2: The Non-Metrical Morphological Characters of the Hawaiian Skull. *Journal of Anatomy* 65:368–78.

———. 1930c. The Non-Metrical Morphological Characters of the Skull as Criteria for Racial Diagnosis, pt. 3: The Non-Metrical Morphological Characters of the Skulls of Prehistoric Inhabitants of Guam. *Journal of Anatomy* 65:438–45.

Zegura, S. L. 1971. A Multivariate Analysis of the Inter- and Intrapopulation Variation Exhibited by Eskimo Crania. Ph.D. diss., University of Wisconsin, Madison.

Appendix 9.A. Dental trait frequencies

Frequency (%)

Dental trait	Grade	Irene	SCDG	SCDGSM	SMDY	Baum	Ledford	King	Little Egypt	Coweeta Creek	Upper Saura Town	Town Creek
Shoveling I1	0	0(0.0)	1(1.6)	0(0.0)	0(0.0)	0(0.0)	0(0.0)	0(0.0)	0(0.0)	0(0.0)	0(0.0)	0(0.0)
	1	1(1.4)	5(8.1)	3(6.9)	2(5.7)	1(20.0)	0(0.0)	1(1.7)	0(0.0)	0(0.0)	0(0.0)	2(7.1)
	2	25(36.2)	25(36.2)	20(46.5)	10(28.6)	2(40.0)	22(28.9)	11(19.3)	1(7.1)	2(8.3)	5(16.1)	7(25.0)
	3	29(42.0)	29(42.0)	14(32.6)	17(48.6)	1(20.0)	28(36.8)	25(43.9)	8(57.1)	10(41.7)	15(48.4)	11(39.3)
	4	14(20.3)	14(20.3)	5(11.6)	4(11.4)	1(20.0)	20(26.3)	17(29.8)	5(35.7)	5(20.8)	7(22.6)	6(21.4)
	5	0(0.0)	1(1.6)	1(2.3)	2(5.7)	0(0.0)	5(6.6)	3(5.3)	0(0.0)	6(25.0)	4(12.9)	2(7.1)
	6	0(0.0)	0(0.0)	0(0.0)	0(0.0)	0(0.0)	1(1.3)	0(0.0)	0(0.0)	1(4.2)	0(0.0)	0(0.0)
Shoveling I2	0	0(0.0)	1(1.2)	5(11.9)	0(0.0)	0(0.0)	0(0.0)	0(0.0)	0(0.0)	0(0.0)	0(0.0)	0(0.0)
	1	1(1.5)	11(12.8)	4(9.5)	2(6.1)	3(27.3)	1(1.4)	1(2.0)	2(14.3)	1(3.4)	1(3.4)	3(6.1)
	2	5(7.5)	33(38.4)	16(38.1)	13(39.4)	2(18.2)	12(16.7)	5(10.0)	5(35.7)	6(20.7)	5(17.2)	10(20.4)
	3	18(26.9)	18(21.0)	10(23.8)	8(24.2)	3(27.3)	28(38.9)	14(28.0)	1(7.1)	8(27.6)	11(37.9)	17(34.7)
	4	22(32.8)	15(17.4)	5(11.9)	4(12.1)	1(9.1)	26(36.1)	16(32.0)	2(14.3)	6(20.7)	7(24.1)	11(22.4)
	5	18(26.9)	4(4.6)	0(0.0)	3(9.1)	1(9.1)	4(5.6)	8(16.0)	3(21.4)	2(6.9)	4(13.3)	6(12.2)
	6	2(3.0)	2(2.3)	0(0.0)	3(9.1)	1(9.1)	1(1.4)	1(2.0)	0(0.0)	5(17.2)	1(3.4)	2(4.1)
	7	1(1.5)	1(1.1)	2(4.7)	0(0.0)	0(0.0)	0(0.0)	5(10.0)	1(7.1)	1(3.4)	0(0.0)	0(0.0)
	8	0(0.0)	1(1.1)	0(0.0)	0(0.0)	0(0.0)	0(0.0)	0(0.0)	0(0.0)	1(3.4)	0(0.0)	0(0.0)
Double shoveling	0	2(2.9)	8(12.3)	11(22.9)	5(15.1)	2(40.0)	3(3.9)	2(3.6)	2(14.3)	1(3.3)	1(4.0)	1(3.0)
	1	0(0.0)	8(12.3)	7(14.6)	2(6.1)	0(0.0)	2(2.6)	0(0.0)	0(0.0)	2(6.7)	1(4.0)	1(3.0)
	2	9(13.2)	15(23.1)	11(22.9)	9(27.3)	1(20.0)	7(9.1)	9(16.1)	1(7.1)	12(40.0)	5(20.0)	4(12.1)
	3	10(14.7)	19(29.2)	2(4.2)	8(24.2)	0(0.0)	20(26.0)	11(19.6)	4(28.6)	3(10.0)	3(12.0)	2(6.1)
	4	20(29.4)	8(12.3)	13(27.1)	3(9.1)	1(20.0)	28(36.4)	21(37.5)	5(35.7)	6(20.0)	6(24.0)	12(36.4)

(continued)

Dental trait	Grade	Irene	SCDG	SCDGSM	SMDY	Baum	Ledford	King	Little Egypt	Coweeta Creek	Upper Saura Town	Town Creek
Interruption groove	5	19(27.9)	7(10.8)	4(8.3)	5(15.1)	0(0.0)	14(18.2)	10(17.9)	1(7.1)	6(20.0)	7(28.0)	13(39.4)
	6	8(11.7)	(0.0)	0(0.0)	1(3.0)	1(20.0)	3(3.9)	3(5.4)	1(7.1)	0(0.0)	2(8.0)	0(0.0)
	0	41(62.1)	28(41.8)	15(34.1)	15(51.7)	0(0.0)	36(58.1)	23(53.4)	9(81.8)	15(57.7)	6(40.0)	14(42.4)
	1	5(7.6)	22(32.8)	8(18.2)	9(31.0)	3(27.3)	17(27.4)	8(18.6)	1(9.1)	5(19.2)	4(36.7)	5(15.1)
	2	19(28.9)	11(16.4)	13(29.6)	4(13.8)	6(54.6)	2(3.2)	11(25.6)	1(9.1)	3(11.5)	5(33.3)	9(27.3)
	3	1(1.5)	2(2.9)	0(0.0)	0(0.0)	2(18.2)	7(11.3)	0(0.0)	0(0.0)	1(3.8)	0(0.0)	1(3.0)
	4	0(0.0)	4(5.9)	8(18.2)	1(3.4)	0(0.0)	0(0.0)	1(2.3)	0(0.0)	2(7.7)	0(0.0)	4(12.1)
Metacone M3	0	1(1.6)	3(2.6)	0(0.0)	2(9.5)	0(0.0)	0(0.0)	0(0.0)	0(0.0)	0(0.0)	3(9.1)	0(0.0)
	1	0(0.0)	1(0.8)	0(0.0)	1(4.7)	0(0.0)	0(0.0)	1(4.0)	1(14.3)	0(0.0)	1(3.3)	1(1.8)
	2	3(4.8)	3(2.6)	2(5.9)	2(9.5)	2(16.7)	0(0.0)	1(4.0)	0(0.0)	5(14.3)	7(22.2)	12(21.4)
	3	11(17.7)	23(19.8)	7(20.6)	2(9.5)	1(8.3)	7(18.9)	5(20.0)	0(0.0)	12(34.3)	5(15.1)	9(16.1)
	3.5	27(43.5)	34(29.3)	12(35.3)	11(52.4)	5(41.7)	17(46.0)	13(52.0)	5(71.4)	6(17.1)	10(30.3)	19(33.9)
	4	20(32.2)	48(41.4)	10(29.4)	3(14.3)	3(25.0)	13(35.1)	5(20.0)	1(14.3)	8(22.9)	6(18.2)	10(17.9)
	5	0(0.0)	4(3.4)	3(8.8)	0(0.0)	1(8.3)	0(0.0)	0(0.0)	0(0.0)	4(11.4)	1(3.0)	5(8.9)
Hypocone M1	3	0(0.0)	1(0.6)	1(1.9)	0(0.0)	0(0.0)	1(1.1)	0(0.0)	0(0.0)	0(0.0)	3(6.0)	1(1.3)
	3.5	2(2.1)	11(6.3)	4(7.8)	4(8.7)	2(12.5)	1(1.1)	1(1.5)	1(5.3)	3(4.8)	1(2.0)	13(16.9)
	4	39(41.0)	68(39.3)	40(78.4)	33(71.7)	8(50.0)	78(86.7)	57(83.8)	14(73.7)	42(66.7)	36(72.0)	48(62.3)
	5	54(56.8)	93(53.7)	6(11.7)	9(19.6)	6(37.5)	10(11.1)	10(14.7)	4(21.0)	18(28.6)	10(20.0)	15(19.5)
Hypocone M2	0	0(0.0)	1(0.7)	0(0.0)	1(2.8)	0(0.0)	0(0.0)	0(0.0)	1(9.1)	2(4.2)	3(8.1)	7(11.5)
	1	0(0.0)	7(4.7)	2(5.3)	1(2.8)	1(7.1)	0(0.0)	1(2.4)	1(9.1)	1(2.1)	1(2.7)	2(3.3)
	2	7(8.6)	5(3.3)	2(5.3)	3(8.3)	0(0.0)	0(0.0)	1(2.4)	0(0.0)	2(4.2)	3(8.1)	8(13.1)
	3	12(14.8)	29(19.5)	8(21.0)	8(22.2)	5(35.7)	19(28.8)	13(30.9)	3(27.3)	6(12.5)	7(18.9)	17(27.9)
	3.5	25(30.8)	74(49.7)	11(28.9)	15(41.7)	5(35.7)	25(37.9)	20(47.6)	2(18.2)	26(54.2)	18(48.6)	23(37.7)
	4	35(43.2)	30(20.1)	15(39.5)	8(22.2)	2(14.3)	22(33.3)	7(16.7)	3(27.3)	11(22.9)	5(13.5)	4(6.6)
	5	2(2.5)	3(2.0)	0(0.0)	0(0.0)	1(7.1)	0(0.0)	0(0.0)	1(9.1)	0(0.0)	0(0.0)	0(0.0)
Metaconule M10	0	62(72.9)	83(73.4)	30(88.2)	26(65.0)	4(25.0)	35(42.2)	38(65.5)	12(66.7)	34(85.0)	34(87.2)	57(82.6)
	1	8(9.4)	7(6.2)	0(0.0)	4(10.0)	6(37.5)	27(32.5)	9(15.5)	4(22.2)	2(5.0)	3(7.7)	3(4.3)

Dental trait	Grade	Irene	SCDG	SCDGSM	SMDY	Baum	Ledford	King	Little Egypt	Coweeta Creek	Upper Saura Town	Town Creek
	2	8(9.4)	5(4.4)	0(0.0)	3(7.5)	4(25.0)	17(20.5)	8(13.8)	0(0.0)	3(7.5)	1(2.6)	5(7.3)
	3	2(2.3)	9(7.9)	3(8.8)	6(15.0)	2(12.5)	4(4.8)	1(1.7)	2(11.1)	1(2.5)	0(0.0)	2(2.9)
	4	0(0.0)	9(7.9)	1(2.9)	1(2.5)	0(0.0)	0(0.0)	2(3.4)	0(0.0)	0(0.0)	1(2.6)	2(2.9)
	5	5(5.8)	0(0.0)	0(0.0)	0(0.0)	0(0.0)	0(0.0)	0(0.0)	0(0.0)	0(0.0)	0(0.0)	0(0.0)
Metaconule M2	0	68(94.4)	78(77.2)	24(96.0)	30(96.8)	9(64.3)	49(84.5)	32(94.1)	10(90.9)	37(97.4)	29(100)	48(98.0)
	1	0(0.0)	4(3.9)	0(0.0)	0(0.0)	3(21.4)	7(12.1)	0(0.0)	0(0.0)	0(0.0)	0(0.0)	0(0.0)
	2	0(0.0)	3(2.9)	0(0.0)	1(3.2)	0(0.0)	2(3.4)	1(2.9)	0(0.0)	0(0.0)	0(0.0)	0(0.0)
	3	0(0.0)	3(2.9)	0(0.0)	0(0.0)	1(7.1)	0(0.0)	0(0.0)	1(9.1)	1(2.6)	0(0.0)	0(0.0)
	4	1(1.3)	8(7.9)	0(0.0)	0(0.0)	1(7.1)	0(0.0)	1(2.9)	0(0.0)	0(0.0)	0(0.0)	1(2.0)
	5	3(4.1)	5(4.9)	1(4.0)	0(0.0)	0(0.0)	0(0.0)	0(0.0)	0(0.0)	0(0.0)	0(0.0)	0(0.0)
Carabelli's trait M1	0	33(35.8)	23(23.7)	18(58.1)	22(55.0)	5(33.3)	11(13.1)	10(16.4)	6(35.3)	6(15.0)	6(20.0)	7(11.1)
	1	8(8.7)	14(14.4)	5(16.1)	5(12.5)	6(40.0)	11(13.1)	3(4.9)	0(0.0)	12(30.0)	5(16.7)	17(27.0)
	2	24(26.0)	20(20.6)	4(12.9)	6(15.0)	3(20.0)	17(20.2)	16(26.2)	6(35.3)	8(20.0)	6(20.0)	17(27.0)
	3	10(10.8)	14(14.4)	4(12.9)	1(2.5)	0(0.0)	14(16.7)	10(16.4)	1(5.9)	10(25.0)	5(16.7)	10(15.9)
	4	11(11.9)	11(11.3)	0(0.0)	4(10.0)	0(0.0)	23(27.4)	16(26.2)	3(17.6)	3(7.5)	3(10.0)	5(7.9)
	5	3(3.2)	13(13.4)	0(0.0)	2(5.0)	0(0.0)	4(4.8)	6(9.8)	1(5.9)	0(0.0)	2(6.7)	7(11.1)
	6	0(0.0)	1(1.0)	0(0.0)	0(0.0)	1(6.7)	1(1.2)	0(0.0)	0(0.0)	1(2.5)	3(10.0)	0(0.0)
	7	3(3.2)	1(1.0)	0(0.0)	0(0.0)	0(0.0)	3(3.6)	0(0.0)	0(0.0)	0(0.0)	0(0.0)	0(0.0)
Carabelli's trait M2	0	74(94.8)	71(98.6)	23(95.8)	29(96.7)	13(100)	57(95.0)	26(78.8)	10(100)	31(86.1)	21(87.5)	41(87.2)
	1	2(2.5)	0(0.0)	0(0.0)	0(0.0)	0(0.0)	1(1.7)	2(6.1)	0(0.0)	5(13.9)	2(8.3)	3(6.4)
	2	1(1.2)	1(1.4)	0(0.0)	0(0.0)	0(0.0)	0(0.0)	4(12.1)	0(0.0)	0(0.0)	1(4.2)	2(4.3)
	3	1(1.2)	0(0.0)	1(4.2)	0(0.0)	0(0.0)	2(3.3)	0(0.0)	0(0.0)	0(0.0)	0(0.0)	0(0.0)
	4	0(0.0)	0(0.0)	0(0.0)	1(3.3)	0(0.0)	0(0.0)	1(3.0)	0(0.0)	0(0.0)	0(0.0)	1(2.1)
Parastyle	0	62(100)	88(92.6)	36(97.3)	20(95.2)	12(100)	36(97.3)	24(92.3)	5(62.5)	23(88.5)	18(100)	37(94.9)
	1	0(0.0)	2(2.1)	0(0.0)	1(4.8)	0(0.0)	0(0.0)	0(0.0)	2(25.0)	1(3.8)	0(0.0)	0(0.0)

(continued)

Dental trait	Grade	Irene	SCDG	SCDGSM	SMDY	Baum	Ledford	King	Little Egypt	Coweeta Creek	Upper Saura Town	Town Creek
	2	0(0.0)	1(1.0)	0(0.0)	0(0.0)	0(0.0)	1(2.7)	1(3.8)	1(12.5)	1(3.8)	0(0.0)	2(5.1)
	3	0(0.0)	2(2.1)	0(0.0)	0(0.0)	0(0.0)	0(0.0)	0(0.0)	0(0.0)	1(3.8)	0(0.0)	0(0.0)
	4	0(0.0)	1(1.0)	0(0.0)	0(0.0)	0(0.0)	0(0.0)	0(0.0)	0(0.0)	0(0.0)	0(0.0)	0(0.0)
	5	0(0.0)	1(1.7)	1(2.7)	0(0.0)	0(0.0)	0(0.0)	1(3.8)	0(0.0)	0(0.0)	0(0.0)	0(0.0)
Peg-shaped incisor	0	67(100)	79(98.7)	50(100)	32(100)	11(100)	73(100)	49(98.0)	13(92.9)	39(92.9)	22(91.7)	49(92.4)
	2	0(0.0)	1(1.2)	0(0.0)	0(0.0)	0(0.0)	0(0.0)	1(2.0)	1(7.1)	3(7.1)	2(8.3)	4(7.6)
Peg-shaped molar	0	61(98.4)	82(91.2)	40(97.6)	22(91.7)	13(100)	39(100)	25(96.1)	6(100)	32(97.0)	21(84.0)	38(79.2)
	1	0(0.0)	19(18.2)	1(2.4)	0(0.0)	0(0.0)	0(0.0)	1(3.9)	0(0.0)	1(3.0)	4(16.0)	10(20.8)
	2	1(1.6)	0(0.0)	0(0.0)	2(8.3)	0(0.0)	0(0.0)	0(0.0)	0(0.0)	0(0.0)	0(0.0)	0(0.0)
Anterior fovea	0	0(0.0)	3(3.6)	3(11.1)	2(8.3)	0(0.0)	0(0.0)	0(0.0)	0(0.0)	0(0.0)	0(0.0)	1(2.9)
	1	0(0.0)	4(4.9)	2(7.4)	2(8.3)	0(0.0)	1(1.2)	0(0.0)	0(0.0)	1(5.3)	0(0.0)	0(0.0)
	2	0(0.0)	6(7.3)	5(18.5)	1(4.2)	0(0.0)	1(1.2)	3(5.7)	1(6.2)	1(5.3)	2(8.3)	1(2.9)
	3	2(3.2)	12(14.6)	9(33.3)	16(66.7)	9(81.8)	19(22.6)	20(37.7)	6(37.5)	7(36.8)	8(33.3)	9(25.7)
	4	61(96.8)	57(69.5)	8(29.6)	3(12.5)	2(18.2)	63(75.0)	30(56.6)	9(56.3)	10(52.6)	14(58.3)	24(68.6)
Groove pattern M1	1	78(95.1)	126(88.7)	27(87.1)	26(76.5)	13(92.9)	78(90.7)	57(96.6)	15(93.7)	32(80.0)	43(93.5)	77(92.8)
	2	0(0.0)	3(2.1)	1(3.2)	1(2.9)	0(0.0)	0(0.0)	0(0.0)	0(0.0)	1(2.5)	0(0.0)	2(2.4)
	3	4(4.9)	13(9.1)	3(9.7)	7(20.6)	1(7.1)	8(9.3)	2(3.4)	1(6.3)	7(17.5)	3(6.5)	4(4.8)
Groove pattern M2	1	9(11.8)	22(15.7)	11(45.8)	12(44.4)	1(9.1)	4(6.8)	6(17.6)	1(10.0)	5(13.2)	2(5.3)	0(0.0)
	2	4(5.3)	12(8.6)	10(41.7)	1(3.7)	0(0.0)	4(6.8)	11(32.4)	0(0.0)	5(13.2)	7(18.4)	16(25.4)
	3	63(82.9)	106(75.7)	3(12.5)	14(51.8)	10(90.9)	51(86.4)	17(50.0)	9(90.0)	28(73.7)	29(76.3)	47(74.6)
Cusp number M1	4	1(1.3)	0(0.0)	1(2.8)	0(0.0)	0(0.0)	0(0.0)	0(0.0)	0(0.0)	0(0.0)	0(0.0)	2(3.3)
	5	56(70.9)	92(70.8)	21(58.3)	27(77.1)	7(50.0)	54(61.4)	35(60.3)	11(61.1)	26(66.7)	21(55.3)	28(45.9)
	6	20(25.3)	35(26.9)	14(38.9)	8(22.9)	7(50.0)	32(36.4)	20(34.5)	7(38.9)	13(33.3)	17(44.7)	31(50.8)
	7	2(2.5)	3(2.3)	0(0.0)	0(0.0)	0(0.0)	2(2.2)	3(5.2)	0(0.0)	0(0.0)	0(0.0)	0(0.0)

Dental trait	Grade	Irene	SCDG	SCDGSM	SMDY	Baum	Ledford	King	Little Egypt	Coweeta Creek	Upper Saura Town	Town Creek
Cusp number M2	4	6(8.3)	8(6.8)	4(14.8)	5(20.0)	1(9.1)	0(0.0)	0(0.0)	0(0.0)	4(19.0)	9(37.5)	9(23.7)
	5	54(75.0)	68(58.1)	16(59.3)	14(56.0)	6(54.5)	45(76.3)	24(72.7)	6(54.6)	14(66.7)	10(41.7)	20(52.6)
	6	12(16.7)	41(35.0)	7(25.9)	6(24.0)	4(36.4)	14(23.7)	9(27.3)	5(45.4)	3(14.3)	5(20.8)	9(23.7)
Deflecting wrinkle	0	9(34.6)	5(8.9)	6(27.3)	11(57.9)	4(80.0)	14(25.4)	17(47.2)	4(28.6)	0(0.0)	1(3.5)	2(4.3)
	1	2(7.7)	11(19.6)	3(13.6)	4(21.0)	1(20.0)	6(10.9)	5(13.9)	3(2.9)	5(10.6)		
	2	8(30.8)	35(62.5)	11(50.0)	2(10.5)	0(0.0)	30(54.6)	11(30.6)	7(50.0)	7(43.7)	15(53.5)	23(48.9)
	3	7(26.9)	5(8.9)	2(9.1)	2(10.5)	0(0.0)	5(9.1)	3(8.3)	0(0.0)	9(56.3)	7(25.0)	17(36.2)
Distal trigonid crest	0	35(87.5)	55(67.1)	21(94.4)	21(100)	5(83.3)	58(86.6)	45(95.7)	12(75.0)	20(90.9)	32(97.0)	34(73.9)
	1	5(12.5)	27(32.9)	1(4.6)	0(0.0)	1(16.7)	9(13.4)	2(4.3)	4(25.0)	2(9.1)	1(3.0)	12(26.1)
Protostylid M1	0	3(3.7)	6(8.4)	3(14.3)	17(50.0)	8(57.1)	16(18.2)	0(0.0)	2(11.8)	6(20.0)	5(15.5)	11(24.4)
	1	34(41.5)	29(40.8)	14(66.7)	17(50.0)	5(35.7)	51(57.9)	34(58.6)	12(70.6)	14(46.7)	8(25.0)	4(8.9)
	2	45(54.9)	36(50.7)	4(19.0)	0(0.0)	1(7.2)	21(23.9)	24(41.4)	3(17.6)	8(26.7)	9(28.1)	11(24.4)
	3	0(0.0)	0(0.0)	0(0.0)	0(0.0)	0(0.0)	0(0.0)	0(0.0)	0(0.0)	2(6.7)	7(21.9)	12(26.7)
	4	0(0.0)	0(0.0)	0(0.0)	0(0.0)	0(0.0)	0(0.0)	0(0.0)	0(0.0)	0(0.0)	3(9.4)	7(15.6)
Protostylid M2	0	5(6.9)	14(24.1)	6(66.7)	12(50.0)	10(90.9)	13(21.3)	5(14.7)	3(27.3)	8(32.0)	4(21.0)	16(41.0)
	1	35(48.6)	25(43.1)	1(11.1)	12(50.0)	1(9.1)	39(63.9)	20(58.8)	7(63.6)	12(48.0)	7(36.8)	16(41.0)
	2	32(44.4)	19(32.7)	2(22.2)	0(0.0)	0(0.0)	9(14.7)	9(26.5)	1(9.1)	2(8.0)	6(31.5)	5(12.8)
	3	0(0.0)	0(0.0)	0(0.0)	0(0.0)	0(0.0)	0(0.0)	0(0.0)	0(0.0)	2(8.0)	1(5.3)	0(0.0)
	4	0(0.0)	0(0.0)	0(0.0)	0(0.0)	0(0.0)	0(0.0)	0(0.0)	0(0.0)	1(4.0)	1(5.3)	2(5.1)
Cusp 5 M1	0	1(1.3)	0(0.0)	1(2.9)	0(0.0)	0(0.0)	0(0.0)	0(0.0)	0(0.0)	0(0.0)	0(0.0)	1(3.0)
	2	0(0.0)	0(0.0)	0(0.0)	0(0.0)	0(0.0)	1(1.1)	2(3.4)	0(0.0)	0(0.0)	0(0.0)	1(3.0)
	3	6(6.7)	18(14.1)	1(2.9)	3(8.8)	0(0.0)	20(22.7)	7(12.1)	2(11.1)	3(11.1)	1(4.3)	0(0.0)
	4	28(35.4)	58(45.3)	27(77.1)	20(58.8)	9(64.3)	32(36.4)	33(56.9)	11(61.1)	11(40.7)	6(28.5)	1(3.0)
	5	44(55.7)	52(40.6)	6(17.1)	11(32.4)	5(35.7)	35(39.8)	16(27.6)	5(27.8)	13(48.2)	14(66.7)	30(91.0)

(continued)

Dental trait	Grade	Irene	SCDG	SCDGSM	SMDY	Baum	Ledford	King	Little Egypt	Coweeta Creek	Upper Saura Town	Town Creek
Cusp 5 M2	0	7(9.7)	9(7.9)	4(16.7)	5(20.0)	1(9.1)	0(0.0)	0(0.0)	0(0.0)	4(20.0)	9(50.0)	9(30.0)
	1	0(0.0)	2(1.7)	0(0.0)	2(8.0)	0(0.0)	0(0.0)	0(0.0)	0(0.0)	0(0.0)	0(0.0)	1(3.3)
	2	3(4.2)	6(5.3)	0(0.0)	2(8.0)	2(18.2)	6(10.2)	5(15.1)	0(0.0)	8(40.0)	1(5.5)	8(26.7)
	3	13(18.0)	32(28.1)	2(8.3)	4(16.0)	2(18.2)	20(33.9)	16(48.5)	7(63.6)	2(10.0)	1(5.5)	6(20.0)
	4	34(47.2)	59(51.7)	15(62.5)	11(44.0)	5(45.4)	23(39.0)	10(30.3)	3(27.3)	5(25.0)	3(16.7)	3(10.0)
	5	15(20.8)	6(5.3)	3(12.5)	1(4.0)	1(9.1)	10(16.9)	2(6.1)	1(9.1)	1(5.0)	4(22.2)	3(10.0)
Cusp 6 M1	0	59(74.7)	92(71.9)	17(56.7)	26(76.5)	7(50.0)	55(62.5)	36(62.1)	11(61.1)	21(61.7)	19(52.3)	29(47.5)
	1	1(1.3)	6(4.7)	3(10.0)	1(2.9)	1(7.1)	1(1.1)	1(1.7)	1(5.6)	1(2.9)	4(11.1)	4(6.6)
	2	5(6.3)	12(9.4)	6(20.0)	4(11.7)	4(28.6)	10(11.4)	11(19.0)	3(16.7)	5(14.7)	7(19.4)	16(26.2)
	3	12(15.2)	6(4.7)	4(13.3)	3(8.8)	2(14.3)	13(14.8)	4(6.9)	2(11.1)	5(14.7)	4(11.1)	8(13.1)
	4	2(2.5)	12(9.4)	0(0.0)	0(0.0)	0(0.0)	8(9.1)	6(10.3)	1(5.6)	1(2.9)	1(2.3)	1(1.6)
	5	0(0.0)	0(0.0)	0(0.0)	0(0.0)	0(0.0)	1(1.1)	0(0.0)	0(0.0)	1(2.9)	1(2.3)	3(4.9)
Cusp 6 M2	0	60(88.3)	76(66.7)	17(80.9)	19(76.0)	7(63.6)	44(74.6)	24(72.7)	6(54.5)	19(82.6)	17(77.3)	27(71.1)
	1	0(0.0)	2(1.7)	1(4.8)	1(4.0)	0(0.0)	0(0.0)	0(0.0)	0(0.0)	0(0.0)	0(0.0)	3(7.9)
	2	1(1.4)	10(8.8)	1(4.8)	2(8.0)	0(0.0)	4(6.8)	0(0.0)	1(9.1)	0(0.0)	2(9.1)	2(5.3)
	3	5(6.9)	7(6.1)	1(4.8)	1(4.0)	2(18.2)	7(11.9)	6(18.2)	1(9.1)	1(4.3)	2(9.1)	3(7.9)
	4	6(8.3)	17(14.9)	0(0.0)	1(4.0)	2(18.2)	4(6.8)	3(9.1)	3(27.3)	1(4.3)	0(0.0)	1(2.6)
	5	0(0.0)	2(1.7)	1(4.8)	1(4.0)	0(0.0)	0(0.0)	0(0.0)	0(0.0)	2(8.7)	1(4.5)	2(5.2)
Cusp 7 M1	0	75(94.9)	123(96)	31(100)	34(100)	14(100)	87(98.9)	55(94.8)	18(100)	33(97.1)	34(87.2)	56(90.3)
	1	0(0.0)	3(2.3)	0(0.0)	0(0.0)	0(0.0)	0(0.0)	0(0.0)	0(0.0)	1(2.9)	3(7.7)	3(4.8)
	2	4(5.0)	1(0.8)	0(0.0)	0(0.0)	0(0.0)	0(0.0)	3(5.2)	0(0.0)	0(0.0)	1(2.5)	2(3.2)
	3	0(0.0)	1(0.8)	0(0.0)	0(0.0)	0(0.0)	1(1.1)	0(0.0)	0(0.0)	0(0.0)	1(2.5)	1(1.6)
Cusp 7 M2	0	71(98.6)	114(100)	23(100)	24(96.0)	11(100)	59(100)	33(100)	11(100)	29(100)	27(100)	44(100)
	2	1(1.4)	0(0.0)	0(0.0)	0(0.0)	0(0.0)	0(0.0)	0(0.0)	0(0.0)	0(0.0)	0(0.0)	0(0.0)
	4	0(0.0)	0(0.0)	0(0.0)	1(4.0)	0(0.0)	0(0.0)	0(0.0)	0(0.0)	0(0.0)	0(0.0)	0(0.0)

Appendix 9.B. Cranial trait frequencies

N (% present)

Cranial trait	Irene	SCDG	SCDGSM	SMDY	Baum	Ledford	Upper Saura Town	Town Creek	Warren Wilson
Ossicle at lambda	70 (34.3)	0 (0.0)	63 (31.7)	18 (5.5)	68 (17.6)	29 (27.6)	15 (33.3)	64 (37.5)	18 (55.6)
Lambdoid ossicles	70 (62.9)	0 (0.0)	63 (42.9)	19 (31.6)	67 (32.8)	30 (36.7)	23 (87.0)	70 (75.7)	23 (73.9)
Ossicle at asterion	62 (37.1)	0 (0.0)	62 (32.3)	20 (30.0)	67 (13.4)	25 (12.0)	16 (43.7)	55 (43.6)	18 (55.6)
Parietal notch bone	64 (15.6)	0 (0.0)	64 (6.2)	20 (10.0)	65 (6.1)	29 (6.9)	17 (5.9)	57 (8.8)	21 (4.8)
Epipteric bone	51 (19.6)	0 (0.0)	36 (2.8)	18 (0.0)	56 (0.0)	26 (11.5)	15 (0.0)	54 (0.0)	20 (0.0)
Bregmatic bone	67 (0.0)	0 (0.0)	62 (1.6)	21 (0.0)	69 (0.0)	32 (0.0)	22 (0.0)	63 (1.6)	22 (4.6)
Coronal ossicle	67 (4.5)	0 (0.0)	62 (1.6)	21 (0.0)	67 (4.5)	32 (3.1)	18 (0.0)	50 (8.0)	20 (0.0)
Metopism	69 (0.0)	0 (0.0)	70 (0.0)	21 (0.0)	69 (0.0)	32 (0.0)	28 (3.6)	73 (5.5)	24 (0.0)
Fronto-temporal articulation	50 (2.0)	0 (0.0)	38 (0.0)	18 (0.0)	60 (0.0)	28 (0.0)	14 (7.1)	42 (4.8)	16 (0.0)
Supraorbital foramen	67 (17.9)	0 (0.0)	66 (18.2)	20 (25.0)	67 (43.3)	32 (12.5)	29 (27.6)	72 (31.9)	17 (52.9)
Frontal notch	66 (13.6)	0 (0.0)	65 (36.9)	20 (60.0)	68 (69.1)	32 (50.0)	25 (24.0)	64 (35.9)	14 (57.1)
Auditory torus	69 (0.0)	0 (0.0)	66 (0.0)	21 (0.0)	69 (0.0)	32 (0.0)	38 (5.3)	97 (17.5)	31 (51.6)
Foramen of Huschke	69 (24.6)	0 (0.0)	68 (32.3)	21 (33.3)	65 (12.3)	32 (15.6)	39 (33.3)	99 (22.2)	31 (9.7)
Condylar facet double	48 (0.0)	0 (0.0)	36 (0.0)	16 (0.0)	45 (0.0)	19 (0.0)	19 (26.3)	36 (17.1)	16 (12.5)
Precondylar tubercle	44 (0.0)	0 (0.0)	33 (12.1)	16 (0.0)	47 (17.0)	18 (11.1)	16 (0.0)	37 (8.1)	18 (5.6)
Foramen ovale	48 (2.1)	0 (0.0)	53 (1.9)	16 (0.0)	62 (11.3)	25 (4.0)	19 (5.3)	53 (7.5)	23 (0.0)
Foramen spinosum	44 (29.5)	0 (0.0)	55 (21.8)	16 (18.7)	60 (26.7)	25 (8.0)	21 (42.9)	48 (41.7)	27 (33.3)
Accessory palatine foramen	45 (75.6)	0 (0.0)	42 (78.6)	12 (41.7)	45 (60.0)	21 (42.9)	9 (100.0)	27 (85.2)	17 (100.0)
Palatine torus	57 (80.7)	0 (0.0)	57 (77.2)	18 (83.3)	54 (31.5)	29 (100.0)	6 (33.3)	24 (91.7)	13 (61.5)
Maxillary torus	59 (3.4)	0 (0.0)	58 (27.6)	18 (11.1)	51 (0.0)	31 (25.8)	22 (0.0)	52 (13.5)	22 (0.0)
Parietal foramen	67 (31.3)	0 (0.0)	65 (44.6)	21 (19.0)	69 (56.5)	32 (50.0)	18 (5.6)	69 (0.0)	21 (0.0)
Posterior condylar canal	39 (33.3)	0 (0.0)	32 (18.7)	7 (57.1)	38 (63.2)	18 (16.7)	23 (43.5)	38 (52.6)	12 (41.7)
Mastoid foramen extrasutural	61 (16.4)	0 (0.0)	63 (12.7)	16 (18.7)	67 (10.4)	24 (8.3)	19 (21.0)	60 (35.0)	16 (56.2)
Ant. condylar canal double	48 (14.6)	0 (0.0)	33 (18.2)	14 (42.9)	50 (16.0)	20 (10.0)	29 (24.1)	50 (28.0)	21 (28.6)
Zygomatico-facial foramen	61 (60.7)	0 (0.0)	56 (66.1)	18 (83.3)	64 (32.8)	29 (75.9)	19 (26.3)	40 (25.0)	11 (18.2)
Accs. infraorbital foramen	47 (6.4)	0 (0.0)	49 (6.1)	12 (0.0)	46 (28.3)	27 (18.5)	0 (0.0)	0 (0.0)	0 (0.0)

10

A Spanish Borderlands Perspective
on La Florida Bioarchaeology

Phillip L. Walker

The quincentenary of Christopher Columbus's inadvertent discovery of the New World stimulated an enormous amount of research on the biological and cultural consequences of the ensuing contacts between the people of the Old and New Worlds. The contributions to the current volume clearly show how much this work has enriched our understanding of the ways in which the Native Americans of La Florida responded to the immense changes European contact brought.

Bioarchaeological studies of Native American responses to European contact in other parts of the Spanish Borderlands offer a revealing comparative perspective on the La Florida experience. This vast region, stretching from California to the Atlantic coast of Florida and Georgia, encompasses a breathtaking diversity of natural environments. It was inhabited by Native Americans with an equally diverse array of cultures. Some groups, such as those in much of the southwestern and southeastern United States, practiced maize agriculture. Hunter-gatherers who supported themselves through fishing, hunting, and collecting wild plants lived in other areas of the Borderlands, including most of California and many of the coastal areas along the Gulf of Mexico and the Atlantic coast of southern Florida. These varied subsistence practices fostered cultures that ranged from highly mobile, egalitarian bands of hunter-gatherers to complex, hierarchically organized chiefdoms with large, sedentary village populations.

The Spanish conquest of the Borderlands spanned more than 250 years from the earliest 16th-century contacts with aboriginal Floridians to the establishment of the first permanent settlements in Alta California (now the state of California) during the last half of the 18th century. Through time, economic, political, and social conditions in the Spanish empire changed markedly and this influenced New World colonial policies. Nevertheless, several consistent motivations shaped Spanish-Indian relations throughout the Borderlands. The goals of Spanish authorities were typically threefold: extract whatever wealth they could from the natural and human resources of the occupied area, establish a sufficient military presence to prevent the area from coming under the control of another colonial power, and convert the Native Americans living in the area into economically productive, Catholic members of the Spanish empire.

This is not to say that the Spanish colonial policy remained static over the nearly 300 years of their colonial experience in the New World. Changing political and economic conditions in Spain had important consequences for the government's ability to exploit the people and resources of their Borderlands holdings (Bannon 1974; Kealhofer 1996). Nevertheless, a common colonial strategy was used throughout North America and this resulted in similar historical progressions in different Borderlands areas. Initial contacts with local Native Americans made by the members of a small expeditionary force were followed by the arrival of a few priests, soldiers, and civilians, who built missions and military garrisons. Since conversion of native people to Catholicism made them willing laborers, the proselytizing efforts of Catholic missionaries played a key role in the Spanish colonial strategy (Milanich 1996).

It was not feasible for a handful of priests and soldiers to subjugate large, well-organized Borderlands tribes through military force, and, in general, armed conflict was avoided. In 1680, this colonial strategy was made explicit in the Laws of the Indies, which stated that "war cannot and shall not be made on the Indians of any province to the end that they may receive the Holy Catholic faith, or yield obedience to us, or for any other reason" (Zavala and Coyne 1943:46).

Although these regularities in Spanish motivations and colonial policy created some broad patterns in the indigenous response, there are many unique aspects to the colonial experience in different Borderlands areas that derive from differences in pre-contact Native American adaptations and cultural histories. The marked demographic and social differences among Borderlands Indian groups have significant implications for the cultural and biological responses they were able to mount to the disease and social disruption Spanish colonists brought. An analysis of the range of responses Spanish contact elicited from different Borderlands groups can, therefore, shed light on the role that local ecological and cultural historical influences had in shaping native responses to European contact. Such a comparative perspective can be obtained by contrasting the contact experiences of Native Americans living in La Florida, the Puebloan area of the American Southwest, and Alta California. The biological and cultural consequences European contact had for the Indians of these areas have been studied extensively, and, in many cases, comparable bioarchaeological data from skeletal studies are available. This makes possible direct comparisons of changes in daily activities, diet, growth and development, and health that reveal much about the underlying processes of biological and cultural change.

Pre-Contact Conditions

To comprehend the effects that Europeans had on Native Americans, it is necessary to know something about the previous living conditions of indigenous peoples. To some extent, these initial conditions can be extrapolated from the reports of the earliest European explorers. However, as is amply illustrated by the heated controversy over the effects of early epidemics on New World populations (Baker and Kealhofer 1996), such ethnohistoric extrapolations are full of uncertainty. The task of determining when Native Americans first began to experience the massive cultural disruption and demographic collapse that came with the introduction of highly lethal diseases such smallpox and measles is far from straightforward. If virulent infections rapidly spread along Indian trade routes into remote areas unvisited by Europeans, for most groups the earliest ethnohistoric and ethnographic descriptions we have refer to populations that had been massively disrupted by devastating epidemics (Dunnell 1991). Owing to this uncertainty, it is important to scrutinize ethnohistoric descriptions with a critical eye and, whenever possible, verify them using archaeological evidence from pre-Columbian times.

Establishing a baseline of conditions against which to measure the effects of European contact is also complicated by the instability of pre-contact societies. Native American cultures were far from static before the arrival of Europeans, and this makes the "ethnographic present" of pre-contact cultures an elusive, constantly moving target. Throughout the Borderlands area, pre-contact populations engaged in a dynamic interaction with their constantly changing natural and sociocultural environments. Through time this process of responding to environmental exigencies resulted in periods of relative stability as well as episodes of extremely rapid cultural change (Jones et al. 1999).

In many areas, the result was a gradual intensification of resource exploitation through which highly mobile hunter-gatherer groups developed strategies for maintaining people in larger, more permanent aggregations. For example, hunter-gatherers in Alta California developed techniques for increasing wild plant yields, such as acorn leaching and grassland burning to increase seed-crop production (Lewis and Bean 1973, Walker 1991–92). In coastal areas such as the Santa Barbara Channel area, intensified resource use resulted in a shift toward heavy dependence upon marine resources and intervillage economic exchange. In the southeastern and southwestern United States, intensification took the form of a shift from hunting and gathering to a heavy dependence on maize and other agricultural produce. Concomitant with these subsistence changes were increases in local population densities and sedentariness. Extensive trade systems began to develop, and the size of social networks increased. Throughout the Borderlands, late prehistoric period demographic and cultural landscapes were both varied and in continual flux; demographic and sociopolitical changes were commonplace and often occurred within the timeframe of a generation.

The changes in diet and demography associated with this late pre-contact period economic intensification had important implications for the spread of contact period diseases. Living in a large, permanent village that is linked to other villages through a regional economic and social exchange system increases a person's direct and indirect contacts with people, and this greatly speeds the spread of infectious disease. Village life would also contribute to a decline in health owing to the sanitation problems that larger aggregations of people create. The presence of such living conditions in many Borderlands areas at contact greatly increased the chances that highly contagious European diseases would spread rapidly over wide areas. Finally, economic intensification typically is accomplished by narrowing the spectrum of foods consumed to a small number of highly productive plant foods. Isotopic studies show that in La Florida (Hutchinson et al. 1998; Larsen et al., this volume) and the Puebloan Southwest (Spielmann et al. 1990; Matson and Chisholm 1991) this occurred through a dietary shift toward greater maize dependence. This had important health-related consequences owing to the well-known protein and iron deficiencies associated with a maize-based diet (Walker 1985; Schultz et al., this volume). Such deficiencies are likely to reduce host resistance and render people more susceptible to infectious disease (Yesner 1980; Cohen 1989; Lambert 1993).

Bioarchaeological studies show that these changes in diet and demography resulted in a decline in the health of many pre-contact period Native American groups. Research reported in this volume shows that beginning several centuries before Europeans arrived, the people of at least some of the regions of La Florida (e.g., Lake Jackson, Irene Mound) experienced increases in population size and social complexity and an economic shift from hunting and gathering to maize agriculture. The health-related consequences of these changes were complicated and differed between the Georgia coast and Florida. One clear trend, however, is the dramatic increase in tooth decay that came with the shift toward a carbohydrate-rich maize-based diet (Larsen et al. 1990). This undoubtedly reflects the fact that decay-producing bacteria thrive in carbohydrate-rich oral environments (Walker and Hewlett 1990). The shift from hunting and gathering to agriculture also brought an increase in infectious disease. By about A.D. 1000, a treponemal disease (probably endemic syphilis) had spread throughout the region (Powell 1990; Hutchinson 1993). Today endemic syphilis is found in societies with impoverished living conditions and poor sanitation (Hudson 1958:28). The frequency of porotic hyperostosis, a condition associated with iron deficiency, does not increase during the pre-contact period (Powell 1990; Larsen and Sering 2000). This suggests that the shift toward greater maize dependence did not disrupt the balance between iron intake and iron loss sufficiently to increase the prevalence of anemia.

Skeletal evidence for poor health makes the Anasazi (pre-contact Puebloan Indians) stand out, not only in comparison to other Borderlands groups but also in comparison to Native Americans throughout the Western Hemisphere (Martin et al. n.d.). Anasazi dental caries rates were high (Stodder and Martin 1992:57). This undoubtedly reflects their carbohydrate-rich, maize-based diet and perhaps also increased susceptibility to dental disease owing to poor health and nutrition. The level of childhood stress, as indicated by disruptions in dental development, appears to have increased significantly between the Basketmaker III and the later Pueblo periods (Malville 1997). Skeletal lesions such as cribra orbitalia that are indicative of infection and nutritional deficiency are especially common in late prehistoric period southwestern skeletal collections (Walker 1985; Stodder and Martin 1992:58; Malville 1997). Cases of treponemal disease (Denninger 1938; Cole et al. 1955; El-Najjar 1979; Stodder 1998) and tuberculosis (El-Najjar 1979; Fink 1985; Ortner and Putschar 1985; Sumner 1985; Buikstra 1999:489) have been documented in several late prehistoric period Anasazi skeletal collections. The earliest of these date to a time of large-scale population growth and aggregation (Buikstra 1999:483). These paleopathological data suggest that before the arrival of Europeans, the Anasazi were living a difficult, stress-filled existence in which infectious disease and malnutrition were commonplace.

The health status of Indians living in Alta California shows some of the same pre-contact period trends found in other Borderlands areas. Owing to the widespread practice of cremation, large skeletal collections are available only from the Santa Barbara Channel and Sacramento River Valley areas where high pre-contact period population densities may have contributed to the maintenance and spread of infectious disease. The health of Indians in these areas undoubtedly differed in some respects from that of people who lived in more sparsely populated parts of California. Short-term declines in health status linked to fluctuations in local environmental productivity appear to have been common. As a result, it is difficult to make sweeping generalizations about pre-contact period conditions (Walker and Thornton n.d.).

Bioarchaeological studies show that the diet and health of pre-contact Alta Californians varied regionally and through time (Walker and DeNiro 1986; Walker 1991–92; Walker 1996; Walker and Thornton n.d.). For example, in the Santa Barbara Channel area, the shift from hunting and gathering to heavy dependence on marine resources was accompanied by a decrease in dental caries and tooth wear rates (Walker 1978; Walker and Erlandson 1986). These changes are paralleled by bone isotope changes indicating increased marine resource dependence (Walker and DeNiro 1986). Dental pathological and isotopic studies suggest that on the Northern Channel Islands, the early prehistoric period diets of women were more terrestrially oriented and less variable than those of men, and that through time the diets of both sexes converged toward greater seafood consumption (Walker and DeNiro 1986; Goldberg 1993).

In both central California and the Santa Barbara Channel area, there is a tendency for disruptions in dental development to increase during the pre-contact period (Walker et al. 1989). In central California dental hypoplasia decreases between the early and middle horizons, but after that time it increases steadily into the historic period (Schulz and McHenry 1975; Schulz 1981). In the Santa Barbara Channel area, the trend toward more dental hypoplasia is unbroken from the early to the late period (Walker et al. 1989). This evidence of more childhood growth disruption through time probably reflects health problems associated with increased late prehistoric period population densities and sedentism (Schulz 1981; Dickel et al. 1984; Walker et al. 1989). The expansion of intervillage and interregional economic interactions during the late period (Moratto 1984) may also have contributed to the decline in health through facilitating the spread of infectious disease.

Paleopathological studies show that bone lesions indicative of streptococcal or staphylococcal infections were fairly common in some pre-contact California Indian populations (Roney 1959, 1966; Suchey et al 1972). There is also evidence that tuberculosis, treponematosis, and possibly coccidioidomycosis were present in California before the arrival of Europeans (Roney 1959; Hoffman 1987; Walker and Lambert 1989). Skeletal evidence for anemia is common in some areas, such as on the offshore islands of southern California, where people had limited access to fresh water and a limited range of food sources (Walker 1986).

In the Santa Barbara Channel area, the frequency of people with bone infections (osteoperiostitis) varies markedly through time. Although burials with skeletal lesions whose histological appearance is suggestive of endemic syphilis occur as early as 2,600 B.C. (Lambert 1993; Walker and Lambert 1998), the frequency of such cases increases dramatically during times of resource stress, warfare, and population aggregation (Walker and Lambert 1989). On Santa Cruz Island, osteoperiostitis increased significantly between the early and middle periods and then became somewhat less prevalent during the late period (Lambert and Walker 1991; Lambert 1993).

In the Channel Island area, there is also a gradual decrease in body size from the early prehistoric period until the middle period, with especially small statures during the late middle period (Lambert 1994; Walker et al. 1996). The late middle period was a time of unstable environmental conditions and frequent outbreaks of warfare and violence (Walker and Lambert 1989; Lambert and Walker 1991; Lambert 1994). It seems likely that the small stature of people during this period reflects stunting owing to these unfavorable environmental conditions (Walker and Lambert 1989). During the late prehistoric period statures increase significantly, perhaps owing to somewhat improved living conditions.

The social organization of Borderlands Indian groups had an important influence on how easy they were to control. In some parts of La Florida and Alta California, chiefdoms developed that integrated the people living in an area under the control of powerful chiefs and a social elite. In such situations, it was often possible for the Spanish to subdue large numbers of people through manipulation of their chief's power. In other areas, less hierarchical forms of pre-contact social organization made gaining control of the local population much more difficult. For example, groups like the Guale were hard to control because of their spatial mobility, and a dispersed settlement pattern that meant they were scattered throughout their territory for part of the year (Barcia Carballido y Zuniga 1970:152; discussion in Jones 1978). The Apalachee chiefdoms, on the other hand, had a well-developed social hierarchy and tribute system that the Spanish could exploit to meet their subsistence and labor needs (Hann 1988; Hann and McEwan 1998). Although the degree of social stratification present in the pre-contact Anasazi population of the Puebloan Southwest is hotly debated (Wormington and Reed 1947; Upham 1982; Saitta and McGuire 1998), it is clear that at the time of European contact, most Puebloan groups possessed complex yet flexible clan-based political systems. This gave them the facultative capacity to aggregate in large villages or to disperse into small settlements depending upon the demands of prevailing social and environmental conditions. Such organizational flexibility posed a formidable obstacle to Spanish control.

Protohistoric Epidemics

This pre-contact Native American diversity in diet, health, social organization, and living conditions set the stage for the earliest encounters with Europeans. Often there was a considerable time lag (227 years in Alta California) separating these initial, often ephemeral contacts with Spanish explorers and the beginning of full-fledged colonization efforts involving the establishment of missions, military garrisons, and permanent settlements.

The possibility that early explorers introduced infectious diseases to Borderlands groups before colonization began in earnest has enormous implications for the interpretation of later events. If early explorers such as Ponce de León in La Florida, Coronado in the Puebloan Southwest, and Cabrillo in Alta California brought with them lethal infectious diseases that decimated Native Americans throughout the Borderlands, the attendant socioeconomic collapse would have important consequences. The social disruption and loss of biological and cultural diversity associated with going through a recent epidemic-induced demographic bottleneck would significantly reduce the survivors' capacity to cope successfully with the challenges posed by later Spanish colonization efforts. The possibility of devastating undocumented protohistoric period epidemics also has significant implications for our ability to use ethnographic analogy to reconstruct pre-contact conditions; if the Native American cultures described in ethnohistoric and ethnographic reports were the remnants of devastated pre-contact cultures, the relevance of these descriptions for reconstruction of pre-contact conditions is unclear (Dunnell 1991).

This issue of the magnitude of protohistoric period demographic collapse is a contentious one that is far from being resolved. According to

some scholars, European disease spread so rapidly through contacts between Native American groups that, in many areas, depopulation occurred
before the appoarance of the first European explorers (Dobyns 1983). For
example, Fairbanks (1985) and Dobyns argue that the Spanish *entrada*
into La Florida resulted in massive social disruption and depopulation.
Other scholars (Thornton et al. 1991; Thornton et al. 1992)—while admit-
ting that some tribes may have experienced episodes of introduced diseases
by the time de Soto arrived in 1540—argue based on epidemiological
grounds that smallpox and other similar diseases are unlikely to have dif-
fused throughout La Florida as rapidly as Dobyns (1983) suggests.

Similar uncertainties exist regarding the effects that early Spanish contacts had on Indians living in the Puebloan Southwest and Alta California.
In the Southwest, few historic documents are available until the 16th century. As a result, epidemics could have ravaged Puebloan groups without
being recorded by Europeans (Upham 1992). Based upon archaeological
data and historical records, Upham (1992:233) estimates that the Pueblo
population of the Rio Grande region dropped to about half of its pre-
contact size during the 16th century. Although historical records do not
refer to epidemics among the Puebloan groups during the last part of the
16th century, few documents are available for this period (Upham
1992:227). Upham (1992) argues that only the acute crowd infections
brought by the Spanish could account for a population decline of this
magnitude.

The consequences of protohistoric period Spanish contacts with Alta
California Indians are unclear (Johnson 1982:49; Walker and Hudson
1993). Several ships carrying goods from the Philippines to Mexico passed
along the California coast during the 1600s (Schurz 1939). Although we
have no evidence that these sailors interacted with the local Native Americans, it is reasonable to assume that the crews of these ships occasionally
had contacts with native Californians while provisioning themselves with
fresh water and food (Walker and Hudson 1993). Such visits would have
the potential to infect California Indians with European diseases. Besides
such direct contacts, infections may also have reached Alta California indirectly through transmission along the aboriginal trade routes that linked
California to the American Southwest and Mexico (Dobyns 1981:49–50).

On the other hand, the theory that Alta Californian Indians were devastated by European diseases before the first permanent Spanish settlements
were established is inconsistent with the behavior of later well-documented
epidemics. As early as 1798, a ship containing smallpox victims landed at

Santa Barbara in the center of the densely populated Chumash territory, yet no smallpox epidemics are known to have occurred in this area until 1844 (Cook 1939:163–64; Walker and Johnson 1994:118). Even then, the epidemic was an isolated phenomenon affecting mainly the northern missions in the Chumash territory. This is strong evidence against the idea that there was widespread, large-scale protohistoric period epidemic-related mortality in Alta California. The failure of smallpox epidemics to occur until the earlier comparative isolation of Spanish settlements in Alta California had been broken is also consistent with the demographic history of the Indians who lived in the isolated interior deserts of southern California. Even though this area is crisscrossed by native trade routes linking the southern California coast to the Puebloan Southwest (Davis 1961), the Indians living there apparently escaped widespread epidemic-related mortality until large numbers of American miners and farmers expanded into this sparsely populated area during the 1840s and 1850s (Harvey 1967; Stoffle et al. 1995).

What conclusions can we draw from these data on protohistoric period epidemics and their possible effects? It is becoming increasingly clear from archaeological and documentary evidence that the rate of the demographic collapse of the Native American population varied greatly from region to region. The likelihood of transmitting communicable diseases is strongly influenced by the distribution of people over the landscape and the intensity of the interactions within and between groups (Johnson and Geoffrey 1996; Noah and O'Mahony 1998). The probability that diseases will spread rapidly through a population is increased by the existence of larger, permanent villages and economic systems that encourage the exchange of people and resources between villages and long-distance trade. Such favorable conditions for the rapid spread of European diseases were not present in the less densely populated areas of the Spanish Borderlands.

Indians living in some areas the American Southwest and eastern North America may have suffered devastating epidemics early during the early contact period. However, recent archaeological research makes the devastating early contact period pandemics that Dobyns (1983) envisages increasingly unlikely. Archaeological and documentary evidence for demographic changes in the Mohawk Valley, for example, suggests that the northeastern region of North America was not affected by exogenous epidemics until the 17th century. When epidemics did arrive in this area, they had horrendous consequences. It is estimated that within just a few months, more than half of the members of some tribes died (Snow 1996).

The massive economic collapse and social disruption associated with so many deaths would greatly facilitate the colonial efforts of any Europeans who followed in the epidemic's wake.

Spanish Colonial Policy

Whatever the effects of protohistoric period diseases, it is clear that the establishment of permanent settlements initiated a process that resulted in enormous biological and cultural changes that devastated Borderlands Indians. These included changes in religion, diet, workload, daily activities, technology, and disease exposure that affected all aspects of their lives. Even though missionization occurred much later in Alta California than it did in La Florida, the results were similar: aggregation of the local Indians at missions led to rapid depopulation and cultural collapse and eventually resulted in their virtual extinction. The consequences of European contact in the Puebloan area were somewhat different. The area's remoteness and lack of strategic importance and the passive resistance of Puebloan groups to Spanish domination meant that attempts at missionization were unsuccessful. As a result, many important elements of pre-contact culture were able to persist into the 20th century.

Spain's colonial policy had profound consequences for Native Americans throughout the Borderlands. In other areas, such as northeastern North America, European contacts typically resulted from private entrepreneurial activities under comparatively weak governmental control (Bryce 1968). Spanish colonial activities, in contrast, were organized and administered under the auspices of an elaborate set of governmental regulations. Although these overarching policies gave some uniformity to the colonial experience throughout the Borderlands, their implementation often faltered in remote areas. These administrative problems often stemmed from the difficulty of controlling government functionaries and settlers living far from the sources of power. There were also frequent conflicts between the sacred concerns of Catholic missionaries and the secular interests of government officials (Gannon 1990; Whitehead and Cutter 1996:73–75). Nevertheless, regulations governing the treatment of Indians were an important force unifying Spain's colonial activities.

Between the 16th and 19th centuries, the Spanish established hundreds of Catholic missions as well as a number of military installations throughout the Borderlands area. The goal of this colonial activity was to bring the local Native Americans under Spanish control and to make them economically productive members of the Spanish empire: in other words, to convert them into "tax paying Christians" (Weber 1992:306–7). Although local circumstances sometimes made it unfeasible, ideally the conversion from paganism would progress through several graduated stages: *reducción,* the process of removing Indians from their native villages to mission communities where they could be given religious instruction by priests; *conversión,* the process of teaching them the fundamental concepts of Christianity; and *curato,* the final stage, which would launch them into a secular community as *gente de razón* (rational beings endowed with a mind and a soul) capable of manifesting personal lawful habits and civic responsibilities (Almaráz 1992:34).

The process of reducción greatly facilitated another element of Spanish colonial policy, the *encomienda* system. Reducción increased the availability of Indian laborers for the Spanish missions and military garrisons. Although the role of forced labor in the decline of Borderlands Native American populations has long been a focus of heated debate (Cook 1976; Gibson 1988; Castillo 1989:378; Costello and Hornbeck 1989:313), the bureaucratic basis for the Spanish use of Indian laborers is clear (Simpson 1982; Yeager 1995; Pastore 1998). Under the encomienda system, the Spanish settlers and soldiers (*encomenderos*) were rewarded for their services to the government by being given the right to collect tribute and to use the personal services of Indian vassals living in a specified area (Simpson 1982). In return, the encomendero was supposed to maintain peace and order within the area, protect it from external threat, and assist the missionaries working there in converting the local Indians to Christianity. The repartimiento was a more severe form of impressment in which Indian labor was used for public purposes or in the mines (Simpson 1982). The human rights of Indians could be further reduced to absolute servitude if they resisted Spanish domination to the point that they were captured as prisoners of war or fugitive criminals. In that case, although they could not be sold, they could legally be forced into slavery for a designated number of years (Haring 1963:53–57; Gibson 1988:410). In the American Southwest, these strictures on the treatment of Indian captives were generally ignored, and they were treated as chattel with an assigned value that could be used to settle debts (Schroeder and Omer 1988:410).

As Worth (this volume) notes, the repartimiento system, which was active in La Florida during the early part of the colonial period, had significant, highly detrimental effects on the Indians under Spanish control. Many villages suffered enormously from having a large proportion of the able-bodied men taken to St. Augustine to work for extended periods as agricultural laborers and construction workers (Worth 1998:21–22). This forced removal would have disrupted Native American subsistence greatly, and it is also likely to have created demographic imbalances that significantly reduced the reproductive capacity of an Indian population already suffering from widespread epidemic-related deaths. As Gannon (1990) points out, the Apalachee were converted into what were essentially pack animals to transport their agricultural produce from their native villages to St. Augustine, a trip from which many of them would never return.

It is unfair to focus all of the blame for inhumane treatment of La Florida's Native American population upon the Spanish. When the Spanish found the costs of defending their holdings in La Florida too onerous, they abandoned them to the English. In the meantime, many Indian neophytes who sought protection from English-sponsored slave raids were either killed or captured and shipped off to a short life of grueling slave labor on a Carolina plantation (Wood 1988; Saunt 1998). These English slave raiders with flintlock rifles greatly hastened the extinction of La Florida Native American populations.

In Alta California, especially after Mexican Independence, the influence of the Laws of the Indies and other regulations designed to protect the rights of indigenous people under the control of the Spanish government was greatly reduced. A letter by Father Vicente Sarria, a Franciscan missionary writing to explain the cause of the 1824 revolt of Chumash Indians in the Santa Barbara Channel area, makes the plight of the mission Indians clear:

> They are extremely overwhelmed with an excessive and unbearable burden of taxes, donations, and required loans to support an unreasonably large number of soldiers in view of the limited resources which this province has to offer. For the troops to be fed and clothed it must be at the expense of the Indians who, in turn, cannot be fed or clothed. It is very sad to see that the laws, (Volume VI, Article III, Law I), which so explicitly and religiously dictate gentleness, fair treatment, and help for the Indians reduced to the missions, do not apply here (Laws of the Indies 1943). It is just the opposite. Instead of experiencing the tenderness of the evangelical law and the holy bond of Jesus Christ, those new Christians, who could serve as an example for the others who have not converted yet, have been burdened with work by the missionaries and their weak necks cannot support it. (Beebe and Senkewicz 1996:280–81)

The combined effects of the policy of reducción and the systems of encomienda and repartimiento were large-scale population displacement, social disintegration, deterioration of health, and in many areas the extinction of local Native American cultures throughout the Spanish Borderlands (Thomas 1989, 1990, 1991).

In view of the devastating effects that Spanish colonial policy had on Borderlands Indians, it is worth asking why they were so successful in subduing most of the Native American groups with whom they came in contact. What enabled a handful of priests and soldiers to take over Borderlands areas inhabited by large, dense, sometimes militaristic Native American groups? Although they were ultimately unsuccessful in the Puebloan Southwest, in La Florida and Alta California one or two Franciscan priests with a few soldiers as escorts made rapid inroads into native communities, persuaded Indians to participate in Christian rituals, and enlisted them as laborers to build churches (Gannon 1990; Walker and Johnson 1992).

Some Native Americans initially welcomed missionaries because of the material and social benefits obtained through getting access to European trade goods (Weber 1990). The Spanish had many attractive things to offer the Native Americans. Perhaps of greatest significance were the metal tools the colonists brought. The value of swords, knives, hatchets, and firearms was readily apparent; from the onset, obtaining such highly desirable items was a high Native American priority. For example, the Indians of the Santa Barbara Channel area were so enamored with the metal tools the Spaniards brought that the members of the 1769 Portolá expedition had difficulty keeping the local Indians from stealing their equipment (Bolton 1927). A few years later, an Indian's attempt to cut off the tail of a soldier's mule and take the soldier's rifle precipitated a fight in which six Indians were killed (Tibesar 1955:295; Lasuén 1965:46). The domestic animals the Spanish brought had more than attractive tails; the advantages of horses, mules, and oxen for transportation and as draft animals were readily apparent to Indian people who were accustomed to carrying heavy loads on their own backs. Domestic animals could also provide a steady supply of meat without hunting, and they also provided valuable raw materials such as hides, wool, and bone (Weber 1990). These values of domestic animals were appreciated early on by Native Americans, and even conservative groups, such as the Puebloan Indians, readily adopted animal husbandry.

These attractions of mission life must also be seen in the context of the appalling post-epidemic conditions many Borderlands Indians were experiencing in their native villages. Mass mortality resulted in intervillage warfare, social disruption, and economic collapse. In comparison to the prospect of continuing to face starvation and death in a native village, moving to a mission would increasingly appear to be an attractive option.

Father José Señán, for example, reported that Indians on Santa Rosa Island in Alta California were eager to come to the missions because they were starving and had heard that meat was plentiful at San Buenaventura (Simpson 1982). The failure of traditional religious leaders to control the epidemics also would have abetted the priests in their conversion efforts. Under such dire circumstances, the priest's promise of the spiritual power necessary for protection from imminent death must have appeared extremely attractive (Walker and Hudson 1993).

Mission Period Demographic Collapse

If we set aside the often intractable issue of the effects of undocumented protohistoric period epidemics and examine the demographic histories of Borderlands populations during the well-documented period of intensive Spanish-Indian interaction, the disastrous effects of Spanish colonial policy become abundantly clear. In most cases, the missionaries' attempts to convert Borderlands Indians into productive Christian members of the Spanish Empire resulted in the rapid decline and extinction of the targeted population. This "harvest of souls," as it was euphemistically called by some of the friars (Engelhardt 1912–29), resulted in strikingly similar patterns of population collapse in Borderlands areas widely separated in space and time.

The collapse of mission period Native American populations throughout the Borderlands was usually a gradual process that occurred over several generations (Walker et al. 1989; Walker and Johnson 1992, 1994; Worth 1998). In La Florida, it required about 200 years; in Alta California somewhat less. Historical records show that La Florida Indians plummeted from a pre-contact population of roughly 200,000 in the area affected by the mission system to virtual extinction in the late 18th century (Worth, this volume). Census data show that a catastrophic population decline occurred between the early 16th and late 18th centuries, in which La Florida's mission Indians declined to less than one-tenth of a percent of the original population. Their final demise occurred in the 1760s when the remaining mission Indians were shipped to Cuba and Veracruz, Mexico (Hann 1988:314–316; Worth 1998:156–157).

The pre-contact Alta California population is estimated to have been at least 300,000 individuals (Cook 1978:93; Thornton 1980; Walker and Thornton n.d.). This minimum population estimate might be doubled by demographers who believe that undocumented protohistoric period epidemics took a heavy toll. With the establishment of the first Spanish settlements in Alta California, mission birth and death registers became available. These documents chart the demographic collapse of California's mission Indian population in great detail. Based in part upon this evidence, Cook (1976:5) estimated that in 1770, at the beginning of Spain's attempt to colonize Alta California, about 135,000 Indians were living there (this figure excludes the Colorado River tribes, Paiute, and Modoc). By 1848 when Mexico ceded Alta California to the United States, this number had been reduced to 88,000. Through the introduction of new diseases and genocidal raids by American settlers, the expansion of miners and farmers into previously unoccupied areas as a result of the 1849 gold rush devastated Indians living in remote areas, who had previously had little contact with Europeans. By the end of this period of American expansion, the Indians remaining in California numbered no more than 30,000 (Cook 1976:5). California's Indian population continued to decline until the beginning of the 20th century, when it reached a nadir of fewer than 25,000 people.

Data from the Puebloan area present a somewhat different picture. The total Puebloan population is estimated to have been about 150,000–200,000 on the eve of European contact (Upham 1992:232). A rapid population reduction appears to have begun soon after the arrival of the earliest Spanish explorers in 1539, and by the end of 16th century these numbers had been reduced to roughly half the pre-contact population. The number of occupied settlements continued to decline precipitously after the establishment of permanent Spanish settlements and missions in the Southwest in the early 1600s. Ethnohistoric census figures, which are available for many of the Pueblos, suggest that after a precipitous 17th-century decline in the Puebloan population, which further reduced it by more than 50 percent, a comparatively stable population of around 8,000–10,000 persisted into the first decades of the 19th century (Zubrow 1974; Kessell 1979; Simmons 1979a:185). During the last half of the 19th century, the Pueblo population began to rebound, and by 1970 it totaled 33,569 individuals (Dozier 1970; Simmons 1979b).

What conclusions can we draw from the mission period demographic histories of Borderlands populations? First, it is clear that the causes of depopulation were complex and varied to some extent both within and between Borderlands areas. Much of the population decline can be attributed to high mortality from introduced diseases combined with secondary disease-related factors that reduced birthrates, such as sterility and reduced fertility. The details of the causes of this imbalance between births and deaths varied from mission to mission. However, the Spanish policy of reducción, whereby Indians were removed from their native villages and concentrated at mission settlements, clearly was a key factor contributing to the population decline in the areas in which it could be effectively applied. From the perspective of the priests, the advantages of reducción were clear: government limitations on the number of priests who could reside at each mission meant that the only way the religious training of Indian neophytes could be supervised effectively was by isolating them from the harmful influences of their heathen colleagues and keeping them close at hand (Whitehead and Cutter 1996:75–76).

Aggregation at mission settlements created problems of waste disposal and water contamination that fostered the spread of disease. Additional problems were created by the attempts the priests made to eradicate pagan practices that they considered repugnant: Indians accustomed to going naked or wearing a g-string were forced to cover their bodies with clothing at all times, and sweat bathing was prohibited because of its association with pagan religious activities (Walker and Hudson 1993). The result was squalid mission living conditions that were a breeding ground for disease: "These miserable habitations [thatched huts], each of which was allotted for the residence of a whole family, were erected with some degree of uniformity, about three or four feet asunder, in straight rows, leaving lanes or passages at right angles between them; but these were so abominably infested with every kind of filth and nastiness, as to be rendered not less offensive than degrading to the human species" (Vancouver and Vancouver 1798:13).

Owing to the priests' desire to regulate the sexual activity of the neophytes under their control, elderly women were enlisted to monitor the activities of unmarried girls above the age of nine and women whose husbands were absent. At night these women and girls were locked up in *mojerios,* or women's quarters (Vancouver and Vancouver 1798:11). Imprisonment in such close quarters created an environment conducive to the maintenance and spread of infectious disease and may be a factor that contributed to the high mortality rates found among women of reproductive age in the Alta California mission period population (Walker and Johnson 1994:116).

Evaluating the role that nutritional inadequacies in the mission diet played in the decline of Borderlands Native American population is complicated by differences between missions and changes through time. In the context of the threat of starvation caused by disrupted subsistence activities in epidemic-ravaged native villages, the availability of food was a strong force attracting Indians to the missions. The Alta California mis-

sions experienced some early crop failures that forced the priests reluc-
tantly to allow their neophytes to return to their native modes of subsistence. However, the missions rapidly began to produce surpluses (Costello
and Hornbeck 1989), and most of the time there was plenty to eat at the
California missions (Milliken 1995:88). At times, beef was so abundant
that animals were slaughtered for their hides and tallow and the carcasses
were burned in the fields (Geiger and Meighan 1976:86). Judging the
amount of food available to mission Indians in other areas of the Borderlands is complicated by the encomienda system, which siphoned off the
productivity of Indian agricultural activities in the form of tribute to Spanish settlers and soldiers (Simpson 1982).

In terms of its nutritional adequacy, it seems clear the mission period
diet was often inferior to that available through native subsistence activities before the arrival of Europeans. In both California and La Florida,
there was a decline in the diversity of food that almost certainly had negative health consequences (Walker et al. 1989; Larsen et al., this volume). In
the Puebloan Southwest, the nutritional adequacy of the diet may have
improved in some respects. For example, the introduction of domestic animals increased the availability of animal protein.

The role that physical coercion and forced labor played in the decline of
the Borderlands Indian population varied significantly through time and
from area to area. Once a person had been baptized, fleeing the mission
system was considered a serious offense and was punished harshly. In such
cases, after recapture, the fugitive faced punishments including deprivation
of food and subjection to lashing, stocks, imprisonment, and a sentence of
hard labor (Engelhardt 1930; Cook 1976:126). Spanish labor and tribute
demands were a principal cause of revolts among the Indians of La Florida,
the Puebloan Southwest, and Alta California (Engelhardt 1932:30–33;
Hackett and Shelby 1942; Cook 1976:60; Jones 1978; Hann 1993; Reff
1995; Beebe and Senkewicz 1996). The executions and other dire consequences these insurrectionists incurred suggest that the Indians viewed
their exploitation through the colonial labor system as a life and death
issue.

Although appalling in their barbarity, the direct effects of the military
actions to quell rebellions, extract tribute, obtain slaves, or simply extermi-
nate Indians to obtain their land were in most cases small in comparison to
the number of epidemic-related deaths (Hackett and Shelby 1942; Cook
1976:1–5; Osio 1996:89–94). However, the indirect effects of these and
other individual acts of brutality could sometimes be quite significant in
terms of their economic consequences. Warfare disrupted native subsis-

tence activities, and this undoubtedly led to malnutrition-related increases in the deaths caused by epidemics.

The effects of introduced diseases were also amplified through the social disruption created within Native American societies. In Alta California, outbreaks of accusations of evil sorcery and witchcraft spread through the mission period Indian population as infectious diseases began take their toll (Bean 1976:119). The Mojave Indians, for example, believed that when Euroamerican whites arrived, "witches" began to "spread disease around," and these Indians executed shamans suspected of causing epidemics (Stewart 1973:319, 323; cf. Engelhardt 1912–29:328). In the Santa Barbara Channel area, a general outbreak of possibly epidemic-related warfare was ongoing during the early contact period (Brown 1967:75–76). Later accounts specifically describe raids between native villages that were justified by claims that enemy shamans had caused an epidemic (Engelhardt 1923:6–8).

Borderlands Bioarchaeology

What insights can bioarchaeological research provide into the causes of the decline of the Borderlands Native American population? Much of what we know about the effects that Europeans had on the Indians of the Borderlands comes from historical sources that are open to multiple or even paradoxical interpretations. The interpretation of historical documents is especially problematic because they are symbolic products of a specific cultural milieu, often telling us more about their authors than about the events they describe. A major obstacle to a balanced understanding of the history of the Borderlands is the fact that almost all of the surviving documents are the writing of missionaries and military authorities and thus reflect the Spanish point of view.

In contrast to historical records, bioarchaeological data derived from human skeletal remains are not culture-dependent symbolic constructs. At a fundamental level, bones do not lie. Encoded within a skeleton's elemental composition and histological structure is a detailed record of that person's childhood development and adult history of metabolic responses to the environment (Walker 1997:145; Walker 2000). If the enamel of a person's teeth contains areas of disorganized prisms, this says something very specific about an episode of metabolic disruption the person experienced during childhood. Similarly, the size and shape and elemental composition of long bones reflect the foods a person ate and the mechanical stress to which the skeleton was subjected during daily activities. This kind of substantive evidence about physical interactions that took place between a person and the environment is extremely valuable as an independent source of evidence for enriching and critically evaluating reconstructions of past events based upon historical sources

The stable isotope research described in this volume provides a good example of how useful bioarchaeological data can be. Stable isotope concentrations in the collagen of bone give an objective measure of the types of foods a person ate. Isotopic studies of La Florida skeletal collections show unequivocally that maize played an increasingly important role in native diet during the post-contact period and that sea foods became less important for coastal populations after the establishment of the La Florida missions. This picture of a reduction in dietary diversity between the prehistoric and mission periods is consistent with the decreased variability in the microscopic scratches found on the teeth of Indians who lived during the mission period (Teaford et al., this volume).

A similar mission period shift from marine to terrestrial resources has also been documented in the Santa Barbara Channel area of Alta California. These studies show that the bones of mission Indians and Spanish settlers have similar, terrestrially oriented isotopic signatures (Costello and Walker 1987; Walker et al. 1989). Bioarchaeological studies such as these in La Florida and Alta California show convincingly that contact period dietary change involved a shift from a heterogeneous pre-contact food base to a comparatively homogeneous mission period diet of agricultural produce and seafood. These data are consistent with historical data indicating that maize, wheat, barley, and a small number of other agricultural products became important mission period commodities.

Isotopic research on skeletal remains of Indians from the Puebloan Southwest offers an interesting counterpoint to the evidence of a shift toward heavy dependence on agricultural produce seen in La Florida and Alta California. Studies of skeletal remains from the Pecos Pueblo show a decrease in carbon isotope values in the historic period, which suggests that either bison meat or maize or both decreased in importance in the Pecos diet and that dependence on wild plants increased (Spielmann et al. 1990). One interpretation of this is that the demands of the encomienda system on Indian labor and food reserves forced the people of Pecos to supplement their diet with wild foods (Spielmann et al. 1990). Alternatively, the economic disruption caused by recurrent epidemics (Kessell 1979:368) may have forced the Pecos Indians to shift to more generalized subsistence strategies that entailed more intensive wild plant use (Reff 1993).

Biomechanical studies of long bone size and shape have produced important insights into the exploitation of Guale laborers in La Florida. Based on changes in femur shape, Ruff and Larsen (this volume) argue that women generally became less mobile when they went to the missions, while males did not. This is what would be expected to result from the repartimiento system, in which Native American men were used to carry heavy loads long distances. On the other hand, the evidence that the mobility of women was restricted at the missions fits well with the documentary evidence that at some Borderlands missions, activities of women were closely controlled by priests in order to prevent extramarital sexual activity (Vancouver and Vancouver 1798:11). The Yamasee are interesting because they do not show the Guale pattern. This suggests that they were not subject to forced labor to the same extent as the Guale, an interpretation consistent with historic documents suggesting that the Yamasee were less affected by Spanish contact than were the Guale (Worth 1995).

Although historic period collections are too small and poorly preserved to provide reliable stature estimates, comparisons of long bone diameters and tooth dimensions indicate that body size of Alta California Indians decreased significantly after the establishment of the mission system. For example, in the Santa Barbara Channel area, a substantial body size reduction relative to pre-contact times is suggested by the small dimensions of historic period skeletal material from Malibu and Mission La Purísima (Walker et al. 1989:356; Walker et al. 1996). The La Purísima skeletons are small even in comparison to diminutive historic period Malibu remains (cf. Walker et al. 1996:86 and Walker et al. 1989:356). These data suggest that during the mission period, Indian children who died at Mission La Purísima were stunted in growth and development in comparison to contemporaneous Indian children who continued to live in native villages.

Studies of defects in enamel histology resulting from childhood growth disruption provide additional information on the biological consequences of European contact. In La Florida, the percentage of episodes of growth disruption increased dramatically between the late prehistoric period (36%) and the early (83%) and late (82%) mission period. A plausible explanation for this increase in growth disruption is diarrheal disease resulting from the contaminated food and water that crowded mission living conditions are likely to have produced (Simpson, this volume). The widths of enamel surface defects are greatest during the late prehistoric and early mission Georgia groups in La Florida. In Florida the width of surface defects is often greatest for the late prehistoric groups.

A similar difference is seen between protohistoric and mission period Santa Barbara Channel area collections. Historic period burials from Mission La Purísima and Malibu have frequencies of enamel defects that are comparable to those in protohistoric and late prehistoric period collections from the same area (Walker et al. 1989:358; Walker et al. 1996). These data show that the developmental problems associated with European contact were complicated and suggest that local environmental variables had an important influence on the frequency of disruptions in dental development.

The striking increase in the frequency of porotic hyperostosis in La Florida skeletal collections during the mission period provides strong evidence for a decline in health associated with the aggregation of Indians at mission centers (Larsen and Sering 2000). Factors contributing to childhood anemia undoubtedly included a decrease in iron intake owing to increased maize dependence and the reduction in iron-rich sea foods that isotopic studies suggest. This decrease in iron intake would be greatly exacerbated by the increases in iron loss and diarrheal disease and parasite infections that are likely to have accompanied the aggregation of large numbers of people at the missions. It is likely that local micro-environmental factors contributed importantly to the increase in anemia suggested by the La Florida data. For example, contamination of drinking water at the missions may well have occurred when shallow wells replaced streams as water sources (Schultz et al., this volume). This in turn would greatly increase the prevalence of iron loss related to diarrheal disease.

The significance of local environmental conditions, especially the quality of water sources, in the etiology of porotic hyperostosis is also suggested by paleopathological data from other Borderlands areas. Data from the Santa Barbara Channel area do not show a clear temporal trend or strong correlation with the availability of iron-rich foods (Walker 1986). Instead, the spatial distribution of the condition strongly suggests that its prevalence is closely related to local living conditions, especially the local availability of good sources of uncontaminated drinking water. Data from the Puebloan Southwest show a similar lack of clear temporal trends, also pointing to the importance of local conditions in the etiology of porotic hyperostosis (Walker 1985; Stodder and Martin 1992).

Although rapid advances are currently being made in the identification of genetic material from pathogens in bone (Arriaza et al. 1995; Nerlich et al. 1997; Crubezy et al. 1998; Drancourt et al. 1998; Rollo and Marota 1999; Taylor et al. 1999), most of the European diseases that devastated Borderlands populations kill so rapidly that they leave no osseous signs. As a result, they cannot currently be diagnosed in human skeletal remains. Two exceptions to this are treponemal disease (i.e., syphilis in its various forms) and tuberculosis. Although they produce skeletal lesions in only a small proportion of afflicted individuals, both diseases leave clear osseous signs. Paleopathological research has convincingly demonstrated that both tuberculosis and syphilis were endemic throughout the Borderlands before the arrival of Europeans and that they persisted into the post-contact period (Baker and Armelagos 1988; Buikstra 1999). However, owing to the low frequency of individuals with clear manifestations of these conditions, it is difficult to say anything definitive about changes in prevalence associated with European contact.

One controversial issue that bioarchaeological research can begin to address is the question of the New World origin of the virulent form of venereal syphilis that devastated Europe during the 17th century. Historic accounts from Alta California repeatedly refer to the scourge of syphilis that afflicted the mission population and the devastating effects it was having in terms of neophyte deaths and reproductive failure (Simpson 1939:32; Geiger and Meighan 1976:74–75). The severity of the mission period Alta California syphilis epidemic and the fact that non-indigenous medical techniques were devised to treat it (Walker and Hudson 1993) both suggest that the mission period syphilis epidemic was caused by a newly introduced pathogen to which the Native Americans had not previously been exposed. One of the osseous hallmarks of both venereal and endemic syphilis is the deposition of layer after layer of new bone under the fibrous layer of connective tissue that encapsulates the long bones, especially the tibia. The pattern of new bone formation seen in historic period skeletons from Malibu appears to differ somewhat from that seen in skeletons from the Malibu cemetery dating to before the arrival of Europeans (Walker et al. 1996). This perhaps reflects the introduction of a new form of treponemal disease to the Malibu population by European colonists.

Conclusions

The sustained exchange of people, goods, and diseases between the Old and New World had disastrous consequences for Native Americans living throughout the Borderlands area. My comparisons of data from La Florida, the Southwest, and Alta California show that European contact brought ill health and catastrophic population decline, regardless of the details of pre-contact socioeconomic organization or local environmental conditions. Both agricultural and hunter-gatherer societies were devastated by European intrusion into the Spanish Borderlands (Miller 1996).

When viewed from a broad spatial-temporal perspective, there is a depressing uniformity in the picture that emerges of Europeans as harbingers of death, disease, and cultural disintegration. This global perspective, however, masks significant local differences that provide key insights into the historical, sociocultural, and environmental variables that allowed human adaptive flexibility and persistence under extremely unfavorable contact period conditions. Native American responses to European contact were far from uniform. It is clear that part of this variability in the biological and cultural consequences of European contact derives in important ways from the preexisting social, economic, and environmental conditions that prevailed in different areas of the New World.

The resistance of southwestern groups to European influences provides an instructive example. In contrast to many Native Americans in other parts of the Borderlands area, the Puebloan cultures of the American Southwest have proven to be remarkably resistant to the effects of European contact. Why have the Pueblo people been able to persist when so many other Native American cultures have vanished? Local environmental conditions clearly provide part of the explanation. The fact that the Southwest is marginal for large-scale, intensive agricultural activity, along with the lack of other attractive resources such as easily accessible gold and silver, made large-scale Spanish efforts to subdue Puebloan groups economically unattractive.

The inhospitable southwestern environment also created cultural impediments to Spanish domination. During the many centuries that preceded the arrival of Spanish colonists, Puebloan groups had evolved agricultural techniques and a flexible form of social organization that allowed them to respond effectively to the adaptive challenges posed by the epidemics and social disruption associated with Spanish attempts to colonize them.

The Puebloan example also illustrates—as do many of the studies presented in this book—how the explanations we devise for the confusing array of biological and cultural responses Native Americans made to European contact depend upon the interpretive framework within which we view our data. Global explanations are inadequate explanations for local phenomena. For example, short-term environmental perturbations can sometimes have important influences on historical developments in a specific cultural context (Jones et al. 1999). The initial colonization of New Mexico occurred during a time of drought and famine (Stodder 1996:148), and these conditions undoubtedly influenced the capacity of Puebloan groups to mount an effective response to newly introduced epidemic diseases. Similarly, paleoenvironmental reconstructions based on tree-ring data from Virginia show that the Lost Colony of Roanoke Island disappeared during the most extreme drought in 800 years (1587–89) and that devastating mortality that nearly forced abandonment of the Jamestown Colony occurred during the driest seven-year episode (1606–12) in almost 800 years (Stahle et al. 1998). Unpredictable environmental fluctuations such as these sometimes play an important role in shaping historical events. These examples underscore how complicated the cultural-ecological interactions were that shaped the varied responses made by Native Americans to the enormous challenges posed by European contact.

The contributions to this volume show how powerful the bioarchaeological approach is in its ability to provide us with a better understanding of the causes of such seemingly unique historical events. They show that by critically evaluating independent sources of evidence from paleoecology, osteology, archaeology, and historical sources, it is possible to increase the reliability of what we know about the past. Studies such as these are encouraging. Although particularistic explanations that highlight the uniqueness of historical events have some validity, there are also clear commonalities in the history of our species that reflect general aspects of the human condition. This is the kind of understanding that has the potential to guide us into the future.

References Cited

Almaráz, F. D. J. 1992. The Legacy of Columbus Spanish Mission Policy in Texas. *Journal of Texas Catholic History and Culture* 3:17–36.

Arriaza, B. T., W. Salo, A. C. Aufderheide, and T. A. Holcomb. 1995. Pre-Columbian Tuberculosis in Northern Chile: Molecular and Skeletal Evidence. *American Journal of Physical Anthropology* 98(1):37–45.

Baker, B. J., and G. J. Armelagos. 1988. Origin and Antiquity of Syphilis: Paleopathological Diagnosis and Interpretation. *Current Anthropology* 29:703–37.

Baker, B. J., and L. Kealhofer. 1996. Assessing the Impact of European Contact on Aboriginal Populations. In *Bioarchaeology of Native American Adaptation in the Spanish Borderlands,* ed. B. J. Baker and L. Kealhofer, 1–13. Gainesville: University Press of Florida.

Bannon, J. F. 1974. *The Spanish Borderlands Frontier, 1513–1821.* Albuquerque: University of New Mexico Press.

Barcia Carballido y Zuniga, A. G. d. 1970. *Barcia's Chronological History of the Continent of Florida . . . from the Year 1512, in which Juan Ponce de León Discovered Florida, until the Year 1722.* Westport, Conn.: Greenwood Press.

Bean, L. J. 1976. Social Organization in Native California. In *Native Californians: A Theoretical Retrospective,* ed. L. J. Bean and T. C. Blackburn, 99–123. Ramona, Calif.: Ballena Press.

Beebe, R. M., and R. M. Senkewicz. 1996. The End of the 1824 Chumash Revolt in Alta California: Father Vicente Sarria's Account. *Americas* 53(2):273–83.

Bolton, H. L. 1927. *Fray Juan Crespi, Missionary Explorer on the Pacific Coast, 1769–1774*. Berkeley: University of California Press.

Brown, A. K. 1967. The Aboriginal Population of the Santa Barbara Channel. *University of California Archaeological Survey Reports* 69:1–99.

Bryce, G. 1968. *The Remarkable History of the Hudson's Bay Company, Including that of the French Traders of North-Western Canada and of the North-West, XY, and Astor Fur Companies*. New York: B. Franklin.

Buikstra, J. E. 1999. Paleoepidemiology of Tuberculosis in the Americas. In *Tuberculosis Past and Present*, ed. G. D. Pálfi, O. Dutour, J. Deák, and I. Hutás, 479–94. N.p.: Golden Book Publisher Ltd.

Castillo, E. D. 1989. The Native Response to the Colonization of Alta California. In *Columbian Consequences*: 1. *Archaeological and Historical Perspectives on the Spanish Borderlands West*, ed. D. H. Thomas, 377–94. Washington: Smithsonian Institution Press.

Cohen, M. N. 1989. *Health and the Rise of Civilization*. New Haven: Yale University Press.

Cole, H. N., J. C. Harkin, B. S. Kraus, and A. R. Moritz. 1955. Pre-Columbian Osseous Syphilis. *Archives of Dermatology* 71:231–38.

Cook, S. F. 1939. Smallpox in Spanish Mexican California 1770–1845. *Bulletin of the History of Medicine* 8:151–91.

———. 1976. *The Conflict between the California Indian and White Civilization*. Berkeley: University of California Press.

———. 1978. Historical Demography. In *Handbook of North American Indians*: 8. *California*, 91–98. Washington: Smithsonian Institution Press.

Costello, J. G., and D. Hornbeck. 1989. Alta California: An Overview. In *Columbian Consequences*: 1. *Archaeological and Historical Perspectives on the Spanish Borderlands West*, ed. D. H. Thomas, 303–31. Washington: Smithsonian Institution Press.

Costello, J. G., and P. L. Walker. 1987. Burials from the Santa Barbara Presidio Chapel. *Historical Archaeology* 21:3–17.

Crubezy, E., B. Ludes, J. D. Poveda, J. Clayton, B. Crouau-Roy, and D. Montagnon. 1998. Identification of *Mycobacterium* DNA in an Egyptian Pott's Disease of 5,400 Years Old. *Comptes Rendus de L Academie des Sciences, Serie III, Sciences de la Vie* 321(11):941–51.

Davis, J. 1961. *Trade Routes and Economic Exchange among the Indians of California*. Reports of the University of California Archaeological Survey, Berkeley, 54.

Denninger, H. S. 1938. Syphilis of a Pueblo Skull before 1350. *Archives of Pathology* 26:724–27.

Dickel, D. N., P. D. Schulz and H. M. McHenry. 1984. Central California: Prehistoric Subsistence Changes and Health. In *Paleopathology at the Origins of*

Agriculture, ed. M. N. Cohen and G. J. Armelagos, 439–61. Orlando: Academic Press.

Dobyns, H. F. 1981. *From Fire to Flood: Historic Human Destruction of Sonoran Desert Riverine Oases.* Socorro, N.M.: Ballena Press.

———. 1983. *Their Number Become Thinned: Native American Population Dynamics in Eastern North America.* Knoxville: University of Tennessee Press.

Dozier, E. P. 1970. *The Pueblo Indians of North America.* New York: Holt, Rinehart and Winston.

Drancourt, M., G. Aboudharam, M. Signoli, O. Dutour, and D. Raoult. 1998. Detection of 400-Year-Old Yersinia *pestis* DNA in Human Dental Pulp: An Approach to the Diagnosis of Ancient Septicemia. *Proceedings of the National Academy of Sciences of the United States of America* 95(21):12637–40.

Dunnell, R. C. 1991. Methodological Impacts of Catastrophic Depopulation. In *Columbian Consequences: 3. The Spanish Borderlands in Pan-American Perspective,* ed. D. H. Thomas, 561–80. Washington: Smithsonian Institution Press.

El-Najjar, M. Y. 1979. Human Treponematosis and Tuberculosis: Evidence from the New World. *American Journal of Physical Anthropology* 51:599–618.

Engelhardt, Z. 1912–29. *The Missions and Missionaries of California.* 4 vols. San Francisco: James H. Barry Company.

———. 1923. *Santa Barbara Mission.* San Francisco: James H. Barry Company.

———. 1930. *San Buenaventura, the Mission by the Sea.* Santa Barbara, Calif.: Mission Santa Barbara.

———. 1932. *Mission La Concepcion Purisma de Maria Santisima.* Santa Barbara, Calif.: Mission Santa Barbara.

Fairbanks, C. H. 1985. From Exploration to Settlement: Spanish Strategies for Colonization. In *Alabama and the Borderlands: From Prehistory to Statehood,* ed. L. A. Clayton and R. Badger, 128–39. Tuscaloosa: University of Alabama Press.

Fink, T. M. 1985. Tuberculosis and Anemia in a Pueblo II–III (ca. A.D. 900–1300) Anasazi Child from New Mexico. In *Health and Disease in the Prehistoric Southwest,* ed. C. F. Merbs and R. J. Miller, 359–79. Arizona State University Anthropological Research Papers 34.

Gannon, M. V. 1990. Defense of Native American and Franciscan Rights in the Florida Missions. In *Columbian Consequences: 2. Archaeological and Historical Perspectives on the Spanish Borderlands East,* ed. D. H. Thomas, 449–58. Washington: Smithsonian Institution Press.

Geiger, M. J., and C. W. Meighan. 1976. *As the Padres Saw Them: California Indian Life and Customs as Reported by the Franciscan Missionaries, 1813–1815.* Santa Barbara, Calif.: Santa Barbara Mission Archive Library, distributed by A. H. Clark Company.

Gibson, C. 1988. Spanish Indian Policies. In *Handbook of North American Indi-*

ans: 4. *History of Indian-White Relations*, ed. W. E. Washburn, 96–109. W. C. Sturtevant, general editor. Washington: Smithsonian Institution Press.

Goldberg, C. F. 1993. The Application of Stable Carbon and Nitrogen Isotope Analysis to Human Dietary Reconstruction in Prehistoric Southern California. Ph.D. diss., University of California.

Hackett, C. W., and C. C. Shelby. 1942. *Revolt of the Pueblo Indians of New Mexico and Otermin's Attempted Reconquest, 1680–1682*. Albuquerque: University of New Mexico Press.

Hann, J. H. 1988. *Apalachee: The Land Between the Rivers*. Gainesville: University Presses of Florida.

———. 1993. *Visitations and Revolts in Florida, 1656–1695*. Tallahassee: Florida Bureau of Archaeological Research.

Hann, J. H., and B. G. McEwan. 1998. *The Apalachee Indians and Mission San Luis*. Gainesville: University Press of Florida.

Haring, C. H. 1963. *The Spanish Empire in America*. New York: Harcourt.

Harvey, H. R. 1967. Population of the Cahuilla Indians: Decline and Its Causes. *Eugenics Quarterly* 14:185–98.

Hoffman, J. M. 1987. *The Descriptive Physical Anthropology of the Cardinal Site, CA-SJO-154; A Late Middle Horizon–Early Phase I Site from Stockton, California*. Colorado College Publications in Anthropology 12.

Hudson, E. H. 1958. *Non-Venereal Syphilis: A Sociological and Medical Study of Bejel*. Edinburgh: Livingstone.

Hutchinson, D. L. 1993. Treponematosis in Regional and Chronological Perspective from Central Gulf Coast Florida. *American Journal of Physical Anthropology* 92:249–61.

Hutchinson, D. L., C. S. Larsen, M. J. Schoeninger, and L. Norr. 1998. Regional Variation in the Pattern of Maize Adoption and Use in Florida and Georgia. *American Antiquity* 63:397–417.

Johnson, J.K.L., and Geoffrey R. 1996. Sociopolitical Devolution in Northeast Mississippi and the Timing of the de Soto Entrada. In *Bioarchaeology of Native American Adaptation in the Spanish Borderlands*, ed. B. J. Baker and L. Kealhofer, 38–55. Gainesville: University Press of Florida.

Johnson, J. R. 1982. An Ethnohistoric Study of the Island Chumash. M.A. thesis, University of California, Santa Barbara.

Jones, G. D. 1978. *The Ethnohistory of the Guale Coast through 1684*. Anthropological Papers of the American Museum of Natural History 55:178–210.

Jones, T. L., G. M. Brown, L. M. Raab, J. L. McVickar, W. G. Spaulding, D. J. Kennett, A. York, and P. L. Walker. 1999. Environmental Imperatives Reconsidered. *Current Anthropology* 40:137.

Kealhofer, L. 1996. The Evidence for Demographic Collapse in California. In *Bioarchaeology of Native American Adaptation in the Spanish Borderlands*, ed. B. J. Baker and L. Kealhofer, 56–92. Gainesville: University Press of Florida.

Kealhofer, L., and B. J. Baker. 1996. Counterpoint to Collapse Depopulation and Adaptation. In *Bioarchaeology of Native American Adaptation in the Spanish Borderlands,* ed. B. J. Baker and L. Kealhofer, 209–22. Gainesville: University Press of Florida.

Kessell, J. L. 1979. *Kiva, Cross, and Crown: The Pecos Indians and New Mexico, 1540–1840.* Washington: National Park Service, U.S. Department of the Interior.

Lambert, P. M. 1993. Health in Prehistoric Populations of the Santa Barbara Channel Islands. *American Antiquity* 58:509–22.

———. 1994. War and Peace on the Western Front: A Study of Violent Conflict and Its Correlates in Prehistoric Hunter-Gatherer Societies of Coastal Southern California. Ph.D. diss., University of California, Santa Barbara.

Lambert, P. M., and P. L. Walker. 1991. Physical Anthropological Evidence for the Evolution of Social Complexity in Southern California. *Antiquity* 65:963–73.

Larsen, C. S., and L. E. Sering. 2000. Inferring Iron Deficiency Anemia from Human Skeletal Remains: The Case of the Georgia Bight. In *Bioarchaeological Studies of Life in the Age of Agriculture,* ed. P. M. Lambert, 116–33. Tuscaloosa: University of Alabama Press.

Larsen, C. S., M. J. Schoeninger, D. L. Hutchinson, K. F. Russell, and C. B. Ruff. 1990. Beyond Demographic Collapse: Biological Adaptation and Change in Native Populations of La Florida. In *Columbian Consequences*: 2. *Archaeological and Historical Perspectives on the Spanish Borderlands East,* ed. D. H. Thomas, 409–28. Washington: Smithsonian Institution Press.

Lasuén, F. F. 1965. *Writings of Fermin in Francisco de Lasuén.* Trans. Finbar Kenneally. 2 vols. Washington: Academy of American Franciscan History.

Laws of the Indies. 1943. *Recopilacion de Leyes de los Reynos de las Indias, Mandadas Imprimir y Publicar por la Magestad Catolica del Rey don Carlos II. Nuestro Senor.* 3 vols. La Viuda de d. J. Ibarra, Impresora, 1791. Madrid: Graficas Ultra, s.a.

Lewis, H. T., and L. J. Bean. 1973. *Patterns of Indian Burning in California: Ecology and Ethnohistory.* Ramona, Calif.: Ballena Press.

Malville, N. J. 1997. Enamel Hypoplasia in Ancestral Puebloan Populations from Southwestern Colorado, pt. 1: Permanent Dentition. *American Journal of Physical Anthropology* 102:351–67.

Martin, D. L., A. L. Stodder, and A. H. Goodman. N.d. Cultural Longevity in the Face of Biological Stress: The Anasazi of the American Southwest (A.D. 800–1400). In *The Backbone of History: Health and Disease in the Western Hemisphere,* ed. R. Steckel and J. Rose. New York: Cambridge University Press. In press.

Matson, R. G., and B. Chisholm. 1991. Basketmaker II Subsistence: Carbon Isotopes and Other Dietary Indicators from Cedar Mesa, Utah. *American Antiquity* 56:444–16.

Milanich, J. T. 1996. Laboring in the Fields of the Lord: The Franciscan Missions of Seventeenth-Century Florida Enabled Spain to Harness the Energies of Tens of Thousands of Native People. *Archaeology* 49:60–67.

Millen, E. 1996. The Effect of European Contact on the Health of Indigenous Populations in Texas. In *Bioarchaeology of Native American Adaptation in the Spanish Borderlands,* ed. B. J. Baker and L. Kealhofer, 126–47. Gainesville: University Press of Florida.

Milliken, R. 1995. *A Time of Little Choice: The Disintegration of Tribal Culture in the San Francisco Bay Area, 1769–1810.* Menlo Park, Calif.: Ballena Press.

Moratto, M. J. 1984. *California Archaeology.* Orlando: Academic Press.

Nerlich, A. G., C. J. Haas, A. Zink, U. Szeimies, and H. G. Hagedorn. 1997. Molecular Evidence for Tuberculosis in an Ancient Egyptian Mummy. *Lancet* 350 (9088):1404.

Noah, N. D., and M. O'Mahony. 1998. *Communicable Disease: Epidemiology and Control.* Chichester, U.K.: Wiley.

Ortner, D. J., and W.G.J. Putschar. 1985. *Identification of Pathological Conditions in Human Skeletal Remains.* Washington: Smithsonian Institution Press.

Osio, A. M. 1996. *The History of Alta California: A Memoir of Mexican California.* Trans. R. M. Beebe and R. M. Senkewicz. Madison: University of Wisconsin Press.

Pastore, M. 1998. Government, Taxation, Coercion, and Ideology: A Comment on Yeager. *Journal of Economic History* 58:511–20.

Powell, M. L. 1990. On the Eve of the Conquest: Life and Death at Irene Mound, Georgia. In *The Archaeology of Mission Santa Catalina de Guale: 2. Biocultural Interpretations of a Population in Transition,* ed. C. S. Larsen, 26–35. Anthropological Papers of the American Museum of Natural History 68.

Reff, D. T. 1993. An Alternative Explanation of Subsistence Change during the Early Historic Period at Pecos Pueblo. *American Antiquity* 58:563–64.

———. 1995. The "Predicament of Culture" and Spanish Missionary Accounts of the Tepehuan and Pueblo Revolts. *Ethnohistory* 42:63–90.

Rollo, F., and I. Marota. 1999. How Microbial Ancient DNA, Found in Association with Human Remains, Can Be Interpreted. *Philosophical Transactions of the Royal Society of London.* Series B: *Biological Sciences* 354 (1379):111–19.

Roney, J. G., Jr. 1959. Palaeopathology of a California Archaeological Site. *Bulletin of the History of Medicine* 33:97–109.

———. 1966. Paleoepidemiology: An Example from California. In *Human Paleopathology,* ed. S. Jarcho. New Haven: Yale University Press.

Saitta, D. J., and R. H. McGuire. 1998. Dialectics, Heterarchy, and Western Pueblo Social Organization. *American Antiquity* 63:334–36.

Saunt, C. 1998. "The English Has Now a Mind to Make Slaves of Them All": Creeks, Seminoles and the Problem of Slavery. *American Indian Quarterly* 22(1).

Schroeder, A.H.S., and C. Omer. 1988. Indian Servitude in the Southwest. In *Handbook of North American Indians: 4. History of Indian-White Relations,* ed. W. E. Washburn, 96–109. W. C. Sturtevant, general editor. Washington: Smithsonian Institution Press.

Schulz, P. D. 1981. Osteoarchaeology and Subsistence Change in Prehistoric Central California. Ph.D. diss., University of California, Davis.

Schulz, P. D., and H. M. McHenry. 1975. Age Distribution of Enamel Hypoplasia in Prehistoric California Indians. *Journal of Dental Research* 54:913.

Schurz, W. L. 1939. *The Manila Galleon: Illustrated with Maps.* New York: E. P. Dutton.

Simmons, M. 1979a. History of Pueblo-Spanish Relations to 1821. In *Handbook of North American Indians*: 9. *Southwest,* ed. W. E. Washburn, 178–93. W. C. Sturtevant, general editor. Washington: Smithsonian Institution Press.

———. 1979b. History of the Pueblos since 1821. In *Handbook of North American Indians*: 9. *Southwest,* ed. W. E. Washburn, 206–23. W. C. Sturtevant, general editor. Washington: Smithsonian Institution Press.

Simpson, L. B. 1939. *California in 1792: The Expedition of Jose Longinos Martinez.* San Marino, Calif.: Huntington Library.

———. 1982. *The Encomienda in New Spain: The Beginning of Spanish Mexico.* Berkeley: University of California Press.

Snow, D. R. 1996. Mohawk Demography and the Effects of Exogenous Epidemics on American Indian Populations. *Journal of Anthropological Archaeology* 15:160–82.

Spielmann, K. A., M. J. Schoeninger, and K. Moore. 1990. Plains-Pueblo Interdependence and Human Diet at Pecos Pueblo, New Mexico. *American Antiquity* 55:745–65.

Stahle, D. W., M. K. Cleaveland, D. B. Blanton, M. D. Therrell, and D. A. Gay. 1998. The Lost Colony and Jamestown Droughts. *Science* 280:564–77.

Stewart, K. M. 1973. Witchcraft among the Mohave Indians. *Ethnology* 12:315–24.

Stodder, A. L. 1996. Paleoepidemiology of Eastern and Western Pueblo Communities in Protohistoric and Early Historic New Mexico. In *Bioarchaeology of Native American Adaptation in the Spanish Borderlands,* ed. B. J. Baker and L. Kealhofer, 148–76. Gainesville: University Press of Florida.

———. 1998. Bone by Bone, Pueblo by Pueblo: Reviewing the Evidence for Treponemal Infection in the Prehistoric Southwest. *American Journal of Physical Anthropology* suppl. 26:210.

Stodder, A.L.W., and D. L. Martin. 1992. Health and Disease in the Southwest before and after Spanish Contact. In *Disease and Demography in the Americas: Changing Patterns Before and After 1492,* ed. J. Verano and D. Ubelaker, 55–73. Washington: Smithsonian Institution Press.

Stoffle, R. W., K. L. Jones, and H. F. Dobyns. 1995. Direct European Emmigrant Transmission of Old World Pathogens to Numic Indians during the Nineteenth Century. *American Indian Quarterly* 19:181–223.

Suchey, J. M., W. J. Wood, and S. Shermis. 1972. Analysis of Human Skeletal

Material from Malibu, California (LAn-264). Report, Archaeological Survey, Department of Anthropology, University of California, Los Angeles.

Sumner, D. R. 1985. A Probable Case of Prehistoric Tuberculosis from Northeastern Arizona. In *Health and Disease in the Prehistoric Southwest*, ed. C. I. Merbs and R. J. Miller, 139–64. Arizona State University Anthropological Research Papers 34.

Taylor, G. M., M. Goyal, A. J. Legge, R. J. Shaw, and D. Young. 1999. Genotypic Analysis of *Mycobacterium tuberculosis* from Medieval Human Remains. *Microbiology* 145:899–904.

Thomas, D. H. (ed.). 1989. *Columbian Consequences*: 1. *Archaeological and Historical Perspectives on the Spanish Borderlands West*. Washington: Smithsonian Institution Press.

———. 1990. *Columbian Consequences*: 2. *Archaeological and Historical Perspectives on the Spanish Borderlands East*. Washington: Smithsonian Institution Press.

———. 1991. *Columbian Consequences*: 3. *The Spanish Borderlands in Pan-American Perspective*. Washington: Smithsonian Institution Press.

Thornton, R. 1980. Recent Estimates of the Prehistoric California Indian Population. *Current Anthropology* 21:702–4.

Thornton, R., T. Miller, and J. Warren. 1991. American Indian Population Recovery Following Smallpox Epidemics. *American Anthropologist* 93:28–45.

Thornton, R., J. Warren, and T. Miller. 1992. Depopulation in the Southeast after 1492. In *Disease and Demography in the Americas: Changing Patterns Before and After 1492*, ed. J. Verano and D. Ubelaker, 187–95. Washington: Smithsonian Institution Press.

Tibesar, A. 1955. *Writings of Junipero Serra*, vol. 2 of 4. Washington: Academy of American Franciscan History.

Upham, S. 1982. *Politics and Power: An Economic and Political History of the Western Pueblo*. New York: Academic Press.

———. 1992. Population and Spanish Contact in the Southwest. In *Disease and Demography in the Americas: Changing Patterns Before and After 1492*, ed. J. Verano and D. Ubelaker, 223–36. Washington: Smithsonian Institution Press.

Vancouver, G., and J. Vancouver. 1798. *A Voyage of Discovery to the North Pacific Ocean, and Round the World; in Which the Coast of North-west America Has Been Carefully Examined and Accurately Surveyed. Undertaken by His Majesty's Command, Principally with a View to Ascertain the Existence of Any Navigable Communication between the North Pacific and North Atlantic Oceans; and Performed in the Years 1790, 1791, 1792, 1793, 1794, and 1795, in the Discovery Sloop of War, and Armed Tender Chatham, under the Command of Captain George Vancouver*. London: G. G. and J. Robinson.

Walker, P. L. 1978. A Quantitative Analysis of Dental Attrition Rates in the Santa Barbara Channel Area. *American Journal of Physical Anthropology* 48:101–6.

———. 1985. Anemia among Prehistoric Indians of the American Southwest. In

Health and Disease in the Prehistoric Southwest, ed. C. F. Merbs and R. J. Miller, 139–64. Arizona State University Anthropological Research Papers 34.

———. 1986. Porotic Hyperostosis in a Marine-Dependent California Indian Population. *American Journal of Physical Anthropology* 69:345–54.

———. 1991–92. An Overview of California Indian History before the Arrival of Europeans. *Journal of Human Ecology* 3:359–70.

———. 1996. Integrative Approaches to the Study of Ancient Health: An Example from the Santa Barbara Channel Area of Southern California. In *Notes on Populational Significance of Paleopathological Conditions: Health, Illness and Death in the Past,* ed. A. Pérez-Pérez, 98–105. Barcelona: Fundació Uriach.

———. 1997. Wife Beating, Boxing, and Broken Noses: Skeletal Evidence for the Cultural Patterning of Interpersonal Violence. In *Troubled Times: Violence and Warfare in the Past,* ed. D. L. Martin and D. W. Frayer, 145–75. Amsterdam: Gordon and Breach.

———. 2000. Bioarchaeological Ethics: A Historical Perspective on the Value of Human Remains. In *Biological Anthropology of the Human Skeleton,* ed. M. A. Katzenberg and S. R. Saunders, 3–39. New York: Wiley-Liss.

Walker, P. L., and M. J. DeNiro. 1986. Stable Nitrogen and Carbon Isotope Ratios in Bone Collagen as Indices of Prehistoric Dietary Dependence on Marine and Terrestrial Resources in Southern California. *American Journal of Physical Anthropology* 71:51–61.

Walker, P. L., and J. Erlandson. 1986. Dental Evidence for Prehistoric Dietary Change on the Northern Channel Islands. *American Antiquity* 51:375–83.

Walker, P. L., and B. S. Hewlett. 1990. Dental Health Diet and Social Status among Central African Foragers and Farmers. *American Anthropologist* 92:383–98.

Walker, P. L., and T. Hudson. 1993. *Chumash Healing: Changing Health and Medical Practices in an American Indian Society.* Banning, Calif.: Malki Museum Press.

Walker, P. L., and J. R. Johnson. 1992. The Effects of European Contact on the Chumash Indians. In *Disease and Demography in the Americas: Changing Patterns Before and After 1492,* ed. J. Verano and D. Ubelaker, 127–39. Washington: Smithsonian Institution Press.

———. 1994. The Decline of the Chumash Indian Population. In *In the Wake of Contact: Biological Responses to Conquest,* ed. C. S. Larsen and G. R. Milner, 109–20. New York: Wiley-Liss.

Walker, P. L., and P. M. Lambert. 1989. Skeletal Evidence for Stress during a Period of Cultural Change in Prehistoric California. In *Advances in Paleopathology,* ed. L. Capasso. Journal of Paleopathology, Monographic Publication 1.

———. 1998. Prehistoric Treponematosis in the Western United States. *American Journal of Physical Anthropology* suppl. 26:224.

Walker, P. L., and R. Thornton. N.d. Health, Nutrition, and Demographic Change in Native California. In *The Backbone of History: Health and Disease in the*

Western Hemisphere, ed. R. Steckel and J. Rose. New York: Cambridge University Press. In press.

Walker, P. L., F. Drayer, and S. Siefkin. 1996. *Malibu Human Skeletal Remains: A Bioarchaeological Analysis.* Sacramento: Resource Management Division, California Department of Parks and Recreation.

Walker, P. L., P. M. Lambert, and M. DeNiro. 1989. The Effects of European Contact on the Health of California Indians. In *Columbian Consequences*: 1. *Archaeological and Historical Perspectives on the Spanish Borderlands West,* ed. D. H. Thomas, 349–64. Washington: Smithsonian Institution Press.

Weber, D. J. 1990. Blood of Martyrs, Blood of Indians: Toward a More Balanced View of Spanish Mission in Seventeenth-Century North America. In *Columbian Consequences*: 2. *Archaeological and Historical Perspectives on the Spanish Borderlands East,* ed. D. H. Thomas, 429–48. Washington: Smithsonian Institution Press.

———. 1992. *The Spanish Frontier in North America.* New Haven: Yale University Press.

Whitehead, R. S., and D. C. Cutter. 1996. *Citadel on the Channel: The Royal Presidio of Santa Barbara, Its Founding and Construction, 1768–1798.* Santa Barbara, Calif: Trust for Historic Preservation, A. H. Clark Company.

Wood, P. H. 1988. Indian Servitude in the Southeast. In *Handbook of North American Indians*: 4. *History of Indian-White Relations,* ed. W. E. Washburn, 407–9. W. C. Sturtevant, general editor. Washington: Smithsonian Institution Press.

Wormington, H. M., and E. K. Reed. 1947. *Prehistoric Indians of the Southwest.* Denver: Colorado Museum of Natural History.

Worth, J. E. 1995. *The Struggle for the Georgia Coast: An Eighteenth-Century Spanish Retrospective on Guale and Mocama.* Anthropological Papers of the American Museum of Natural History 75.

———. 1998. *The Timucuan Chiefdoms of Spanish Florida*: 1. *Resistance and Destruction.* Gainesville: University Press of Florida.

Yeager, T. J. 1995. "Encomienda" or Slavery? The Spanish Crown's Choice of Labor Organization in Sixteenth-Century Spanish America. *Journal of Economic History* 55:842–60.

Yesner, D. 1980. Nutrition and Cultural Anthropology. In *Nutritional Anthropology: Contemporary Approaches to Diet and Culture,* ed. G. H. Pelto, N. W. Jerome, and R. F. Kandel, 85–116. Pleasantville, N.Y.: Redgrave.

Zavala, S. A., and J. Coyne. 1943. *New Viewpoints on the Spanish Colonization of America.* Philadelphia: University of Pennsylvania Press.

Zubrow, E. B. 1974. *Population, Contact and Climate in the New Mexican Pueblos.* University of Arizona Anthropological Papers 24.

Contributors

Elizabeth Monahan Driscoll
Research Laboratories of Archaeology and Department of Anthropology
University of North Carolina
Chapel Hill, NC 27599–3120

Mark C. Griffin
Department of Anthropology
San Francisco State University
San Francisco, CA 94132

Dale L. Hutchinson
Department of Anthropology
East Carolina University
Greenville, NC 27858

Kerstin Kreutz
Anthropologisches Institut
University of Giessen
Giessen, Germany

Patricia M. Lambert
Department of Sociology, Anthropology, and Social Work
Utah State University
Logan, UT 84322

Clark Spencer Larsen
Department of Anthropology
The Ohio State University
Columbus, OH 43210-1364

Jerald T. Milanich
Department of Anthropology
Florida Museum of Natural History
Gainesville, FL 32611

Vivian E. Noble
Department of Cell and Molecular Biology
Northwestern University Medical School
Chicago, IL 60611

Lynette Norr
Department of Anthropology
University of Florida
Gainesville, FL 32611

Robert F. Pastor
Department of Archaeological Sciences
University of Bradford
Richmond Road
Bradford, West Yorkshire BD7 1DP, U.K.

Christopher B. Ruff
Department of Cell Biology and Anatomy
Johns Hopkins University School of Medicine
725 North Wolfe Street
Baltimore, MD 21205

Margaret J. Schoeninger
Department of Anthropology
University of California, San Diego
La Jolla, CA 92093

Michael Schultz
Zentrum Anatomie
University of Göttingen
Kreuzbergring 36
D-37075 Göttingen, Germany

Scott W. Simpson
Department of Anatomy
School of Medicine
Case Western Reserve University
Cleveland, OH 44106

Mark F. Teaford
Department of Cell Biology and Anatomy
Johns Hopkins University School of Medicine
725 North Wolfe Street
Baltimore, MD 21205

Phillip L. Walker
Department of Anthropology
University of California
Santa Barbara, CA 93106

John E. Worth
Coosawhattee Foundation
3217 Redbud Road, N.E.
Calhoun, GA 30701

Index

References in italics refer to illustrations.

Town Creek Mound (N.C.), 230, 250; genetic isolation of, 250, 254; and Upper Saura Town population, 245, 246
Toxemia, effect on dental enamel, 149
Trabeculae, cranial, 213–14, 216, 218
Traits, morphological, correlation of, 240, 241. *See also* Cranial morphology; Dental morphology
Transportation system, Timucua province in, 12, 28
Treponemal disease, 35, 278, 280; osseous signs of, 295–96
Tryptophan deficiency, 220
Tuberculosis: in Alta California, 280; archaeological evidence of, 35; osseous signs of, 296; pre-Columbian, 22
Tukey Multiple Comparison tests, 119, 127–28
Tuscarora, population affinities of, 230

Upham, S., 282
Upper limbs, mechanical loadings on, 136–37, 138
Upper Saura Town (N.C.), 230, 231, 250; and Town Creek Mound population, 245, 246

Vásquez de Ayllón, Lucas, 6
Villages, aboriginal: *congregación* from, 18; mission convents at, 7
Vitamin deficiencies, 34, 221; effect of, on dental enamel, 149

Waddells Pond site: bone samples of, 63; diet at, 65, 67
Wage laborers, 16, 18
Ward, J. H., 244; Minimum Variance method, 246
Warfare: biological consequences of, 8; epidemic-related, 291–92
Warren Wilson site (N.C.), 231, 250
Water, contamination of, 208, 210, 222, 295
Weber, D. F., 147
Westos (northern Indians), 13
Whittaker, D. K., 147
Wilson, D. F., 147
"Wilson Bands." *See* Striae of Retzius
Witchcraft, 292
Women: in labor system, 18; mortality rates among, 290
Woodland culture: late, 230; middle, 84, 230
Workloads: effect of maize production on, 75; effect of, on skeleton, 25, 199, 294; following contact, 137; pre-contact, 23
Worth, John, 285; *The Timucuan Chiefdoms of Spanish Florida*, 2

Yamasee people: on Amelia island, 28; dental enamel hypoplasia among, 183, 194; effect of missionization on, 141; kinship of, to Guale, 230, 254, 255; mechanical loading of limbs, 140; relocation of, 13, 19, 34; sexual dimorphism among, 138, 139; skeletal remains of, 115, 123, 124, 126–33, 137–41, 230. *See also* Santa Maria de Yamasee

Ripley P. Bullen Series
Florida Museum of Natural History
Edited by Jerald T. Milanich

Tacachale: Essays on the Indians of Florida and Southeastern Georgia during the Historic Period, edited by Jerald T. Milanich and Samuel Proctor (1978); first paperback edition, 1994

Aboriginal Subsistence Technology on the Southeastern Coastal Plain during the Late Prehistoric Period, by Lewis H. Larson (1980)

Cemochechobee: Archaeology of a Mississippian Ceremonial Center on the Chattahoochee River, by Frank T. Schnell, Vernon J. Knight, Jr., and Gail S. Schnell (1981)

Fort Center: An Archaeological Site in the Lake Okeechobee Basin, by William H. Sears, with contributions by Elsie O'R. Sears and Karl T. Steinen (1982); first paperback edition, 1994

Perspectives on Gulf Coast Prehistory, edited by Dave D. Davis (1984)

Archaeology of Aboriginal Culture Change in the Interior Southeast: Depopulation during the Early Historic Period, by Marvin T. Smith (1987); first paperback edition, 1992

Apalachee: The Land between the Rivers, by John H. Hann (1988)

Key Marco's Buried Treasure: Archaeology and Adventure in the Nineteenth Century, by Marion Spjut Gilliland (1989)

First Encounters: Spanish Explorations in the Caribbean and the United States, 1492–1570, edited by Jerald T. Milanich and Susan Milbrath (1989)

Missions to the Calusa, edited and translated by John H. Hann, with an introduction by William H. Marquardt (1991)

Excavations on the Franciscan Frontier: Archaeology at the Fig Springs Mission, by Brent Richards Weisman (1992)

The People Who Discovered Columbus: The Prehistory of the Bahamas, by William F. Keegan (1992)

Hernando de Soto and the Indians of Florida, by Jerald T. Milanich and Charles Hudson (1993)

Foraging and Farming in the Eastern Woodlands, edited by C. Margaret Scarry (1993)

Puerto Real: The Archaeology of a Sixteenth-Century Spanish Town in Hispaniola, edited by Kathleen Deagan (1995)

Political Structure and Change in the Prehistoric Southeastern United States, edited by John F. Scarry (1996)

Bioarchaeology of Native American Adaptation in the Spanish Borderlands, edited by Brenda J. Baker and Lisa Kealhofer (1996)

A History of the Timucua Indians and Missions, by John H. Hann (1996)

Archaeology of the Mid-Holocene Southeast, edited by Kenneth E. Sassaman and David G. Anderson (1996)

The Indigenous People of the Caribbean, edited by Samuel M. Wilson (1997); first paperback edition, 1999

Hernando de Soto among the Apalachee: The Archaeology of the First Winter Encampment, by Charles R. Ewen and John H. Hann (1998)

The Timucuan Chiefdoms of Spanish Florida: vol. 1, *Assimilation*; vol. 2, *Resistance and Destruction*, by John E. Worth (1998)

Ancient Earthen Enclosures of the Eastern Woodlands, edited by Robert C. Mainfort, Jr., and Lynne P. Sullivan (1998)

An Environmental History of Northeast Florida, by James J. Miller (1998)

Precolumbian Architecture in Eastern North America, by William N. Morgan (1999)

Archaeology of Colonial Pensacola, edited by Judith A. Bense (1999)

Grit-Tempered: Early Women Archaeologists in the Southeastern United States, edited by Nancy Marie White, Lynne P. Sullivan, and Rochelle A. Marrinan (1999)

Coosa: The Rise and Fall of a Southeastern Mississippian Chiefdom, by Marvin T. Smith (2000)

Archaeological Studies of Gender in the Southeastern United States, edited by Jane M. Eastman and Christopher B. Rodning (2001)

Religion, Power, and Politics in Colonial St. Augustine, by Robert L. Kapitzke (2001)

Bioarchaeology of Spanish Florida: The Impact of Colonialism, edited by Clark Spencer Larsen (2001)

The Archaeology of Traditions: Agency and History Before and After Columbus, edited by Timothy R. Pauketat (2001)